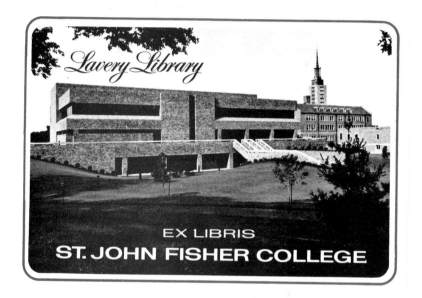

D1285647

States, Labor Markets, and the Future of Old-Age Policy

States, Labor Markets, and the Future of Old-Age Policy

EDITED BY

John Myles and

Jill Quadagno

Temple University Press
Philadelphia

Temple University Press, Philadelphia 19122
Copyright © 1991 Temple University. All rights reserved
Published 1991
Printed in the United States of America

Library of Congress Cataloging-in-Publication Data
States, labor markets, and the future of old-age policy / edited by
    John Myles and Jill Quadagno.
        p.   cm.
    Includes bibliographical references and index.
    ISBN 0-87722-790-X
    1. Old-age pensions.   2. Aged—Government policy.   3. Aged—
Employment.   4. Early retirement.   5. Social security.   I. Myles,
John.   II. Quadagno, Jill S.
HD7105.3.S74   1991
331.3'98—dc20   91-9678

Contents

Part II. The Restructuring of Old Age: Older Workers in the Economy

States, Labor Markets,
and the Future of Old-Age Policy

1/Introduction: States, Labor Markets, and the Future of Old-Age Policy

Jill Quadagno and John Myles

Throughout this century, the structure of the social and economic life cycles of men and women has changed dramatically. The expansion of secondary and postsecondary education has delayed entry into paid employment, while retirement and other forms of early labor-force exit have lowered the age when people leave the workforce. Women have increased their rate of participation in the paid labor force dramatically, with the result that the organization of male and female life cycles has become more similar.[1]

All these changes, which we now take pretty much for granted, are comparatively recent. The expansion of higher education, the growing labor-force participation of women, and the practice of retirement are post–World War II phenomena. All were shaped by two forces: politics and markets.[2] The expansion of the welfare state, on the one hand, and the changing character of labor markets, on the other, made possible and determined the way education, work, and retirement have evolved in the second half of the twentieth century. Without rising productivity in agriculture and goods production, it is unlikely that the practice of retirement would have become the norm for older people; without the old-age security programs of the modern welfare state, it would have been impossible.

As these changes were occurring, they seemed natural, almost inevitable outcomes of processes associated with modernization, industrialization, and a rising standard of living. Until the mid 1970s, the spread of retirement and the expansion of income security and other programs to maintain a large retired population were typically welcomed as taken-for-granted consequences of social development and human progress. No sooner were the institutions related to retirement and the welfare state put in place, however, than they began to be called into question. These new concerns were related to a growing awareness of three long-term developments.

Table 1.1/Percentage of Population Aged 65 or Over, 1960–2040

COUNTRY	1960	1986	2000	2020	2040
Australia	8.5	10.5	11.7	15.5	20.0
Austria	11.9	14.5	14.9	19.4	24.4
Belgium	12.0	14.1	15.0	18.5	22.3
Canada	7.6	10.7	12.9	18.8	22.7
Denmark	—	15.3	14.9	20.1	25.2
Finland	7.5	12.7	14.6	21.7	23.2
France	11.6	13.2	15.2	19.5	23.1
Germany	10.6	15.1	17.0	21.7	28.0
Greece	8.1	13.0	15.0	17.9	21.2
Iceland	8.1	10.1	10.9	14.4	20.3
Ireland	11.1	10.9	11.2	12.7	17.2
Italy	9.1	13.1	15.4	19.1	24.9
Japan	5.7	10.5	15.1	21.0	22.7
Luxembourg	—	13.4	16.8	20.3	22.3
Netherlands	8.6	12.3	13.5	19.0	25.0
New Zealand	8.6	10.5	11.1	15.2	21.9
Norway	11.1	16.0	15.0	18.2	23.1
Portugal	—	12.2	13.3	15.4	20.6
Spain	—	12.8	14.6	17.9	23.3
Sweden	11.8	17.5	16.6	20.8	22.8
Switzerland	11.0	14.7	16.8	24.4	28.6
Turkey	—	4.1	5.1	6.9	10.5
United Kingdom	11.7	15.3	14.5	16.4	20.6
United States	9.2	12.1	12.2	16.2	20.0
OECD average	9.7	12.7	13.9	18.0	22.2

Source: OECD, *Social Expenditure Trends and Demographic Developments* (Paris: OECD, 1988).

1. Population aging. The populations of Western industrial nations have been aging almost from the dawn of industrialization, but slowly. With the dramatic decline in fertility in the latter part of the twentieth century, however, population aging accelerated dramatically. Population projections through the year 2040 (Table 1.1) show the percentage of the population over 65 years of age in the member countries of the Organization for Economic Cooperation and Development (OECD) rising from an average of 9.7 percent in 1960 to 22.2 percent in 2040.

2. Public expenditures. Assuming Western populations age under similar economic and social conditions, as they do now, then inevitably public expenditures to support the elderly will also rise dramatically. With today's benefit levels, pension expenditures alone are projected to increase their share of the

Table 1.2/Influence of Demographic Change on the Share of Pension Expenditure in National Income, 1984–2040

COUNTRY	1984	2000	2020	2040
Australia	6.0	6.7	9.1	12.4
Austria	16.5	17.6	23.7	31.7
Belgium	14.0[b]	13.8	17.0	22.7
Canada	6.1	7.6	11.6	15.2
Denmark	10.1	9.5	13.5	18.7
Finland	8.5	9.7	16.0	17.8
France	14.3	16.5	21.6	27.0
Germany	13.7	16.4	21.6	31.1
Greece	10.8	13.0	15.7	19.5
Ireland	6.7	6.2	6.8	9.9
Italy	16.9	19.7	25.6	35.7
Japan	6.0	9.4	14.0	15.7
Netherlands	12.1	13.4	19.6	28.5
New Zealand	8.9	9.3	13.0	20.3
Norway	9.6	9.0	11.0	15.0
Portugal	8.2	10.6	12.1	16.9
Spain	10.0	11.7	13.6	20.4
Sweden	12.9	12.1	15.9	18.0
Switzerland	8.8	10.6	16.9	21.1
United Kingdom	7.7	7.5	8.6	11.2
United States	8.1	8.2	11.3	14.6
OECD average[a]	10.3	11.4	15.1	20.2

Source: OECD, *Social Expenditure Trends and Demographic Developments* (Paris: OECD, 1988).
Note: The projections show only the impact of demographic change. They assume constant benefit levels per beneficiary relative to national income per worker, constant labor force participation rates, and constant proportions of elderly people in receipt of benefits. Figures are based on the OECD medium fertility variant.
[a]Arithmetic mean.
[b]Expenditure ratio for 1983.

national income from an average of 10.3 percent in 1984 to over 20 percent in 2040 (Table 1.2). And pension expenditures reflect only part of the impact of population aging on the public purse. Expenditures on health care and other social services can also be expected to rise significantly.

3. *The trend toward early retirement.* Most long-term projections of the consequences of a changing population structure have been made under the conventional assumption that, for the majority, old age begins at 65. Since the early 1970s, however, there have been dramatic declines in labor-force participation rates of 50–64-year-olds in many OECD nations, a trend documented and analyzed in detail in this volume.

A growing awareness of these developments—in government, in business, and among the general public—has given rise to a number of controversies since the middle of the 1970s. Will we be able to "afford" all these old people? Will the welfare state go broke? Will the young people of tomorrow revolt against the inevitably rising tax burden looming in their future? Will the combination of changing demography, labor markets, and states lead to yet another rearrangement of the life course?

These questions have been raised, moreover, in a political and economic climate in which conventional assumptions about the welfare state and the role of markets more generally have been questioned. The 1980s brought a swing to the political right in a number of countries, symbolized by the Thatcher revolution in the United Kingdom and the presidency of Ronald Reagan in the United States. A new philosophy of acquisitiveness, one that praised inequality and condemned government intervention to promote social change, gained a level of respectability not seen since the 1920s.

On closer inspection, however, the apparent similarity among these developments is part illusion. Reaganism and Thatcherism were localized, not general, phenomena among Western capitalist democracies, a fact often lost on those who view the world largely from the vantage point of the Anglo-American nations and through the lenses of the English language. Reaganism and Thatcherism were important national experiments, but they were not the only game in town. Otherwise similar demographic and economic developments have met with a variety of political and social responses and outcomes since the mid 1970s. Population aging has been defined as more of a problem in some nations than others; the past decade has brought the expansion of early retirement in some countries and an increase in the retirement age in others; the decline in labor-force participation has been precipitous in Germany and France, moderate in Canada and the United States, and negligible in Sweden and Japan.

We think the reason for this variation reflects the fact that we are in a period of transition. It has become increasingly apparent that the developed Western economies are going through an economic transformation of major significance. The globalization of capital, the emergence of new international trading blocks, the adoption of knowledge-intensive technologies, and the shift in employment from goods to services have all been associated with the end of a postwar boom during which prosperity was led by growing levels of mass consumption produced by the technologies of mass production. Under these conditions, old verities have been challenged, and the future has become less certain. In response to this uncertainty, the past decade brought a variety of national social, economic, and political experiments—with a variety of results. In Europe, real employment growth in the 1980s was extremely modest despite a long and sustained economic boom. As a result, the prospect of "jobless growth" appeared, and with it serious discussion of the possibility that in the future we will all retire at age 38. Alternatively, productivity gains and new forms of work organization associated with a postindustrial society arguably will bring about a "flexible life course" as people enter and exit paid work for retraining or the care of dependents and the end of retirement as we now know it.[3]

The shape of the future is established in the present. Our purpose in assembling this volume is to document actual developments since the mid 1970s with particular attention to variations in the way different countries have responded to and addressed otherwise similar demographic, political, and economic changes. Much of our current understanding of the character of old age was formed in the light of events prior to the 1970s—the growth of the welfare state and the institutionalization and spread of retirement. The focus of the essays we have assembled here is on what has been happening since then.

Our emphasis on comparative differences follows from the assumption that during periods of transition the future is inherently indeterminate. The national variants described in the following chapters represent the outcomes of national experiments to construct a social, economic, and political paradigm capable of solving new problems in the organization of production and of social life. But no one "experiment" has yet emerged as the clear victor or successor to social forms we seem to be leaving behind. Under these conditions, it is extremely hazardous to project likely future patterns on the basis of a single and idiosyncratic national experience such as that of the United States under Reagan or the United Kingdom under Thatcher.

Our assumption that transformations in the structure of the life course occur at the intersection of labor markets and states led us to focus on both dimensions. In Part I, we present a set of essays on the politics of old age; in Part II, on the elderly in the labor market. The division is sometimes artificial, since many authors attempt to bridge the gap to establish linkages between the two.

The essays presented here are by no means cut from a single cloth, nor do they constitute a synthetic whole. In inviting authors to prepare articles for this volume we deliberately avoided the impulse to impose a single framework or even a single problematic on their work. Such synthesis, theoretical or empirical, was premature in our view. Our purpose at this stage was to document the variants, not to explain them. To impose a common theoretical framework presumes the variations are known and reasonably well understood. Our more immediate goal was to establish what needs to be explained. In this respect, we think these essays bring us closer to our goal.

The Politics of Old Age

The decade of the 1980s was ushered in by a seemingly dominant new conservativism represented by Margaret Thatcher and Ronald Reagan, who were elected to office on the promise of rolling back the welfare state. In Part I, Alan Walker, Jill Quadagno, and Carroll Estes examine political developments in Britain and the United States, presenting two scenarios regarding how old-age politics was ideologically constructed during this period.

Alan Walker traces the development of the politics of old age under the Thatcher governments and describes the impact of Thatcherism on social policies toward elderly people, with particular reference to pensions. First, Walker evaluates the postwar consensus on welfare for elderly people, based on the Keynes–Beveridge mixed economy, and outlines the structure of pensions and other benefits inherited by the Conservatives in 1979. He argues that the consensus was precarious, disguising opposing interests in Britain's structurally fractured pension system. He goes on to analyze the ideological basis of the social and economic strategy pursued by the Thatcher government and the new conflict-based politics of pensions it introduced. Walker identifies a two-pronged campaign against state pensions together with an assault on state pensioners themselves. Next, he examines the prospects for intergenerational conflict in Britain and concludes that the economic and demographic imperative has been amplified artificially by the government in order to legitimate ideologically motivated policies aimed at residualizing the state's role in welfare. The Thatcher government's primary concern with the public burden of aging is also highlighted. Finally, Walker considers the outlook for the politics of old age in the 1990s in the light of a continuation of Thatcherite policies. Although he sees continuing conflict over public welfare for the elderly and both intra- and intergenerational conflict, these are likely to remain covert.

Jill Quadagno examines the changing configuration of interest groups that have provided a seemingly invincible base of support for the social security system in the United States. Quadagno argues that social security developed in the context of class-based politics centered in a coalition between organized labor and program bureaucrats, which created cross-class solidarity as social insurance became the one welfare program to provide income security.

During the late 1960s and early 1970s an age-based interest-group politics was activated, as evidenced by the numbers of formal organizations whose membership is dominated by older citizens. The rise of interest-group politics does not mean that class issues disappeared from U.S. policymaking but that the parameters of the debate were restructured. Since the 1980s, the politics of old age has been constructed around the concept of generational equity, the idea that benefits are unequally distributed between the young and the old. The generational-equity theme is designed to undermine the cross-class strength of the old-age alliance and counter the power of the elderly lobby. Its combined messages of class and generational conflict were played out in the failure of the Medicare Catastrophic Coverage Act, which illustrated the fragility of interest-group politics when upper- and middle-class elderly were asked to sustain a program that primarily benefited the elderly poor.

What makes the United States unique among the welfare states of Western capitalist democracies is its failure to legislate a universal program of national health insurance. Instead, the United States provides public health insurance only for the elderly (Medicare). The result is that only in the United States is health care part of the politics of old age. Carroll Estes examines health and aging policy in the United States as an outcome of crisis construction and crisis management by the Reagan administration, which, she argues, is a product of tensions between capital, the state, and democracy. In Estes's analysis, President Reagan's success in promoting the twin philosophies of neoliberalism and neoconservativism amounted to an ideological revolution that generated a paradigm shift in the direction of a promarket and profamily social-policy agenda. She argues that the three forces of austerity, federalism, and deregulation were central in shaping the direction of public policy on aging and health care during the 1980s. Estes identifies two legacies of the Reagan administration. One is the shift toward cost containment, competition, and privatization in health and social services, which represented part of the state's response to its own legitimation problems in the crisis context. The other legacy concerns the social struggles kindled across generational, gender, and class lines. Estes closes with a discussion of the problems related to constructing aging in crisis terms, specifically the public burden associated with demographic aging, and an analysis of the restructured welfare state that is emerging.

Since the economic downturn of the 1970s and early 1980s, the politics of old-age policy in Canada has been quite unlike that in the United States and the United Kingdom. The main issue that dominated Canadian public policy debates until the beginning of the 1980s was how to expand the income-security system for Canada's elderly, not how to contract it. And since then, there has been little evidence of the "crisis" or "intergenerational conflict" motifs that have characterized American debates on old age. John Myles and Les Teichroew explore the reasons for the comparatively tranquil character of recent old-age politics in Canada. Their reconstruction of policy debates shows that Canada's "dualistic" welfare state for the elderly is widely viewed by both business leaders and government officials as providing a more general prototype for future social-policy reform in all areas of social life. The reasons for this have to do with an expanding low-wage service economy in which social expenditures will increasingly have to be directed toward the poor and away from workers with average and above-average incomes. Income security for the latter is to be returned to the market, albeit supported by substantial state subsidies. Paradoxically, however, this "privatization" of income security is creating a new and expanded role for the state in the regulation of private markets.

During the 1980s the Australian welfare state saw a dramatic return to means testing for income-security benefits, reversing a century-long history of development from selective toward universal entitlements. Responding to the collapse of postwar prosperity and Australia's increased vulnerability in the international economy, the return to selective social policy, as Sheila Shaver explains, reflects a resurgence of class interests in welfare politics. The age pension, paradigm setter for Australian income security, has led the turnaround.

The age pension was originally framed as needs-based social assistance for the working class. From its inception, however, it was given ideological status as a social right flowing from citizenship and labor service. Its originators dismissed the contradictions inherent in a means-tested social right as "considerations of mere logic." These contradictions fueled the drive toward incomplete universalism in the age pension during the "long boom," as middle-income groups protested their exclusion from social rights freely given to the working class. They also underlie contemporary resistance to the Labor government's program of pension "reform," by which the age pension is to be limited to lower-income groups, while tax-subsidized occupational superannuation provides income-related benefits to the middle class.

Beginning with a presentation of the public–private interplay in present pension packages and an overview over the main stages in their historical evolution, Fritz von Nordheim Nielsen outlines the major elements of similarity and divergence in pension provisions in the Scandinavian countries. With the exception of Denmark, pension politics in the Nordic countries has been remarkably tranquil. Contrary to popular interpretations, this has less to do with inter-Nordic differences in the power position of Social Democratic labor movements than with the extent to which the reform spurt of the 1960s achieved consensus regarding the balance between public and private pensions. Differences in political settlements about two-tiered pensions in the 1960s largely accounted for dissimilarities in political pension scenarios of the 1980s. With their ability to mute conflicts of interest, public pension systems in Sweden, Finland and, until 1989, Norway have proven resistant to negative forces, and pension mixes have been stable.

The implications of the buildup of large public pension funds for the political economy have been hotly contested in Scandinavia. The weight of Swedish and Finnish funds in national savings and investments seems to have added greatly to their political stability, whereas the unexpected underfunding of Norwegian two-tiered pensions has created agreement about the need to cut replacement rates for upper-income groups and has given political currency to the rhetoric of the new demographics.

In Denmark, where proposals for a similar two-tiered scheme repeatedly were defeated, public pensions stagnated while occupational and private schemes proliferated. Macroeconomic concerns about savings and investment have superseded consideration of pensioner needs in recent discussions about proposals for a system of mandated occupational pensions. Traditional pension politics has been turned into a deadlocked struggle about the future contours of Danish political economy.

Ewa Morawska, in her chapter on Poland, provides a unique look at how the momentous changes in Eastern Europe have affected the economic security of the elderly. During the late 1940s when Poland nationalized production and distribution, it also instituted a comprehensive program of old-age security. Since the program covered only those employed in state-owned enterprises, excluding peasants and the self-employed, only 47 percent of the population were eligible, and the degree of economic security offered the elderly was modest. In addition to the national system for the socialized sector, a second tier of public welfare, administered like charity, was available for the elderly poor.

Initially, welfare goals were subordinate to production goals, but during the 1960s the state was able to release more funds for social needs, improving coverage but not adequacy. During the 1970s the economic situation of the elderly (especially elderly women and the rural elderly) deteriorated when benefits failed to keep pace with inflation.

According to Morawska, the macrocrisis of an overcentralized and overendebted economy in the 1980s—characterized by even greater rates of inflation and severe budget deficits—led to a further deterioration of the social security program. An early-retirement act, designed to resolve Poland's employment problems, added thousands to the social security rolls and led to a labor shortage. Although subsequent amendments allowed retirees to work, old-age payments continued to increase at a rapid pace, by 480 percent between 1980 and 1985. Contributions failed to keep pace, and as a result more than half of Poland's elderly have incomes below the official minimum. What has thus far taken the place of public support has been private care through the family.

Morawska's analysis was written just before the political upheaval that so dramatically transformed Eastern Europe in 1989. If anything, the economic crisis that has followed political transformation has accentuated the difficulties of the elderly throughout Eastern Europe. Responding to the needs of the elderly is among the most pressing problems facing Eastern European societies in the 1990s.

Older Workers in the Economy

In Part II of this book, Anne-Marie Guillemard argues that a radical restructuring of old age is already under way. She notes that in most industrialized countries, labor-force participation rates for persons 55–64 years old have decreased significantly since the mid 1970s, signaling a shift in the boundary between economic activity and retirement. Guillemard analyzes and interprets changes in labor-force withdrawal based on a comparative study of the United States, United Kingdom, Netherlands, France, West Germany, and Sweden. She finds that the various institutional arrangements (in particular, disability insurance and unemployment compensation) most frequently used for authorizing aging workers to withdraw early from the labor force indicate deep changes affecting the social organization of the end of the life course. Since public old-age pension funds, which have been the major means of regulating definitive withdrawal, have lost much of the power to do so, the chronological threshold of retirement is no longer clear, and functional (instead of age) criteria are increasingly used to regulate withdrawals. In effect, the changes under way cannot be interpreted merely as early retirement. Instead, she argues, the way in which these early exits from the labor market are being organized is dissolving the tripartite life course (education/work/retirement) organized on the basis of chronological age. The life course is being "dechronologized," and old age is being reconstructed around definitions of functional capacity in the labor market.

Gösta Esping-Andersen and Harald Sonnberger also compare labor-force trends of older workers, focusing particularly on Germany, Sweden, and the United States. Arguing that trends in early labor-force withdrawal are governed by both "push" and "pull" factors, they find that variations between the three countries can be understood in the context of the relationship between social policies and labor markets.

Germany's relatively high rate of early labor-force withdrawal by men is the result of legislation that has made early retirement both feasible and attractive given the lack of employment growth and the absence of job opportunities for older workers. Although legislation also made early retirement attractive in Sweden, an active employment policy has given the older worker an alternative, resulting in high labor-force participation rates for older male workers. Labor-force participation rates of older male workers in the United States fall in between those of Germany and Sweden. According to Esping-Andersen and Sonnberger, the U.S. pattern has emerged from the lack of social legislation making early retirement attractive but no compensating employment policy to maintain participation rates. Esping-Andersen and Sonnberger conclude that early retirement in the United States is governed less by market constraints, an idea that Harold Sheppard addresses in his essay, which points to the influence of a culture of leisure as a factor affecting retirement patterns.

Klaus Jacobs and Martin Rein provide a detailed look at how Germany's high rates of early retirement have been produced. Like Guillemard, they note that a significant amount of labor-force withdrawal takes place outside the public pension system through other programs, such as unemployment insurance, sick pay, and preretirement programs. In Germany, legislation creating early-exist possibilities provided the social infrastructure subsequently used by firms in periods of high unemployment and weak labor markets to forge early-retirement policies. Social policy, in effect, became a tool of labor-force management for the private sector.

Jacobs and Rein argue that the high levels of labor-force withdrawal by older workers temporarily resolved economic problems but that the long-term effect of shortening working life may place a burden on the solvency of the social security system and create a future labor scarcity. Recent efforts by the German government to reverse these trends have failed, both because of the alternative pathways outside the pension system and because of the reluctance of firms to hire older workers.

Toshi Kii explains how the retirement system operates in Japan where it is controlled primarily by industry. Until recently, retirement age in Japan has been set at 55 with employees receiving a lump sum at retirement instead of a pension. Recently, under pressure from both the government and the labor unions, some larger companies have raised the retirement age to 60. The push for later retirement stems from the fact that the government's old-age pension does not begin until age 60 and that the lump sum paid to employees on retirement is inadequate as a source of support. In spite of mandatory retirement rules, labor-force participation rates for males aged 55–64 remain high—higher even than in Sweden—because of the reemployment system and the extension-of-employment system.

Under the reemployment system, which is found mainly in large firms, management retires older workers, rewards them with a lump-sum payment, and then rehires selected workers in lower positions at lower salaries. The extension-of-employment system, which is found in smaller firms, means that management allows selected workers to continue working past retirement age, often with some reduction in income and status, although not as severe as under the reemployment system. Given the lack of government programs that encourage early exit, Japanese firms have developed a flexible labor-management system to retain needed older employees and retire surplus workers.

Although the United States has not witnessed as great a decline in labor-force participation rates among older workers as Germany, Harold Sheppard points out that a significant downward trend exists nonetheless and that early exit is appearing even among those in the 50–55 age cohort. Although a predicted future labor shortage may increase the demand for older workers, Sheppard suggests several reasons why future retirement trends may not be affected by the anticipated labor shortage. These include the possibility of exporting labor abroad through advanced technology, increased productivity that may lessen labor demands, and the continued "pull" of private pension programs. Sheppard argues that the United States is witnessing the institutionalization of early retirement, which has made retirement a valuable life goal. Thus, Sheppard's arguments support Esping-Andersen and Sonnberger's explanation of why high rates of labor-force withdrawal have occurred in the United States despite the lack of public policies that provide alternative income sources.

In summarizing the main themes of this book, James Schulz returns to the intersection of politics and markets. Picking up on themes developed by Guillemard and by Jacobs and Rein, he points out that the practice of using the elderly as a buffer group to balance the demand and supply of labor has been with us for some time and that governments have adjusted their retirement and pension policies accordingly. He notes that we need to remind ourselves of why there are welfare states and the important impact they have had on retirement policies. Economic insecurity created by market mechanisms, the "graying" of populations, rising prosperity among some elderly, and increased international competition all raise questions about future roles for the aged. According to Schulz, a growing tension is arising in policy arenas, given the desire for leisure among the elderly and the concerns of others about the need for more older workers to stay in the labor force. Schulz is skeptical, however, that future increases in labor demand will bring older workers back into the labor force. Nor is it clear that anticipated labor shortages will ever emerge. As he ironically points out, "Everyone is in favor of keeping older people in the labor force except the unions, government, business, and older people."

Many of the essays in this volume began as papers for a conference entitled *The Politics of Aging in the Eighties* held at Florida State University in March 1989. Many were extensively critiqued and revised to fit this volume. The conference received support from the Mildred and Claude Pepper Foundation, the International Exchange Center on Gerontology at the University of South Florida, and the Institute on Aging and the Center for Professional Development and Public Service, both of Florida State University. The quality of the conference and essays in this collection was greatly enhanced by the commentary of several colleagues who participated as discussants in the conference. They include Melissa Hardy, William Serow, Charles Cnudde, Warren Peterson, Larry Isaac, Richard Rubinson, and Madonna Harrington Meyer. We especially want to thank Susan Lampman for her assistance in organizing the conference.

Notes

1. For a detailed and provocative analysis of the changing organization of the life course, see Judah Matras, *Dependency, Obligations, and Entitlements* (Englewood Cliffs, N.J.: Prentice-Hall, 1989).

2. On the role of politics, see Karl Urlich Mayer and Urs Schoepflin, "The State and the Life Course," *Annual Review of Sociology* 15 (1989): 187–209. On the intersection of politics and markets, see John Myles, "States, Labor Markets and Life Cycles," in *Beyond the Marketplace: Rethinking Economy and Society*, ed. Roger Friedland and A. F. Robertson (New York: Aldine de Grueyter, 1990).

3. On the topic of postindustrialism and the life course, see Fred Block, *Revising State Theory: Essays in Politics and Postindustrialism* (Philadelphia: Temple University Press, 1987), Introduction and chap. 6.

The Politics
of Age

2/Thatcherism and the New Politics of Old Age

Alan Walker

Before 1979, the policies of postwar British governments toward elderly people were characterized by a consensus between the two main political parties, Conservative and Labour. The system of pensions and other benefits introduced after the Beveridge Report (1942) survived largely unchanged for thirty years. Both parties espoused, though never committed sufficient resources to, a policy of community care. There was always *competition* over policy, with each party vying for electoral success in the pledges they made to pensioners about increases in pensions and the specific benefits of the new pensions structure they were proposing. This consensus-style politics of old age reached its pinnacle in the mid 1970s when Labour was last in power. Here was a sympathetic government engaged in corporatist power sharing with the trade-union movement, and through this latter channel, pensioners were able to lobby effectively for better pensions. It was during this period that the only substantial addition to Beveridge's pension scheme was made, with all-party support.

The election of a New Right–inspired Conservative government in 1979 marked a watershed for both social policy and the politics of old age in Britain. Conventional wisdom, sustained by more than thirty years of consensus politics, was that no government would dare risk the wrath of the pensioner vote.[1] The anti-welfare-state predisposition of the Thatcher governments was soon confronted by the fact that, as in all welfare-state systems, elderly people are by far the largest group of beneficiaries. Thus, if the much-trumpeted goal of "rolling back the frontiers of the state" was to be achieved, this risk, if indeed it was one, would have to be taken. Characteristically, the first Thatcher administration did not shrink from this self-imposed task and acted quickly to break the link between pensions and average earnings, though more radical measures were to wait for the government's third term in office.

The twin purposes of this chapter are to trace the development of the politics of old age in Britain in the 1980s and to describe the impact of this new regime on policies toward elderly people. This agenda begs questions about the nature of Thatcherite ideology and the specific form of the pre-Thatcher political consensus, and these issues are also discussed, albeit briefly. Underlying this analysis is a critique of dominant liberal–pluralist accounts of the politics of old age that disguise divisions of interest and power among elderly people. They have failed to examine the conflict underlying the political consensus of old-age policies and have proven wholly inadequate as a basis for examining conflict-led strategies such as Thatcherism. The primary focus of attention is social security policy because that was the main canvas on which the new politics of old age was sketched in the 1980s (though in the 1990s, policies on health and social services are likely to be the most prominent). The Thatcher government did continue and enhance the policy, introduced by the previous Labour government, of disengaging older male workers from the labor market in response to unemployment,[2] but that was strongly supported by public opinion. It was in the field of social security, and pensions in particular, that a more radical departure was made. My starting point is the system of social security provision for elderly people that the Thatcher government inherited in 1979.

Postwar Pension Policy: The Precarious Consensus

Although Britain has a "mixed economy" of public and private pension provision, as in other West European welfare states public transfers are, by a long way, the major source of pensioners' incomes: around two-thirds compared with one-half in Canada and the United States.[3] But two distinctive features of this provision for elderly people set the British social security apart from the prevalent pattern in most other European Economic Community (EEC) countries. On the one hand, there is its dual system of flat-rate national insurance (NI) pensions and additional earnings-related benefits, in contrast to the more common pure insurance system of earnings-related benefits. On the other hand, there is the relatively low replacement rate:[4] 31 percent for a single person in 1980, compared with 66 percent in France, 69 percent in Italy, and 44 percent in the United States. For married couples, the figures were 47 percent in Britain, 75 percent in France, 69 percent in Italy, and 66 percent in the United States.[5] Another indication of the low level of the state pension in Britain is that it is set *below* that of social assistance (known in Britain as income support).

Not surprisingly, the majority of elderly people in Britain have relatively low incomes. They have been shown to constitute the largest group in the population living in poverty ever since such statistics were first collected in the late nineteenth century. In 1985, the latest year for which official statistics are available, just over one-third of elderly people were living on incomes at or below the official income-support poverty line, compared with one in ten of those under pension age. This includes more than a million people living on incomes below this poverty line (largely because they are not claiming income support).[6]

Why are the incomes of British pensioners so significantly lower than those of pensions in most other comparable EEC countries? It is, perhaps, tempting to conclude that replacement rates are merely a function of the particular kind of pension scheme in operation in different countries. This view would be mistaken. Although the relatively high replacement rates found in France and Italy are based on an earnings-related pension formula, Britain shares with Sweden a two-tiered pension system, and Swedish replacement rates are the highest in the Organization for Economic Cooperation and Development (OECD) (83 percent for a married couple), while the British rates are among the lowest. Thus, as in other realms of social policy, pension levels are primarily a function of political decision making rather than a technical artifact. In Britain they are the product of a postwar political consensus that emphasized narrow economic efficiency rather than equity, the containment of public expenditures rather than the abolition of poverty in old age.

The Keynes–Beveridge Regime

This consensus and the mixed economy of welfare it produced had their roots in the postwar settlement, through which the accommodation of the organized working class into capitalism was achieved by commitments to full employment, improved welfare provision, and consultations with trade unions in a quasi-corporatist policymaking process. The vehicle for these changes was provided by the partnership between Keynesian interventionist economic management and William Beveridge's liberal-inspired social security reforms. Our primary concern in this chapter is with the foundations the Beveridge Report laid for pension provision up to the present day.[7]

Beveridge built on the insurance principle established by the National Insurance Act of 1911 and the Widows, Orphans and Old Age Contributory Pensions Act of 1925, rather than the noncontributory, means-tested model provided by the Old Age Pensions Act of 1908 or other, more radical alternatives. This means that, despite the appearance of universality, pensions are not granted as a right but are contingent on the establishment of eligibility through employment, or "work testing."[8] Moreover, pensions and other social security benefits provide only the minimum subsistence floor specifically in order to encourage additional private welfare provision.[9] These fundamental principles—contributions through employment and the state safety net—which have guided the construction and subsequent operation of the postwar social security system, were enshrined in the following passage:

Social security must be achieved by co-operation between the State and the individual. The State should offer security for service and contribution. The State in organising security should not stifle incentive, opportunity, responsibility; in establishing a national minimum it should leave room and encouragement for voluntary action by each individual to provide more than the minimum for himself and his family.[10]

It will not be a surprise to learn that this passage was much quoted by the Thatcher government during its major review of social security in 1985. As well as the contribution condition, Beveridge proposed and the National Insurance Act of 1946 institutionalized a second important condition for the receipt of the NI pension: retirement.

The dominant official concern in the preparation of Beveridge's recommendations on state pensions had been their financing, particularly limiting the size of the Exchequer contribution, and this proved to be the overriding political issue in subsequent pensions policy. Because the full benefits of the state pension scheme were introduced in 1948, far sooner than Beveridge and the Treasury officials who scrutinized his proposals had intended, the national insurance fund quickly went into deficit; consequently, the NI pension scheme has always operated on a pay-as-you-go basis.

Reform of the State Pension Scheme

As a result of the continuance of widespread poverty in old age, despite the introduction of the NI pension, the necessity for millions of retired people to claim social assistance and the social divide that began to emerge between public- and private-sector pensioners as a result of the burgeoning of occupational pensions in the 1950s and 1960s, several attempts were made to improve the basic pension. For example, a nonindexed graduated pension scheme was initiated in 1961, and in 1970 a small pension was provided for those aged 80 and over who were too old to join the NI scheme in 1948. At the same time, encouragement was given to the private and occupational pensions sector by allowing contracting out from the state's graduated scheme and by various tax concessions. Although in the 1950s, 1960s, and 1970s both Labour and Conservative parties proposed structural reforms of the Beveridge pension scheme, the only one to reach the statute book was the State Earnings Related Pension Scheme (SERPS) introduced in 1975.

SERPS represented a compromise between the more radical plan prepared by the previous Labour government and the Conservative opposition's proposals. The trade-union movement exerted considerable influence on the form of the new pension scheme, particularly in supporting the contributory principle, which was then regarded as a guarantee of protection from government cuts (a view that was to change rapidly when the Thatcher government started cutting national insurance benefits in 1980). As well as the employment test, the new pension scheme retained earnings-related benefits and earnings-related contributions from the pre-1975 scheme. The scheme will not reach full maturity until 1998 and then an individual's state earnings-related pension will be calculated on the basis of the best twenty years of earnings, revalued, and added to the flat-rate pension.

The most important aspect of the new pension scheme was the measure of integration it forged, in the Beveridge mold, between the public and private sectors. Thus occupational pension schemes were allowed to "contract out" of SERPS in return for a rebate of NI contributions, and the state accepted the responsibility for inflation-proofing these pensions once they were being paid, up to the maximum entitlement under SERPS. In view of the longstanding failure of the private pension industry to protect pensioners from inflation and the closure of many pension funds, particularly during the hyperinflation of the mid 1970s, this policy was, not surprisingly, endorsed by both the pension companies and the Conservative party.

Where did this major pension reform leave the politics of old age at the end of the 1970s? In the first place, it diverted official and public attention away from the needs of existing pensioners toward the pension provision of the future. The argument that pensions were inadequate was accepted, but only for those retiring in twenty years' time. Second, it institutionalized the existence of "two nations" in old age: those with access to earnings-related inflation-proofed pensions, and those, such as part-time women workers, people with disabilities, racial minorities, and others prone to experience disadvantage in the labor market, who continue to rely on the flat-rate pension supplemented by income support.[11]

In other words, the politics of old age may have been characterized by consensus between the two main political parties, a fact emphasized by the Labour government's decision in 1977 to index state pensions to earnings *or* prices, whichever rose faster, despite stagflation and implementation in the wake of the fiscal crisis of a policy of reducing public expenditure on other programs. But this consensus was built on a foundation of fundamentally opposed interests among both pensioners and contributors to the different sectors of Britain's structurally fractured pension system. The main social divisions were along socioeconomic group and occupational class lines, with white-collar core employees having access to occupational and private pensions and blue-collar peripheral employees, along with those outside the labor market, relying on state pensions and benefits. Thus there is no unified "age interest" among Britain's elderly people, as functionalist/pluralist accounts would have us believe.[12] Instead, dominant class interests have been protected in pension policy by the hegemony of the Keynes–Beveridge public-burden model of welfare.[13] The postwar party political consensus on age policies was sustained by the class relations of power and particularly the economic insecurity and powerlessness of the majority of poor elderly people; therefore, in this limited sense, it was precarious. But the consensus and the social security structure it built were even more vulnerable to a change in economic ideology, from Keynesian-style demand management to supply-side monetarist policies—and so it proved.

Thatcherism and the Politics of Pensions

The Conservative government elected in 1979 was cast in a different ideological mold from the "one-nation" Conservatives that had shared in consensus government over the previous thirty years. Its leader, Margaret Thatcher, espoused New Right ideology and placed similarly ideologically committed politicians in key cabinet posts. As with Reagan in the United States, Thatcher provided a focus for the disparate elements of New Right opinion in her crusade against social democracy and the extended state and thereby helped create a new right-wing agenda in Britain.

The strategy pursued by the Thatcher governments—the free economy and the strong state—derived from a weaving together of the distinct liberal and conservative threads in New Right ideology.[14] The market-liberal warp focuses on the requirements for a free economy, while the neoconservative weft is more concerned with the conditions for maintaining and restoring authority throughout the key institutions of society. Both accept the need for the economy to be free and the state to be strong, but the respective emphasis is reversed.[15] Thus, in the 1980s the state took an increasingly interventionist role and at the same time withdrew from key areas of responsibility.

The New Right, or neoliberals, in Britain are most closely identified with the macroeconomic prescriptions of monetarism (or, after 1985, when the policy was substantially modified, neomonetarism). At a technical level, monetarism is concerned with the control of the money supply to generate noninflationary economic growth. This was the macroeconomic policy adopted, in a weak form, by the Labour government in 1976–1977. Moreover, this supply-side approach has increasingly come to dominate the macroeconomic policies of other Western (and former Eastern bloc) countries and is the established orthodoxy in the international monetary agencies.[16] But, under Thatcherism, monetarist policies have been the macroeconomic element of a much broader and longer-term economic and social strategy aimed at promoting inequality, reducing the role of the state in a wide range of long-accepted areas, encouraging free enterprise and individual intiative, and undermining the power of the trade unions.

The main economic component of this strategy has been the limitation of the growth of public expenditures on the grounds that it crowds out private investment and necessitates high taxation, which in turn damages incentives; the use of high interest rates to dampen demand; and privatization, particularly of public utilities but also in the field of welfare in areas such as municipal housing, residential and nursing homes for the elderly, and the contracting out of ancillary health services. The proceeds from public expenditure and privatization policies have been used chiefly to fund cuts in taxation. As the embodiment of the social democratic sentiments of the postwar settlement, the welfare state has attracted much of Thatcherism's philosophical and practical attention. On the one hand, it offends the belief in the primacy of the market in responding to demand, ensuring choice, and containing costs; on the other, it is said to create dependency by making people reliant on welfare. The main thrust of government policy in the field of social security has been toward the replacement of universal-style national insurance benefits with means-tested, or, in the Thatcherite euphemism, "targeted" benefits.

Public expenditures have been a primary focus of attention from the outset. The first sentence of the Thatcher government's first white paper on public spending proclaimed: "Public expenditure is at the heart of Britain's economic difficulties." [17] Although public spending has increased year on year, as it is bound to do, the government has succeeded in reducing the proportion of national output it spends, from 42 percent in 1978–1979 to 39 percent in 1988–1989. This is a remarkable achievement in view of the fact that some programs, such as defense, have been increased substantially and the need for benefits and services has risen rapidly as a result of the combined effects of the government's own economic policies and sociodemographic changes. The main cuts have fallen on social spending with, for example, a cumulative total of over £17 billion being taken from the social security budget since 1979 (a cut of 26 percent).[18]

The Campaign against State Pensions
How did this neoliberal economic and social strategy impinge on elderly people and, more generally, the politics of old age? Once a policy of cutting public expenditures had been adopted, as pointed out above, it was difficult to avoid the largest public spending program: social security, and in turn, the group that receives by far the largest chunk of that budget: elderly people. Social security expenditures on elderly people were £23.9 billion in 1988–1989, just over half of the total social security budget. Moreover, population projections show continuing growth in the numbers of elderly people, particularly very elderly people, though not as rapid growth as in some other Western countries, such as Canada.

Thus, in contrast to discussions in the 1960s and 1970s of expansionist plans for pension reform, in the 1980s attention focused almost exclusively on the government's plans to residualize the basic state pension, target resources on the poorest, and privatize the earnings-related scheme. State pensions were attacked as part of the general onslaught on public spending and, over the course of the 1980s, the specter of the economic burden of old age was used more and more openly to justify restraint in, first, social security expenditures and, subsequently, health and social services spending.

The new politics of pensions began to take shape early in the life of the government as what in retrospect can be seen to have been a two-pronged attack on state pensions was begun. First, soon after taking office, with the 1980 Social Security Act the government broke the upraising link between the NI pension and earnings or prices and tied it to price rises alone. This was part of a general squeeze on the public sector, though fears were also expressed, in moderate terms at this stage, about the rising cost of pensions. The cumulative effect of this change (by April 1989) was a reduction in the NI pension for a couple of more than £17.50 per week (or 25 percent) compared to what it would have been had the previous practice continued. This important change has not been reversed, even though, at the time, pensioners were promised a share in rising prosperity as the economy improved. Thus this policy has had the effect not only of significantly reducing the cost of state pensions but also of serving a warning on future generations of older people that the residualized state pension will not be sufficient to maintain their living standards.

This message was emphasized in the second prong of the campaign, which began at the same time. This time the object was SERPS, and the intention was severely to curtail and possibly to abolish the scheme and to encourage the growth of private and occupational pensions in its place. This part of the campaign began quietly and took the overt form of several official statements highlighting the future cost of pensions. Then, in 1983, following the reelection of the Thatcher government, an inquiry was announced into provision for retirement—the first part of what subsequently turned out to be a full-scale review of all social security provision. This inquiry provided a focus for public discussion of the pension issue, and as far as the government was concerned, this meant the rising cost "burden" of pensions. Both the initial request for evidence and the final report of the inquiry were full, to the point of obsession, of references to this issue. The long-term demographic trends were highlighted, and an adverse shift in the "dependency ratio" between the employed and the retired was predicted for the first quarter of the next century, in spite of the well-known deficiencies of such forecasts. In doing so, the government portrayed state pensions as a "burden" and a threat to Britain's future economic performance. In contrast, the income needs of pensioners were discussed only summarily.

The report of the pension inquiry (published as part of the general review of social security) also contained one of the first official references in Britain to the generational-equity issue that was to figure far more outspokenly in the parallel debate in the United States: "Our belief in One Nation [*sic*] means recognising our responsibilities to *all* the generations represented within it. . . . It would be an abdication of responsibility to hand down obligations to our children which we believe they cannot fulfil." [19]

The main cause of official concern was the rising long-term cost of the SERPS: "The certain and emerging cost of the state earnings-related pension scheme should give everyone—of whatever persuasion—pause for thought." [20] (The scheme was also criticized for being too generous to women by allowing spouses to inherit the full SERPS entitlement and providing home responsibility credits for those looking after children.) Because SERPS is a relatively new scheme being phased in over twenty years, it entails the maturation effect associated with all such earnings-related schemes.[21] But this increase in costs was not due to take place until the turn of the century. Nonetheless, the government's response to this projected increase was to propose its phasing out over three years for all men under age 50 and women under age 45 and to replace it with compulsory occupational and private pensions. The motivation behind this approach, clearly in tune with the Thatcher government's overall strategy outlined above, was spelled out as follows: "The purpose of these proposals is to achieve a steady transition from the present dependence on state provision to a position in which we as individuals are contributing directly to our own additional pensions and in which we can exercise greater choice in the sort of pension provision we make." [22]

The government's proposals met with almost universal opposition, including from its own official social security advisers, who argued that the abolition of SERPS would be, at best, premature, the Confederation of British Industry (the leading employers organization), and the private pension industry and insurance companies, as well as, more predictably, the trade unions, the Labour party, and pensioners' organizations. The weight of this influential opinion against abolishing SERPS caused the government to rethink its plans (one of the very few examples of its doing so). Although, when the final proposals for reform were published, in December 1985, there were no doubts as to the government's continuing belief that SERPS represented an unacceptable "burden" on future generations, they constituted modification rather than abolition. Their effect was to cut the projected cost of the scheme in half, though, in deference to public opinion, their introduction was postponed until 1988. This issue figured in the intervening 1987 general election but had little salience in relation to the preeminent issues of the economy and defense. As a consequence, there was no sustained debate of the opposition parties' policies on pensions, which favored the retention of SERPS and a more prominent role for state provision.

The reelection of the Thatcher administration for a third term of office indicated that it had achieved a substantial reduction in the role of the state in pension provision at very little political cost, and, therefore, the myth of the power of the pensioner vote was finally laid to rest. The main emphasis in this third term has been on the encouragement of the private sector by generous additional tax incentives for private, so-called personal pensions, and occupational schemes that contract out of SERPS before 1993. This incentive, together with the poor long-term prognosis for the value of the state scheme and a massive advertising campaign by the pension industry, has already boosted the membership of private schemes by 3.25 million and occupational schemes by 1 million—more than eight times the growth rate officially estimated in 1986.

The Official Depreciation of Need in Old Age
The campaign against state pensions was also, in part, an assault against state pensioners. The language of the economic "burden" of pensions and of old age was established very early as a feature of Thatcherite rhetoric on the welfare state. In addition, the government's offensive included the proposition that the incomes of pensioners had improved recently by comparison with other groups living in poverty.[23] Thus, despite official and independent evidence to the contrary, cuts in elderly people's benefits were legitimated by the myth that they were relatively well off and that Britain might actually be overproviding for old age.

As a result of the growth of mass unemployment in the early 1980s and the proselytization of this myth of affluence in old age, a significant shift occurred in the longstanding consensus about the deprived status of elderly people and, to some extent, about their position as the most deserving of the poor. At the time of the pension inquiry, official reports and some independent social scientists started to point to relative improvements in the position of pensioners in the income distribution. In fact, there has been an improvement in the relative incomes of pensioners, albeit a modest one overall and one accompanied by much more unequal incomes among the elderly; but the main point of interest here is that this was translated into policy proposals that redistributed income from poor elderly people to other groups in poverty.[24]

The main factors behind the improvement in the disposable income of pensioners relative to nonpensioners are, on the one hand, a slowing down in the growth of real disposable income among those below pension age, caused mainly by the reduction in the numbers in full-time employment in the early 1980s, and, on the other, the increase in the value of the basic pension, in the 1970s, in relation to average earnings. Their improvement with regard to other social security claimants chiefly reflects the growth of unemployment and the substantial cuts in unemployment benefits made by the Thatcher government.

In other words, the "advantageous" position of pensioners among the poor and near-poor has largely been manufactured by the government's own monetarist and neomonetarist policies. These caused a surge of mainly unemployed people and their families into the bottom quintile of the income distribution in the early 1980s, which had the effect of displacing many low-income elderly people into the next-to-bottom quintile. Furthermore, because of public expenditure constraints imposed by the government, which in effect posit the social security budget as a zero-sum, elderly people are now regarded as the *source* of finance for redistribution to other groups in poverty. Thus the social security changes implemented in April 1988 were openly designed to make 2.2 million state pensioners worse off and redistribute some of the savings to families with children.

The government's depreciation of need among Britain's elderly people took a bolder and even more threatening form in late 1988 when the chancellor of the exchequer gave a now infamous briefing to the press on pensioners' incomes. He advanced the case for further reductions in pensions by arguing that only a "tiny minority" of elderly people "genuinely" experience "difficulty making ends meet." [25] This argument was a variation on a consistent theme denying the existence of poverty that has gained in prominence over the past decade. It was widely interpreted as a thinly veiled attack on the NI pension, presaging a further restructuring of the social security system away from universalism and toward more means testing.

The chancellor's briefing was greeted by a public outcry in the media, which was followed by an unseemly squabble between him and the journalists present about the precise words that had been used. As a result of sustained media pressure on the chancellor, the government was forced to act to get him off the hook and did so by announcing the introduction, in October 1989, of a small addition to the incomes of pensioners aged 75 and over claiming income support. The considerable embarrassment that this incident caused to the Thatcher government suggests that, in the face of its propaganda effort, the old consensus on the deservingness of the elderly is still surviving.

The New Politics of Old Age: Toward Intergenerational Conflict?

The chancellor's remarks on pensioners' incomes, echoing in more outspoken terms the sentiments expressed by the report on the pensions inquiry, opened up for the first time in Britain the serious prospect of political conflict between the generations. I am not suggesting that it is likely to reach the same pitch as in the United States where the pressure group Americans for Generational Equity was formed to promote policies intended to reduce the present and future cost of retirement on younger generations.[26] In Britain there is no evidence, as yet, of any resentment on the part of younger generations toward paying contributions to the pensions of older people.[27] Moreover, the distribution of welfare-state expenditures between young and old is roughly equal, so there is no empirical basis for resentment.[28] But the current thrust of Thatcherite social security policy and the rhetoric surrounding it may create the same backlash against elderly people that has occurred in the United States. By suggesting that only a "tiny minority" of elderly people are poor, the chancellor made the latest contribution to the creation of an inaccurate picture of the financial circumstances of elderly people. This is likely to have two implications.

First, it might weaken the demonstrably strong resolve of the British public to provide adequate pensions without a test of means. No doubt this is in part what was intended. But if the government succeeds in sowing the seeds of doubt about the extent of poverty in old age, it may create a new political cleavage between young and old and so pave the way for overt intergenerational conflict. Ironically, if this happens, it would be founded on an erroneous stereotype of affluence when the reality for the majority of British pensioners continues to be poverty and low incomes.

Second, the stigma experienced by the poorest and most materially deprived will worsen. If they are told by opinion formers that a majority of pensioners are well provided for, their feelings of inadequacy at having to claim state benefits are likely to heighten. The current take-up rate of means-tested income support among pensioners is 67 percent. If it is perceived by poor elderly people that most of their counterparts can get by without claiming a means-tested benefit, they too will be reluctant to do so, regardless of the extent of their need. Of course, this is an example of the social construction of stigma as a deterrent to claiming social security.[29]

The Creation of an Economic Imperative
The fact that the government appears to be prepared to run the risk of open intergenerational war raises the question of the motivation underlying Thatcherite pension policy. Why has the politics of old age been reconstituted in a new, conflict-oriented form? Were the government's expressed fears about the future cost of pensions well founded? We have seen that the Thatcher government chose to take action to curtail the SERPS despite opposition from its own social security advisers and the major interests involved. Even the normally conservative OECD indicated that it was not necessary to contemplate this sort of step until 2010.[30] Moreover, in comparison with the far greater projected costs of pensions in some other EEC countries, the action was premature. As a consequence of the deindexation of pensions from earnings and lower growth in the retired population than in most other EEC countries, the projected share of national income devoted to pension expenditures for the next fifty years is likely to increase only modestly: from 7.7 percent in 1984 to 7.6 percent in

2010 and 11.2 percent in 2030. Whereas in other countries still contemplating radical restructuring of their pension systems, such as France and Italy, a continued upward trend in the proportion of gross domestic product (GDP) allocated to pensions is forecast. For example, in France the share of pension expenditures in national income is projected to increase from 14.3 percent in 1984 to 17.3 percent in 2010 and 27 percent in 2040.[31]

In fact, it is not the burden of aging as such that concerns the Thatcher government, or even the economic cost of pensions; it is the *public* burden.[32] The public sector in this context is narrowly constructed to mean only direct public transfers (private pensions have received generous tax subsidies). This suggests that it is not sociodemographic change nor indeed a fiscal crisis of the state that underpins the new politics of old age, but ideology. This conclusion is supported by retrospective evidence concerning the postwar expansion in social expenditures, which shows that it was political decisions concerning eligibility for and levels of benefits, rather than demography, that were the main factors.[33]

The Thatcher government's opposition to state provision is the driving force behind the changes in pensions outlined earlier. This means that the public-burden concept of welfare that formed such an important part of the Keynes–Beveridge welfare hegemony has been elevated to a preeminent position by the neoliberal ideology of Thatcherism. Thus it is this ideology and the changed assumptions it entails about the role of the public sector with regard to welfare that underlie the current economic pessimism about aging emanating from the British government. To put it another way, concern about the aging of the population in Britain has been amplified artifically as an economic and demographic imperative in order to legitimate ideologically driven policies aimed at reducing the state's role in welfare.[34]

The Future Politics of Old Age

What are the implications for the politics of old age in the 1990s of a continuation of the welfare strategy being pursued by the Thatcher government? In the first place, the increasing polarization between affluent retired people with access to substantial private pensions at one extreme and materially deprived elderly people reliant solely on state pensions at the other is likely to increase the potential for *intra*generational conflict along social class, particularly consumption class lines.[35] The social division between public and private pensioners has been long entrenched in the British social security system, but the residualization of the former and the subsidization of the latter will widen this division still further. Moreover, there are signs that a similar strategy is being pursued in other realms of social policy, notably health and social services. For example, the 1989 budget introduced a tax subsidy for pensioners who take out private medical insurance, and the government has given notice of its intention to tighten controls on the budgets of local public health and social services and encourage the private sector.[36]

Second, as the impact of the government's strategy is felt more in the health and social services, this might fuel the conflict between the sexes and generations within the family over the provision of care to disabled elderly people. Again, this potential conflict will be structured along social and consumption class lines, with only poor families relying on residualized state provision, but gender may also be an important dimension of conflict.

Third, there is likely to be a continuation of the social construction of elderly people as an economic burden. Because pensioners will remain for the foreseeable future the main users of the welfare state, and neoliberal ideology will continue to oppose state welfare, state pensioners can expect to be increasingly stigmatized. Indeed, further attempts by the Thatcher government to reconstitute the social contact between the generations and portray the elderly as a burden may themselves inspire intergenerational conflict.

Although the 1990s are likely to see continuing conflict over public provision for old age, at least for as long as a neoliberal government remains in power, with a series of intra- and intergenerational conflicts following in its wake, these are unlikely to take the form of open struggle. Apart from the party political arena, the politics of old age in Britain has taken a characteristically covert form. It is essentially structured conflict over resources within the policy system. Apart from pockets of militancy among working-class pensioner-action groups, old-age politics in Britain is marked by its acquiescence.[37] Moreover, there is no unified politics of old age. The reasons for this lie in the divisions of interest among elderly people, along with the economic insecurity of the majority and the less participative political system in Britain than, say, North America. This helps explain why the resistance among pensioners to the Thatcher government's assault on their pensions was so muted. It contrasts, for example, with the campaign mounted by Canadian pensioners against the proposal in the 1985 budget to index only partially Old Age Security payments.[38]

Conclusion

The 1980s in Britain represented a period of severe retrenchment in the welfare state. Social security for elderly people was cut back significantly, even though, at the start of the decade, the incomes of British pensioners were among the lowest in northern Europe. In contrast to Myles and Teichroew's speculation that the Canadian pension scheme may have escaped cuts because it was so modest (see Chapter 5), the paucity of the British state pension system did not help it to escape assault. Notwithstanding the deleterious impact of the government's policies on elderly people, to a quite unprecedented extent in the postwar period, it would be mistaken to regard Thatcherism as an attack on old age as such; instead, it is against state pensions and state pensioners. (After all, the Conservative leader herself is well over retirement age.)

This distinction emphasizes the inadequacy of liberal–pluralist accounts of the politics of old age in failing to demonstrate that Thatcherism, and neoliberalism in general, operates in the interests of some affluent elderly people whose incomes are derived chiefly from property investment and private pensions, as well as those of future pensioners in secure employment and contributing to occupational and private schemes. Conversely, it works to the considerable disadvantage of poor elderly people, especially very elderly women, who are reliant solely on increasingly residualized state pensions. For all its many faults,[39] at least the Keynes–Beveridge regime, as it developed up to the end of the 1970s, provided universal pensions for the majority, and the maturation of SERPS would have raised the average income of Britain's pensioners from their lowly position in comparison with other leading OECD countries.[40] But, again, the liberal–pluralist approach failed to analyze the divisions underlying social democratic welfare provision for the elderly. In other words, structural conflict is ever present in welfare systems. Of course, it is not necessarily overt; more often, it is buried in the policy system and the covert operation of power and ideology.[41] This conflict is principally structured by social class, but there are also generational, gender, and racial dimensions, reflecting the fact that welfare provision is administratively organized according to such criteria. It may be that a more overt form of conflict over pensions and other old-age policies will emerge in Britain, but this seems unlikely. If it does, the main impetus will be the Thatcher government's divisive policies.

The preceding analysis suggests that, although the 1980s represented a distinct departure from the consensus era, there were also important continuities between Thatcherism and what went before it. Indeed, the Keynes–Beveridge regime was a necessary precondition for neoliberalism because it firmly entrenched the public-burden conception of welfare. Thus, on one dimension Thatcherism represents an extreme version of this neoclassical economic assumption. There is little prospect of a return to the pre-Thatcherite consensus on welfare, even if a social democratic government is elected in the 1990s. Moreover, in response to Thatcherism and similar neoliberal policies in other countries, a more critical analysis of aging and social policy has developed apace.[42] In Britain we can be sure that, after Thatcherism, the politics of old age will never be the same again.

Notes

1. Although it is questionable how far, in practice, the elderly population ever represented a "pensioner vote," senior politicians from both main political parties

often acted in public as if it did. The social divisions on which this consensus was based are discussed below and at greater length in A. Walker, "The Politics of Ageing in Britain," in *Dependency and Interdependency in Old Age: Theoretical Perspectives and Policy Alternatives*, ed. C. Phillipson, M. Bernard, and P. Strong (London: Croom Helm, 1986), 30–45.

2. A. Walker, "The Social Consequences of Early Retirement," *Political Quarterly* 53, no. 1 (1982): 61–72; F. Laczko et al., "Early Retirement in a Period of High Unemployment," *Journal of Social Policy* 17, no. 3 (1988): 313–33.

3. OECD, *Reforming Public Pensions* (Paris: OECD, 1988), 55.

4. Pensions as a proportion of earnings in the year before retirement for workers with average wages in manufacturing.

5. OECD, *Reforming Public Pensions*, 50.

6. For a full account, see A. Walker, "The Social Creation of Poverty and Dependency in Old Age," *Journal of Social Policy* 9, no. 1 (1980): 45–75; idem, "Pensions and the Production of Poverty in Old Age," in *Ageing and Social Policy*, ed. C. Phillipson and A. Walker (London: Gower, 1986), 184–216.

7. W. Beveridge, *Social Insurance and Allied Services* (London: HMSO, 1942).

8. E. Shragge, *Pensions Policy in Britain* (London: Routledge, 1984).

9. Beveridge, *Social Insurance*, 93.

10. Ibid., 6–7.

11. A. Walker, "Towards a Political Economy of Old Age," *Ageing and Social Policy* 1, no. 1 (1981): 85.

12. See, for example, D. Nelson, "Alternative Images of Old Age as the Bases for Policy," in *Age or Need?* ed. B. Neugarten (Beverly Hills: Sage, 1982), 131–70.

13. R. M. Titmuss, *Essays on "the Welfare State,"* 2nd ed. (London: Allen & Unwin, 1963), 35; A. Walker, *Social Planning* (Oxford: Basil Blackwell, 1984), 45–69.

14. A. Gamble, *The Free Economy and the Strong State* (London: Macmillan, 1988).

15. A. Gamble and A. Walker, "Introduction: Bringing Socialism Back In," in *The Social Economy and the Democratic State*, ed. Sheffield Group (London: Lawrence and Wishart, 1989), 15.

16. A. Walker, "The Economic Impact of Ageing: A Critical Assessment" (Paper presented to the Canadian Association on Gerontology's Seventeenth Annual Scientific and Educational Meeting, Halifax, Nova Scotia, October 23, 1988).

17. H. M. Treasury, *The Government's Expenditure Plans, 1980–81* (London: HMSO, 1979).

18. J. Hills, "What Happened to Spending on the Welfare State?" in *The Growing Divide*, ed. A. Walker and C. Walker (London: CPAG, 1987), 100.

19. DHSS, *Reform of Social Security*, Cmnd. 9517 (London: HMSO, 1985), 18.

20. Ibid., 21.

21. OECD, *Reforming Public Pensions*, 37.

22. DHSS, *Reform of Social Security: Programme for Change*, Cmnd. 9518 (London: HMSO, 1985), 6.

23. DHSS, Cmnd. 9517, 12–13.

24. The basic NI pension increased from 19 percent of gross average male earnings for a single pensioner in 1948 to 22 percent in 1986. The main improvement in the

value of the NI pension has been against some other social security benefits, notably unemployment benefits, rather than average earnings. Up to 1972–1973, unemployment benefits and retirement pensions were paid at the same rate; by 1984–1985, the latter was worth 26 percent more than the former, as it was in 1989.

25. Gamble and Walker, "Introduction."

26. J. Jones, "Ageing and Generational Equity: An American Perspective" (Paper presented to the Futuribles International Seminar on the Ageing of the Population, Paris, October 4–5, 1988).

27. E. Binney and C. Estes, "The Retreat of the State and Its Transfer of Responsibility: The Intergenerational War," *International Journal of Health Services* 18, no. 1 (1988): 83–96.

28. P. Johnson and J. Falkingham, *Intergenerational Transfers and Public Expenditure on the Elderly in Modern Britain* (London: Centre for Economic Policy Research, 1988).

29. P. Golding and S. Middleton, *Images of Welfare* (Oxford: Martin Robertson, 1982).

30. OECD, *Reforming Public Pensions*, 37.

31. Ibid., 35.

32. House of Commons, *Hansard* (London: HMSO, May 9, 1988), col. 30.

33. OECD, *Ageing Populations: The Social Policy Implications* (Paris: OECD, 1988), 30; see also J. Myles, "Conflict, Crisis, and the Future of Old Age Security," *Millbank Memorial Fund Quarterly* 61, no. 3 (1983): 462–72.

34. Gamble and Walker, "Introduction," 28.

35. Walker, "Politics of Ageing."

36. Department of Health, *Working for Patients* (London: HMSO, 1989); Secretary of State for Health, *Statement on Community Care* (London, Department of Health, July 12, 1989).

37. Walker, "Politics of Ageing."

38. M. Maclean, "Ageism in the United Kingdom and Canada," *Critical Social Policy*, no. 18 (1986): 52–57.

39. See, for example, Shragge, *Pensions Policy*; R. Mishra, *The Welfare State in Crisis* (London: Wheatsheaf Books, 1984); N. Johnson, *The Welfare State in Transition* (London: Wheatsheaf Books, 1987).

40. P. Hestrom and S. Ringen, "Age and Income in Contemporary Society: A Research Note," *Journal of Social Policy* 16, no. 2 (1987): 227–39.

41. S. Lukes, *Power: A Radical View* (London: Macmillan, 1974).

42. See, for example, C. Phillipson and A. Walker, "The Case for a Critical Gerontology," in *Social Gerontology: New Directions*, ed. S. di Gregorio (London: Croom Helm, 1987), 1–13; C. Estes, "The Politics of Ageing in America," *Ageing and Society* 6, no. 3 (1986): 121–34; A.-M. Guillemard, "Social Policy and Ageing in France," in Phillipson and Walker, *Ageing and Social Policy*, 263–79.

3/Interest-Group Politics and the Future of U.S. Social Security

Jill Quadagno

When Ronald Reagan was elected to the presidency in 1980, he initiated a series of budget cuts directed at every social program. In 1981 Congress enacted the Omnibus Budget Reconciliation Act, which eliminated the entire public-service jobs program, removed 400,000 individuals from the food stamp program, and reduced or eliminated welfare and Medicaid benefits for the working poor.[1] In addition, residents of public housing were required to pay 30 percent of their income toward rent instead of 25 percent. Cuts directed at social security focused on the politically vulnerable: elimination of the minimum benefit for low-income earners, an end to the modest death benefit for most recipients, and phasing out benefits for older children of deceased workers.[2] Congress legislated these cuts in July 1981 with the full support of the Senate Budget Committee, including such liberal senators as Howard Metzenbaum (D-Ohio), Daniel Moynihan (D-N.Y.), Donald Riegle (D-Mich.), and Gary Hart (D-Col.).

A more sweeping proposal aimed at social security that Reagan unveiled at the same time the welfare reductions slid through Congress touched off a storm of controversy. Its main recommendations were a 10 percent cut in future benefits, a 31 percent cut in early-retirement benefits, and a further narrowing of eligibility for disability.[3] This second set of cuts attacked middle-class entitlements (not the working and welfare poor), and reprisals were swift and harsh. Days after Reagan's proposal appeared, his public approval rating dropped sixteen points.[4] In two congressional elections held after the Reagan proposals, Ohio Republican Michael Oxley barely held on to a seat Republicans had occupied since the 1930s, and a secure Mississippi Republican seat went to the Democrats.[5]

What accounts for the seeming invincibility of social security compared to other welfare programs? In this chapter I argue that the answer lies in the concept of "middle-class incorporation." Middle-class incorporation occurs when social benefits are based on a "social security" model rather than a "social assistance" model. Social assistance stems from a poor-relief tradition. Its hallmark is means testing, which is both punishing and stigmatizing.[6] Historically, the working classes, those most likely to fall into need over the life course, have had a vested interest in expanding the right to benefits and eliminating their punitive aspects.

The social security model provides true income security through the principles of universality and wage replacement. Universality guarantees the right to benefits for all citizens, while wage replacement signifies continuity in living standards over the life course.[7] When a social security system is in place, it provides benefits not only for the working class but also for the middle class. What social security does, then, is to merge working-class and middle-class interests by creating cross-class solidarity behind a single program. This is the essence of middle-class incorporation. It engages the middle class in a solidaristic agenda supporting the welfare state.

The concept of middle-class incorporation meshes with the argument that political interest groups, organized around a variety of ascriptive characteristics that transcend class-based distinctions, are the force behind welfare expansion. Pampel and Williamson, for example, argue that those in a demographic category, like the aged, may provide just as salient a base for demands for benefit improvements as those in a class-based category.[8] In their view, the emergence of aged-based interest-group politics derives from two factors: the growth of the aged population and the homogenization of interests of the aged. While this argument appears to reflect recent events in the United States, the problem is that neither factor can explain why the old-age lobby emerged in the United States in the 1970s rather than earlier or later, nor whether interest groups of the elderly have been successful in fact in protecting social security. The issues that remain to be resolved are to delineate the conditions under which interest-group politics are likely to emerge and to evaluate possible outcomes of interest-group politics.

In this chapter I argue that the late 1960s and early 1970s represented a turning point for Social Security politics that activated an age-based interest-group politics. This occurred because of two separate but related factors. First, the benefit increases and program improvements enacted between 1969 and 1972 incorporated the middle class into the welfare state by providing true income security in a welfare program for the first time in U.S. history.[9] Second, the breakdown of the organized labor–Social Security Administration coalition created class fragmentation that removed organized labor as a factor in future social security decisions. The result was the growth of interest-group politics around social security issues, a form of politics that resided in the vast numbers of formal organizations whose membership was dominated by older citizens.

The rise of interest-group politics does not mean that class issues disappeared from policymaking, for during the 1970s the business community, alarmed by the decline in America's international competitiveness, came to view social security as an impediment to economic growth. Since the 1980s, the politics of old age has been constructed around the concept of generational equity, the idea that public benefits are unequally distributed between the young and the old. The generational-equity theme, designed to undermine the cross-class strength of the old-age alliance, has been promulgated by Americans for Generational Equity (AGE). Organized along the lines of interest-group politics, AGE has dedicated its agenda to countering the power of the elderly lobby. Its combined message of class and generational conflict was played out in the controversy surrounding the Medicare Catastrophic Coverage Act of 1988.

In the first section of this chapter, I trace the role of organized labor in the gradual expansion of social security from one providing minimal benefits to a small proportion of the labor force to an inclusive measure that guaranteed true income security. I then discuss the emergence of the old-age lobby as well as the counterforces that came to oppose social security. Incorporated here is an analysis of the passage and eventual near-demolition of the Catastrophic Care Act. Finally, I evaluate alternative scenarios for the future of social security.

Social Security Expansion and the Role of Organized Labor

By the early 1930s, the United States was undeniably on the brink of passage of some form of national pension, as a depression-torn nation surveyed its existing measures for old-age security. Many industrial pension plans that had seemed promising during the 1920s were discontinued, closed to new employees, or suspended. Labor-union pension funds had insufficient reserves to pay the benefits promised. And bankrupt state treasuries had no revenues to pay their aged pensioners.[10]

The Social Security Act of 1935 initiated a national system of old-age security. It provided national contributory old-age insurance (OAI) for all industrial wage workers with payroll taxes as the financing mechanism, as well as a federal–state provision for immediate payment of means-tested old-age assistance. In the 1930s, however, public sentiment favored a flat pension, not a wage-based insurance system, a justifiable sentiment given that social security initially covered less than half the working population and provided only meager benefits, less than those paid by the more popular Old Age Assistance. Thus, while the public was pleased that Congress had passed pension legislation, most of the positive sentiment was for old age assistance. The eligibility requirements excluded the majority of citizens from coverage, making the measure too narrow to garner a wide base of support from either the working or the middle class.[11]

Beginning with the addition of dependent benefits in 1939, Congress gradually improved the availability of social security benefits. Between 1950 and 1960, coverage was expanded to include most of the labor force, benefits were increased, and disability benefits were added.[12] The force behind program expansion was the Social Security Administration with the support and active participation of organized labor. As Derthick explains:

In building the social security program, organized labor was by far the most important ally of the Social Security Administration. It supported the SSA inside the advisory councils and lobbied and testified for the agency's legislative proposals. It largely conducted and financed the public campaigns for Medicare. . . . Perhaps most important of all, labor was an unofficial outlet for proposals that SSA officials were not free to promote themselves because they lacked approval from political superiors.[13]

From the program's inception, the Social Security Board actively sought the cooperation of the American Federation of Labor (AFL), and by the early 1940s both the AFL and the Congress of Industrial Organizations (CIO) had become active supporters of social insurance, although the stronger liaison was with the AFL until the two unions merged in 1955.[14] As early as 1941, the AFL argued the need for health and disability insurance, and sponsored a number of bills over the next twenty years. The 1950 amendments to the Social Security Act, which increased benefit levels and expanded program coverage, also resulted from both the active support of the AFL and the collective-bargaining successes of the CIO, which placed pressures on the state to expand public benefits.[15]

In spite of program improvements legislated during the 1950s, by 1960 one-third of older men and 40 percent of older women still had incomes below the poverty level.[16] Benefit increases were under the control of Congress, occurring inconsistently, usually right before an election, and health-care expenses placed an enormous financial burden on millions of uninsured of all ages.

Organized labor had become the national campaign organization for the Democratic party during the 1944 elections, and labor's program successes were contingent on which party was in office.[17] By 1960 the political scene had shifted to the left with Democrats holding a 2.5–1 majority in Congress, enough to give northern Democrats a majority without the South. In 1965 Congress enacted Medicare, a legislative success that owed much to labor's efforts. Much of the staff work supporting Medicare was done at AFL-CIO headquarters, where unionists drafted bills, planned arguments, and wrote speeches for congressional sympathizers. The AFL-CIO also founded and helped finance the National Council of Senior Citizens (NCSC), a nationwide organization of retired unionists that lobbied for Medicare and other program improvements.[18]

The Medicare victory was the last sustained joint effort for old-age legislation between organized labor, the Social Security Administration, and the Democratic party. The breakup of the organized labor–SSA coalition began in 1965 when Walter Reuther, president of the United Auto Workers (UAW), introduced a resolution at the AFL-CIO convention calling for extensive improvements in social security: substantial increases in benefits, a higher wage base, and contributions from general revenues. Reuther's vision of reform went beyond the more moderate proposals of the AFL-CIO, and at his urging, Senator Robert Kennedy introduced a more radical bill than that presented to Congress by President Lyndon Johnson and supported by the AFL-CIO. In 1968 the UAW withdrew from the AFL-CIO, which Reuther believed was unresponsive to wider issues, such as organizing the unorganized, civil rights, and the Vietnam war.[19] Thus, internecine warfare within the union movement fractured labor's social-policy agenda.

Other issues—for example, the welfare explosion and urban unrest of the late 1960s—further alienated unionists from a sense of broader class solidarity. Organized workers became increasingly resentful of the tax burden of the nonworking poor, while "the emergence of demands for power-sharing and positive discrimination for blacks, hispanics and women directly threatened the exclusivist operation of ethnic patronage politics and craft union apprenticeships." [20] The 1968 elections, in which the "new liberals" of the antiwar movement captured the Democratic party, further estranged organized labor, and in 1969 AFL-CIO President George Meany went so far as to explore the possibility of links with the Republican party. The 1972 elections confirmed the breach between the Democratic party and the AFL-CIO when the union's executive committee voted not to support the party's nominee, George McGovern.[21] Organized workers deserted the Democratic party and its 1972 presidential candidate, fragmenting the coalition that had been the source of support for social security expansion.

Although organized labor's internal conflicts, as well as its dissatisfaction with the Democratic party, reduced its political effectiveness in pressing for improvements in social security, other forces continued to move Congress toward major reform. In 1971 the Advisory Council on Social Security reported that the program was greatly overfinanced and would produce cumulative reserves approaching $1 trillion by the year 2025. Included in the Advisory Council's recommendations were automatic benefit adjustments to keep pace with price increases, liberalization of the retirement test, and improved disability protection, many of the proposals initiated by Reuther.

In 1972 Congress legislated the most substantive structural change in the program since 1935. It increased benefits by 20 percent, indexed benefits to inflation (COLA's) and maximum taxable wages to future wage movements, and abandoned the level-wage assumption.[22] The 1972 amendments represented a turning point for social security, a watershed for U.S. welfare-state development. Between 1967 and 1984, the average income of elderly family units rose by 55 percent, despite a large drop in the average amount of earned income, while poverty rates dropped from over 25 percent to less than 15 percent. Further, social security benefits gained in importance as the total share of elderly income derived from social security increased from 28 percent in 1967 to 36 percent in 1984.[23] For the first time in U.S. history, the middle class was fully incorporated into a national welfare program whose benefits determined the well-being of a large proportion of the nation's elderly.

The Growth of the Elderly Lobby

Although organized labor had lost its prominent position in social security policymaking, the elderly apparently no longer needed labor's support. By the mid 1970s, more than 80 percent of those over age 65 were receiving some income from social security. Social security also helped widows and widowers with dependent children and provided income security for the disabled. Because social security was the sole welfare program (including Medicare) where the middle class as well as the poor received something tangible back for their taxes, public support for social security was high. Virtually every public-opinion poll between 1977 and 1983 indicated that the American people supported social security.[24] Middle-class incorporation created a vested interest group that was to become the program's sustaining factor.

Throughout the 1970s, a significant growth of senior-citizen organizations occurred. Founded in 1958 mainly to provide insurance to retirees, the American Association of Retired Persons (AARP) had grown to 28 million members by 1988, with one out of nine Americans paying the $5 annual membership fee. Other powerful senior-citizen organizations include the Gray Panthers at 80,000 members and the National Council of Senior Citizens with approximately 4 million members in 1982.[25]

Senior-citizen organizations have been highly effective in protecting social security because of their successful lobbying tactics. The largest organization, AARP, publishes *Modern Maturity*, the nation's third-highest-circulation magazine, which includes voters' guides on candidate positions on issues of relevance to the aged, runs a wire service that provides newspapers with reporting on elderly issues, and sponsors a weekly television series. During the 1988 presidential election, in New Hampshire alone AARP mailed out 250,000 pieces of literature detailing the candidates' positions on social security, long-term health care, and other issues of relevance to older people. Yet the size and diversity of AARP's membership has limited its ability to take a position on most issues, a factor that has placed constraints on the organization's political power and caused politicians to overestimate its impact.

Even more effective as a lobbying force has been the NCSC, organized around 4,000 active local clubs. NCSC has access to the full lobbying power of the AFL-CIO. Moreover, its smaller size and the shared background of its members (trade unionists) make it more capable of taking a stance on particular issues than the unwieldy AARP.[26]

The power of the elderly lobby became highly visible in 1979 when President Jimmy Carter attempted some minor cuts in social security. Save Our Security (SOS), made up of a coalition of senior-citizen groups, responded with vehement protest. Then in 1981, when President Reagan suggested cutting basic benefits, the dormant organization revived, expanding its membership from less than two dozen elderly groups to over a hundred by the end of the year. By 1982 SOS could claim approximately 125 labor and elderly advocacy organizations with 35 to 40 million members.[27]

What is most significant about the senior-citizen lobby is not its sponsorship of particular candidates, for the size and cross-class nature of the lobby makes agreement on issues other than old-age security unlikely, but rather its impact on the political agenda. Sixty-five year olds vote at nearly three times the rate of eligible voters under age 24, and politicians are fearful of their political potential.[28] The public outcry against Reagan's attempts to cut social security has made it virtually untouchable. Even when the 1987 stock market crash put every social program under scrutiny, social security remained off the bargaining table. It had become, in the words of *Time* magazine, the budget's sacred cow, a "sacroscanct program unassailable by cost cutters." [29]

The Attack on Social Security

The year 1971 marked the first trade deficit of the century, indicating the loss of the competitive advantage the United States had sustained since World War II.[30] The 1973 energy crisis and subsequent stagflation further eroded profit rates. Although business leaders saw themselves as the victims of a failing economy, public opinion seemed to blame them.[31] To counter not only this negative public image but, more important, what they perceived as the domination of the media, universities, and government by an antibusiness "new class," corporate leaders financed a vast network of conservative think tanks, policy centers, research institutes, and probusiness "public interest" law firms. The result of this new intellectual base was a huge outpouring of books, articles, research, and "expert" congressional testimony demonstrating the benefits of promarket policy.[32] By the late 1970s, "the corporate lobbying community . . . had gained a level of influence and leverage approaching that of the boom days of the 1920s." [33]

While the enactment of Medicare and the addition of COLAs solidified middle-class support for social security, the business community became increasingly critical of these programs. *Business Week* quoted economists' views that "Social Security financing depresses private savings and thus impedes the capital accumulation and investment necessary to insure adequate economic growth," a factor that "appeared to be intensifying with the expansion of the system." [34] Payroll taxation also had adverse inflationary and employment effects.[35] A *Fortune* magazine editorial quoted Martin Feldstein's view that social security had seriously retarded capital formation.[36]

Beginning in the late 1970s, prominent journals, books emanating from conservative think tanks, and the popular news media began an attack on social security, echoing the message that the program was in crisis and near bankruptcy.[37] What gave credibility to these claims was the declining reserve in the trust fund, the result of several factors, including high unemployment, which reduced the funds going into the treasury, and inflation, which triggered large cost-of-living increases. Social security reached its low point on November 5, 1982, when the trust fund was forced to borrow $581 million from the Medicare and disability accounts to pay benefit checks on time, a measure that was repeated twice in the next thirteen months. If some resolution was not achieved by July 3, 1983, benefit checks would be delayed for the first time in the program's history.[38]

By October 1982, polls indicated that 70 percent of the public disapproved of Reagan's handling of social security.[39] Yet the issue had become so politicized that any proposal carried political risk. The result was that all social security debate came to a halt, preventing Congress from reaching an agreement on how to restore the trust fund to solvency.

With Congress stalemated, the only hope for reform lay with the bipartisan National Commission on Social Security Reform, appointed by Reagan the previous year. The commission held its first meeting in February 1982. Conservative members (who represented the interests of a number of business organizations) advocated benefit cuts, while liberals (taking the stance favored by organized labor and senior-citizen organizations) pressed for tax increases. After a lengthy negotiation period during which a few of the commission members held secret meetings in hopes of reaching a compromise, a proposal was put before Congress. The package included a six-month COLA delay, increased tax rates, the inclusion of federal workers, and the taxation of benefits for upper-income retirees.[40] The 1983 amendments also included four measures designed to curb early retirement: (1) a greater penalty for retiring before age 65 (from 80 percent to 75 percent by the year 2005 and to 70 percent by 2022); (2) a gradual increase in the age for full benefits, from 65 to 67; (3) an increased bonus to defer retirement; (4) a lower penalty for continuing to work on a reduced basis while in receipt of retired worker benefits.[41] Minor tinkering had resolved the "crisis."

Among the large number of groups that testified before Congress on the amendments, the elderly (represented by AARP and the NCSC) and small business groups were most active. Yet neither side could claim a victory, for the 1983 amendments represented a compromise of benefit cuts and tax increases, which put into effect a number of proposals previously rejected as politically unfeasible.[42] The long-run implications are more significant than the short-term tinkering, however, for two groups will lose future benefits. Since the amendments did not tie the maximum taxable income levels to any economic indicators, each year a higher proportion of recipients will find their benefits subject to taxation. This provision has the potential to undermine middle-class support, as social security begins to decrease its contribution to the total income package of higher-income elderly. At the same time, the increase in the age of eligibility for early retirement and the decrease in early-retirement benefits will hit manual workers and union retirement funds particularly hard. Blue-collar workers in many industries now retire well before reaching the eligibility age for early benefits. The age increase in eligibility for benefits is not likely to reverse this trend but to place greater pressure on pension funds, many in troubled industries, which will be forced to carry workers longer.[43]

The Generational-Equity Message
Defining the Parameters of the Debate
With social security opponents seemingly unable to make significant program cuts either through a media assault or through direct political action, a new strategy designed to compete with the highly effective senior lobby emerged. The goal of Americans for Generational Equity (AGE) became that of altering the character of the public discussion surrounding social security through the dual messages of class conflict and generational conflict.

The seeds of an attack on social security based on generational conflict had been sown in the early 1970s as part of the business community's response to the 1972 tax hike and benefit increases. A 1972 analysis of the social security system published by the Federal Reserve Bank of New York described it as a "huge Ponzi scheme" that depends on the power of the tax collector to extract increasing taxes from today's already overtaxed workers.[44] And the funding problems the system faced in the late 1970s and early 1980s honed the argument. Bendix Corporation chairman William Agee direly predicted that "procrastinating until the burden forces the breaching of the promises will only make the problem worse. Young and old will be pitted against one another in a fearful battle over the remains of a shrinking economy."[45] By

1982, *Fortune* magazine warned its readers: It is part of the sorrowful lot of the baby-boom generation that it will have to finance both its parents' retirement and a substantial portion of its own.[46]

The theme of generational equity initially reduced the critique of social security to the simple premise that the generosity of entitlements to the old created poverty among children. "The old," Phillip Longman wrote in the *Washington Monthly*, "have come to insist that the young not only hold them harmless for their past profligacy, but sacrifice their own prosperity to pay for it."[47] Because of entitlements, older people, only 7 percent of whom were in poverty in 1982, according to Longman's calculations, were taking resources from the young, squandering the nation's limited wealth instead of investing in future economic growth. In contrast, 23 percent of children were in poverty, and funding for programs that support children had been subject to budget cuts as expenditures for the aged increased.

The attack on entitlements became formalized in 1984 when Senator Dave Durenberger (R-Minn.), one of the three leading recipients of corporate political action committee (PAC) money in the 1982 elections, founded AGE.[48] Durenberger's management intern, Paul Hewitt, became president and executive director, and Phillip Longman was brought on board as research director.[49] In its first year in operation, AGE attracted 600 members and had a budget of $88,000. By 1987, AGE revenues had increased to $367,316, with most of the funding coming from social security and Medicare's prime private-sector competitors: banks, insurance companies, defense contractors, and health-care corporations, a total of eighty-five organizations and businesses.[50] And AGE's goal? "To promote the concept of generational equity among America's political, intellectual and financial leaders. . . . The more America's leaders talk about and think in terms of generational equity, the more effective AGE will be in its education program, and the better chance we will have of making the difference on crucial legislative issues."[51]

In his keynote address at a conference held at the University of Minnesota on January 13, 1987, Senator Durenburger espoused the AGE theme: "We have entered an era in which the date of one's birth has become the prime determinate of one's prospects for realizing the American dream. Younger Americans—regardless of their class or ethnic origin—are in the grip of what seems like a permanent and compounding downward spiral."[52] Included among AGE's topics of concern were Medicare reform, educational priorities, savings and investment policy, deficit reduction options and "a national strategy for the Baby Boom generation's retirement."

As AGE sought to expand its political constituency, it refined the concept of class conflict implicit in its discussion of generational conflict. The theme of class conflict was already prominent among conservative critics of social security. Peter Ferrara, senior member in the White House Office of Policy Development in 1982 and 1983 and social security consultant to the Heritage

Foundation, a conservative think tank, argued that the payroll tax "imposes a particularly harsh burden on low-income jobs—a burden that no one consciously would have contemplated." [53] Similarly, James Dale Davidson, head of the National Taxpayers Union, declared, "It's time we told the widow in the East Side luxury condominium that she's getting what amounts to welfare at the expense of the low-wage worker in the South Bronx." [54]

In its *Generational Journal* AGE published articles suggesting that social programs should target the poor. One such article, focusing on the problems of schools in inner cities, espoused "quality education for all children by the year 2000." Another article, appearing in the same issue, addressed the problem of health insurance for the poor.[55] Thus, AGE publications suggested that the poor were the victims of misappropriated societal funds, which went disproportionately to the aged.

The notion of targeting the poor appealed to liberal Democrats, such as Wisconsin Congressman Jim Moody, who became AGE co-chairman. Moody hailed from a district that reelected him to office on the argument that taxes placed an unfair burden on the working class. At a speech to the Allied Council of Senior Citizens in Milwaukee, Moody claimed that "many people receiving Social Security benefits are better off than those taxed to pay them. The federal deficit is out of control, and the young are too heavily taxed; everyone must sacrifice; Social Security must be curbed." [56]

AGE was able to expound a thesis that crossed party lines by capitalizing on the fractured class interests that had split the Democratic party and turned working-class Democrats to the Republicans. By focusing on middle-class discontent over the growing tax burden, the AGE theme had appeal for young, educated Republicans. At the same time, the emphasis on the penalty poor children were paying aroused the resentment of low-income groups in traditional Democratic strongholds over cuts in welfare benefits. This combination of a conservative ideology attached to legitimate concerns of antipoverty liberals gave AGE the political capital to build a broader coalition than one based solely on an attack on entitlements.

The Strategy of AGE

Initially perceived as an organization dedicated to abolishing social security or, worse, "a new kind of yuppie lobby," AGE worked at changing its image to an organization "pursuing a constructive, responsible program." [57] So successful was AGE in its strategy that in the two weeks after the stock market crash, AGE was contacted for interviews or background information by NBC, CBS, PBS, the *New York Times*, the *Wall Street Journal, Newsweek, Time, U.S. News and World Report, Fortune, Forbes*, the *Chicago Tribune*, and the *Des Moines Register*.[58]

How did AGE manage to accomplish this image change? The organization's strategy included a number of tactics designed to enhance its credibility and provide a public forum. First, AGE expanded its boundaries beyond the narrow "yuppie" fringe of staff, adding a board of directors and an advisory board consisting of representatives from such right-wing think tanks as the Hoover Institution, the Heritage Foundation, and the American Enterprise Institute, but also more moderate conservatives, officers from banks, life insurance companies and health-care corporations, and a few academics from prestigious institutions, including Donald Kennedy and Michael Boskin of Stanford University and Samuel Preston of the University of Pennsylvania. AGE also expanded its political base by establishing a bipartisan congressional advisory council.[59] By 1987, AGE could claim among its advisers former chief actuary of the Social Security Administration, Robert Myers.[60]

A second AGE strategy was to sponsor a series of conferences, which brought in a wider array of mainstream intellectuals. The first, held in 1986, on the "Baby Boom Generation's Retirement," was followed by three in 1987 and three more in 1988 on such topics as growth and productivity, Medicare reform, deficits and demographics, and downward mobility in America.[61] AGE's Autumn 1987 conference, "Ties That Bind: Debts, Deficits, and Demographics," specifically addressed the impact of social security on the private savings rate, a topic of concern to banks and savings and loan institutions.[62] The conferences enhanced the credibility of the organization while providing a public forum for AGE.

AGE made one attempt at political lobbying through a letter-writing campaign. On January 18, 1988, AGE members received a letter from Tom Rodman, marketing vice-president with Smith Barney in New York, warning that "our children's future is going to explode," because of the huge budget deficit. Budget-cutting efforts have failed, according to Rodman, because of continued growth in entitlement programs: "Our children should burn their Social Security cards today." Rodman suggested that each AGE member find five friends who would "send one snapshot of a child—any child—to their five elected officials" along with a letter asking to "put entitlement spending reform back on the table."[63] The Rodman letter was accompanied by a memo from Paul Hewitt encouraging AGE members to respond.[64] There is no evidence that this tactic generated any significant response.

Finally, AGE sought to get its message out through a series of books, articles, and Op-Ed pieces. A 1985 *Atlantic Monthly* article by Phillip Longman expanded the AGE message to incorporate several new themes. First, it revived the "crisis" scenario under a new guise. Although the social security trust fund was no longer insolvent and was, in fact, accumulating reserves, the system was still in trouble because Congress was likely to adopt interfund borrowing to reduce the anticipated deficit in the Medicare trust fund.[65] Depending on how quickly Medicare exhausted its reserves, the trust fund could go broke anyway.

Second, Americans were warned that future benefits would be less generous, with the result that most baby boomers would pay more into the system than they collect.[66] And third, since recent poverty statistics indicated that the elderly as a group had a higher standard of living than the working population, Longman argued that there was no need to subsidize them so generously.[67]

The increased budget deficit and reports of a declining relative level of economic growth in the United States in the mid 1980s provided further fuel for attacks on social security, and AGE arguments came to focus more on economic issues. The month prior to the stock market crash, Peter G. Peterson, now research director for AGE, published an *Atlantic Monthly* article coupling the generational-equity message with broader economic issues. Peterson warned that as a result of feeble productivity growth, we have "witnessed a widening split between the elderly, among whom poverty is still declining, and children and young families, among whom poverty rates have exploded— a development with dire implications for our *future* productivity." [68] Although Americans, according to Peterson, endorsed smaller and leaner government, federal spending increased significantly between 1979 and 1986, with most of the growth concentrated in middle-class entitlements, which had grown from 5.4 percent in 1965 to 11.5 percent of GNP.[69] By contrast, federal spending for America's public infrastructure, for research and development in industry (R&D), education, job skills, and remedial social services have been cut.[70]

Within recent policy debates, there are a number of indications that the AGE message has gained credibility. One indicator is that other politicians have cautiously begun to echo the AGE message. For example, Senator Jack Danforth (D-Mo.) told an audience of trustees from children's hospitals that 35 percent of the federal budget goes for programs directed at the elderly, while only 2 percent is spent on education. "The decision we've made as a country," declared Danforth, "is that our children come last." [71] Similarly, Anthony Beilenson, a Democratic representative from California, declared that social security should be included in deficit-reduction negotiations because "retired persons as a class are not worse off than other groups of Americans." [72]

The AGE message has also been picked up by the media. A July 5, 1987, article in the *Washington Post* entitled "Fooling Around" claimed that "not only are today's young workers facing an insecure retirement, but they are being asked to fund more than their share of government." [73] In a similar vein, the *Wall Street Journal* suggested that "major reforms of Social Security cannot be ducked indefinitely. . . . Either policymakers will have to slash benefits or raise payroll taxes to undreamed of levels." [74] In 1987 the liberal *New Republic* also launched a series of articles echoing the AGE message.[75]

Yet in spite of the proliferation of the generational-equity theme, public support for entitlements remains high. A 1987 survey conducted for the American Association of Retired Persons concluded that there are "no signs of waning support for programs targeted for the elderly." Even among young adults (ages 21 to 29), 77 percent believe the government should spend more money on Medicare, 74 percent favor higher social security benefits, and 76 percent say the government is "not doing enough for older people." [76]

With no grass-roots constituency, AGE is at a political disadvantage compared to the elderly lobby. It cannot place the same sort of political pressure on politicians, nor can it mobilize a mass campaign to generate support for its agenda. In this way, it is limited in its ability to use the kinds of political opportunities available through the structure of partisan politics. Nonetheless, a recent policy issue, framed in generational-equity terms, demonstrates how readily social programs that do not spread the costs across the entire population can erode public support.

The Medicare Catastrophic Coverage Act of 1988

The Medicare Catastrophic Coverage Act of 1988 was signed into law on July 1, 1988, with strong support in the Senate and the House. In October 1989 a vastly altered bill was accepted in a compromise proposal that barely salvaged the program. The events that transpired in the interim illustrate the fragility of interest-group politics as a means of sustaining a social security agenda.

In 1985 Otis Bowen, secretary of Health and Human Services, drafted a basic proposal for insurance against catastrophic health expenses. Initially shelved, President Reagan asked Bowen to revive the proposal in 1987 in an attempt to undo damage from criticism by Democrats against his administration's proposals to delay the scheduled cost-of-living increases in social security benefits. In supporting the proposal, Reagan stipulated that the program be financed entirely by the elderly.[77]

The following year, a much-revised proposal emerged from the Health Subcommittee of the Senate Finance Committee, chaired by Senator Durenberger. The Medicare Catastrophic Coverage Act of 1988 represented the largest expansion of the Medicare program since its creation. Under the original act, all Medicare recipients would have paid a flat premium of $4 a month, scheduled to increase to $10.20 a month in 1993. Although nursing-home-care coverage was extended only from 100 to 150 days, other benefits were extensive. They included long-term hospital care (365 days of coverage after payment of a one-time deductible of $560), a prescription drug benefit for medication not covered by preexisting Medicare policies, mammography screening, hospice care, caregiver support for anyone caring for a sick relative, and the extension of Medicaid benefits to poor pregnant women and infants. As the first health-care bill in many years, it became a vehicle for the deferred agenda in health care.

In addition, about a third of the Medicare recipients—those who pay at least $150 in annual income taxes—would have been required to pay a surtax. The surtax would have worked in this fashion: For every $150 paid in federal income tax, a person on Medicare would pay an additional $37.50 surtax. A tax liability of $1,500 would trigger a surtax of $375; a tax liability of $3,000 would mean a surtax of $750, and so on, up to a ceiling of $800, to increase to $1,050 by 1993. If husband and wife were both on Medicare, each would have paid the surtax.[78]

The significance of the total package cannot be underestimated. The costs for middle-income elderly taxpayers were substantial, while the potential benefits they would have received were paltry. First, a small fraction of Medicare recipients (less than 1.5 percent) exceeds the present 150-day limit on covered care, and only 16.8 percent were expected to benefit from the prescription-drug coverage. Second, because of previous gaps in Medicare coverage, a large portion of older people either purchased or received from employers Medigap policies from private insurance companies. These policies pay benefits similar to those the Catastrophic Coverage Act would have covered and fill many of the holes in health-care coverage that the new legislation would not have filled.[79] Finally, the only present source of public funding for extended nursing home care is Medicaid, a means- and asset-tested social assistance program. Neither working-class nor middle-class aged have any help in financing the astronomical costs of nursing home care, except by spending down their income and assets to become impoverished. Thus, middle- and upper-income elderly would have had to pay increased taxes for insurance coverage they did not need, while not receiving help for the major benefit they did need.

While the surtax received all the public attention, the financing of the new benefits represented a significant departure from previous policy. For the first time in history, the costs of a social insurance program was structured to be borne totally by the better-off beneficiaries. As Durenberger proclaimed, "Medicare insurance costs will be paid for by those who receive the benefits. In other words, this law will not penalize one generation for the sake of another."[80] The significance of this policy change—implemented with a generational equity message—can hardly be overstated. The new Medicare legislation represented the first successful attempt to desocialize an entitlement program. Instead of spreading the costs across the entire working population, it placed them solely on the shoulders of the elderly, with the middle class paying the most.

Not surprisingly, the Catastrophic Coverage Act triggered an explosive reaction from the elderly lobby. Across the country, petition drives and other protests arose almost instantaneously. In just sixty days, the Nevada-based Senior Coalition Against the Catastrophic Act claimed to have gathered 410,000 signatures on a repeal petition.[81] According to newspaper reports, 6,000 older people canceled their membership in AARP, which had supported the legislation and opposed its repeal. And Washington legislators had their offices flooded with letters and calls from constituents, infuriated that middle-income elderly would be paying the highest tax rates in the nation as a result of the legislation.[82] What they wanted was either repeal of the legislation, a significant reduction of the tax burden to the middle class, or the right to withdraw from the new benefits (and costs) with no penalty on other health-care coverage.

Even though Medicare has been funded historically through payroll taxes, which socialized its costs, critics of the Catastrophic Coverage Act did not advocate resocializing Medicare by increasing payroll taxes. Such an option would seem to have been a possibility given that Medicare includes the long-term disabled of all ages and that until this legislation, all program funding came from payroll taxes. Yet such an agenda, which had been a core issue for organized labor, did not emerge from the old-age lobby, either from supporters or opponents of the act. This suggests that policies shaped by interest-group politics have a different dynamic than those shaped by class politics, one that is less solidaristic and more oriented toward particularistic demands.

On October 4, 1989, the House voted to repeal the program it had approved just sixteen months earlier. Two days later, the Senate voted to repeal the surtax and retain only the long-term hospital benefits, eliminating the ceiling on doctor bills, the expanded nursing-home benefits, and the drug benefits. Thus, the insistence of the Reagan administration on financing by the elderly essentially destroyed a program that would have provided needed health benefits to the least-prosperous aged, to the disabled of all ages, and to poor women and children.

Middle-class incorporation has generated both broad public support and interest-group activity that has thus far made social security seemingly impermeable to attacks against it. Yet both the 1983 amendments, which taxed benefits of higher-income retirees and raised the future retirement age, and the Medicare Catastrophic Coverage Act of 1988, which laid the tax burden on the middle- and upper-income aged, have the possibility for decreasing cross-class solidarity for social security. One consequence already visible is a split between middle- and upper-income elderly (who would have paid the costs of these changes in reduced income and higher taxes) and the poor (who would have benefited more). The final outcome may be a reduced sense of middle-class entitlement and the erosion of middle-class support.

The events of the 1980s suggest several possible directions in which the social security system might move. The next section explores possible scenarios for the future of social security.

The Future of Social Security

AGE proponents propose a number of alterations in social security that would reduce middle-class incorporation. Several proposals suggest eliminating the entitlement component of social security to make it more similar to social assistance. This could be accomplished by either reducing or eliminating COLAs,[83] raising the retirement age, and encouraging private insurance through tax policy so that "Social Security and Medicare might be replaced gradually." [84] Universal rights to benefits would be replaced by means testing, which would require returning eligibility decisions to local authorities.[85] What would be left would be "generous public provision for the elderly poor" over age 70.[86] The AGE agenda, then, would provide only subsistence to the aged poor while eliminating the middle class from access to benefits.

What are the implications of a welfare state designed by generational-equity proponents? The most certain impact would be to increase the labor-force participation rates of older people. With fewer of the aged guaranteed benefits at adequate wage-replacement levels, there would be no option for many but to work. Although increased labor-force participation by older people is not necessarily a negative impact, the real issue is *who* would have to work and what kinds of jobs would be available for these older workers. In recent decades, the basic shift in the American economy has been from mass production to services. While the economy has grown, nearly all the growth has come in the service sector with no expansion in goods production. Among the many new jobs generated in the 1980s, most were in service-sector jobs paying less than the median wage, while the number of high-stratum jobs declined.[87]

Although middle-aged workers have been relatively protected from these trends, new entrants to the labor market, young men and women, have ended up in these low-wage jobs.[88] The focus on young people, however, ignores a second transition that is also occurring—the reentry of formerly retired workers into the labor force. Since 1972, there has been a significant trend toward labor-force reentry for both men and women after age 55 with those in secondary occupations (i.e., low-wage, unskilled, low-status jobs) most likely to experience reentry. All older labor-force reentrants, regardless of previous labor-force location, however, are likely to spend their postretirement second careers in secondary jobs.[89] With reduced benefits available at later ages only to those who qualified through means tests, the subsistence wages in low-wage service industries would become a more attractive income supplement than they are at present.

Because workers in the core manufacturing sector of the economy already retire even before reaching the minimum-benefit age of 62, the impact on this diminishing segment of the American economy would be relatively less than it would be on others. Further, mass production workers in unionized core industries would work to negotiate increases in private pension agreements to make up the difference in social security reductions. Most vulnerable would be present service-sector workers, primarily women, those with little private pension coverage and already heavily represented in that sector of the economy where a labor shortage is developing.[90]

A welfare state designed by AGE would eliminate the generational and class solidarity generated by the present social security system. Further, although AGE proponents claim to be advocates of the poor, the loss of middle-class support would lead to a reduction in income security. As events following the passage of the Catastrophic Care Act illustrate so elegantly, taxation with no benefits quickly erodes support.

Conclusion

Between 1935 and 1972, administrators within the social security system worked with organized labor to construct a social insurance program that was universalistic in scope and that guaranteed a basic measure of income security. In the process they created a constituency that served as a broad base of support for the program. When the "new class" movements of the late 1960s alienated organized labor from the Democratic party, the social security system lost its most consistent supporter, but this loss seemed irrelevant given the strength of the old-age lobby that emerged to take its place.

Recent legislative changes foreshadow the different social-policy outcomes that result when interest-group rather than class politics predominates. Because interest groups have self-protection rather than universalism as their dominant motivator, their support is contingent on continued high spending. Any challenge to the program's solidaristic base does not necessarily lead to tactics to resocialize the program but rather to the withdrawal of support.

The Catastrophic Care Act illustrates both how contingent middle-class support can be and how readily class fragmentation can be activated. When programs are socialized across the entire population, their costs for any category of individual is small compared to the benefits received. But when upper- and middle-income individuals, in this case the aged, are asked to sustain a program that primarily benefits the poor, the relationship between costs and benefits is reversed. The act also demonstrates the risks of substituting private insurance for public benefits. Privatization is an equally powerful factor in fragmenting the class solidarity that sustains social programs, since it reduces benefits relative to costs for those capable of paying for private coverage.

Social security and Medicare are at present the only national welfare programs that cut across the dualism present in other social benefits, a dualism in which the poor receive means-tested benefits from taxes paid by a resentful middle class. The common stake in social insurance has eliminated generational and class issues of equity. AGE has attempted to reinsert generational and class conflict into social security debates, and while its attempts have met with only minimal success, the fragility of interest-group-based support suggests that only minor alterations are needed to fracture the coalition that has made social security a "sacred cow."

Notes

Acknowledgments: I would like to thank James Schulz, Edward Berkowitz, Andrew Achenbaum, Theodore Marmor, John Myles, and Frances Fox Piven for comments on an earlier version of this essay and Madonna Harrington Meyer both for her comments and for her excellent library research.

1. Thomas Byrne Edsall, *The New Politics of Inequality* (New York: Norton, 1984), 17.

2. Wilbur J. Cohen, "The Bipartisan Solution: Securing Social Security." *New Leader*, February 7, 1983, 5.

3. Ibid.

4. Paul Light, *Artful Work: The Politics of Social Security Reform* (New York: Random House, 1985), 124.

5. "The Battle over Repairing Social Security." *Business Week*, September 28, 1981, 116.

6. Gösta Esping-Andersen, "The Three Political Economies of the Welfare State," *Canadian Review of Sociology and Anthropology* 26 (February 1989): 22.

7. John Myles, "Decline or Impasse? The Current State of the Welfare State," *Studies in Political Economy* 26 (Summer 1989): 87.

8. Fred C. Pampel and John B. Williamson, "Welfare Spending in Advanced Industrial Democracies, 1950–1980," *American Journal of Sociology* 93 (May 1988): 1425.

9. The idea that 1972 represented a turning point in social security is taken from John Myles, "Postwar Capitalism and the Extension of Social Security into a Retirement Wage," in *The Politics of Social Policy in the United States*, ed. Margaret Weir, Ann Shola Orloff, and Theda Skocpol (Princeton: Princeton University Press, 1988), 274.

10. Jill Quadagno, *The Transformation of Old Age Security, Class and Politics in the American Welfare State* (Chicago: University of Chicago Press, 1988), 66, 72, 95.

11. Ibid., 119.

12. Martha Derthick, *Policymaking for Social Security* (Washington, D.C.: Brookings Institution, 1979), 431.

13. Ibid., 110.

14. Quadagno, *Transformation of Old Age Security*, 119.

15. Derthick, *Policymaking for Social Security*, 120; Quadagno, *Transformation of Old Age Security*, 166.

16. Greg Duncan and Ken Smith, "The Rising Affluence of the Elderly: How Far, How Fair, and How Frail?" *Annual Review of Sociology* 15 (1989): 262.

17. J. David Greenstone, *Labor in American Politics* (New York: Vintage Books, 1969), 51.

18. Nelson Cruickshank, *Memoirs* (New York: Butler Library, Columbia University Oral History Collection, n.d.), 43; Quadagno, *Transformation of Old Age Security*, 166.

19. Quadagno, *Transformation of Old Age Security*, 173.

20. Mike Davis, *Prisoners of the American Dream* (London: New Left Books, 1986), 223.

21. John Barnard, *Walter Reuther and the Rise of the Auto Workers* (Boston: Little, Brown, 1983), 41–43.

22. Derthick, *Policymaking for Social Security*, 259.

23. Duncan and Smith, "The Rising Affluence of the Elderly," 268–69.

24. Light, *Artful Work*, 59.

25. "Gray Power," *Time*, January 4, 1988, 36–37; "Grays on the Go," *Time*, February 22, 1988, 69. Light, *Artful Work*, 77.

26. Light, *Artful Work*, 77.

27. Ibid., 82, 124.

28. "Gray Power," 36–37.

29. "Sacred Cow," *Time*, November 9, 1987, 24.

30. Paul Blumberg, *Inequality in an Age of Decline* (New York: Oxford University Press, 1980), 109.

31. Seymour Martin Lipset and William Schneider, *The Confidence Gap: Business, Labor and Government in the Public Mind* (New York: Free Press, 1983).

32. Edsall, *The New Politics of Inequality*, 117.

33. Ibid., 107.

34. "Propping Up Social Security." *Business Week*, July 19, 1976, 34. See also "The Social Security Bite: Deeper, Deeper, Deeper . . .," *Nation's Business*, September 1972, 34–35.

35. "The Social Security Time Bomb Is Still Ticking." *Business Week*, January 9, 1978, 79.

36. "Social Security Needs More Than a Quick Fix." *Fortune*, June 1977, 97.

37. John Myles, "The Trillion Dollar Misunderstanding," in *Growing Old in America*, ed. Beth Hess and Elizabeth Markson (New Brunswick, N.J.: Transaction, 1985), 507.

38. Light, *Artful Work*, 33.

39. Ibid., 160.

40. Mildred and Claude Pepper Library, RG 309B, Box 87, File 20: "The Green Sheet." For a complete recounting of the history of the 1983 amendments, see Light, *Artful Work*.

41. The federal government began efforts to restrain the drift toward early retirement in the 1970s. In 1978 Congress passed amendments to the 1967 Age Discrimination in Employment Act, raising the allowable retirement age from 65 to 70. See Harold Sheppard, "The Early Retirement Age Issue in the United States," for the Committee on U.S.–Europe Early Exit Project, Tampa, Florida, November 12–14, 1987, 6; Rachel

Florsheim Boaz, "The 1983 Amendments to the Social Security Act: Will They Delay Retirement? Summary of the Evidence." *Gerontologist* 27 (1987): 151.

42. Light, *Artful Work*, 196.

43. Madonna Harrington Meyer and Jill Quadagno, "Ending a Career in a Declining Industry: The Retirement Experience of Male Auto Workers," *Sociological Perspectives* 33 (1990): 51–62.

44. Quoted in Peter G. Peterson, "The Salvation of Social Security," *New York Review*, December 16, 1982, 50; "Social Security: The Real Cost of Those Rising Benefits," *Fortune*, December 1973, 80.

45. A. F. Ehrbar, "How to Save Social Security," *Fortune*, August 25, 1980, 36.

46. A. F. Ehrbar, "Heading for the Wrong Solution," *Fortune*, December 13, 1982, 36.

47. Phillip Longman, "Taking America to the Cleaners." *Washington Monthly*, November 1982, 24.

48. Edsall, *New Politics of Inequality*, 88.

49. American Association of Retired Persons, "Yankelovich Survey Finds Conflict among Generations Mostly Fiction." *AARP News Bulletin*, April 1987; see also AARP, "Poll Finds Little Friction between Young and Old," *Highlights* 5 (July 1987): 13.

50. Americans for Generational Equity, Second Annual Report, 1986–87.

51. Letter from Dave Durenberger to AGE directors and members, December 1, 1986, 2.

52. Remarks by Senator Dave Durenburger to the conference "An Agenda for the Aging Society," Minneapolis, January 13, 1987, 9.

53. Peter Ferrara, "Put a Permanent Lid on Payroll Taxes," *New York Times*, January 25, 1987, 1.

54. James Dale Davidson, "Social Security Rip-Off," *New Republic*, April 7, 1987, 15.

55. Ernest L. Boyer, "An Imperiled Generation," *Generational Journal* 1 (April 15, 1988): 37; Uwe E. Reinhardt, "U.S. Health Policy: Errors of Youth," *Generational Journal* 1 (April 15, 1988): 45.

56. Paula Schwed, "A Dirty Little Secret," *Campus Voice*, August/September 1986.

57. James Jones, "Letter from the President," *Of Age*, Fall 1987, 8.

58. Ibid.

59. AGE, Second Annual Report, 1986–87, 7.

60. "AGE Adds Four Policy Experts to Board," *Of Age*, Fall 1987, 7.

61. Letter from Dave Durenberger to AGE directors and members, December 1, 1986, 1; Americans for Generational Equity, *Fiscal 1988 Plan of Operation*, 2–3.

62. "Age Conference Looks at the Economics of an Aging Society," *Of Age*, Fall 1987, 3.

63. Letter from Thomas Rodman to Fellow Baby Boomers, January 18, 1988.

64. Memo to AGE members from Paul Hewitt, February 4, 1988.

65. Phillip Longman, "Justice between Generations," *Atlantic Monthly*, June 1985, 74; see also Lee Smith, "The War between the Generations," *Fortune*, July 20, 1987, 78.

66. Ibid., 75.

67. Ibid., 78–79.

68. Peter G. Peterson, "The Morning After," *Atlantic Monthly*, October 1987, 44.

69. Ibid., 44, 60.

70. Ibid., 60.

71. "Senator Pessimistic on Health Care," *Kansas City Star*, May 3, 1987.

72. Anthony Beilenson, "Let's Put Social Security Back on Deficit-Negotiations Table," *Tallahassee Democrat*, November 11, 1988, 13a.

73. "Washington Post Changes Editorial Stance on Social Security," *Of Age*, Fall 1987, 7.

74. Ibid.; for other examples, see "The Dawning of the Age of Emeritus," *Kansas City Star*, April 5, 1987, 1a, 12a; the cartoon "The Reading of the Will," *Kansas City Times*, April 27, 1987; James Kilpatrick, "For Blacks, the System Is a Ripoff," *Kansas City Star*, July 12, 1987; "Social Security's Ticking Time Bomb," *Tallahassee Democrat*, March 6, 1988, 3a.

75. Mickey Kaus, "The Right's Free Lunch," *New Republic*, March 9, 1987, 14; "Tradeamok," *New Republic*, April 27, 1987, 7–9; "An Exchange on Social Security," *New Republic*, May 18, 1987, 20–23; "Reagan's Correction," *New Republic*, November 16, 1987, 7–9; "You Call This Austerity," *New Republic*, December 7, 1987, 4, 41.

76. *AARP News Bulletin*, April 1987.

77. Martin Tolchin, "Health Act Doomed from Outset," *Kansas City Times*, October 9, 1989, A-1.

78. James Kilpatrick, "Catastrophic Was a Catastrophe." *Tallahassee Democrat*, August 24, 1989, 10A.

79. Among the gaps at present covered by Medigap policies that the new legislation does not cover are the one-time deductible for Part A hospital coverage, the daily copayment for the first eight days of skilled nursing home care, the 20 percent portion of out-of-pocket expenses for doctors' visits and other outpatient services, and the difference between Medicare's allowable charges and the amount the doctor actually charges. Gregory Spears, "Medicare Payments Go Up," *Tallahassee Democrat*, January 1, 1989, 1A.

80. "Catastrophic Health Insurance Debuts in New AGE Report Series," *Of Age*, Fall 1987, 2; "Medicare Catastrophic Coverage to Start in 1989," *A Portfolio of Articles about Americans for Generational Equity*, July 1988.

81. Spears, "Medicare Payments Go Up," 1A; "Catastrophic Care Act Headed for Revision," *Tallahassee Democrat*, August 4, 1989, 10.

82. Joan Beck, "Catastrophic Needs to Be Repealed," *Tallahassee Democrat*, July 29, 1989, 12A; Tolchin, "Health Act Doomed," A-1.

83. Schwed, "Dirty Little Secret," 74; Peterson, "Morning After," 69.

84. Longman, "Justice between Generations," 81.

85. Phillip Longman, *Born to Pay: The New Politics of Aging in America* (Boston: Houghton-Mifflin, 1987), 249.

86. Ibid.; Smith, "War between Generations," 80; "Social Security: Will You Get Yours?" *Reader's Digest*, June 1988, 145.

87. Barry Bluestone and Bennett Harrison, "The Great American Jobs Machine:

The Proliferation of Low-Wage Employment in the U.S. Economy" (Study prepared for the Joint Economic Committee, 1987), 5, 21.

88. Ibid., 31.

89. Mark D. Hayward, William R. Grady, and Steven D. McLaughlin, "Changes in the Retirement Process among Older Men in the United States: 1972–1980," *Demography* 25 (1988): 371–86. Mark D. Hayward, William R. Grady, and Steven D. McLaughlin, "The Retirement Process among Older Women in the U.S.: Changes in the 1970s," *Research on Aging*, 10 (1988): 358–82.

90. William J. Serow, "The Effects of an Aging Population on Immigration Policy," *Journal of Applied Gerontology* 1 (1982): 27.

4/The Reagan Legacy: Privatization, the Welfare State, and Aging in the 1990s

Carroll L. Estes

President Ronald Reagan successfully shifted the focus of U.S. discourse on social policy from activism and improvement to crisis and budget cutting.[1] This was accomplished with the support of an ideological revolution reinstating the primacy of the economy as the driving rationale for state action and a romanticized notion of individualism and the family as a justification for shifting social responsibility to the private sector. This chapter explores the Reagan legacy, lays out the paradigm shift that occurred, examines its symbolic and material consequences, and assesses the implications for old age in the U.S. welfare state, with particular attention to health care.

The theme of crisis was a central motif resonating throughout the Reagan presidency. Aging policy was a central part of the schema of crisis definition and the resulting outcomes. Understanding the contemporary welfare state requires theoretical and empirical attention to crisis construction and crisis management by the state. The "Reagan revolution" was a product of tensions between the state and capital in working through the crisis tendencies and contradictions of late-twentieth-century American capitalism.[2]

Under Reagan, economic crisis was used to justify the imposition of cost-containment policies in health care that shifted costs from the state to individuals (including the elderly) and transferred funding from public and nonprofit health-provider organizations to for-profit enterprises.[3] Furthering a process that commenced with the passage of Medicare and Medicaid in 1965, Reagan administration policies fueled the growth in the for-profit components and costs of the medical-care system.[4] Although 40 percent of the cost of U.S. health care is financed by a largely private-sector medical–industrial complex, the state has limited its activities in health and social services to those that support and complement the market through limited public financing of health insurance, primarily for the aged (Medicare) and the poor who cannot afford to pay for private insurance (Medicaid).

Through the regulation and financing of medical care and social services, state policy under Reagan augmented efforts to stimulate market investment opportunities for private capital that promised the greatest likelihood of profit (e.g., hospital and home health services). This created competition for government funds in areas of service delivery that had been traditionally controlled by nonprofit health-care organizations.[5] State policy also provided productive opportunities for private capital through civil law and regulation protecting the market and the encouragement of proprietary health entities (e.g., the Omnibus Reconciliation Act of 1980) including the federal tax subsidy of the purchase of private health insurance. Under Reagan, public subsidies (tax cuts) for capital, combined with the promotion of medical care for profit under deliberate strategies to increase privatization and competition, acted in contradictory fashion, exacerbating the fiscal problems of the state.

These state actions and policies contributed to (1) the deepening of divisions in the de facto rationing system of U.S. health care based on ability to pay;[6] and (2) a largely unchecked rise in federal health-care costs.[7] Finally, under Reagan the state intensified constraints on funding for social and community-care services[8]—areas of the greatest dependency by nonprofit service organizations on the government.[9] The state-financed services that experienced the most severe cuts under Reagan were the social and supportive services that are less attractive for business investment because they tend to be less profitable as a result of their labor intensity, lower technological content, and general unpredictability.[10] Each of these state actions altered the terrain of health and aging policy, and each generated consequences.

In the Reagan era, health and aging policy exemplified the contradictions facing the state as it finds itself pressed to regulate and contain government costs in medical care and simultaneously required to deregulate and promote economic expansion and profit through a robust state-financed but privately run and extremely costly medical–industrial complex.

The Reagan Legacy: An Ideological Revolution

One of the most striking and significant features of the Reagan legacy is its phenomenal success in advancing the ideologies of neoliberalism and neoconservatism as strategies in the production of crisis, subsequent crisis management, and restructuring the welfare state. Although it is too early to estimate the magnitude or permanence of its social-policy changes, the ideological legacy of the Reagan administration is a profound paradigm shift in the Kuhnian sense.[11]

All political regimes use ideology to communicate and impose a reflection of material relations. As deeply held systems of beliefs, ideologies are generally unexamined as both evidential and moral truths.[12] They frame the possible and the ethical, orienting us to what is, who we are, and how we relate to the world. Ideologies influence what we conceive of as imaginable and as right and wrong.[13] The production and uses of ideology are integral to three processes by which dominant views are sustained: (1) successful creation of cultural images by policymakers, experts, and the media; (2) appeal to the necessities of the economic system; and (3) implementation of policy and application of expertise to transform conflicts over goals and means into systems of rational problem solving in familiar organizational structures and professions in ways that obfuscate class, gender, and racial content.[14]

In weaving together the threads of neoliberalism and neoconservatism, Reagan's ideological revolution simultaneously promoted the revival of the free market and the now-mythical patriarchal autonomous family. Neoliberalism is distinctly oriented toward a "minimalist state" and hostile to anything that may impede the order of the market (and its natural superiority). Neoconservatism appeals to authority, allegiance, tradition, and "nature." The allegiance of the citizen to the state is seen as transcendent. "A corollary . . . is that [a particular vision of] the family is central to maintaining the state."[15] The attractiveness of this New Right model is that it moves toward "squaring the circle between an intellectual adherence to the free market and emotional attachment to authority and imposed tradition."[16] Further, the New Right reminds us that the primary, if not the only, justification for government intervention is national defense and law enforcement. One accomplishment of the Reagan administration was the effective blurring of the concepts of national security with the national economic interest.

In the United States, natural-rights individualism is the "ideological cement" that binds together contemporary neoconservative and neoliberal ideas and politics,[17] supporting notions of self-help based on economic initiative and productivity, individual autonomy, and voluntary association. The difficulty in restoring "both the giant corporation and the autonomous family . . . to their 'rightful place' in American life [requires] . . . faith and patriotism,"[18] but the stunning success of this project was one of Ronald Reagan's most significant hallmarks.

Reagan's ideological project became operational through a policy agenda designed to promote both privatization and competition, as well as the isolation of the "family" from "society."[19] Privatization policies promote the belief that the "proper" and best form of the delivery of health and social services to the elderly is nongovernmental, but obscure the (inherently ideological) assumptions on which this belief is based. In U.S. health and social policy, privatization operates hand in glove with the rhetoric of competition and deregulation.

One aspect of the success of Reagan's ideological mission was its remarkable capacity to shape public consciousness by limiting a vision of the "possible" to inherently promarket solutions. An example was the Reagan administration's claim that the only route to universal health care was through competition and market strategies. What was obscured by this rhetoric is the fact that the U.S. health system is a pluralistically financed and essentially private delivery system dominated by a powerful medical profession and medical industries that impede effective state action to control costs or ensure access.

The fact that Reagan's agenda of intensified privatization in health care generated little national attention or opposition illustrates the power of the neoliberal ideology in American thought;[20] the weakness of the American welfare state;[21] the strength of the private nonprofit sector and the political advocates who support and sustain it;[22] the logic of capital accumulation that favors the expansion of investment capital into new markets, particularly those subsidized by the state;[23] and the power of the reigning paradigm of neoclassical economics and cost containment in public policy.[24]

Ideology and Legitimacy Problems of the State

The Reagan administration's ideological assault on government reflected the difficulties of the U.S. state in maintaining legitimation for its activities in the face of its own politically defined economic crisis. Federal funding cuts and Reagan's health-policy agenda of cost containment, competition, and privatization were explicable as part of the state's response to its legitimacy problems. The transfer of state-funded medical-care dollars from nonprofit to for profits and from small entities to multifacility corporate ones had the dual advantage of addressing one aspect of the economic crisis—the need for new investment opportunities and profit potential—and simultaneously bolstering the legitimacy of state decisions to the extent that they were perceived as rationalizing and lowering the costs of the delivery of care.

The economic, political, and social changes that occurred in the 1980s reflected the fact that the legitimacy of the state can no longer be assumed. One marker of the success of the Reagan period was the pronounced shift in state actions toward market norms and market solutions. For the elderly, major issues became the continued availability of legitimating beliefs supporting the two cornerstones of aging policy—social security and the notion of universal health care for the elderly (Medicare's assurance of access to health care without respect for ability to pay). Both policies depend on expert and public opinion as to the fiscal capacity of the state to support them, and, increasingly, on the perceived social justice and generational equity involved in these and other publicly financed programs.

Reagan Theses and Aging Policy

Four major claims, or theses, were advanced by the Reagan administration as the basis for reshaping public policy in aging and health care. These theses are captured in themes that dominated the Reagan years: (1) austerity, (2) federalism, (3) deregulation, and (4) privatization.

Austerity

The impact of austerity (both real and constructed) and its political processing can be demonstrated in President Reagan's skilled use of a national recession, high unemployment, and a skyrocketing federal deficit to legitimate tax cuts for the wealthy, social spending reductions, and defense spending increases.

Aging policy was an integral part of the economic, political, and ideological struggle over austerity throughout the Reagan years. Austerity is both objective and subjective. The objective basis of austerity lies in the crisis tendencies of capitalist economies and specifically in the U.S. economic decline in relation to the global economy. The subjective basis of austerity lies in the political claims-making and social construction of crises (with or without objective crisis conditions). Both have contributed to the legitimacy problems of the American state. When the state does not sustain a healthy economy, legitimacy questions that arise are likely to prompt renewed and energized state efforts to promote economic growth and favorable conditions for capitalist expansion. Sacrifices are required and arrived at through political struggles likely to culminate in the reallocation of resources to "productive uses" and away from areas seen as "nonproductive." In times of economic crisis, expenditures for the elderly and the poor are especially prone to being identified as nonproductive.

An important example of "using" the aged was the claim that federal spending for the elderly was depressing the economy. But, contrary to the rhetoric and Reagan's call for austerity, cross-national evidence provided no support for the claim that public-sector health expenditures for the elderly were a causative factor in the U.S. economic decline. Certainly, the overall rise in U.S. health-care spending has been inordinate for more than twenty years, at an annual rate of three to five times the cost of living. But this is clearly a result of private-sector dominance in American health care and the inability of a "weak state" to regulate effectively or to control health-care prices. Significantly, the United States ranks behind almost every major industrialized country in terms of the percentage of health expenditures financed by the public sector (4.4 percent of GNP). The United States also ranks last in public health expenditures as a percentage of total health expenditures (41.1 percent).[25] In fact, a much higher percentage of U.S. health-care spending occurs in and benefits the private sector than in comparable countries. While some analysts have argued that the percentage devoted to medical care is unacceptably high, these expenditures have fueled a medical–industrial complex of more than $500 billion per year, one that is highly profitable for a number of powerful economic interests including the medical, hospital, equipment and supply, and pharmaceutical industries. The not-so-hidden profits contained in our nation's escalating medical expenditures suggest that arguments about the "crisis" in health-care costs, especially as caused or fueled by the elderly, need reexamination.

A growth in public expenditures between the 1960s and 1980s was common to all advanced capitalist countries, but there was considerably less growth in U.S. public expenditures as a percentage of GNP than in any other advanced capitalist country. Throughout the 1980s, the United States had lower public expenditure levels than any advanced nation except Japan. Public outlays for education, social and health services, and social security were lower in the United States (20 percent of GNP) than in any of these countries. Further, between 1975 and 1981, U.S. expenditures on social security exhibited one of the lowest growth rates (3.7 percent) of these nations.[26]

Federalism

The struggle over federal, state, and local responsibility is older than the Republic and continues to have important meaning and consequences for the elderly. From the earliest days of the Reagan administration, a major goal was to reverse the historical trend of national governmental expansion by devolving domestic policy responsibility to state, local, and private levels. A companion goal was the reduction of public spending.

Beginning with the introduction of President Nixon's strategy of new federalism in the mid 1970s, decentralization of federal responsibility has been employed with the intent of budget cutting and government "downsizing." Initially targeted at stemming the proliferation and growth of categorical programs that flourished in the 1960s, the first round of new federalism (the Nixon period) took the form of block grants, small federal budget reductions, and the adoption of federal revenue sharing. Round two (the Reagan period) was characterized by more block grants, significant cutbacks in the block-granted federal programs, deregulation, and the extinction of general revenue sharing with the states. Reagan's vision was a literal (some said, radical) effort to separate the powers of the different levels of government. As he stated in his 1981 inaugural address, "It is my intention to curb the size and influence of the federal establishment and to demand recognition of the distinction between the powers granted to the federal government and those reserved to the states or to the people."

At least two meanings were inferred: first, "in the absence of overriding national needs, local taxpayers and voters would be the ones to decide which public programs they would support and how much; and second, local citizens should have control over the way . . . federal programs are implemented." [27] The ambiguity in the interpretation of an "overriding national need" permitted challenges to the justification for any national responsibility for meeting basic human needs, particularly in view of the testimony by David Stockman, then Office of Management and Budget (OMB) director, that new federalism would put an end to the idea that citizens have "any basic right to legal services or any other kinds of service." [28]

The Reagan administration's strong and sustained support achieved what the Advisory Committee on Intergovernmental Relations (ACIR) called a return to "the more traditional brand of federalism of the pre-Great Society era"—a "fend for yourself [new] federalism" characterized by a slowdown in the growth of federal aid to the states and localities [29] and augmented responsibilities for state and local governments. With substantial federal reductions in grants to state and local governments and increased state discretion, an important question for state-only and federal–state programs of import to the aging (e.g., Supplemental Security Income (SSI), mental health, and Medicaid) concerns the capacity and commitment of state jurisdictions to deal with their growing responsibilities, particularly in the context of their own fiscal problems. [30] Reagan administration policies diminished federal grants-in-aid to state and local governments as a percentage of GNP from 3.4 percent in 1980 to 2.4 percent in 1989. In real dollar terms, however, federal expenditures for intergovernmental programs fell so much that their share of GNP shrank by one-fourth and "their contribution to state and local budgets dropped by one-fifth." [31]

Other forces of fiscal consequence to the states were introduced through changes in the tax law in 1982 and 1986. One observer notes that the combined effect of Reagan's policy was that "states that pursue Robin Hood tax policies will be under heavy competitive pressure to pull in their progressive tax horns" because "the dramatic drop in federal personal and corporate income tax has sharply reduced the value of state and local tax deductions claimed by business firms and individuals." [32] States that tax and spend heavily are likely to be compromised in interstate competition to attract and retain capital enterprise.

It has been argued that the impact of Reagan's decentralization strategy was blunted by the "bias for centralization" and opposition to radical change inherent in the basic structure of the federal system. [33] New federalism in the 1980s did not engineer the abandonment of the categorical system because of the stakes that both Congress and the "vast intergovernmental bureaucracy" have in it. Because policies of centralization are in the electoral interest of members of Congress of both parties, it is argued that the "system is stacked against unified control of the national and state governments, and unified control is a virtual prerequisite for substantial reform of the current federal system." [34] Both "the absence of [Reagan administration] guiding principles for making changes in federal policy" and a political infrastructure dedicated to marginal change are said to have limited the long-term effects of Reagan's new federalism. [35]

Observers from a less sanguine perspective do not underestimate the long-term impact of new federalism. [36] First, and most important, decentralization assures that the dominant economic and political interests operating at the national level will not be challenged by fragmented and divergent state and local policies that are variably created and inconsistently implemented. Second, the divestment of federal (public-sector) responsibility through deregulation and decentralization of policy goal setting increases the influence of private-sector interest groups on policymaking. Old-age policies, particularly those for the sick and poor aged, are mediated in important and largely invisible ways by business and provider interests. Third, with highly discretionary state and local programs, the possibility of effective political action for all but the most well organized and well funded organizations is neutralized and weakened because they lack the capacity to mobilize across multiple and dispersed geopolitical jurisdictions. Fourth, increased state and local fiscal and regulatory responsibility for human services places these demands on the most fiscally vulnerable and politically sensitive decision-making levels, since jurisdictions have more variable and limited fiscal resources than the federal government. Hence, decisions about services for the poor are located precisely where pressures to control social expenses are greatest and necessarily most conservative. Fifth, decentralization supplants national policy goals and commitments with more autonomous and variable state and local policy choices, particularly with regard to programs for the poor, blunting the most progressive changes effected at the national level. Sixth, decentralization raises important accountability issues, while the availability of comparable data across multiple jurisdictions is more difficult to obtain, and assessments of the effects of policies implemented are more difficult to make.

Deregulation

On both ideological and policy levels, deregulation was selectively implemented to extend the Reagan administration's transfer of federal responsibility to other levels of government and to promote the goals of privatization and the instigation of market forces. Among the effects of deregulation were the elimination of state requirements for matching federal dollars for services, the relaxation of eligibility, affirmative action and civil rights requirements in health and social services, and the return of regulatory authority to states and localities. [37] Zealous federal deregulators went even further, limiting the regulatory prerogatives of states because of insufficient trust that states could resist political pressures to invent their own regulations in ways that might undermine the Reagan agenda. In what can only be called a series of contradictory moves, "the federal government harnessed its considerable power to disempower the states . . . [by] mandat[ing] nonintervention by the states, despite an ideological commitment to federalism." This "deregulatory federalism" was carried forward in different ways by each of the three branches of government—Congress, administrative agencies, and the courts.[38] Some observers have assessed the states' responses to their discretion as "less than creative." [39]

The "regulatory vacuum" created by the Reagan administration when it abandoned areas of regulation (e.g., occupational safety and environmental protection) and mandated that states disengage from their own regulatory processes raised serious questions concerning the appropriateness of preemptive efforts of nonelected federal administrative agencies to curtail state involvement in economic and social regulation.[40]

In health and social services, as in economic policy, regulation was identified by Reagan as an important cause of the poor performance of the economy.[41] Nevertheless, even a cursory examination of the administration's inconsistent actions on the regulatory front renders transparent its highly strategic and political uses of deregulation. For example, increased regulatory actions were designed to cut federal health costs under Medicare through the imposition of fixed reimbursements for hospital care according to diagnosis-related groups (DRGs), the adoption of restrictions on recipients' freedom to choose providers, and the intensification of federal Health Care Financing Administration (HCFA) regulations that dramatically increased claim denials for home health by Medicare fiscal intermediaries. Under the Older Americans Act, augmented regulatory initiatives were used to stimulate "market forces" as area agencies on aging were required to institute competitive bidding practices that indirectly favored "for-profits" in the traditionally nonprofit world of social services.

Other examples of deregulation affecting the aged demonstrate its utility as a tool in cutting government costs and enhancing prospects of participation and profits by business in federal programs: eradication of Medicare restrictions prohibiting reimbursement of for-profit home health agencies in states without licensure (opening a previously barred sector of health-service provision to proprietaries);[42] loosening of eligibility and service requirements under Medicaid, permitting states to adopt more stringent and varied standards to reduce the number of poor elderly eligible for the program;[43] abolition of the 25 percent state match for social services (reducing state incentives to fund these services) and of report requirements (making it difficult to ascertain program, client, and expenditure data) under the social services block grant;[44] and eradication of restrictions limiting for-profit social service providers under the Older Americans Act.

While the long-term success of the Reagan administration's regulatory federalism campaign did not generate profound and permanent structural changes, it was nonetheless an extremely important force in insinuating Reagan's ideology into a wide array of programs that affect the elderly. Perhaps most important was the immediate favorable political impact achieved by what became a largely administrative (rather than legislative) strategy in deregulation.[45]

Privatization

In 1981, President Reagan accelerated the substantial privatization of health and social services that had been an integral and growing feature of the U.S. welfare state in the two previous decades. The 1960s and 1970s introduced a form of privatization built on the voluntary sector.[46] Reagan dramatically shifted the weight of ideological and fiscal resources to a new kind of privatization—privatization characterized by state subsidy of for-profit (in the place of nonprofit) enterprises in state-contracted and -financed services[47] and privatization in the form of increased provision of services by the informal sector.[48] Both represented a marked shift away from the privatization that characterized the earlier two decades in which a growing nonprofit sector flourished as a result of federal funding. In the earlier period, the rationale was that a strong nonprofit sector would permit publicly needed services to be provided with state support, but in a manner that permitted expansion in the provision of welfare-state benefits without the commensurate growth in the state bureaucracy that occurred in European welfare states.[49] Thus "nonprofit federalism"[50] was envisioned as permitting the simultaneous growth of both the welfare state and the nonprofit form of private provision.

The 1980s were characterized by an intensification of privatization and a series of explicit and implicit policies designed to (1) increase the conduct of state business through the auspices of for-profit corporations; and (2) shift the responsibility of caregiving for the elderly from formal paid provision to the informal sector of the family (primarily women). In health and social services, a number of regulatory and legislative devices were important, including the Omnibus Reconciliation Act (ORA) of 1980 and the Omnibus Budget Reconciliation Act of 1981 (OBRA). Both contributed in different ways to increasing competition and deregulation, private contracting, and the growth of for-profit provision of health and social services—services traditionally dominated by nonprofit or public providers.

Privatization in the twentieth-century U.S. context describes a direction of change more than its destination or origin.[51] In the 1960s, Great Society policies fostered dramatic growth in the nonprofit sector. But the long-term historical import of the private nonprofit sector in U.S. health and social services, since the earliest days of the Republic, and the rapid organizational changes of the 1980s (e.g., vertical and horizontal integration) further blurred boundaries between sectors. Conceptual and structural complexities multiplied, rendering meaningless any simple differentiation of the "public" from the "private." Before the 1980s, the most common form of privatization was public-sector contracting with the private nonprofit sector. The Reagan administration proposed to shift the tax status of state-financed and -contracted provider entities toward organizations in the for-profit sector. Thus it is no longer appropriate to limit the concept of U.S. privatization to the not-for-profit organizational form.

Contrary to classical economic theory of privatization, however, state-initiated privatization strategies do not necessarily reduce government involvement in terms of either public subsidy or regulation.[52] Indeed, privatization may actually enhance the role of the state insofar as privatization policies of the state either maintain or increase public spending or the regulation of services. Policies that promote privatization may serve as a vehicle for the transfer of more, rather than less, state subsidy into particular components of the welfare state, as was the case with medical-care provision during the Reagan era. In such instances, it is more accurate to say that the state is being restructured than that there is a retrenchment by the state.[53] An example is the Reagan administration's successful reversal of the direction of long-term trends in expanding eligibility and benefits[54] through entitlement policy changes, without reducing either the share of GNP allocated to entitlement programs or the total federal deficit.

The Health Legacy of Ronald Reagan: 1981–1988

Between 1981 and 1987, the president was responsible for cuts of $20 billion in the Medicare program for the elderly and $15 billion in Medicaid for the poor. At the same time, health-care cost sharing increased dramatically for the elderly as Medicare covered a declining proportion (approximately 44 percent) of the costs of their health care. Recent research substantiates that there has been both a decline in access to health care in the general population and a positive relationship between insurance coverage and medical-service use.[55] Hence, access to needed care for both young and old is a more pressing problem than at any time since the passage of Medicare in 1965.

Reagan's strategy in health care was to continue former President Carter's focus on cost containment in Medicare and Medicaid and advance market principles in health (competition, deregulation, and privatization). Although Reagan's policies stimulated a revolution in the organization of health care and its corporatization and privatization, medical costs continued to rise at two to three times the rate of inflation.

A companion strategy was to cut Medicaid. Medicaid cuts were implemented through reductions in the federal share of the costs (FY 1982–1985) and incentives provided to states to constrain expenditures and access to this program for the poor. Federal budget tightening aimed at Medicaid from 1981 to the present has pressed states to curtail eligibility and utilization, generating greater variability among the states in eligibility for and access to Medicaid services and an increased burden on the poor.[56] The percentage of the poor covered by Medicaid declined from 63 percent to 46 percent between 1975 and 1985.[57]

The net result was that the number of Americans without health insurance reached the highest levels since the early 1960s, with more than one in seven Americans lacking health insurance altogether.[58] The number underinsured, of which the elderly constitute a significant element, has also grown. The under-insurance of the elderly is attributable to the underlying medical model of care that specifically prohibits Medicare reimbursement for long-term chronic-illness care and to rapidly rising out-of-pocket costs for acute care. Virtually all long-term care is excluded from Medicare coverage, including nursing-home care (except for brief periods of highly skilled care), nonmedical in-home services such as personal care and rehabilitation for the chronically ill, dental care, eyeglasses, hearing aids, preventive physical examinations, and support-ive services (e.g., transportation, meals on wheels, and case management). Medicare's acute-care emphasis is clearly mismatched with the needs of the older population in a society characterized by increasing life expectancy and growing "population frailty."[59]

During the Reagan years, two major policy changes occurred in Medi-care: (1) introduction of prospective payment systems (PPS) for hospitals in 1983 and (2) passage of the Medicare Catastrophic Coverage Act of 1988 (which was subsequently repealed in large part). Significantly, neither altered the basic approach of Medicare nor the basic structural arrangements (e.g., fee-for-service medicine and pluralistic financing) that inhibit government cost control. Further, neither policy change altered the incentives for the application of costly (and often inappropriate) technologically oriented care. Other major health policy changes successfully implemented were actions to increase the share of the costs borne by the elderly, and to put a lid on expanding Medicaid costs and eligibility.

The introduction of the PPS for hospitals (paying by diagnosis-related groups, or DRGs) was designed to contain costs with incentives to shorten hospital stays. Although the rate of cost increases slowed in PPS hospitals,[60] the system did not stem the overall rise in the cost of medical care, which continues at two to three times the rate of inflation. Although implemented under the guise of cost containment, the PPS demonstrates a major contradic-tion of the Reagan years, for the actual policy did little to stem rising health costs, but increased federal oversight and regulatory control through hospital rate setting and the regulation of physician behavior. Other Medicare (Part B) costs increased as medical procedures were shifted to ambulatory settings and doctors' offices not restricted by the PPS. In particular, Medicare expenditures for physicians exploded. Consequently, the limited savings the PPS achieved in slowing the rate of Medicare (Part A) hospital cost increases were off-set by increases in Part B expenditures, which rose more than 15 percent a year throughout the post-PPS period. In addition, there was no abatement in beneficiary cost sharing, which continued to rise sharply.

The "ripple effects" of the PPS were experienced throughout the community-based care system.[61] With the immediate two-day reduction in the average length of hospital stay for Medicare patients in the first year of the PPS, more than 21 million days of care were shifted from the formal hospital-care system to the informal care of home and family.[62] Simultaneously, HCFA further restricted Medicare's already limited home health benefits through a series of regulatory and interpretive revisions. Both changes occurred in the context of other deregulatory and austerity policies that had reduced the already meager social service funding and increased women's caregiving responsibilities.

The second major Medicare policy change was the passage of the catastrophic coverage bill expanding hospital insurance benefits, providing coverage for outpatient prescription drugs and Medicaid coverage for copayments and deductibles for the elderly below poverty, and protecting elders from spousal impoverishment in the event that one partner is institutionalized and must "spend down" assets to receive Medicaid assistance. Notable omissions from the act were the lack of coverage for long and expensive nursing-home stays and other in-home and community long-term care needed by old and chronically ill persons, including coverage for social support services, mental health, disease prevention, and health promotion. Political opposition among the elderly to the method of paying for catastrophic care and its provisions contributed to its repeal prior to implementation by a rattled Congress in the early days of the Bush administration.

As the only health program that finances long-term care, Medicaid is particularly important to the aged in its coverage of nursing-home care, but only for those who "spend down" to the poverty level. Stringent eligibility standards (below poverty in many states) and a welfare stigma explain why only 36 percent of the old poor are on Medicaid.[63] As a result of its stringent eligibility and focus on institutionalization, Medicaid has been described, with some justification, as a policy that promotes both impoverishment and dependency for the aged.

The Rising Costs of Medical Care

Overall, 1987 national health-care spending exceeded $500.3 billion,[64] claiming 11.1 percent of the nation's GNP. In spite of the health-care reforms of prospective payment, deregulation, and state policies designed to promote competition throughout the 1980s, health-care costs continued to outpace the general inflation.[65] Every component of aggregate costs grew, and it is projected that, between the years 2005 and 2010, annual Medicare outlays will exceed yearly spending for social security.[66] For elders, the rising cost of health care has meant rising copayments and deductibles under Medicare; for example, the Medicare Part A hospital deductible paid out-of-pocket by the elderly rose 155 percent in the first half of the 1980s alone, more than five times the rate of inflation, and Part B deductibles and premiums were not far behind.[67] Out-of-pocket health expenses now exceed 16 percent of elders' annual incomes (more than at the time of the passage of Medicare) and are projected to rise to 20 percent in the 1990s.[68]

Medicare beneficiary costs are rising almost twice as fast as social security cost-of-living adjustments, and the burden of these costs are disproportionately borne by low- and lower-middle-income elders who have poorer health status and more illness than middle- and upper-income elders. There are severe class disparities in the burden of out-of-pocket health costs for which the poor and near-poor spend more than one-quarter of their income (26.6 percent), compared to a mere 2.9 percent for high-income elders. Minorities and women are most likely to fall into these low-income categories and hence to have high personal health-care costs. These costs rise with age, and single elderly persons aged 85 and older spend almost 42 percent of their income for out-of-pocket health costs.[69] The precarious economic status of most elderly people and the financial catastrophe that nursing-home costs can bring are evident in the startling findings of a congressional study showing that, within thirteen weeks of nursing-home admission, nearly one-half (48 percent) of single persons aged 65 or over in the United States would be impoverished, and an equal proportion of couples would reach poverty by the end of one year.[70]

With the structure of service delivery, the methods of financing, and the orientation of Medicare essentially intact, the Reagan administration deepened and extended the nation's commitment to the commodification and "medicalization" of aging through state policy.[71] The former was achieved through the ideological production of rhetoric and policies that promoted health care as a market good rather than a right. The latter is reflected in the construction of "aging as illness," the exclusive targeting of federal reimbursement for medical treatment rather than social supportive care, the biomedical emphasis of federal research priorities and medical education.

The most important effects of the Reagan legacy in health care for the aged are (1) a fueling of the commodification and medicalization of care for the aging in ways that are consistent with the expansion of the for-profit medical–industrial complex; (2) the continuing refusal of the state to provide meaningful long-term-care benefits to the elderly and disabled; (3) the accumulation of multiple pressures on a beleaguered network of traditionally nonprofit home and community-based health and social service providers thinly stretched by the demands of very sick and very old patients discharged from the hospital earlier than ever before;[72] and (4) the use of policy to increase family responsibility and dependence on the work of women through the informalization of care. These efforts to restore and regulate family life (particularly to control the lives of women) are congruent with the deep concerns of the state and capital to minimize state costs for the elderly and the intentions of the New Right to restore patriarchical family arrangements to assure a continuing supply of free female labor essential to the reproduction and maintenance of the workforce.[73] The Reagan administration's resistance to a federal policy solution to the problem of long-term care and its unstated policy of informalization must be understood as part of a larger austerity strategy in the context of the state's need for women (regardless of their labor-force participation) to continue to perform large (and increasing) amounts of unpaid servicing work.[74]

Health Care as a Market Good
The health-policy goals of equity, access, and accountability that were hallmarks of the 1960s died in the Reagan White House, and America's elders found themselves caught in the middle between (1) the dual interests of the state and capital, each of which was attempting to constrain and reduce its own costs and neither of which was necessarily concerned about inequities in access to care; and (2) the tensions between the shared goals of the state and segments of capital that wanted to reduce medical-care costs versus segments of capital (the large medical–industrial complex) that pressed for the expansion of a state-guaranteed and profitable market in high-tech medical care. The result has been a costly and deeply stratified health-care system for all Americans.

Social Services
The second part of the Reagan legacy as it pertains to health concerns the agenda on social services. Social services can be said to serve at least three major functions. They often provide the "glue" that holds together an array of federal, state, and local programs and the lives of the individuals and caregivers they serve. Second, they often provide the means by which an individual can remain independent in the community without total reliance on family or the alternative of institutionalization. The third purpose of many social service programs is client advocacy, especially when clients are unable or not sufficiently informed to advocate for themselves.[75] During the 1960s and early 1970s, federal support for social services grew, peaking in 1978. Between 1978 and 1981, there was a modest decline in support for social services, a decline that was to weaken the foundation and set the stage for future cuts imposed by the Reagan administration.

The Reagan administration's social service policy was motivated from the start by broad concerns about the need for budgetary restraint in domestic programs, the appropriate division of responsibility between federal and state governments, and pressure from profamily forces. After the first two years of the Reagan administration, federal support for social services was cut by 20 percent in real dollars, and there was a movement toward increasing state flexibility and block grants.[76] The Omnibus Budget Reconciliation Act of 1981 changed the name of Title XX to the Social Services Block Grant (SSBG), reduced its funding, and eliminated most of the state matching requirements. The final budget reduction resulted in about a 20 percent decline in federal funding for both FY 1981 and FY 1982. In FY 1982, the funding for the Administration on Aging declined for the first time, from $748 million to $720 million and then to $652 million in FY 1983.[77] The early 1980s abruptly curtailed any hope of significant expansion in social services. For example, Social Services Block Grants increased by only .8 percent from 1984 to 1986, well below the inflation rate, and Older Americans Act services suffered a similar fate.[78]

The transfer of federal responsibility to the states and localities is a crucial element in the Reagan legacy to social services. SSBG and concomitant budget cuts shifted a large burden for multiple programs to state and local governments under the assumption that they would replace the funding for essential programs. The result was that states that had taken on more responsibility for federally aided entitlement programs were particularly hard hit with cuts that ranged from 10 percent to over 50 percent.[79]

Overall, federal aid to states for health and human services (excluding social security) suffered three years of cuts (1982, 1986, and 1987), cuts in absolute dollars of $343.4 million in 1982 and $194 million during 1986 and 1987. The overall budget for these services rose only a total of 8.1 percent from 1981 to 1987, limiting the ability to maintain even the levels of service available when Reagan entered office (see Table 4.1). Social services reflect the overall trend in Reagan's federalism strategy—calling for a transfer of federal responsibility to state and local governments while cutting overall federal aid to these entities. Part of the context is that, during the Reagan administration, there were two major cuts in federal aid to the states (1982 and 1987); and in the first seven years of the Reagan administration, federal aid to states and localities rose only 14.3 percent, far below the rate of inflation.

Crisis, Social Struggles, and the Reagan Legacy

A significant part of the Reagan legacy is contained in the social struggles that characterized the 1980s: generational, gender, racial–ethnic, and class struggles. The concept of generational equity was manufactured and fueled as

Table 4.1/Social Service Outlays as a Percentage of GNP, Fiscal Years 1976 to 1992

YEAR	OUTLAY ($\times$ 1,000)	TOTAL ($\times$ 1,000)	PERCENTAGE OF GNP
1976	$4,526	$302,170	1.50
1980	6,116	476,591	1.28
1981	6,861	543,013	1.26
1982	5,950	594,302	1.00
1983	6,133	662,352	0.92
1984	7,145	695,968	1.00
1985	6,728	769,509	0.87
1986	7,246	806,318	0.89
1987	7,543	821,074	0.91
1988	7,885	821,900	0.96
1989	8,099	857,284	0.94
1992 (est.)	7,870	935,063	0.84

Source: Adapted from Executive Office of the President and Office of Management and Budget, *Budget of the United States Government, 1990* (Washington, D.C.: Government Printing Office).

a public and political issue in the 1980s. The idea that generations "owe" one another and pointed questions of fairness between different age cohorts have penetrated and now threaten to dominate political discourse on income and health policy for the aged. The specter of "intergenerational war" emerged as an important product of the Reagan years.

The Reagan legacy also kindled a gender war. Neoconservative ideology laid the affective base for increased pressures for family responsibility. Three social trends further heightened the latent gender issues in eldercare: (1) the increase in family responsibilities for posthospital care of the elderly as a result of Medicare's hospital prospective payment system; (2) the demographic revolution of the growing aging population accompanied by a "baby dearth" and a growing female labor force; and (3) the continuing lack of social-policy alternatives in long-term care and support of the elderly. Each of these trends encouraged millions of American women to return to "home and hearth" to meet the rising burden (and expectation) of unpaid caregiving work. Not surprisingly, more than one-half of caregivers of the elderly also work outside the home, and more than one-third of these make significant sacrifices, including severe financial penalties, work conflicts, and the loss or reduction of paid employment.[80]

Indeed, the 1980s were years of reassessment of women's place in society. Women are needed in the labor force for both the public reason of fulfilling service roles, including temporary low-paid work without benefits, and the private reason of maintaining individual standards of living; yet women are essential in filling the nation's growing need for long-term care, since their work constitutes the bulk of the nation's long-term care. During the Reagan period, the contradictions in women's lives were starkly apparent and their roles in the labor market and the home were simultaneously but differentially reinforced and expanded (but not necessarily supported) so that women were sandwiched not only between paid work and uncompensated caregiving but also between multiple generations, exemplifying "the crazy quilt" described by Laura Balbo.[81]

Reagan policies exacerbated class divisions along the health-care-access dimension. Privatization policies not only failed to stem the rising cost of medical care but spurred reductions in coverage by public and private insurance and excluded more and more of the U.S. population from access to coverage.[82] Since 1980, there has been a significant rollback from early achievements in health-care access following the passage of Medicare and Medicaid in 1965. With the reemergence of a two-tiered system of health care,[83] the present class war in health is experienced in declining access to care for the poor, rising infant mortality, and the erosion of health insurance benefits for the working population.[84]

Another aspect of the deterioration of access is the reversal of decades of legitimacy and state support for the nonprofit provision of health and social services. As the role of for-profit enterprises in health flourished in the 1980s, nonprofits found themselves in a beleaguered, uncertain, and highly competitive environment that eroded their capacity to continue providing charity services.[85] Nonprofit health and social services themselves became part of the restructuring of delivery that affected all aspects of the formal and informal care system, including the nature and scope of services provided, the clientele served and their access to care, the composition of the labor force, and organizational financing.[86] With changes in the structure, ownership, and control of health-care organizations, there has been an increase in fragmentation of service delivery, provider targeting to clients who can pay privately, and emphasis on services that are profitable, or at least reimbursable by the state or by private insurance.[87]

Conclusion

Social policy in aging and health is an important battleground on which the social struggles currently engulfing the state are being fought as the state attempts to address growing tensions between capitalism and democracy. The construction of the aging of the population in crisis terms has served two ideological purposes. First, the "demographic imperative" has been a rallying point for those who argue that the elderly are living too long, consuming too many societal resources, and robbing the young—justifying rollbacks of state benefits for the aged. Additional antistatist sentiments have been expressed in the unfounded contention that state policy to provide for formal care will encourage abdication of family responsibility for the aging, which in turn will bankrupt the state. This line of reasoning is consistent with the state's continuing refusal to provide for long-term care, reinforcing the nation's long-term-care policy that such care is (and should remain) the responsibility of the informal sector and the unpaid labor of women.

Second, the projections of a chronic-illness burden that is of "pandemic" proportions (another version of the crisis) have been used in ideological attacks on health care as a right for the elderly, particularly by the politicians, the media, and the others who are promoting the intergenerational war. The elderly are accused of crippling the state and capital with unsupportable demands. A case in point is Daniel Callahan's argument for "setting limits" that indicts those who advocate for elderly rights as encouraging "unreasonable," "unfair," and "selfish" expectations by the old for life expectancy, quality of life, and the allocation of societal resources.[88] One aspect of the intergenerational struggle is a battle for the intellectual high ground in constructing resource and equity issues for the elderly. The seriousness and import of this struggle lies in the crucial role that intellectuals play in both maintenance of the status quo and in meaningful sociohistorical change.[89]

Both crisis constructions support what may be called a "reluctant welfare state" that requires the rationalization of health care through the transfer of state-financed resources from nonprofit to for-profit entities and from little capital to big capital (i.e., from small business, including individual fee-for-service physicians, to large corporate, multifacility systems and chains).

Aging people in the United States and the policies designed to deal with them are in a war zone. This is so because the real and constructed crises of both capital and the state have been transported into the field of health and aging policy. At the ideological level, the elderly are accused of being well-off "greedy geezers" ripping off the country's youngsters. The material consequences of this assault are reflected in a complex struggle between (1) forces seeking drastic cutbacks in state financing for the aged, a major retrenchment of the welfare state, and the resurgence of patriarchy; and (2) forces seeking a restructured welfare state, with publicly financed resources redirected to rationalized and efficient health providers through the restitution of market forces in health care. One result, and one source of contradiction, is the simultaneous commodification of care for the elderly (increased privatization) where profits are to be made and decommodification (increased family care/responsibility) where costs are high and women's work is involved.

Another contradiction is that successful efforts to rationalize and privatize a medical model of health care (and to transfer resources from the nonprofit service sector to the for-profit sector) will lead, under the guise of cost savings to the state by contracting to proprietary organizations, to the state's bearing increased costs for services and technologies. State costs are likely to grow both as a result of contracting out and from the additional costs incurred by the necessity to underwrite the most difficult (and least profitable) clients being dumped on the public sector. Pressures will continue to mount to shift care from the formal to the informal sector, the private world of home and family.

The current economic crisis was constructed and transported into and resolved through political processing by the state. Although overall state expenditures increased, resources for different categories of expenditures were reallocated according to the policy agenda of the Reagan administration. From Reagan to the present day, within the domestic budget, federal spending on the poor is down, while federal medical-care financing is the most rapidly growing component of the domestic budget. Programs experiencing the greatest federal budget reductions are income maintenance (especially Aid to Families with Dependent Children, AFDC), housing, and social services for the poor. Notably, Reagan policies have effected a restructuring of health and social service delivery at the local level in the direction of privatization, rationalization, and medicalization.[90]

Gramsci believed that those who possess the means of cultural production can influence or even determine the course of history because of their crucial role in both maintenance of the status quo and creation of meaningful change.[91] The most immediate legacy of Ronald Reagan is the symbol of the Reagan revolution, the cultural product of an actor/politician whose tour de force was the use and manipulation of the media for political, policy, and ideological goals. This legacy may be best known in the future as the most important modern example of what Gramsci theorized concerning ideological hegemony. Gramsci acknowledged that hegemony and class domination can be imposed through consent more than force by those who possess the means of cultural production (as much as by the lived historical experience of capitalist material relations of production). The ability to realize common interest and catalyze common power will be the telling factor in what history will recognize as the Reagan legacy.

Notes

1. Thomas Byrne Edsall, "The Reagan Legacy," in *The Reagan Legacy*, ed. Sidney Blumenthal and Thomas Byrne Edsall (New York: Pantheon, 1988), 3–50.

2. See James O'Connor, *Fiscal Crisis of the State* (New York: St. Martin's Press, 1973); idem, *The Meaning of Crisis: A Theoretical Introduction* (Oxford: Basil Blackwell, 1987); Jurgen Habermas, *Legitimation Crisis* (Boston: Beacon Press, 1975); Claus Offe, "The Abolition of Market Control and the Problems of Legitimacy," in *Kapital-*

state, pts. 1 and 2 (1973), 114; idem, *Contradictions of the Welfare State* (Cambridge, Mass.: MIT Press, 1984).

3. John Ehrenreich and Barbara Ehrenreich, *The American Health Empire* (New York: Vintage, 1971).

4. Victor Fuchs, "The Competition Revolution in Health Care," *Health Affairs* 7, no. 3 (1988): 5–24.; Uwe E. Reinhardt, "The Battle Over Medical Costs Isn't Over," *Wall Street Journal*, October 22, 1986.

5. Theodore R. Marmor, Mark Schlesinger, and Richard W. Smithey, "Non-Profit Organizations and Health Care," in *The Nonprofit Sector: A Research Handbook*, ed. Walter W. Powell (New Haven: Yale University Press, 1987), 226.

6. Helen Darling, "The Role of the Federal Government in Assuring Access to Health Care," *Inquiry* 23 (1986): 286–95.; Margaret B. Sulvetta and Katherine Swartz, *The Uninsured and Uncompensated Care: A Chartbook* (Washington, D.C.: National Health Policy Forum, 1986).

7. Reinhardt, "The Battle Over Medical Costs Isn't Over"; Fuchs, "The Competition Revolution in Health Care," 5–24.

8. Alan Abramson and Lester Salamon, *The Nonprofit Sector and the New Federal Budget* (Washington, D.C.: Urban Institute, 1986), 70.

9. Lester M. Salamon, "Of Market Failure, Voluntary Failure, and Third-Party Government: Toward a Theory of Government–NonProfit Relations in the Modern Welfare State," in *The Shifting Debate: Public/Private Sector Relations in the Modern Welfare State*, ed. Susan A. Ostrander, Stanley Langton, and Jon VanTil (New Brunswick, N.J.: Transaction, 1987), 29–49; idem, "Partners in Public Service: The Scope and Theory of Government: Nonprofit Relations," in Powell, *Nonprofit Sector*, 99–117.

10. Carroll L. Estes, "The Politics of Ageing in America," *Ageing and Society* 6 (1986): 121–34.

11. See Thomas Kuhn, *The Structure of Scientific Inquiry* (Chicago: University of Chicago Press, 1970).

12. R. L. Heilbroner, *The Nature and Logic of Capitalism* (New York: Norton, 1985); Karl Mannheim, *Ideology and Utopia* (New York: Harcourt, Brace & Co., 1936).

13. Goran Therborn, *What Does the Ruling Class Do When It Rules?* (Thetford, Norfolk: Lowe and Brydone, 1978); idem, *The Ideology of Power and the Power of Ideology* (London: Verso, 1980).

14. Vic George and Paul Wilding, "Social Values, Social Class and Social Policy," *Social and Economic Administration* 6, no. 3 (1972). Quoted in Nick Manning, *Social Problems and Welfare Ideology* (Brookfield, Vt.: Gower, 1985), 166.

15. Ruth Levitas, "Competition and Compliance: The Utopias of the New Right," in *The Ideology of the New Right*, ed. Ruth Levitas (Cambridge, Mass.: Polity Press, 1986), 93.

16. David Edgar, "The Free or the Good," in Levitas, *Ideology of the New Right*, 74–75.

17. James O'Connor, *Accumulation Crisis* (New York: Basil Blackwell, 1984), 232.

18. Ibid., 237.

19. John Myles, personal communication, March 1989.

20. Peter F. Drucker, "Beyond the Bell Breakup," *Public Interest* 77 (Fall 1984): 21.

21. Jill Quadagno, "Theories of the Welfare State," *Annual Review of Sociology* 13 (1987): 109–28.

22. Steven R. Smith and Deborah A. Stone, "Privatization: Retrenchment or Entrenchment of the Welfare State?" (Working Paper for Conference on the Unravelling of the Welfare State, University of California, Santa Cruz, 1985).

23. O'Connor, *Fiscal Crisis of the State*.

24. Linda A. Bergthold, Carroll L. Estes, and Augusta Villanueva, "Public Light and Private Dark: The Privatization of Home Health Services for the Elderly," *Home Health Care Services Quarterly*, Fall 1990.

25. Vicente Navarro, "Federal Health Policy in the U.S.: An Alternative Explanation," *Milbank Memorial Fund Quarterly* 65, no. 1 (1987): 81–111.

26. Ibid.

27. George E. Peterson, "Federalism and the States: An Experiment in Decentralization," in *The Reagan Record*, ed. John L. Palmer and Isabel Sawhill (Cambridge, Mass.: Ballinger, 1984), 223–24.

28. David Stockman, Testimony in U.S. Senate Hearings, 1983, 363.

29. J. Shannon, "Fend-For-Yourself (New) Federalism," in *Perspectives on Federalism*, ed. H. Scheiber (Berkeley: Institute for Governmental Studies, University of California, 1987), 31.

30. U.S. Congress, House of Representatives, Committee on the Budget, 101st Cong., 1987, 79. Data from the "Fiscal Survey of the States 1986" of the National Governors' Association and the National Association of State Budget Officers illustrate the difficulty since the year-end budget balance was projected at 1.6 percent for 1987, while the normative measure of state fiscal health is a budget balance of at least 5 percent of overall expenditures.

31. John E. Chubb and Paul E. Peterson, "Realignment and Institutionalization," in *The New Directions in American Politics*, ed. John E. Chubb and Paul E. Peterson (Washington, D.C.: Brookings Institution, 1985), 26.

32. Shannon, "Fend-For-Yourself (New) Federalism," 35.

33. John E. Chubb, "Federalism and the Bias for Centralization," in Chubb and Peterson, *New Directions in American Politics*, 277–281.

34. Ibid., 305.

35. Paul E. Peterson, Barry G. Rabe, and Kenneth K. Wong, *When Federalism Works* (Washington, D.C.: Brookings Institution, 1986), 228.

36. Carroll L. Estes and Robert Newcomer, "The Future for Aging and Public Policy: Two Perspectives," in *Fiscal Austerity and Aging*, ed. Carroll L. Estes, Robert J. Newcomer, and Associates (Beverly Hills: Sage, 1983), 256–59.

37. See, for example, Bradford Gray, ed., *For-Profit Enterprise in Health Care* (Washington, D.C.: National Academy Press, 1986).

38. S. B. Foote, "New Federalism or Old Federalization: Deregulation and the States," in Scheiber, *Perspectives on Federalism*, 42.

39. Chubb, "Federalism and the Bias for Centralization," 301.

40. Foote, "New Federalism or Old Federalization," 44–45.

41. George C. Eads and Michael Fix, *Relief or Reform: Reagan's Regulatory Dilemma* (Washington, D.C.: Urban Institute, 1984), 17–44.

42. Pamela Hanes-Spohn, Linda A. Bergthold, and Carroll L. Estes, "Cottages to Condos: The Expansion of the Home Health Care Industry under Medicare," *Home Health Services Quarterly* 8, no. 4 (Winter 1987/88): 25–55.

43. John F. Holahan and Joel W. Cohan, *Medicaid: The Trade-off Between Cost Containment and Access to Care* (Washington, D.C.: Urban Institute, 1986), 33–52.

44. David Lindeman and Alan Pardini, "Social Services: The Impact of Fiscal Austerity," in Estes, Newcomer, and Associates, *Fiscal Austerity and Aging*, 133–56.

45. Eads and Fix, *Relief or Reform*, 236.

46. Carroll L. Estes and Linda A. Bergthold, "Unravelling the Welfare State," in *The Service Economy*, ed. Joel I. Nelson, Special Issue of the *International Journal of Sociology and Social Policy* 9, nos. 2–3 (1988): 18–31; Carroll L. Estes and Robert A. Alford, "Systemic Crisis and the Nonprofit Sector: Toward a Political Economy of the Nonprofit Service Sector," *Theory and Society*, Spring 1990.

47. Bergthold, Estes, and Villanueva, "Public Light and Private Dark."

48. Elizabeth A. Binney, Carroll L. Estes, and Susan E. Humphers, "Informalization and Community Care for the Elderly," ms., University of California, San Francisco, 1989.

49. Ralph M. Kramer, *Voluntary Agencies in the Welfare State* (Berkeley: University of California Press, 1981).

50. Lester Salamon, "The Nonprofit Sector: The Lost Opportunity," in Palmer and Sawhill, *Reagan Record*, 261–85.

51. Paul Starr, "The Meaning of Privatization." Working Paper No. 6, National Conference on Social Welfare, Project on the Federal Social Role, Washington, D.C., 1985.

52. Julius LeGrand, "The Privatisation of Welfare," Conference on Public Expenditure and the Private Sector, Institute for Public Administration, Dublin, 1987.

53. R. Robinson, "Restructuring the Welfare State," *Journal of Social Policy* 15 (1986): 1–22.

54. R. Kent Weaver, "Controlling Entitlements," in Chubb and Peterson, *New Directions in American Politics*, 308.

55. Howard E. Freeman, Robert J. Blendon, Linda H. Aiken, Seymour Sudman, Connie F. Mullinix, and Christopher R. Corey, "Americans Report on Their Access to Health Care," *Health Affairs*, Spring 1987, 6–18.

56. Holahan and Cohan, *Medicaid*, 5–31, 33–52.

57. Darling, "Role of the Federal Government in Assuring Access to Health Care," 286–95.

58. Jack Meyer and Marilyn Moon. "Health Care Spending on Children and the Elderly," in *The Vulnerable*, ed. John L. Palmer, Timothy Smeeding, and Barbara Boyle Torrey (Washington, D.C.: Urban Institute, 1988), 179.

59. Lois M. Verbrugge, "Recent, Present, and Future Health of American Adults," in *Annual Review of Public Health*, ed. J. E. Breslow, J. E. Fielding, and L. B. Lave (Palo Alto, Calif.: Annual Reviews, 1989), 10:333–62.

60. Judith J. Feder, Jack Hadley, and S. Zuckerman, "How Did Medicare's PPS Affect Hospitals?" *New England Journal of Medicine* 317, no. 14 (1987): 867–72.

61. Juanita B. Wood and Carroll L. Estes, "The Impact of DRGs on Community-Based Service Providers: Implications for the Elderly," *American Journal of Public Health* 80 (1990): 840–43.

62. F. H. Stark, "Introductory Remarks to Hearing on Medicare Hospital DRG Margins," U.S. Congress, House of Representatives, Subcommittee on Health of the Ways and Means Committee, 101st Cong., February 26, 1987.

63. Villers Foundation, *On the Other Side of Easy Street* (Washington, D.C.: The Foundation, 1987).

64. William Roper, press release, HHS, Washington, D.C., November 18, 1988, 1–3.

65. Reinhardt, "Battle over Medical Costs Isn't Over."

66. Roper, press release, 1–3.

67. Villers Foundation, *On the Other Side of Easy Street.*

68. U.S. Congress, House of Representatives, *Twentieth Anniversary of Medicare and Medicaid: Americans Still at Risk, Hearings before House Select Committee on Aging,* 99th Cong., 1985.

69. Mark Schlesinger and Pamela Brown Drumheller, "Beneficiary Cost Sharing in the Medicare Program," in *Renewing the Promise: Medicare and Its Reform,* ed. David Blumenthal, Mark Schlesinger, Pamela Brown Drumheller (New York: Oxford University Press, 1988), 37–38.

70. U.S. Congress, House of Representatives, *Long Term Care and Personal Impoverishment: Seven in Ten Elderly Living Alone Are at Risk* (Report of the Select Committee on Aging, 100th Cong., October 1987), 22–32.

71. Carroll L. Estes and Elizabeth A. Binney, "The Biomedicalization of Aging," *Gerontologist* 29, no. 5 (1989): 587–96.

72. Wood and Estes, "Organizational and Community Responses to Medicare Policy."

73. Mimi Abramovitz, *Regulating the Lives of Women* (Boston: South End Press, 1988), 349–79.

74. Anne Showstack Sassoon, ed., *Women and the State* (London: Hutchinson, 1987), 13–42.

75. Michael F. Gutowski and Jeffery F. Koshel, "Social Services," in Palmer and Sawhill, *Reagan Experiment,* 307–8.

76. Ibid., 313–14.

77. Palmer and Sawhill, *Reagan Experiment,* 320.

78. U.S. Congress, Senate, Special Committee on Aging, *Developments in Aging,* 100th Cong., 1986, 335–411.

79. Richard P. Nathan, Fred C. Doolittle, and Associates, "Overview: Effects of the Reagan Domestic Program on States and Localities" (Working paper, Princeton University Urban and Regional Research Center, 1984); cited in Chubb, "Federalism and the Bias for Centralization," 301–5.

80. American Association of Retired Persons (AARP) and Travelers Insurance Companies Foundation, *National Survey of Caregivers: Summary of Findings* (Hartford, Conn.: AARP and Travelers, 1988); Robin Stone, Gail Lee Cafferata, and Judith Sangel, "Caregivers of the Frail Elderly: A National Profile," *Gerontologist* 27, no. 5 (1987), 616–26; AARP Andrus Foundation, 1989.

81. Laura Balbo, "Crazy Quilts," in Sassoon, *Women and the State*, 45–71.

82. Darling, "Role of the Federal Government in Assuring Access to Health Care," 286–95.

83. Freeman et al., "Americans Report on Their Access to Health Care," 6–18.

84. Sulvetta and Swartz, *Uninsured and Uncompensated Care*; P. Farley, *Selectivity in the Demand for Health Insurance and Health Care* (Hyattsville, Md.: U.S. NCHSR, 1985).

85. Carroll L. Estes and James H. Swan, "Privatization, System Membership, and Access to Home Health Care for the Elderly," ms., University of California, San Francisco, 1989.

86. Estes, "Politics of Ageing in America," 121–34.; Linda A. Bergthold, Carroll L. Estes, Pamela Hanes-Spohn, and James H. Swan, "Running as Fast as They Can: Organizational Changes in Home Health Care," ms., University of California, San Francisco, 1988.

87. Estes, "Politics of Ageing in America," 121–34; Carroll L. Estes, Robert R. Alford, and Elizabeth A. Binney, "Restructuring of the Nonprofit Sector," ms., University of California, San Francisco, 1987.

88. Daniel Callahan, *Setting Limits* (New York: Simon and Schuster, 1988).

89. Antonio Gramsci, *Selections from Prison Notebooks* (New York: International Publishers, 1971).

90. Wood and Estes, "Organizational and Community Responses to Medicare Policy."

91. Gramsci, *Selections from Prison Notebooks*.

5/The Politics of Dualism: Pension Policy in Canada

John Myles and Les Teichroew

In Canada, as elsewhere, the period from the end of World War II to the early 1970s was one of putting in place the basic components of the Canadian version of a Keynesian welfare state. And, as in many other countries, this was accomplished with a flurry of legislation in the late 1960s and early 1970s to patch up and fill in the gaps left from the reforms of the 1940s and early 1950s. In most respects, the Canadian experience since then has also tended to mirror the international pattern. With the end of the postwar boom in the early 1970s, the construction of the Canadian welfare state came to a halt. And while there has been a great deal of what Michael Wolfson calls "modest tinkering"[1] since then, the basic legislative and policy infrastructure put in place in the quarter century or so following World War II has remained largely intact.

In other respects, the politics of social policy since the 1970s has been unlike that in other countries, particularly if other Anglo-American democracies such as England and the United States are taken as referents. There has been no all-out assault on the welfare state. And although the rhetoric of the "welfare state crisis" came to Canada in the late 1970s and early 1980s, it is difficult to find empirical referents to support any easy application of such a metaphor to the Canadian experience.[2] To the contrary, the main preoccupation of Canadian policy elites and, to a lesser degree, the general public, until the early 1980s, was the Great Pension Debate. This was not a debate over how to dismantle the Canadian welfare state but how to expand it. At the time, Canadian old-age security programs were generally considered inadequate and in need of reform. The contrast with the American experience is especially striking if one recalls that during the same period American attention was focused on the "Crisis of Social Security" and claims that it would be necessary to slash social security in order to save it.

In 1984, the "crisis of the welfare state" as a political phenomenon did come to Canada, but briefly, and ended in political disaster for a group of would-be neoconservative reformers. This was the attack on Canada's universal demogrant programs for children and the elderly launched by an important wing of the newly elected Progressive Conservative government under Prime Minister Brian Mulroney. The basic thrust of the universality debate, as it came to be called, was to dismantle social programs that provided benefits to the middle class in order to target better social expenditures on those most in need. It met opposition from organized labor, women's organizations, antipoverty lobbies, and the general public. As a result, Finance Minister Michael Wilson was forced by his prime minister to withdraw proposals to deindex universal old-age benefits, and the new Conservative government experienced what has arguably been its single most important political setback to date.

Finally, in 1989, the Conservatives achieved their first significant change in Canada's public old-age security system. This took the form of a "clawback" that will tax back benefits provided by the universal old-age benefit program from elderly persons with incomes greater than $50,000 per year.[3] The rhetoric of this reform, however, was not an attack on the welfare state as such. Instead, it reflected the main project of both the Liberal and Conservative parties throughout the 1980s—to make the welfare state more efficient by targeting scarce transfer dollars to those most in need.

Equally interesting for a nation huddled along the American border and one that imports American culture and fads in vast quantities is the fact that the main themes that permeated American discussions of old-age issues in the 1980s have had little impact in Canada. The prospect of the fiscal burden expected as a result of a long-term process of population aging has been received with relative equanimity by public, corporate, and policy elites. The conclusion that population aging poses no inherent threat to Canada's economic future has been reiterated even when those involved looked very hard for and, one suspects, were predisposed to finding such a threat.[4] Nor has the debate over intergenerational equity—claims that the young are being sacrificed to maintain the privileges of the old—had any success north of the U.S. border.[5] This is not because child poverty has not become an issue. It has. And the magnitude of the problem is not unlike that in the United States.

What accounts for the comparatively privileged character of Canada's old-age security system? One explanation is the middle-class incorporation thesis: Universal social programs that "incorporate" the middle classes, providing them with benefits or services of high quality, are immune from political tampering. Politicians who threaten to do so court electoral defeat. The Reagan administration's failed attempt to dismantle social security in the United States during the early 1980s is typically invoked as the classic example of this phenomenon.

By this standard, however, Canada's public old-age security system ought to be more, rather than less, vulnerable than the American. For middle-income earners, the level of income replacement available through Canadian public old-age security schemes is substantially lower than in the United States.[6] As a result, Canadian workers must rely to a greater extent on occupational pensions and on personal savings to maintain continuity in living standards in old age.[7] And the "clawback" of Old Age Security (OAS) benefits will exacerbate this dependency on private pensions. Though the "clawback" will affect relatively few seniors in the short run, because of indexing procedures the proportion subject to the clawback will progressively increase in the future.[8]

But herein lies a possible clue to the answer: Perhaps because of its comparatively underdeveloped character, Canada's economic and political elites have less reason to worry about Canada's old-age security system. And, indeed, a recent International Monetary Fund (IMF) study supports this view.[9] IMF projections to the year 2025 indicate that population aging will produce a "significant increase in the ratio of government social expenditures to GDP in most of the countries except Canada,"[10] the result of "a relatively lower level of government social benefits, particularly in the area of pensions."[11] In short, perhaps the assault on Canada's welfare state for the elderly has been so modest because there has been so little to attack!

There is more than a germ of truth to this interpretation. In 1985, Canada spent a smaller percentage of GDP (5.4 percent) on public old-age pensions than every other OECD country except Australia (4.9 percent) and Japan (5.3 percent).[12] This is in part because Canada has proportionately fewer old people than many European nations but also in part because of low real per capita benefits. The United States, with a similar age profile, spent 7.2 percent of GDP on old-age pensions in 1985. Comparatively speaking, Canadian income-security programs for the elderly are not a very large target on which to turn neoconservative guns.

We argue, however, that it is not just the size of the welfare state that matters. As the debate over the welfare state evolved in the 1980s, it became increasingly clear that the main issue was not whether there should be a welfare state or not, but rather what *kind* of welfare state. And in Canada's "welfare state for the elderly," market-oriented critics of postwar social programs discovered an almost ideal-typical design for the classical liberal vision of the welfare state: one that complements and sustains the market by dealing with its failures but allows the market—with appropriate subsidies—to determine the fate of the rest of the population. Canada's income-security system for the elderly provides the model for what is now widely seen as the desirable design for Canada's welfare state of the future. In a curious way, then, actors who elsewhere might be found attacking welfare states for the elderly found themselves in the position of defending the status quo and even arguing in favor of improved income supplements for those whose benefits continue to lag behind quasi-official subsistence levels.

To develop this argument requires that we first describe the architecture of Canada's old-age welfare state—an architecture we characterize as dualistic—and the attempts in the late 1970s to transform it. We then proceed to locate this history within the larger debates over the reform of Canada's welfare state and the broader economic shifts that have informed this debate.

Building Dualism: Canada's Welfare State for the Elderly

Social Assistance for the Elderly: The Old Age Pensions Act

Canada's first national pension legislation for the elderly was the Old Age Pensions Act of 1927. This was a classic piece of "social assistance" legislation in that its provisions were neither universal nor generous. It provided a pension of $20 per month to those over the age of 70 with yearly incomes less than $365. In its last year of operation (1951), less than half the population over 70 were receiving benefits, and the maximum means-tested benefit was $480 per year at a time when the average production worker was earning $2,460 per year and office employees $3,300.

As with all such early legislation, the intent was not to provide a "retirement wage" that would allow older workers to exit from the labor market. Instead, it was conceived as a classic form of poor relief, designed to provide subsistence to older workers forced to exit from the labor market and to their spouses and widows. The notion that welfare states should provide more than subsistence to the poor had not yet arrived. The *social security* welfare state—one that provides income security and continuity of living standards after retirement—was, in Canada as elsewhere, a decidedly post–World War II construction.

Universality: The Old Age Security Act

The first step into the social security era came with the passage of the Old Age Security Act (OAS) in 1951. Though benefit levels remained fixed at $40 per month, the means test for those over the age of 70 was removed, making benefits universal. This provided the first tier in Canada's emergent income-security system for the elderly. In the same year, the Old Age Assistance Act (OAA) extended means-tested benefits to those aged 65–69. It remained in place until 1970, by which time eligibility for the universal pension had been reduced to age 65.

Income Security: The Canada Pension Plan

By themselves, universal flat benefits were insufficient to allow most elderly workers to leave the labor force without a significant drop in living standards.

In Canada, as in other countries where the flat-benefit principle was adopted (e.g., Britain, Sweden), income security required a second tier of contributory pensions. This was achieved in 1965 with the introduction of the Canada Pension Plan and the Quebec Pension Plan (C/QPP). The effect of the legislation was to create a national, contributory pension scheme in which benefits are linked to past contributions.

The C/QPP was a shift in the direction of income security but one that did not greatly offend liberal principles concerning the primacy of the market. The maximum level of insured earnings—25 percent of the average industrial wage—was low enough to ensure that supplementary occupational pensions would still be necessary for the majority.

The addition of the C/QPP did, however, transform the meaning and significance of the universal OAS. Prior to this point, OAS provided no more (indeed less) than a subsistence standard of living. But when combined with the C/QPP, it became the first tier of a two-tiered income-security program for workers and one that provided for a substantial level of redistribution, since the OAS component is independent of market capacity. It did not take long for this fact to be recognized. In the election campaign of 1968, Pierre Trudeau, newly elected leader of the Liberal party and warrior for the Just Society, assured Canadians that, if he was elected, there would be "no more of this free stuff." [13] In this case, campaign rhetoric was followed by action. In the 1970 white paper *Income Security for Canadians*, the Liberals proposed to shift the system away from the universal OAS and to rely more on the income-tested Guaranteed Income Supplement (GIS), a program first introduced as a temporary measure in 1967. [14]

The Guaranteed Income Supplement
Since it would take some years for workers to accumulate benefits under C/QPP, the Guaranteed Income Supplement (GIS) was introduced as an interim measure in 1967. It provided income-tested benefits to elderly individuals and couples, a sort of guaranteed annual income for Canada's seniors. Unlike the means-tested Supplemental Security Income (SSI) in the United States, GIS benefits are income tested. As a result, the elderly are not required to sell off assets or otherwise spend their way into poverty to be eligible. But, unlike OAS, it goes only to seniors whose income from other sources falls below a specified income floor. In 1989, the effective guaranteed annual income (OAS and GIS) was $9,432 per year for a single pensioner and $12,288 per year for a couple.

Though initially intended as an interim measure to be phased out when the C/QPP matured in the mid 1970s, the GIS quickly became the preferred vehicle for further pension enhancement for both ideological and political, "state structural," reasons. Trudeau's opposition to universality was articulated in the 1970 white paper not only with respect to old-age pensions but social programs in general. As Bryden points out,[15] the importance of this view was highlighted by the fact that the following quotation was printed in italics: "Greater emphasis should be placed on anti-poverty measures. This should be accomplished in a manner which enables the greatest concentration of available resources upon those with the lowest incomes. Selective payments based on income should be made where possible in place of universal payments which disregard the actual income of the recipient."

This philosophy, a vision of the welfare state confined to poor relief, dominated official thinking on social policy thereafter. In the area of old-age security, the GIS provided the ideal model for implementing such a strategy. The structure of the Canadian state also favored the GIS over other solutions. Because provincial governments have effective veto power over C/QPP reforms, electioneering strategies by federal politicians were almost of necessity confined to bidding up the value of the federally controlled GIS.

Trudeau's initial attempt to shift the burden of income support to the GIS, however, ended in failure. In the election of 1972, the Liberals returned as a minority government. In exchange for their support in Parliament, Canada's New Democratic party (NDP) demanded that upward adjustment of the OAS be continued.[16] In the long run, this defense of OAS by Canada's social democrats was only a partial success. The 1972 legislation provided for automatic annual indexing of OAS benefits based on the increase in the Consumer Price Index. While this maintains the real purchasing power of benefits intact, it ensures that their relative value (i.e., relative to average wages) will decline over any period when there is real wage growth in the economy (i.e., whenever wages rise faster than prices). GIS benefits are also indexed to prices, but for reasons alluded to earlier, they have been continuously adjusted upward with ad hoc legislation (1971, 1972, 1979, 1980, 1984). The result has been relative stagnation of OAS but both real and relative growth in GIS benefit levels, as shown in Figures 5.1 and 5.2.

The data charted in the figures show OAS and GIS benefit levels as a percentage of the average industrial wage for 1967 to 1985 for single pensioners and a pensioner couple.[17] At the beginning of the 1960s, a single OAS benefit represented 20 percent of the average industrial wage. The data capture the downward drift in relative OAS levels during the 1960s when real wages were rising. This downward trend was arrested with the 1972 legislation, and since then, the single OAS benefit has been relatively constant at about 14 percent of average wages. The reason for this stability has been the absence of real wage growth since that time. To the extent that expected productivity gains bring real wage growth in the future, relative OAS benefits will once again begin their downward trend. Largely because of this projected long-term decline in the relative importance of OAS benefits, long-term projections of the impact

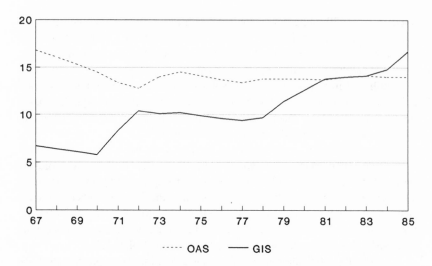

Figure 5.1 Old-age security and maximum guaranteed income supplement, single pensioner, as a percentage of average wage, 1967–1985. *Source:* National Council of Welfare.

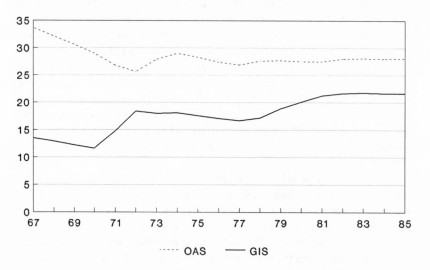

Figure 5.2 Old-age security and maximum guaranteed income supplement, pensioner couple, as a percentage of average wage, 1967–1985. *Source:* National Council of Welfare.

of population aging on public expenditures for the elderly in Canada are comparatively modest. Allowed to continue in this way (i.e., without additional upward adjustments), OAS will represent a relatively trivial component in the income packages of the retired elderly in the next century. By design, the universalistic component of Canada's income-security system for the elderly is expected to wither away with the slack to be taken up by GIS, on the one hand, and an expanded "semiprivate" welfare state on the other.

The Semiprivate Welfare State
By design, the Canada and Quebec Pension Plans were never intended to provide income-replacement levels sufficient to allow the elderly to maintain continuity in living standards after retirement.[18] Instead, the public system was meant to provide a base that would be completed by occupational pensions (Registered Pension Plans, or RPPs) negotiated in the workplace and through private savings for retirement (Registered Retirement Savings Plans, or RRSPs). When the C/QPP was created in 1965, approximately 39 percent of paid workers were covered by occupational plans. The presumption was that in the years ahead, this number would grow to incorporate the majority of those not covered. The hope was never realized. The proportion of the employed labor force covered by occupational plans peaked at 48 percent in 1980 and has since slipped back to 46 percent. RRSPs, which are individual savings accounts much like IRAs in the United States, have mainly benefited high-income earners and the self-employed. In 1989, just over 19 percent of all those who filed tax returns had made RRSP contributions.

Together, RSPs and RRSPs constitute what could be thought of as Canada's semiprivate welfare state for the elderly. Most Canadians think of these programs as falling outside the public sector, since they are privately organized and administered. They exist and flourish, however, because of extensive public subsidies in the form of tax concessions on contributions and earnings that accrue inside the plan. There is comparatively little information on the size of this subsidy because tax expenditure data are only occasionally released by the government. The last year for which such information is available is 1983 when total tax subsidies for RPPs and RRSPs amounted to $5 billion. To estimate the relative importance of this amount it is sufficient to note that in the same year, government expenditures for the C/QPP were $3.5 billion and for OAS approximately $8 billion.

A Dualistic Welfare State

This combination of public and "semiprivate" welfare states is what gives the Canadian income-security system for the elderly its dualist structure. On the one hand, there are those elderly who receive benefits only from the public system (OAS, GIS, C/QPP) and, on the other, those who also receive benefits from privately administered but publicly subsidized occupational pensions and retirement savings plans. The division this creates in the labor market broadly corresponds to the typologies familiar to us from the dual or segmented labor-market theorists. Those covered by both private and public pensions tend to be in the public sector and the larger manufacturing and financial institutions. Those who must get by on the public system (and eventually get income assistance from GIS) tend to be in the "secondary" labor market made up of retail and consumer services, part-time employees, and small, labor-intensive firms. In view of sex differences in patterns of labor-force participation and occupational mix, the principal victims of this dualistic structure are also the fastest-growing sector of the labor market—women. Women (and men) who enter the wrong industry, have interrupted work histories, or have a high level of job mobility simply are largely excluded from the benefits of the semiprivate welfare state and the public funds bestowed on it.

The result of such a system is a classic instance of the insider–outsider problem. "Insiders," those who benefit from both the public and semiprivate welfare states, can expect to retire with a level of income replacement sufficient to maintain continuity of living standards in old age. "Outsiders," employees and those outside the labor market with no access to the semiprivate welfare state, cannot expect income security in old age, but neither are they allowed to perish. Such an outcome is prevented by GIS benefits, which are set close to, or just below, Canada's semiofficial poverty lines (Statistics Canada's "low-income" cutoffs).

Situations such as these are often difficult to change since the insiders have little incentive to push for reform and the outsiders typically have few organizational resources, power, or influence to demand change. And since the outsiders are not allowed to starve (a result of GIS), an aura of legitimacy pervades the system. Nevertheless, in the mid 1970s a segment of the insiders—organized labor—did launch an assault on this arrangement and, as a result, set the terms of debate over old-age pensions until the beginning of the 1980s.

The Attack on Dualism: The Great Pension Debate

By the mid 1970s, the shortcomings of the system put in place during the 1960s were increasingly apparent and well documented.[19] The private sector had not delivered as expected and did not seem about to do so. As a result, the Canadian Labour Congress (CLC) called for expansion of the C/QPP, and the Great Pension Debate was under way. Motivations were not entirely altruistic (i.e., concern for the problems of the outsiders). By the mid 1970s, it was also clear that, dollar for dollar, the public system and especially the C/QPP provided a superior product to private-sector alternatives. Employer pensions were not indexed, were not easily portable when workers changed jobs, and typically had very restrictive vesting provisions. In short, for organized labor, employer pensions were a "bad buy." Everyone would be better off if they were allowed to shift their private pension contributions into the far superior C/QPP.

The majority of experts agreed with this assessment. In 1979, the Special Senate Committee on Pension Reforms called for a massive expansion of the C/QPP along with a major overhaul of the private pension system.[20] And a government task force in the federal bureaucracy reached a similar conclusion, with mandated private pensions (obligatory coverage for all paid workers) as a possible but more costly alternative.[21]

Business response was immediate and clear: Not only was pension reform unnecessary, it was dangerous. Both theses were advanced in a study written by Geoffrey Calvert, commissioned by a coalition of Canada's leading financial and industrial firms (the Canadian Pension Conference) and published by the *Financial Post*, Canada's leading business newspaper.[22] Pension reform was unnecessary, Calvert argued, because the elderly did not need more money. This was demonstrated by the fact that consumer expenditure surveys showed the elderly spent less on food, housing, clothing, and other basics than people in younger age groups. This brilliant logic discredited the study even in the cautious, conservative world of Canada's pension experts. But it did not undermine his claim that expansion of the public pension system was dangerous—for Canadian business.

Calvert pointed out that the money provided by private pension funds had become the single largest source of new investment capital in the Canadian economy and was bound to expand in importance in the future.[23] If the C/QPP were to begin crowding out private pensions, this important source of investment capital could dry up. And, more important, because the C/QPP is a partially funded pension system, it would actually result in a major transfer of control over capital from the private sector to the state. This was no idle threat. In its original design, the CPP, like the vast majority of public pension systems, was to have been funded on a pay-as-you-go basis with no buildup of a capital pool. It was put on a funded basis at the insistence of the Quebec government, which wanted the capital to finance Quebec's "Quiet Revolution." And this is precisely what happened. The Caisse de Dépôt et Placement du Québec was put in charge of managing the funds and became the engine used by the Quebec government to direct capital flows in the province and create an indigenous business class. By 1986, the Caisse controlled $25.2 billion in assets, was the eighth-largest financial institution in the country and the single largest player in Canadian financial markets.[24] Over the same period, the other provincial governments had used the corresponding funds from the CPP to finance provincial debt at preferred rates. Indeed, guaranteed access to this capital pool appears to have been a major motivator for their participation in the first place.[25]

This threat to both the process and control of capital formation in Canada largely explains the implacable opposition of the business community to expansion of the C/QPP and the eventual failure of the reform movement. In the past, business opposition to pension reform had been concentrated in the financial sector, whose business is eroded by public plans. Now, the threat of more state control over capital flows brought industrial capital into the fray as well.[26] The result was a coalition and degree of class solidarity among Canadian capitalists unlike any previous confrontation over pension reform.

The late 1970s and early 1980s saw a flurry of Royal Commissions; hearings and government reports inundated the country with assessments of the Canadian pension system and recommendations for its reform. Throughout, the Liberal government of the day continually reasserted its commitment to pension reform. And the committed and forceful minister of health and welfare, Monique Bégin, made it clear that if the private sector could not get its act together, government would do it for them. Even Pierre Trudeau, the old opponent of universality, agreed in 1981 that the fact that 50 percent of old-age pensioners were receiving income supplements from the GIS was a major source of concern.[27] It was clear, moreover, that expansion of the C/QPP was the cheapest and most effective way of resolving the many problems identified with the current system. It had all the features that employers continuously reiterated they were unable or unwilling to make available in private plans: universal coverage of the labor force, immediate vesting and portability, indexed benefits, and much better provisions for women. It had the added advantage of being efficient, that is, cheap to administer.[28]

Reinforcing Dualism

By 1981, the Great Pension Debate had congealed around three broad strategies for reform.

1. The first strategy was to introduce new regulations designed to overcome the most severe shortcomings of existing private pension plans. In the main these had to do with issues of earlier vesting, easier portability, obligatory survivor benefits, credit splitting between spouses, access to pension programs by part-time workers, and some degree of inflation protection. All this would improve the quality of private pensions for those already covered but would do nothing to solve

the initial problem that fostered the debate—the fact that a majority of workers had no access to such plans. In sum, the effect of this strategy would reinforce the very dualism that was the source of the problem but address traditional complaints over "product quality" of private-sector plans.

2. The second strategy was a compromise solution. This would involve mandatory private coverage for all employees combined with the reform of private pensions covered in strategy 1.

3. The third strategy was that originally proposed by Canadian labor, namely, to deal with the problems of coverage and product quality by significantly expanding the scope of the C/QPP, making a large part of the private pensions industry redundant.

Strategies 2 and 3 offered real solutions to the initial problem that fostered the Great Pension Debate. They differed over whether pension expansion would occur in the private or the public sector. In contrast, the first strategy would deepen rather than solve the problem.

In the end, the first strategy prevailed. Opposition to any dramatic pension reform had always been strong within the powerful and market-oriented Department of Finance, which, after 1981, gained the upper hand.[29] This was in part a result of the department's own maverick budget introduced by the populist minister of finance, Allan MacEachen. In November 1981 he introduced a budget designed to dismantle Canada's welfare state for the rich, that is, the plethora of tax benefits for corporations and high-income Canadians that previous Liberal finance ministers had constructed during the 1970s.[30] The reaction of Canada's business and professional elite was loud and swift. Fearing to alienate Canada's business leaders further after the disastrous failure of the National Energy Policy (NEP) that brought the Canadian oil industry under greater government control, MacEachen was quickly moved to another ministry, and the main proposals of his budget were withdrawn.

The result was to reinforce Liberal wariness over doing anything that might further antagonize Canadian business. The death knell for the pension reform movement came with the advent of the 1982–1983 recession. Labor had all it could do to defend jobs and unemployment benefits for workers, and the Liberal government of the day was even less willing to do anything that might depress "business confidence" and delay recovery. Instead, pension politics entered a new era of "reform," one that by design if not intent would deepen and reinforce the very dualism the earlier proposals had been designed to overcome.

The shift of focus in pension politics was quickly apparent in both the media and the pension industry. A review of the *Globe and Mail* (Canada's national newspaper), the business press, and bulletins of William Mercer Ltd. (Canada's leading pension actuarial house) shows that after 1981, the main issues discussed concerned alternative reforms in the private sector (especially of indexing and coverage of part-time workers).[31] The specter of C/QPP expansion was raised only to highlight the fact that costly and otherwise undesirable changes in private-sector plans were the lesser of two evils from the business community's point of view.

In 1982, the government of Canada introduced its "green paper" on pension reform.[32] The major proposal with respect to reform of the C/QPP was to allow the level of maximum pensionable earnings to return to the level of the average industrial wage over a three-year period. The average industrial wage had been the level established for pensionable earnings under the original 1965 legislation. Since 1965, however, it had been allowed to erode slightly. The balance of the proposals focused on reforming private pensions already in place. The issue of improved coverage and higher replacement rates, whether through C/QPP expansion or mandated pensions, was sidestepped because, as the government argued, "at this time there is no consensus" on how this might be accomplished.[33] Instead, the torch was passed to a parliamentary task force that brought in its recommendations in the fall of 1983. The task force proposals were described by its chair, Douglas Frith, as "an acceptable, workable and affordable compromise," which meant once again that the issue of income replacement and coverage was avoided.[34]

The main body of legislation to come out of almost ten years of debate was the Pension Benefits Standards Act in 1985, directed at improving the quality of occupational plans. It required all federally regulated industries to provide vesting of employer contributions after two years, to provide for the transfer of pension credits when employees change jobs, to make it easier for part-time employees to join corporate plans, and to provide a survivor benefit equal to 60 percent of the retirement pension on the death of a spouse.[35] The majority of provinces that had not already done so subsequently introduced similar legislation,[36] the result of a consensus reached between Ottawa and the provinces in the winter of 1984–1985. In the May budget of 1985, Finance Minister Wilson also introduced a series of improvements and reforms to Canada's Registered Retirement Savings Programs (RRSPs) to make them more attractive and allow individuals to invest larger amounts in these subsidized savings vehicles.[37] In sum, after a decade of debate, the result was to reinforce the economic divisions that generated the debate in the first place: better-quality occupational pensions (for those covered), more tax shelters for the well-to-do (RRSPs), and little or nothing for those whose retirement income depends almost exclusively on the public sector. Throughout, all political parties have maintained their commitment to addressing the problem of "poverty" among the elderly through upward adjustments of GIS benefits.

Why Dualism?

Though old-age pensions form the largest part of the contemporary welfare state, they are not its only component. And pension reform does not take place in isolation from more general considerations and debates over the role and future of social programs. Since the early 1970s, the dominant policy model not just for pensions but for the welfare state generally, and for both Liberal and Conservative governments, has had two components. The first is to cap further expansion of social insurance programs (such as the C/QPP) and to encourage expansion of private-sector alternatives (RPPs and RRSPs). The second component is to shift the emphasis away from universal programs toward income-tested programs such as the GIS. As our narrative indicates, there are many reasons, not all of which have been discussed here, why efforts to counteract this trend, as in the Great Pension Debate, have failed. The desire and capacity of business elites to resist efforts to move toward an alternative welfare-state model and a federal state structure that makes it difficult for the central government to do so are simply among the more prominent reasons.[38]

While these factors help us understand the failure of the reform movement, they do not explain the other side of old-age politics in the 1980s: the growth and consolidation of what is in essence a Guaranteed Income (GI) for the elderly, on the one hand, combined with a reformed and increasingly highly regulated system of occupational pensions, on the other. This development, and with it the comparatively privileged character of old-age security programs in Canada, we argue, has followed a larger shift in welfare-state politics over the past decade. It is a shift in which the principles of a generalized Guaranteed Income (GI) version of the welfare state has emerged as the model of choice for Canada's welfare state of the future.[39]

There are several variants of the GI (or negative income tax) model of the welfare state, but according to Moynihan its basic principles were first elaborated by the U.S. Treasury Department economist Milton Friedman in 1943. The idea was simple: In good years workers would pay taxes to the Treasury, and in bad years the Treasury would pay taxes to workers.[40] This is the notion of a negative income tax, or guaranteed annual income. It has great appeal because it has the potential to eradicate poverty among both the working and nonworking poor and still leaves incentives for the poor to increase their incomes (i.e., to work). The latter is a key ingredient: It eliminates the so-called welfare trap produced by effective marginal tax rates of up to 100 percent that now characterize programs for the poor and unemployed. A Guaranteed Income or negative income tax does this by lowering the effective marginal tax rates on social-assistance benefits.[41] As a result, disincentives for those on unemployment insurance and social assistance to take a job are removed. It is fundamentally different from social security, however. It prevents poverty but makes no guarantee of income security for workers earning above poverty levels. In this sense, it is fundamentally different from the social security welfare state. The key shift is not from the universality principle, as is often implied by critics of the GI model. Instead, what changes is what is universally guaranteed: subsistence instead of wage replacement. Systems of wage replacement such as unemployment, retirement, and accident insurance and horizontal transfers (e.g., family allowances that transfer income from families without children to those with children) are replaced with a system of transfers to the "poor," and most important to the "working poor." It is an "efficient" welfare system because scarce tax-transfer dollars are not wasted on the middle classes, who are expected to purchase income security in the market like any other commodity.

Since the mid 1970s, the GI version of the welfare state has become the preferred model among Canadian business elites as well as liberally minded policy reformers. It has been the implicit policy model underlying the vast majority of social-policy legislation in Canada since the early 1970s.[42] Conservatives see it as a substitute for virtually all existing social legislation, while liberal reformers see it as a supplement to existing programs. Nevertheless, the shared enthusiasm for this model is based on a common assumption that future employment growth in a postindustrial labor market will be concentrated in the labor-intensive, low-wage and unskilled sectors of the service economy.[43] Hence, a fundamental requirement of the welfare state of the future is to accommodate this development. According to the Canadian Council on Social Development, a liberally minded social-policy agency, the challenge now is "to find acceptable ways of accommodating this form of economic development,"[44] that is, to provide an income conduit from high-wage workers to a growing pool of low-wage workers. In the face of this real and anticipated transformation of the labor market, a welfare state organized on principles of income security for a high-wage working class becomes less and less affordable. Instead of income security, scarce transfer dollars are needed to provide income supplementation.

It is against this backdrop that the comparatively privileged character of recent old-age security politics in Canada can be understood. Rather than a target of opprobrium of business elites or conservative reformers, Canada's GI welfare state for the elderly—a population outside the labor market—is widely hailed as embodying the principles of distribution that should inform the welfare state of the future for those in the labor market. For this reason, GIS receives broad support, while universal programs such as OAS are typically reviled in the popular media and the business press.

Conclusion: The Paradox of Liberal Interventionism

We have argued that Canada's old-age security system has been privileged since the mid 1970s not because of middle-class incorporation—a thesis that could be applied to Canada's health-care and educational systems—but the reverse. Following the failure of the reform movement in the 1970s, pension politics congealed around the reform of the semiprivate welfare state of occupational pensions and RRSPs, from which the majority are excluded. As a result, the projected *public* costs of population aging have not been a source of concern, and corporate access to the savings of Canadian workers has been maintained. "Market failures"—those excluded from the semiprivate welfare state—are provided with subsistence through GIS.

Under such a system, the politics of old age tends to become structured in two domains: the public politics of "poverty" and the semiprivate politics of corporate welfare. In the first, "poverty lines," "low-income cutoffs," and even "subsistence" need to be socially and politically constructed and are a focus of ongoing debate and negotiation. But once established, this sphere of the welfare state—helping "the poor"—is available to political parties of all stripes for electioneering purposes and, in this sense, the politics of old age is "depoliticized." Moreover, the "politics of poverty" does not generally get constructed along lines where the main cleavage is between business and organized labor. Instead, business–labor disputes appear in the second domain, in the ongoing reconstruction of the semiprivate welfare state of occupational pensions—a subject to which we return below.

The two spheres also tend to be sex specific. The public GI welfare state is predominantly a welfare state for women. The semiprivate welfare state of occupational pensions and RRSPs is mainly, if not exclusively, a welfare state for men—organized workers and the predominantly male occupations of employed professionals and managers.

But there is a curious paradox here we should not overlook, the "paradox of liberal interventionism" identified in Mary Ruggie's analysis of the American health-care system.[45] As she points out, the consequence of a political strategy to limit state intervention in the delivery of health care is producing new forms of state intervention and a more, not less, intrusive state to contain costs and control the treatment practices of America's "private" health-care providers. The most notable example was the introduction of the diagnostic-related Group (DRG) system, in which payment is determined by a schedule based on 467 categories of disease or illness. The DRG system has altered the prescribing practices of physicians, hospital admission and discharge patterns, and modes of treatment. All are resulting in a fundamental restructuring of the American health-care system.

Canadian pension politics have followed a similar trajectory. Since the failure of the reform movement, the politics of old age has moved to a new terrain, that of the semiprivate welfare state of occupational pensions. Organized labor and its allies lost their battle to provide an adequate retirement wage for workers across the whole of the labor market, and the business community won its battle to prevent expansion of the public pension system. But the cost, for business, has been increasing public regulation and public scrutiny of private pension benefits and pension fund management. As Finlayson shows, the state has become increasingly intrusive in the world of the private pension industry and in the way firms manage their corporate pension funds. There has been an exponential increase in public legislation to define the pension entitlements employers must provide—those having to do with vesting, portability, survivor benefits, credit splitting between spouses, and so forth. And it is not just entitlements that are at issue. The most acerbic business–labor confrontations since the mid 1980s have emerged over the ownership and use of corporate pension funds. Corporate raiding of pension fund "surpluses" and their use of "contribution holidays" when "surpluses" accumulate have been an intense point of confrontation, forcing the state to become involved in the regulation of this capital in a most unliberal way. Moreover, unlike the reform movement of the late 1970s, this battle is being fought from "below" and not just by the policy elites of the labor movement, business, and the state.[46]

The point of all this is to highlight the fact that the consolidation of a fundamentally "liberal" welfare state should not be confused with a return to the past. New forms of "liberal interventionism" in the semiprivate welfare state are a marked departure from traditional forms of classical liberalism, the main purpose of which was to safeguard a strict boundary between "private" and "public" spheres and to create the political, legal, and social conditions that allow markets to function without state intrusion. It is simply not the case that by limiting the scope and development of the public pension system that the state has limited the scope of its involvement in pensions *tout court*. In this respect, the "privatization" of income security has made pensions more, not less, "political."

Notes

1. Michael Wolfson, ed. "The Arithmetic of Income Security Reform," in *Approaches to Income Security Reform*, ed. S. Seward and M. Iacobacci (Ottawa: Institute for Research on Public Policy, 1987).

2. For a more extensive discussion of this point, see John Myles, "Decline or Impasse? The Current State of the Welfare State," *Studies in Political Economy* 26 (Summer 1988): 73–107.

3. Had the "clawback" been in effect in 1989, for example, seniors with net

incomes of $76,332 would have had the entire benefit taxed back; those with incomes between $50,000 and $76,332 would have received partial benefits.

4. Most notably in the report by the Economic Council of Canada, *One in Three: Pensions for Canadians to the Year 2030* (Ottawa: Ministry of Supply and Services, 1979). This conclusion was recently reiterated by Canada's chief statistician, a truly authoritative source in any Canadian policy debate. See Ivan Fellegi, "Can We Afford an Aging Society," *Canadian Economic Observer*, October 1988, 4.1–4.34.

5. This does not mean similar opinions have not been expressed. See, for example, Gordon Gibson, "One Day We Shall Have to Listen to the Messenger with Bad News," *Financial Post*, January 23, 1989, 12. The point is that as the despairing title of Gibson's article indicates, such views have acquired no political currency.

6. Income-replacement rates for Canadian workers with a lifetime history of average earnings in manufacturing in 1980 were .34 and .49 for single workers and one-earner couples, respectively. The corresponding figures in the United States were .44 and .66. See Jonathan Aldrich, "Earnings Replacement Rates of Old-Age Benefits in 12 Countries, 1969–80," *Social Security Bulletin* 45, no. 11 (1982): 3–11.

7. Because of universal health insurance, Canadian workers do not have to be concerned with health-care expenses in old age. And health care in Canada is subject to the middle-class incorporation argument. This, however, explains the immunity of health insurance to attack, not old-age security, for which the vast majority must go outside the public system to get adequate coverage.

8. Like many social program and tax benefits, the OAS clawback is subject to what has become known in Canada as the "3 percent solution." The level at which the clawback takes effect will increase in the future, but only to the degree that inflation exceeds 3 percent. This means that in real terms the cutoff level will decline each year so that over the long run most if not all seniors will become subject to the clawback.

9. Peter Heller, Richard Hemming, and Peter Kohnert, *Aging and Social Expenditure in the Major Industrial Countries, 1980–2025* (Washington D.C.: International Monetary Fund, 1986).

10. Ibid., 4.

11. Ibid., 5.

12. Organization for Economic Cooperation and Development, "Social Expenditure Trends and Demographic Developments" (Paper delivered at the meeting of the Manpower and Social Affairs Committee, July 6–7, 1988), 7.

13. Kenneth Bryden, *Old Age Pensions and Policy-Making in Canada* (Montreal and London, 1974), 176.

14. The white paper was not just about pensions. The objective was to implement the principles of a GAI across the entire social-support system. See James Rice, "Politics of Income Security: Historical Developments and Limits to Future Change," in *The Politics of Economic Policy*, ed. B. Doern (Toronto, 1985), 221–50.

15. Bryden, *Old Age Pensions and Policy-Making in Canada*, 176.

16. Ibid., 177. This was a replay of Canada's first old-age legislation, the Old Age Pension Act of 1927, introduced by MacKenzie King's Liberal government in exchange for the support of two newly elected labor representatives during a period of minority government.

17. OAS benefits for a pensioner couple will always be exactly twice that of a single pensioner. As a universal benefit, both members receive exactly the same amount. GIS benefits, however, are designed for the relief of poverty, and it is (correctly) assumed that two persons living together can achieve a similar living standard of a single person for less money. As a result, the maximum GIS benefit for a couple ($521 per month in 1989) is substantially less than twice the maximum for a single pensioner ($400 per month).

18. If, for example, we assume that a worker will require 70 percent of preretirement earnings to maintain continuity of living standards after retirement, it is clear that the Canadian system falls far short of the target. In 1984, for example, combined OAS/CPP benefits for a worker retiring at the average wage of $22,800 would have been $7,870, about half the amount required to reach the 70 percent replacement rate.

19. Joan Brown, *How Much Choice? Retirement Policies in Canada* (Ottawa: Canadian Council on Social Development, 1975); Kevin Collins, *Women and Pensions* (Ottawa: Canadian Council on Social Development, 1978).

20. Special Senate Committee on Retirement Age Policies, *Retirement without Tears* (Ottawa: Canadian Government Publishing Centre, 1979).

21. Task Force on Retirement Income Policy, *The Retirement Income System in Canada: Problems and Alternative Policies for Reform* (Ottawa: Ministry of Supply and Services, 1980).

22. Geoffrey Calvert, *Pensions and Survival: The Coming Crisis of Money and Retirement* (Toronto: MacLean Hunter, 1977).

23. By 1986, private pension funds were supplying 55 percent of the funds raised in Canada's capital markets and accounted for seven out of every ten trades on the Toronto Stock Exchange. See "Pension Funds Dominate Stock Markets," *Ottawa Citizen*, January 6, 1989, D12.

24. Ann Finlayson. *Whose Money Is It Anyway? The Showdown on Pensions* (Markham, Ontario: Penguin, 1988), 40.

25. As one provincial official remarked: "The main reason for us was the creation of a large fund. It would provide money for development here and give us more liberty in the money markets. The fund was certainly the main reason for me; it was the reason." Quoted in Richard Simeon, *Federal-Provincial Diplomacy: The Making of Recent Policy in Canada* (Toronto: University of Toronto Press, 1972), 176.

26. Calvert, *Pensions and Survival*, lists the following as the most important corporations involved in financing his study: Alcan, Bank of Montreal, Canada Packers, Canadian Industries, Limited, Canadian National Railways, Domtar, Dupont, Elliot and Page, Inco, Morguard Trust, Noranda Mines, Royal Trust, Saskatchewan Wheat Pool, Shell, Steel Company of Canada, Sun Life, Tomeson-Alexander, and Woody Gundy.

27. Pierre Trudeau, "Opening Remarks to the National Pensions Conference," Ottawa, March 31–April 2, 1981, 3.

28. All of this had been clearly established in the report prepared by a task force of senior bureaucrats. See Task Force on Retirement Income Policy, *Retirement Income System in Canada*.

29. The dominant role of the Department of Finance in regulating fiscal, social, and labor-market policy in Canada is discussed in David Wolfe, "The Canadian State in

Comparative Perspective," *Canadian Review of Sociology and Anthropology* 26, no. 1 (1989): 95–126.

30. For a discussion of the construction of this "welfare state for the rich" in the preceding decade, see David Wolfe, "The Politics of the Deficit," in Doern, *Politics of Economic Policy.*

31. Our review covered all articles appearing in the *Globe and Mail*, those indexed in the *Canadian Periodical Index*, and the bulletins of William Mercer Ltd. for the period 1980 to 1987.

32. Canada, *Better Pensions for Canadians* (Ottawa: Ministry of Supply and Services, 1982). A "green paper" is a way of putting forth ideas and proposals for discussion and is less serious than a "white paper," which indicates the government seriously intends to bring forward legislation.

33. Ibid., 39.

34. House of Commons, Canada, *Report of the Parliamentary Task Force on Pension Reform* (Ottawa: Ministry of Supply and Services, 1982).

35. The legislation covers only federally regulated industries, or about 10 percent of the workforce. The assumption, however, is that such legislation provides the model for provincial reform, an assumption that is generally correct. For details on the current status of provincial legislation, see Finlayson, *Whose Money Is It Anyway?* Appendix A.

36. See ibid.

37. Ironically, changes in the legislation covering RRSPs—a form of income subsidy for the rich—were introduced in the very budget in which partial deindexing of universal Old Age Security benefits were proposed.

38. The fact that the debate was not popular at all but conducted "over the heads" of most Canadians by policy elites from business, government, labor, and the "social movements" is one of these. Another is a division that emerged between policy elites in the labor movement and the women's movement over the issue of pensions for housewives.

39. This argument has been developed in some detail in Myles, "Decline or Impasse?"

40. Daniel Moynihan, *The Politics of a Guaranteed Annual Income* (New York, 1973), 50.

41. Under GIS, the maximum monthly supplement is reduced $1 for each $2 of other monthly income for widowed, divorced, and separated pensioners. For couples, the amount is reduced $1 for every $4 of their other combined monthly income. GIS benefits are nontaxable.

42. The most prominent advocacy for a GI welfare state came in the Report of the Royal Commission on the Economic Union and Development Prospects for Canada, the so-called Macdonald Commission, which also proposed the recently implemented free-trade agreement with the United States as an economic strategy for Canada. But it is also the preferred model of Canada's leading economic think tanks, leading Canadian economists, and has been the implicit model informing social legislation in Canada for over a decade. See, for example, Thomas Courchene, *Social Policy in the 1990s: Agenda for Reform* (Montreal: C. D. Howe Institute, 1987).

43. As Marjorie Cohen observes, a second, often implicit, assumption of GAI

proponents is that we are moving into a postemployment or postwork economy and that we require a distributive system independent of the world of work, a view that is also emergent on the left (e.g., André Gorz, Claus Offé). See Marjorie Cohen, "A Good Idea Goes Bad: Guaranteed Income or Guaranteed Poverty," *This Magazine*. And on the postemployment literature, see Steven McBride "The State and Labour Markets: Towards a Comparative Political Economy of Unemployment," *Studies in Political Economy* 23 (Summer 1987): 141–54. This is a complex issue that requires a paper in itself. Surely a major gain from the enhancement of the productive forces is a reduction in the total amount of socially necessary labor time. But for a whole variety of reasons, it is extremely important that this not take the form of a social division between those in the paid labor force and those outside it, as is sometimes envisioned by progressive supporters of GAI-like programs. As Monica Townson points out in her discussion of the GAI, a likely basis of division will be gender, a result of using the family rather than individuals as the relevant income unit. See Monica Townson, "Income Security," *The Facts* 8 (March–April 1986): 27–30.

44. Canadian Council on Social Development, *Proposals for Discussion: Phase One: Income Security Reform: Work and Income in the Nineties (WIN)*, Working Paper No. 8, August 1987.

45. Mary Ruggie, "The Paradox of Liberal Interventionism: Health Policy and the American Welfare State" (Paper presented at the annual meeting of the American Sociological Association, Atlanta, 1988).

46. The details of this increased public scrutiny are documented in Finlayson, *Whose Money Is It Anyway?*

6/"Considerations of Mere Logic": The Australian Age Pension and the Politics of Means Testing

Sheila Shaver

During the 1980s, the Australian welfare state saw a dramatic return to means testing for income-security benefits, reversing a century-long history of development from selective toward universal entitlements. The age pension, the largest single item in the income-security budget and the paradigm setter for welfare politics, led the turnaround. Responding to the collapse of postwar prosperity and Australia's increased vulnerability in the international economy, the return to selective social policy reflected a resurgence of class interests in welfare politics.

Australia's oldest income-security provision, the age pension was originally framed as needs-based social assistance for the working class. From its inception, however, it was given ideological status as a social right flowing from citizenship and labor service. The odd conjunction bridged a gap in the politics of social policy, not only between capital and labor but also between ideal and practical liberalism. Means-tested social rights have since formed a central principle of the Australian welfare state. Initially dismissed as "considerations of mere logic," the contradictions inherent in joining inequality of need to equality of right have structured Australian welfare politics for nearly eighty years.

The history of Australian income security follows the dynamic T. H. Marshall traced in his essay "Citizenship and Social Class." Marshall maintained that the evolution of civil and political rights in the eighteenth and nineteenth centuries gave rise in the twentieth to social "citizenship," the right to "live the life of a civilized being according to the standards prevailing in the society," primarily through public education and the social services.[1] While civil and political rights were clearly compatible with the simultaneous evolution of English industrial capitalism, social rights were potentially in conflict with its basic framework of economic inequality. But as the representative basis of parliamentary democracy became essentially individual, the equality of social citizenship proved to be self-limiting. In the event, an (imperfect) equality of social rights in citizenship became complementary to economic inequality.

Marshall assumed that political rights would be used to create a welfare state on the European or British model, but this was not the only theoretical or historical possibility. Political equality might also be used to establish institutions regulating economy and employment, securing "civilized" standards of living through state intervention in labor markets and the determination of wages and working conditions. Australia represents one such possibility. Castles attributes the weakness of the Australian welfare state to working-class political strategies centered on arrangements such as wage fixation through an independent judiciary, describing it as a "wage-earner's welfare state." [2] Its reliance on means-tested income security is part of a wider pattern of comparatively limited provision for persons and circumstances outside the workforce.

Selectivism represents an ambiguous compromise in welfare politics in which state intervention in market society is at once sanctioned as legitimate and minimized in scope. The establishment of a social right to subsistence effectively decommodifies labor power, providing sustenance outside the labor market. The terms and conditions under which labor is decommodified are political constructions of class relations. In means-tested income security some labor power is decommodified, yet the obligation to work for wages is maintained in principle. The politics of means testing focuses on the terms of interchange between privately gained resources and publicly provided income. These terms concern the implications of access to income security for incentives to work and save, and the calculus of redistribution among taxpayers and beneficiaries.

Joining selective allocation with the symbolism of universal entitlement, the Australian formulation compounds the tension between inequality in economic life and political equality in the state. Need and citizenship qualify each other as the operative basis of entitlement to social rights. An affirmation of community replaces the stigma of poverty.[3] But the means test penalizes the economic virtues of providence and financial independence. Social justice contradicts economic justice.

Esping-Andersen has examined the collective class interests embodied in the principles of selectivism and universalism and the strategic issues involved in policy choices between them. The use of means testing has long been seen as in the interests of the working class because it redistributes economic resources by concentrating public expenditures among low-income groups. It represents the opportunity for a ransom of capital. Esping-Andersen calls this the "class ghetto strategy" and points to the divisiveness of means testing for class solidarities. He contrasts it with social democratic strategies favoring universal benefits, which give up immediate potentials for redistribution in the interest of building wider political solidarity with adjacent income classes.[4]

Nelson has observed that claiming benefits from the state is a political as well as an administrative relationship and that beneficiary status is connected with voters' evaluations of government performance. She concludes that "modern political life includes distributive as well as classically democratic components."[5] This is the political side of Marshall's "social rights." Income security, centerpiece of the welfare state, is a framework that defines legitimate claims to social rights. Such rights, once in existence, become objects of budgetary and ballot-box politics; hence, their terms, conditions, and values are always subject to contention among competing policy agendas and citizen constituencies.

These agendas and constituencies are not defined simply or only in class terms. As Marshall observes, the redistributive equity of the social security safety net operates through categories of life-cycle and human contingency. "Equalization is not so much between classes as between individuals within a population which is now treated for this purpose as though it were one class."[6] People identify their own and mutual interests on a variety of grounds, including stakes in the programs of the welfare state.[7] The welfare state has constructed a complex mesh of cross-cutting interests grounded in age and life cycle, family and household composition, race, ethnicity, region and culture, health and disability, employment status, and income group.[8] This more complex pattern of pluralist welfare politics cuts across the underlying framework of class interest identified by Esping-Andersen, replacing its logic of class solidarity with coincidences of interest among individuals.

In Australia, as elsewhere during the postwar period, sustained economic growth allowed these political forces comparatively free play in the expansion of the welfare state. Contradictions inherent in the means-tested social right lent their own force to this expansion, most actively with respect to the age pension. Popular feeling focused on the means test for the age pension and unequal treatment of elderly citizens. With an expanding tax base these pressures could be accommodated by weakening the means test. When growth stopped in the early 1970s, existing expenditure levels became difficult to finance; moreover, comparative equity was in visible disarray. "Reform in the 1980s focused on the means test and the "considerations of mere logic" inherent in reasserting the notion of a means-tested social right. The reassertion of selective social policy was successful in part because of the more pluralist basis of welfare politics established through the development of the welfare state. As when the age pension was first established, contemporary emphasis is on the "wage earner's welfare state," and the contradictions of means-tested social rights have spread into public support for retirement saving.

Means Tests and Social Rights

The age pension was born with Australian nationhood. The six British colonies federated in a single independent nation in 1901, following a decade of poverty and turbulent class conflict. The Poor Laws had not been imported to the colonies. Destitution did not carry the threat of the workhouse, but neither did it confer the right to subsistence. The gap was filled by charitable societies of the colonial bourgeoisie, liberally supported by the public exchequer. The prolonged depression of the 1890s exhausted their capacities, and liberal opinion began to favor some form of regular relief for the aged poor. In the same decade the labor movement, bitterly defeated in a series of industrial challenges, formed the Australian Labor party (ALP) and turned to "civilize capitalism" through politics and the state. It was widely agreed that an age pension should crown the new federation.

Two colonial governments had already established age pensions. In 1896 a New South Wales Parliamentary Select Committee had considered what kind of pension would be appropriate to Australia. Compulsory social insurance, though under active discussion in Britain at the time, was quickly dismissed as Bismarckian and objectionable to people of British heritage. Voluntary social insurance was preferable, but would leave most of the working class uncovered. Charles Booth's proposal for a universal pension was much admired, for it treated all citizens equally and cast no stigma on the recipient. Regrettably, its costs were unthinkable.

In the event, the committee recommended a means-tested pension, but sought to give it the flavor of a social right. Eligibility would require proof of need, but statutory entitlement would remove any taint of charity. The New South Wales Pensions Act of 1900 repeated this formulation. Its preamble affirmed that "it is equitable that deserving persons who during the prime of life have helped to bear the public burdens of the Colony by the payment of taxes, and by opening up its resources by their labour and skill, should receive from the Colony pensions in their old age." [9] A pragmatic compromise, it was nevertheless deeply felt. Its supporters recognized the contradictions inherent in a means-tested social right, where poverty and citizenship qualify each other as the operative basis of entitlement. But since the alternative was to do nothing, they dismissed these as "considerations of mere logic." [10]

The new federal Parliament was evenly divided among Labor, Protectionists representing manufacturing industry, and Free Traders representing primary producers. The age pension was one of several mutual accommodations between Labor and the Protectionists giving distinctive foundations to the Australian welfare state. Industry would be accorded tariff protection, but this was made conditional on the payment of fair and reasonable wages to workers. Wages were fixed through a Commonwealth Court of Arbitration and Conciliation. In the first years after federation, the court embraced the concepts of need and family to define a fair and reasonable "living wage." The age pension followed logically, as a concession to Labor and a means of providing for older, slower workers unemployable at the fixed minimum wage.[11] It was an early version of the retirement wage.[12]

A Commonwealth Royal Commission on Old-Age Pensions briefly rehearsed the arguments about contributory, universal, and means-tested pensions. It reached much the same conclusion as the New South Wales Parliamentary Select Committee, endorsing its solution in the pension as a means-tested social right. The Commonwealth old-age pension was introduced in 1908 and was similar to the New South Wales pension it replaced. It paid a maximum pension of £26 ($52)[13] per year to both men and women at the age of 65 years. (Women were made eligible at age 60 in 1910). At 10 shillings ($1) per week, this was about one-quarter of the amount the Arbitration Court had fixed the year before as the minimum wage adequate for a family of four. A means test applied to both income and property. The pension was not payable to a person having income over £52 ($104) per year or property valued at more than £310 ($620). An early amendment excluded the value of a claimant's home from the test on property. Further conditions required thirty years' residence in Australia and good character. Unnaturalized aliens, "Asiatics," and aboriginal persons were ineligible. An invalid pension with similar provisions was legislated at the same time.

By 1912, the proud compromise was already in question. Costs were proving higher than expected, for the aged population was growing and the pension was popular. About one-third of those over 65 were receiving it.[14] Liberal opinion had meanwhile forgotten its earlier objection to contributory social insurance; weighed against "Bismarckian" compulsion was the worse prospect of "free" pensions undermining working-class thrift and self-respect. Great Britain had recently legislated for contributory health and unemployment insurance, and Australia began to consider schemes of this kind.

Parliamentary politics now worked as an opposition between Labor and the other parties. The Labor party, then in government, crystalized political positions on what became known as the "contributory question" when it introduced legislation for a maternity allowance. This was a one-time payment of £5 ($10) to the mother upon the birth of a child. Coming at a time of anxiety about low birthrates and "race suicide" of the white settler society, the allowance was available without a means test.[15] Its immediate electoral popularity affirmed Labor's commitment to extending social benefits, on a universal basis wherever practicable. The search for a tenable basis of opposition settled liberal conviction in favor of contributory social insurance.

This debate lasted for some thirty years, and except for veterans' benefits blocked further development of Australian social security until World War II.

It was straightforward class politics argued around economic interests and ideological symbols. Both sides accepted the need for benefits covering unemployment, sickness, and widowhood, mainly for the working class. The non-Labor parties favored contributory social insurance because it would ensure that the working class paid for its benefits and in the process learned providence and possessive individualism. This was the way to make entitlement to social benefit a clear social right free of any taint of charity. Labor saw the matter differently: The working class labored for the nation and was entitled to its protection. Class right could carry no stigma. During the 1930s, Labor became committed to financing social services from a progressive income tax, securing a modest ransom of capital.

The non-Labor parties drew up proposals for contributory insurance twice, in 1928 and 1938, but even in government lacked the power and unity to implement them. Australia weathered the Great Depression with minimal social provision. In the fiscal emergency of 1931 banking interests forced a Labor government to reduce existing age and invalid pensions along with wages. The only new Commonwealth benefits to emerge during the interwar period were for veterans and their dependents.[16] War pensions were compensation for war-caused disability and were not means tested. The means-tested service pension gave benefits equivalent to an early age pension to veterans who had served in a theater of war.

The political stalemate was broken only with the war, when both sides came to see the development of social security as essential to national mobilization. Welfare became a key political symbol of a future worthy of wartime sacrifice, one that "never again" would see its citizens experience the unmitigated hardship of the past. The war gave Labor the moment to move on income security and the opportunity to define its shape. In 1941 the government appropriated the Labor opposition's 1940 election proposal for universal child endowment, a weekly payment for each dependent child except the first. This was a maneuver to persuade the Arbitration Court to restrain male wages, rising rapidly in the wartime economy, by persuading it that the needs of the family were already being met.[17] Shortly afterward, government fell to Labor. The exigencies of war and especially war finance gave the federal government a new and permanent ascendancy over the states, including a monopoly on income taxation. The momentary political unity of the war emergency enabled Labor to secure opposition consent to financing social security from taxation.[18]

The wartime Labor government established a comprehensive income-security system on the existing social assistance foundations. To the existing age and invalid pensions, maternity allowance, and child endowment were added widows' pensions (1942) and sickness and unemployment benefits (1944). Child endowment and maternity allowance were universal; all other benefits were subject to a means test. All were funded from taxation. During the war, one-quarter of the proceeds of the Commonwealth income tax were channeled through a new National Welfare Fund. This was a device of war finance as much as welfare funding, disguising increased taxation of working-class incomes with promises of future benefits.[19] At the end of the war Labor put the finance of social services on what it considered a properly "contributory" basis. A separate graduated income tax levy was to be used exclusively for financing social services; labeled the "social services contribution," it identified welfare with the rights and obligations of citizenship and symbolized nation as community.

The implementation of Labor's design for income security effectively ended the debate over the contributory question, with Australia resisting the transition to social insurance undertaken by almost all other advanced capitalist countries. Pension rates had maintained their real value through the interwar period, but there was no ransom of capital. By war's end, the income tax had become an important source of Commonwealth revenues, and the working class paid a significant share. The effect was not unlike contributory finance.[20] The conservative coalition that governed from 1949 abandoned its formal commitment to social insurance. Dissolving the separate "social services contribution" into general income tax, it reduced welfare funding and spending to routine categories of public finance.

An Incomplete Universalism

Expanded income security formed part of a wider postwar class settlement rooted in Keynesian principles of full male employment and a limited welfare state.[21] The open expression of class interest and class feeling that had been common before the war became uncommon in the long period of prosperity following it. Sustained full employment, steady economic growth, and rising real incomes blurred the older boundaries, while immigrants filled the lower ranks of expanding domestic manufacturing. The cities spread with a suburban, family-centered way of life; by 1966, homeownership had reached 72 percent. Class became popularly understood as a ladder of income groups in the middle rungs of which blue- and white-collar workers overlapped in economic well-being if not necessarily status and culture.

The wartime welfare state transformed Australian income security from limited social assistance for the relief of poverty to a comprehensive tax/transfer system for redistributive equity. This gave a new and double salience to the means test and the contradiction inherent in its original formulation. The effect was to construct the aged as a category with its own legitimacy of entitlement. The "considerations of mere logic" that little troubled its federation creators now took on stronger meaning, as a contradiction between universalism of taxpayer status and selectivism of beneficiary entitlement.

The age pension became the vehicle for a new form of welfare politics.

A vocal middle class, aware of its higher tax burden, now resented its exclusion from the "free" pension available to an undeserving working class. The grounds for objection to the means test had changed from the shame of the pauper to the penalty on thrift. The means test conferred a social right on some that it withheld from others. It made citizenship itself unequal. By the late 1940s, both major parties were internally divided over the means test, and they remained so throughout the postwar period. Labor was officially committed to eventual abolition, but a substantial section supported retention in favor of higher rates for pensioners with little other income. The philosophy of the conservative Liberal party generally endorsed means testing as a way of limiting the welfare state, but the party had a vocal minority demanding a universal pension. Its most outspoken member openly opposed the means test even while serving as the minister responsible for its administration.[22]

Postwar liberalization of the means test was a bipartisan affair. Labor began in 1946, increasing the limits of income and property permitted to full-rate pensioners. The conservative coalition in government from 1949 until 1972 reshaped the Australian welfare state to make middle-income groups significant beneficiaries of public expenditures, in health, housing, and aged care.[23] During this period, it eased the means test repeatedly, most visibly when electoral competition was close. Income and property limits were increased several times. In 1961 the separate tests on income and assets were merged in a single test giving more favorable treatment to invested capital. The pace escalated during the late 1960s and early 1970s, when a new Labor leadership began to compete for suburban middle-income voters. In 1969 the test was "tapered" so that the maximum rate of pension would be reduced by only half the amount by which income or assets exceeded permissible limits. The pension had previously been reduced dollar for dollar, and the change nearly doubled the range of private income over which a partial pension was payable. In 1972 the amount of income and property that could be held without affecting pension entitlement was further doubled.[24]

By then, the means test was remarkably generous. It excluded a house owned and occupied by a pensioner, its land and contents, a car, jewelry, and other personal property. Gifts from relatives and friends were also ignored. "Means as assessed" included earnings, annuities, and other private income plus 10 percent of the value of other assets in excess of $400 for a single pensioner or $800 for a married couple. A single age pensioner could have means equivalent to $20 per week and still receive a full pension of $20, a married couple means of $34.50 and a pension of $34.50. Each additional $2 of means as assessed reduced pension entitlement by $1. These levels represented an accumulation of assets well beyond the capacity of most workers even after almost a generation of full employment, and an increasing share of the aged population gained access to at least a partial pension. In 1933 about one-third of men over 65 and women over 60 received an age pension. By 1960, half were pensioners, and by 1973, almost two-thirds. During most of the postwar period, the rate of full pension kept pace with rising wages. Periodic increases maintained the rate for a single pensioner at about 40 percent of the minimum male wage and 20 percent of average weekly male earnings including overtime. By the mid 1960s, however, the relative value of the pension had begun to decline, causing a rising incidence of poverty among the aged.[25]

Each relaxation of the means test merely focused attention on the income group above which the test continued to exclude. By the 1972 election, the conservative coalition was losing its twenty-three-year hold on government. As political competition escalated, the parties were tempted to exploit middle-income politics of envy, proposing to abolish the means test altogether. The conservative parties promised to phase it out over six years. Labor joined the bidding, proposing to abolish it in three. The irony of Labor's victory was that the postwar boom was already over. The long-running combination of high employment, low inflation, and stable growth was starting to come apart by the end of the 1960s and had visibly done so by the mid 1970s.[26] Having won the bidding, Labor had also to be first to resile from bipartisan commitment to a universal age pension.

Labor took office committed to both raising the base pension rate and making it universal. These were in addition to an ambitious program for reform of the welfare state with expanded public services in health, education, welfare, and urban infrastructure. In 1973 the means test was abolished for all persons aged 75 and over, and in 1974 for those aged 70–74. Pensions were made taxable, with rates set so that a pensioner with little or no nonpension income paid no tax. Pensions were increased significantly, from $21.50 for a single person in 1972 to $31 in 1974. By then, however, the fiscal crisis had struck. Wages had been rising since the late 1960s, as had inflation. Worldwide recession caught up in the early 1970s, and as growth faltered, unemployment and inflation began to spiral together. By 1975, the government was moving to restrain wages and welfare expenditure, and the third round of means-test abolition was "postponed." Labor's dream ended bitterly when the government was illegitimately forced from office.[27]

The next conservative coalition government tackled the fiscal crisis with monetarist rhetoric and class politics. It gave substantial tax concessions to capital and high-income groups, including the pursuit of an ultimately illusory minerals boom, while manufacturing continued to move offshore. Tight monetary policy was intended to "fight inflation first," leaving high rates of unemployment to discipline labor. Ad hoc cutbacks in welfare were borne most heavily by the unemployed, mainly young single people. Child endowment was reconstructed, with the tax rebate for dependent children abolished and the same value paid out in a much bigger child endowment, renamed family allowance. This benefited low-income families, who had not previously received full value from tax concessions.[28]

Hindsight shows the retreat from universalism had already begun under Labor. In the shorter term, however, it was interrupted by a period of contradictory means-test reform. The conservative government had pledged itself to abolish the means test "at an appropriate time." It acted immediately to replace the existing test on income and property with a test on income only, with actual income replacing the 10 percent return on assets assumed previously. This would treat earned and unearned incomes more equally. The measure had been recommended as part of a wider program to rationalize and ultimately integrate the income-security and taxation systems.[29] Implemented alone, it gave rise to a new series of problems. Australia had no capital gains tax, and gave favorable tax treatment to private superannuation settled as lump sums. The income test facilitated "double dipping" in which some people were able to claim public pensions while substantial investments also accrued untaxed future income. Effects were felt in markets for both capital and real estate.

By 1981, the situation was ridiculous. The pension was nearly universal: Some 87 percent of the total aged population and 99 percent of those over 70 were receiving at least a partial pension.[30] Yet the citizenship of the pension was not shared by all, and the means test that excluded these few was riddled with anomaly. Meanwhile, the government's social-policy think tank was drawing attention to demographic trends forecasting the aged as a growing population share.[31] By this time, both parties clearly regretted their rush toward a universal age pension. Both were arguing the need for expenditure restraint and for benefits more closely geared to need. The government had quietly resumed the retreat in 1978 when it froze the universal pension for persons aged 70 and over; henceforth, increases in pension rates over this ceiling would be subject to a means test, and the universal pension would decline in real value.

A Means Test for the 1980s

By 1983, economy and fiscal crisis were visibly out of control. The Labor party again won government, this time in a corporatist alliance with the trade-union movement. The government abandoned key symbols of Labor's "socialist" legacy, such as party commitment to socialization and opposition to uranium mining, in favor of technocratic reform of state and economy. In a historic break with Australian protectionism, it opened the economy to international capital, deregulating banking and floating the currency. A tax-reform program lowered personal and company taxes while rationalizing tax concessions and introducing mild taxes on capital gains and employee fringe benefits. Industry policies were directed at making industry competitive internationally, reducing tariff protection while upgrading technology; these had been cut across by a sharp deterioration in the international terms of trade for Australia's primary exports, especially wheat, iron, and coal. By August 1988, the federal budget had been brought into surplus.

Labor's accord with the trade-union movement exchanged wage restraint for policies maintaining the social wage. The wages side of this agreement had been renegotiated several times since 1983, exacting additional pay and productivity concessions in the light of tax cuts and deteriorating international terms of trade. Real wages fell over the period. Employment had grown steadily, increasing by at least 2 percent per year since 1984, but the new jobs were mainly in the service sector and many are part-time or casual. Unemployment remained at about 8 percent.[32] On the social-wage side, the government reintroduced universal health insurance, abolished by the previous government. Otherwise, it took the view that its commitment to maintain the social wage did not preclude reforming it.

It began with the age pension mess. In its first six months the government announced three important changes in retirement income policy. An income test would be applied to the previously universal pension for persons over 70. The tax on lump-sum superannuation payments was to be increased. Finally, in the future a means tests would apply to assets as well as income. The proposed test would be similar to the one used before 1976, disregarding the pensioner's home, car, personal property including furniture and household effects, a caravan, a boat, jewelry and works of art, and other assets to the value of $1,500 for a single pensioner and $2,500 for a couple.

Accumulating the heat of the first two measures, the announcement of the third provoked a much greater furor than the government had expected.[33] The exclusion of nominated forms of property was a source of obvious anomaly; moreover, it discriminated between people of different tastes and cultures. Why should personal property be treated more favorably than financial assets such as stocks and bonds? Why should one person lose the pension on account of a bush cottage when another's Picasso was overlooked? A government proposal to exempt a "lifestyle package" of up to $30,000 in leisure assets[34] only provoked further outrage and was in turn withdrawn.

Pensioners had some reason to be concerned. Their working lives had coincided with the sustained prosperity of the postwar period, when employment, overtime work, and low-cost credit were plentiful. Many had accumulated a small nest egg. Moreover, the rules of the income-only means test applied after 1976 had encouraged them to hold their assets in non-income-producing forms. Thus seaside cottages and second homes, often let to children rent-free, were not uncommon even among working-class pensioners. Opposition to the proposed assets test joined aged persons' lobby groups across class and income lines.

To quell the controversy, an academic economist was asked to convene a panel of community representatives including the aged lobbies to devise a fair and acceptable test. His panel was concerned that over 30 percent of pensioners were renters, who would be discriminated against by exempting a home.[35] It settled on the only logical possibility: a test based on total assets, including owner-occupied housing.[36] This was dynamite for the Labor party in New South Wales, facing an election while the Sydney real estate market was booming. The panel's recommendation was dismissed within a week. It was replaced by an assets test setting alternate asset figures, indexed for inflation, for pensioners with and without owner-occupied homes.

In all, it took over eighteen months to settle a politically acceptable formula for the assets test. In the end, however, means testing was reestablished. In August 1989 the rate for a single age pensioner on full pension was $129.20 per week, and for a married couple $215.40. Pension rates are indexed to the Consumer Price Index and are adjusted twice yearly after a lag of six months. In recent years the single pension has represented about 23 percent of male average weekly earnings, themselves falling in real terms.[37]

The means test begins to affect pension entitlement when private income reaches $40 per week for a single person or $70 for a married couple. Thereafter, the pension is reduced by 50 cents for every dollar of income above the allowable limit, with no pension payable when income exceeds $280 (single) or $470 (couple). The assets test begins to apply when a single homeowner has other assets[38] valued at $96,000 or more or a single non-homeowner $164,500. Figures for a married couple are $137,000 and $205,500. Pension payable is reduced by $2 per week for every $1,000 of assets above the allowable limit. No pension is payable when assets exceed $160,750 (homeowner) or $229,250 (non-homeowner) for single persons and $245,000 or $313,500 for a couple. When a person's assets are below the allowable level, only the income test applies. When assets exceed this limit, both tests are applied, and the pension is paid under the test giving the lower entitlement. There are hardship provisions and arrangements for pensioners to borrow against their estate. Persons 70 and over are tested on income only, and more generous limits apply to eligibility for a partial pension.[39]

The government overcame opposition to resumed means testing by beginning with very permissive tests. The number of pensioners actually affected was relatively small. Some 68.9 percent own a house or apartment, but this is left out of the calculation. While the majority of pensioners have some non-pension resources, comparatively few (26.5 percent in 1988) have enough to preclude their receiving the pension at the full rate. But time is changing this picture. Although the assets components of the means test are indexed for inflation, income components are not. Inflation has sharpened their teeth, and they bite harder as each year passes. The proportion of pensioners among the age-eligible population fell from 87 percent in 1983 to 78 percent in 1987, and

Table 6.1/Decomposition of Annual Growth Rate of Expenditures on Age Pensions, by Year (annual average percentage changes)

TIME PERIOD	NOMINAL EXPEN- DITURE	INFLATION	REAL EXPEN- DITURE	DEMOG- RAPHY	COVERAGE	AVERAGE REAL PENSION
1959–60 to 1965–66	6.63	2.14	4.39	1.83	1.38	1.12
1965–66 to 1970–71	9.46	3.32	5.94	2.11	2.50	1.22
1970–71 to 1975–76	29.54	11.00	16.71	2.98	4.32	8.64
1975–76 to 1980–81	13.07	10.21	2.60	2.65	0.64	−0.69
1980–81 to 1985–86	8.42	8.26	0.15	2.72	−2.78	0.29
1959–60 to 1985–86	12.88	6.74	5.75	2.43	1.19	2.03

Source: Peter Saunders, *Growth in Australian Social Security Expenditures, 1959–60 to 1985–86*, Background/ Discussion Paper No. 19 (Canberra: Social Security Review, 1987), table 9; reprinted by permission of the author.

the proportion of age pension expenditures in gross domestic product from 3.5 to 3.1 percent.[40]

Numbers of age pensioners and levels of total and real expenditures have risen steadily throughout the postwar period. During the 1980s, expenditures continued to rise, but pensioner numbers fell. Total expenditures on age pensions grew from $3.9 million in 1981 to $5.9 million in 1986, while total numbers declined from 1.33 to 1.27 million. Increasing expenditures were a combined product of growth in the aged as a proportion of the total population (demography), the proportion of age eligible persons receiving pensions (coverage) and real levels of full and partial pension payments. Table 6.1 presents an analysis of this increase for the 1959–1960 to 1985–1986 period, breaking down the increase in expenditures into these components. Growth in real expenditures, having escalated to more than 16 percent per annum in the early 1970s, were brought almost to a complete stop in the 1980s. Growth in real pension payments has been halted since the mid 1970s. The increase in expenditures due to demographic factors has risen slowly over the past three decades. The rate of growth in pension coverage, having expanded as rapidly as 4 percent per year in the early 1970s, were reduced sharply enough in the 1980s to absorb demographic growth.[41]

A Contradiction for the 1990s

Even as social policy has succeeded in reestablishing means-tested pension, a new contradiction has been emerging. The "considerations of mere logic" that motivated the long drift toward a universal age pension have been replicated in tax incentives to private retirement saving. This time, the claim to universalism has been voiced by working people through the trade-union movement: All are properly entitled to the tax subsidies once primarily the property of the middle class. Established when the means test was more severe, these once represented concessions to income groups excluded from the pension. As they become universal benefits, they entail substantially expanded public expenditures on retirement income; moreover, they open a new door to universal enjoyment of the age pension.

Originators of the age pension did not intend pensioners to depend on the pension alone. It was to supplement other income.[42] The reality has always been otherwise, and the bare pension soon came to represent a minimum standard of living. But neither was it expected to be more than this. As with the English Beveridge Plan, low levels and flat rates were intended to leave scope for individual saving.[43]

Occupational superannuation arrangements began to emerge early in the century, but until comparatively recently these were limited to small groups of white-collar and public-sector employees.[44] Employee contributions were tax deductible up to a ceiling, and employer contributions treated as a business expense. Coverage has become widespread only in the last fifteen years or so, during which tax incentives have also become more generous. In 1974, only 40.8 percent of male and 16.5 percent of female wage and salary earners had superannuation coverage. By 1987, these figures had risen to 49.9 and 26 percent. Most recently, the trade-union movement has begun to campaign for universal superannuation cover for the Australian workforce. Under its accord with the Labor government, wage increases attributable to gains in productivity have been exchanged for the establishment of industry-based superannuation schemes. Industrywide agreements were to be endorsed by the Arbitration Commission. The first such bargain, paying 3 percent of wages of full-time workers as new or improved superannuation entitlements, was struck in 1985 and substantially implemented in 1988 and 1989. By mid 1989, some 65 percent of wage and salary earners worked under Arbitration Commission rulings obliging their employers to provide superannuation. A second round has been mooted for the early 1990s.[45]

So far, superannuation coverage remains uneven. It is most widespread among full-time wage and salary workers, and is associated with higher income levels, public-sector employment, and industry unionization. Occupational superannuation is supported by generous tax incentives to employers and employees, at significant cost to public revenues. The cost of tax concessions for private superannuation has been estimated as reaching $4 billion by 1989. This can be compared to $10 billion in direct Commonwealth outlays for assistance to the aged, mainly the pension, in the same year. Distribution of tax benefits is highly regressive.[46]

These arrangements grew up in the context of a means-tested age pension, a steady trend toward early retirement, and favorable tax rates for retirement savings taken as a lump sum rather than an annuity. Workforce participation of men aged 60 to 64, nearly 80 percent in the late 1960s, fell to 45 percent in the mid 1980s. Some retrenched older workers are retiring involuntarily when they are unable to find new employment in a savage labor market. Many, however, appear to be retiring voluntarily, at least some of them encouraged by access to superannuation benefits at age 55. Almost all funds, representing 89 percent of members, settle benefits as lump sums. This is the form preferred by retirees, in large part because of tax rates as low as 3 percent.[47] These arrangements have become the basis of "double dipping" by early retirees. Nearly half of lump-sum payments to early retirees are used in ways that do not provide retirement incomes.[48] Though the evidence is patchy, it seems likely that lump sums are being used to finance early retirement, allowing up to ten years for assets to be run down to levels permissible under pension rules. One-quarter of early retirees use lump sums to pay off mortgages and clear other debts. An investment-planning industry has arisen to advise on investment options and pension requirements. There is a clear trend for people retiring early on superannuation and other savings to become dependent on income-support payments later.[49]

The government has begun to rationalize these arrangements, mainly through changes in the taxation system. In the longer term it intends to make individuals finance a larger share of their retirement income and gives more than passive support to union moves to make occupational superannuation a universal workforce benefit. At the same time, fiscal pressures and an increasingly technocratic welfare lobby are forcing it to rationalize the tax treatment of superannuation. The government has begun to tax fund earnings and employer contributions, with offsetting reductions in taxes on benefits at retirement. It is closing loopholes to ensure that benefits are fully vested[50] and retained in the fund until the minimum age of 55, and to limit employer tax deductions to reasonable maximum levels of benefit. While modifying tax and means-test arrangements to improve the relative attractiveness of annuities, it has resiled from earlier proposals to tax lump-sum benefits at full rates. Instead, it has affirmed that "the Federal Government is committed to maintaining an individual's current free choice to receive a lump sum superannuation benefit."

The contradiction between universalism and selectivism remains alive in continuing asymmetry between equality in citizenship and inequality in allocation of benefits funded from resources of the state. Given Australian labor-market conditions, the trend to early retirement is likely to continue for the foreseeable future. Nor will the Australian predilection for the lump sum be easily overcome. The furor over the assets test showed how closely it is tied to important elements of Australian political culture, including high values put on homeownership and leisure. It has come to be seen, like the pension itself, as a social right of labor service.[51] Those "considerations of mere logic," now displaced into the preretirement years, are likely to continue generating pressures for universal access to the age pension.

Means Testing, Redistribution, and Class Stakes in the Welfare State

Changes in the age pension have foreshadowed wider change in the paradigm for Australian income security, systematically closing access of upper- and middle-income groups to cash social benefits. The purpose of income security is being redefined from relative equity among social groups to the relief of poverty. Payments are increasingly targeted through means tests and other criteria.

Family allowances, universal since their introduction in 1941, are now subject to a means test on the joint income of husband and wife. Given the 1976 replacement of tax concessions by family allowances, this removes from the tax/transfer system the only universal measure for horizontal equity between taxpayers with and without dependent children. Student children between 18 and 25 years, paid family allowances since the 1970s, are no longer eligible. A new, means-tested family-allowance supplement has been introduced for the working poor. The most dramatic changes affect benefits to children and sole-parent families. Base levels of pension support for sole parents are being improved, while loopholes enabling noncustodial parents to shift the burden for child support on to the state are being closed. At the same time, the period of pension dependency permitted to sole parents is being reduced, requiring the parent to reenter the workforce when the youngest child reaches 16. Unem-

Table 6.2/Decomposition of Annual Growth Rate of Expenditures on Various Pensions and Benefits, by Year (annual average percentage changes)

PENSION OR BENEFIT	NOMINAL EXPEN- DITURE	INFLATION	REAL EXPEN- DITURE	DEMOG- RAPHY	COVERAGE	AVERAGE REAL PENSION
Invalid pension	13.70	8.26	5.02	1.61	1.80	1.54
Sole parents' pensions[a]	15.30	8.26	6.50	2.71	2.51	1.16
Unemploy- ment benefit	25.68	8.26	16.09	6.37	5.79	3.17
Sickness benefit	17.56	8.26	8.59	1.61	5.66	1.15
Family allowance	10.10	8.26	1.70	0.04	0.12	1.56

Source: Peter Saunders, *Growth in Australian Social Security Expenditures, 1959–60 to 1985–86,* Background/ Discussion Paper No. 19 (Canberra: Social Security Review 1987), tables 12–16; reprinted by permission of the author.
[a]Class A widow's pension and supporting parents' allowance.

ployment benefits, historically created for short-term circumstances and means tested on income only, have in recent years become the basis of longer-term support; an assets test now applies, with greatest implications for those with lump-sum settlements for retrenchment or superannuation.

The most dramatic policy shifts are too recent to be reflected in expenditure statistics, but figures for the years immediately preceding them show a pattern of budgetary constraint already established by the early 1980s (Table 6.2). Increases in real expenditures and average level of payment were relatively small, with the important exception of unemployment benefits, which had fallen significantly in real value in the later 1970s. A large share of the increase for all benefits was accounted for by demographic factors. This is most marked for unemployment benefits and sole-parents' pensions, where high incidences of unemployment and marriage breakdown have prevailed since the mid 1970s. Increases in coverage for these provisions do not reflect easier access but rising take-up rates within eligible categories.[52]

Even then, the reduction in the rate of growth was significant by international standards. Table 6.3 compares Australian expenditures on pensions

Table 6.3/Decomposition of Annual Growth Rate of Expenditures on Pensions, by Year and Country (annual average percentage changes)

	NOMINAL EXPEN- DITURE	REAL EXPEN- DITURE	DEMOG- RAPHY	COVER- AGE	AVERAGE REAL PAYMENT
1960–1975					
Seven major OECD countries[a]	14.1	8.2	2.4	1.8	3.8
Australia	14.3	8.5	2.2	2.6	3.5
1975–1981					
Seven major OECD countries	17.0	6.8	2.1	1.1	3.5
Australia	14.7	4.0	3.1	−0.3	1.2

Source: Organisation for Economic Cooperation and Development, *Social Expenditure 1960–1990: Problems of Growth and Control* (Paris: OECD, 1985), tables 5 and A1.
[a]Seven largest OECD countries: Canada, France, Germany, Italy, Japan, United Kingdom, and United States.

(age, invalid, widows, and supporting parents) with the seven largest countries of the Organization for Economic Cooperation and Development. From 1960 to 1975, Australian rates of growth were close to the average for these countries. From 1975 to 1981, expenditures were rising markedly more slowly, with almost the whole increase attributable to demographic factors. Labor's movement to reform income security began from this standstill position.

The reestablishment of selectivism is in some respects a return to the "class ghetto" strategy that has prevailed for most of its history. Since the extension of income taxation to the working class in the 1940s, redistribution between income groups has depended almost entirely on selective allocation of social security benefits. Within those limits, it has been comparatively effective.[53] But the contemporary version of the strategy is newly limited. The redistributive framework of modern selectivism is individualized. The means test establishes relations of equity not between classes but among individuals across a series of graded income categories. Class interest is represented only in the narrowest terms of low income and poverty. Coming in association with tax reductions, contemporary selectivism represents less a ransom of capital than an accommodation of the welfare state to diminishing scope for redistribution. This accommodation in turn reflects the corporatist basis of the current Labor government, in which redistributive equity is less important than economic growth and job creation. The reassertion of selective social policy represents class interest as defined by the "wage earner's welfare state": the interests of worker taxpayers take precedence over those of dependent beneficiaries.

At the same time, the Australian conception of selective welfare as a social right has constructed the aged as a population group sharing social-policy interests as much as divided by them. As Marshall noted, the redistributive framework of the welfare state treats the population as one economic class sharing the vicissitudes of personal and social life. Age is a primary category of this redistribution. While the economy was expanding, the people represented by "middle-class welfare" were also the political middle ground competed for by rival parties. Pensioner organizations identified themselves with the sections of both parties supporting universalism, and saw themselves as having a common interest in defending the gains of the aged as a group. This unity was maintained through more than a decade of economic debility, breaking down only when the final means-test proposal was forced on the group as a whole.

Meanwhile, the contradiction between equality of social rights and inequality of economic rewards is emerging in a new form in state support for retirement savings. The old claim to equality of treatment is here reversed, with trade unions and the working class asserting an equal right to the taxation perquisites of the rich. Numerous "considerations of mere logic" inhabit the nexus where economic inequality and tax policy adjoins social equality and public pensions. It would be ironic if these gave rise to the development of a new universalism in retirement income.

Notes

1. T. H. Marshall, "Citizenship and Social Class," in *Sociology at the Crossroads and Other Essays* (London: Heinemann, 1963), 74.

2. Francis G. Castles, *The Working Class and Welfare* (Sydney: Allen and Unwin, 1985).

3. Richard M. Titmuss, "The Residual Model in Social Policy," in *Social Policy: An Introduction* (London: Allen and Unwin, 1974).

4. Gösta Esping-Andersen, "Citizenship and Socialism: De-Commodification and Solidarity in the Welfare State," in *Stagnation and Renewal in Social Policy*, ed. Martin Rein, Gösta Esping-Andersen, and Lee Rainwater (Armonk, N.Y.: M. E. Sharpe, 1987).

5. Barbara Nelson, "Women's Poverty and Women's Citizenship: Some Political Consequences of Economic Marginality," *Signs* 10, no. 2 (1984): 217, 224.

6. Marshall, "Citizenship and Social Class," 107.

7. Frances Fox Piven and Richard A. Cloward, *The New Class War*, rev. ed. (New York: Pantheon, 1985).

8. For discussions of gender and race in the Australian welfare state, see Sheila Shaver, "Race and Gender in the Welfare State," Anthropology Program Colloquium, Graduate School and University Center, City University of New York, November 1988; and idem, "Gender, Class, and the Welfare State: The Case of Income Security," *Feminist Review* 32, no. 2 (1989).

9. Quoted in Thomas H. Kewley, *Social Security in Australia, 1900–1972*, 2nd ed. (Sydney: Sydney University Press, 1973), 46.

10. Ibid., 47.

11. Ray Markey, "The ALP and the Emergence of a National Social Policy, 1880–1910," in *Australian Welfare History: Critical Essays*, ed. Richard Kennedy (Melbourne: Macmillan, 1982).

12. John Myles, "Postwar Capitalism and the Extension of Social Security into a Retirement Wage," in *The Politics of Social Policy in the United States*, ed. Margaret Weir, Ann Shola Orloff, and Theda Skocpol (Princeton: Princeton University Press, 1988).

13. Australian currency was changed from the pound to the dollar in 1966.

14. Michael A. Jones, *The Australian Welfare State* (Sydney: Allen and Unwin, 1980), 16; John McCallum, "The Assets Test and the Needy," *Australian Journal of Social Issues* 19, no. 3 (1984): 232.

15. It was available to both married and unmarried women. "Asiatic," aboriginal, Papuan, and South Sea Islander women were not eligible.

16. Some new social provisions were introduced by state governments, the most important of which were widows' pensions in New South Wales and Victoria and unemployment insurance in Queensland.

17. Kewley, *Social Security in Australia*, 190–200; Rob Watts, *The Foundations of the National Welfare State* (Sydney: Allen and Unwin, 1987), 46–61.

18. Sheila Shaver, "Design for a Welfare State: The Joint Parliamentary Committee on Social Security," *Historical Studies* 22, no. 88 (1987).

19. Kewley, *Social Security in Australia*, 234–37; Watts, *Foundations of the National Welfare State*, 84–103.

20. Watts, *Foundations of the National Welfare State*, 92–103.

21. As in the United States, active use of the public economy, for example, by creating public employment to fill shortfalls in private employment, was resisted in favor of a weaker "commercial Keynesianism" confining intervention to fine tuning through fiscal and monetary policy. See Theda Skocpol, "The Limits of the New Deal System and the Roots of Contemporary Welfare Dilemmas," in Weir et al., *Politics of Social Policy in the United States*. See also Winton Higgins, "State Welfare and Class Warfare," in *Critical Essays in Australian Politics*, ed. Graeme Duncan (Melbourne: Edward Arnold [Australia], 1978).

22. Kewley, *Social Security in Australia*, 407–8.

23. Richard B. Scotton, "Voluntary Health Insurance in Australia," *Australian Economic Review* 68, no. 2 (1968); Leslie Kilmartin and David C. Thorns, *Cities Unlimited* (Sydney: Allen and Unwin, 1978), 114; Kewley, *Social Security in Australia*, 471–78.

24. But as the basic means test became less important, additional tests began to be applied to subsidiary benefits. During the 1950s, means tests were introduced for free medical care and supplementary assistance, a housing allowance available to pensioners not owning their homes and paying rent. These tests have been eased but never abandoned in the years since and remain sources of continuing tension in welfare politics.

25. Ronald F. Henderson, Alison Harcourt, and Raymond John Albert Harper, *People in Poverty* (Melbourne: Cheshire, 1970).

26. Robert Catley and Bruce McFarlane, *Australian Capitalism in Boom and Depression* (Sydney: Alternative Publishing Co-operative, 1981), 91–93.

27. Labor had not controlled the upper house. Deteriorating economic conditions and political scandal encouraged the opposition to break with convention and use its majority in the upper house to refuse passage to budget legislation. In perhaps the most bitter event in Australian political history, the governor general terminated the government's commission and forced an election for both houses. The opposition won this election overwhelmingly.

28. Bettina Cass, "Redistribution to Children and to Mothers: A History of Child Endowment and Family Allowances," in *Women, Social Welfare and the State in Australia*, ed. Cora V. Baldock and Bettina Cass (Sydney: Allen and Unwin, 1983).

29. Commission of Inquiry into Poverty, R. F. Henderson, Chairman, *Poverty in Australia* (Canberra: Australian Government Publishing Service, 1975), 58.

30. P. R. Kaim-Caudle, *Cross-National Comparisons of Social Service Pensions for the Elderly*, SWRC Reports and Proceedings No. 15 (Sydney: University of New South Wales Social Welfare Research Centre, 1981).

31. Social Welfare Policy Secretariat, *Alternative Strategies to Meet the Income Needs of the Aged* (Canberra: Australian Government Publications Service, 1982).

32. Budget Statements, 1987–88, *Budget Paper No. 1* (Canberra: Parliament, Commonwealth of Australia, 1987); John Burgess, "The Accord, Wages Policy, and Social Security," *Australian Journal of Social Issues* 23, no. 2 (1988): 129–41.

33. McCallum, "The Assets Test and the Needy."

34. This amount was to be applied to the aggregate value of a holiday home, boat, caravan, bush block, or hobby farm. The assets test would apply to the value over this amount.

35. As they have been throughout the history of the age pension.

36. "Report of the Panel of Review of the Proposed Income and Assets Test, F. Gruen Chairman," Canberra, 1984, 64. Mimeographed.

37. Burgess, "The Accord, Wages Policy and Social Security."

38. Excluding a car and certain other personal effects.

39. Persons aged 70 and over having private income of less than $195.50 (single) or $329.20 (married couple) use the same test as applies to younger claimants. Between incomes of $195.50 and $200 (single) or $329.20 and $333 (married couple), the old rates of universal pension of $51.45 (single) and $85.80 (married couple) apply. Thereafter, pension is reduced by 50 percent of income over the limit.

40. Chris Foster, *Towards a National Retirement Incomes Policy*, Issues Paper No. 6 (Canberra: Social Security Review, 1988), 15–16.

41. The reduction in coverage is less marked when account is taken of the service pension available to ex-servicemen and women, a relatively larger share of whom qualify for pensions under the means test. Figures adjusted to take account of service pensioners show coverage growing at the lower rate of −2.20 per year in the years 1980–1981 to 1985–1986. See Peter Saunders, *Growth in Australian Social Security Expenditures, 1959–60 to 1985–86*, Background/Discussion Paper No. 19 (Canberra: Social Security Review, 1987), 32–33.

42. John Dixon, "Australia's Policy Towards the Aged," M.Ec. thesis, Australian National University, Canberra, 1976, 60.

43. Inter-departmental Committee on Social Insurance and Allied Services, *Social Insurance and Allied Services: Report by Sir William Beveridge* (London: HMSO, 1942).

44. John McCallum and Sheila Shaver, "Industry Superannuation: A Great Leap Forward?" *Australian Social Welfare/Impact* 20, no. 6 (1986).

45. Foster, *Towards a National Retirement Incomes Policy*, 205–8; Minister for Social Security, *Better Incomes: Retirement Income Policy into the Next Century* (Canberra: Australian Government Publishing Service, 1989), 6.

46. Foster, *Towards a National Retirement Incomes Policy*, 61, 122–34, 145–48; Minister for Social Security, *Better Incomes*, 3.

47. Michelle Gunasekera, and John Powlay, *Occupational Superannuation Arrangements in Australia*, Background/Discussion Paper No. 21 (Canberra: Social Security Review, 1987).

48. Foster, *Towards a National Retirement Incomes Policy*, 62.

49. John McCallum, "How Queensland Public Servants Spend Their Lump Sums," *Australian Journal on Ageing* 3, no. 2 (1984); Foster, *Towards a National Retirement Incomes Policy*, 61–68.

50. This is to ensure that workers have title to both their own and employers' contributions to superannuation schemes and all income earned by funds invested in their names.

51. McCallum, "How Queensland Public Servants Spend Their Lump Sums."

52. Saunders, *Growth in Australian Social Security Expenditures*.

53. Sheila Shaver, "Sex and Money in the Welfare State," in Baldock and Cass, *Women, Social Welfare, and the State in Australia*. See also Ann Harding, *Who Benefits? The Australian Welfare State and Redistribution*, SWRC Reports and Proceedings No. 45 (Sydney: University of New South Wales Social Welfare Research Centre, 1984).

7/The Politics of Aging in Scandinavian Countries

Fritz von Nordheim Nielsen

As did most of the highly developed OECD countries during the 1980s,[1] Denmark, Norway, Sweden, and Finland witnessed significant economic, political, and demographic changes that challenged the foundation of public pension schemes and altered the backdrop to pension politics. The economic performance of the Scandinavian[2] nations was poorer, or at least more precarious, than in the decades when the present public pension systems were established.[3] The political forces most dedicated to the welfare state[4] and the ones traditionally given credit for the high standard of public pensions[5] (i.e., the social democratic labor movements) were weakened. In previous decades, reforms had placed Scandinavian public pension systems among the best and most costly in the world. In the 1980s, the combined effects of early retirement, aging, and scheme maturation increased the costs of these schemes far beyond original estimates. Demographic forecasts, moreover, indicate that the situation will get worse. Given this setting, one might have expected Scandinavian pension politics to be characterized by pressures for cutbacks and intense strife.

In fact, with the exception of Denmark, pension politics in the Nordic countries were remarkably tranquil over the past decade. The public pension systems of Sweden, Finland, and until very recently Norway were largely insensitive to major changes in their economic and political environment. The only significant cuts in public pensions occurred in affluent, oil-rich Norway where demographic prospects are the least gloomy in the region. By contrast, the struggle over the future shape of pensions waged in Denmark in the 1980s was exceptionally intense.

While the Danish case breaks the rule of Nordic tranquility, there were important variations in the general pattern as well. Finnish pension politics in the 1980s were remarkable chiefly because they did not generate conflict along traditional left–right lines. Unlike the other Nordic countries, Finland made major improvements in public pension benefits in the 1980s, and these were passed with broad support. In Sweden, class conflict was more obvious, but for the most part it was successfully contained. Public and private pension systems command a great deal of popular support, so much so that even minor cuts and adjustments to both were vigorously resisted. Because of the way public pension funds are managed in Norway, conservative critics there were more effective, and despite less than alarming demographic prospects, the country instituted cutbacks in benefits. More surprising perhaps is the fact that a Social Democratic government introduced those cuts and did so with the support of all major parties.

Although pension politics in Finland, Sweden, and Norway certainly differed in many curious ways in the 1980s, the three scenarios had one thing in common. Pension politics was reasonably subdued and on the fringes of the main agendas of politics. In Denmark, in contrast, pensions were the most persistent single item on the political agenda. In the latter part of the 1980s the contested pension reform actually tended to dominate the political agenda, where it had surprisingly little trouble competing for attention with issues such as tax reform and European integration. Pension reform was sought and opposed primarily because of its potential contribution to political realignment and its effects on savings rates, capital formation, and long-term active investments. Protagonists on both sides of the struggle had long ago eliminated pensioner needs from the discussion. For them, the real struggle was about the merits of "popular capitalism" versus those of "fund socialism," about the future contours of Danish political economy, rather than the adequacy of pension income.

In what follows I have tried to outline the historical development of pension politics in the Scandinavian countries over the past thirty years, with the intention of explaining why tranquility prevails in Sweden, Finland, and Norway, and why Denmark has proven to be such an exception. I begin by describing in broad comparative terms the pension arrangements that exist in the four Nordic countries, focusing on the institutional structure of pension provision and the relationship between public and private forms. I argue that the experience of the Scandinavian countries does not confirm the common assumption that private and public pension systems are of necessity in competition. Sweden in particular seems to bear out the opposite hypothesis, that is, that the adequacy of public pensions in no way interferes with growth and expansion of private forms of provision but that the two can in fact be complementary.

The political compromises of the 1960s around pension questions provide the key to understanding how stable, complementary relationships between public and private pension systems were achieved. The resolution in Sweden, Finland, and Norway of struggles over the establishment of a statutory earnings-related pension laid the basis for such stability, as I next discuss. It was initially feared that earnings-related pensions would reinforce income inequalities by reproducing them after retirement. They were thus seen as potentially divisive. Yet a broadly based earnings-related system also seemed the most effective way of guaranteeing adequate income in old age. The systems that arose thus tried to address themselves to the problems of equality and adequacy. This in turn made it possible to construct broad cross-class alliances in support of pension reform. Middle-class support was guaranteed by giving white-collar workers, the self-employed, and employers themselves a stake in the stability of the pension systems.

In Denmark, the failure to resolve the earnings-related pension issue conclusively in the 1960s led to years of indeterminacy. Next in this chapter I discuss pension politics in the 1980s and argue that the failure to get a settlement in the boom period mitigated against finding an acceptable solution to Denmark's pension problems during the decade of retrenchment. In the 1980s pension politics everywhere reflected a growing concern with questions of equity, especially intergenerational equity. The question of who will pay for the pensions of those in the demographic bulge tended to overshadow concerns about whether pensioners have or will have sufficient income. Elsewhere, this concern led to some adjustments, but in Denmark the introduction of equity concerns into the debate made it extremely difficult to reach any consensus on the issue of earnings-related pensions, and pension politics became extremely divisive.

Finally, while pension politics in Sweden, Finland, and Norway were considerably less divisive than in Denmark, they are destined to be less tranquil in the future. In all four Nordic countries demographic forecasts have so far had relatively little political impact, but demographic change may soon present serious challenges to Scandinavian pension systems. In my concluding section I discuss the strategies that are available to the Nordic countries and try to suggest how they may cope with the demographic time bomb.

The Present Pension Packages

While the relative importance of the type of provision varies considerably between the four Nordic countries, the formal structures are largely parallel. Universal, flat-rate pensions with a general income-tested supplement and personal needs- and means-tested increments form the first level. In Sweden, Finland, and Norway, the second tier consists of earnings-related pensions. The Danish second tier is made up of a service-related scheme with flat-rate benefits. In all four countries, early-retirement provisions are included in the first two tiers and in the unemployment insurance scheme, or in separate plans. Occupational pensions acquired as part of the conditions of employment and remuneration form the third tier. Individual pension insurance and pension savings contracts constitute the fourth tier of the pension structure.

Some of the crucial differences between the four countries are found in the configuration and administration of second-tier schemes. In turn, differences in their design influence the extent and shape of occupational and individual plans. While second-tier provisions are contained in a single national scheme in Denmark, Norway, and Sweden, the Finnish system of second-tier pensions, which covers all the gainfully employed, consists of a number of separate schemes for the major occupational groups. The Norwegian and Swedish systems are administered by special departments in the public sector, whereas the Danish scheme is run by a semipublic institution under tripartite management, and the Finnish second-tier plans are handled either by separate, nonprofit pension institutes or by private insurance companies.

The mix between these various elements in the total pension package can be measured in a number of ways.[6] Table 7.1 presents a comparative, time-series table of the mix between public, occupational, and individual provisions in the four countries expressed in pension payments.

Measured in current pension payments, the Danish pension package is clearly the most polarized of the four. Three-quarters of all pension payments in 1985 came from the basic first-tier pension scheme, while individual annuity payments amounted to more than 8 percent, or four to sixteen times as much as in the other countries. The main reason for this anomalous distribution is the sorry state of the Danish second-tier scheme. The plan offers service-related flat-rate pensions for flat-rate contributions, but as these have not been indexed, payments from the scheme account for less than 2 percent of overall pension expenditures. The absence of an earnings-related scheme in the statutory part of the packages obviously makes Danish public provisions inferior to those of the other Nordic countries.

Both the basic and the second-tier public pension systems in Scandinavia are financed from a broader tax base than the selective public pension schemes in many other countries.[7] But there are great variations in the mix of social security and other taxes that fund public provisions. Table 7.2 indicates how the costs for statutory pensions have been shared between the insured, the employer, and the general taxpayer from 1960 to 1984.

In Denmark, pensions are largely financed from general revenues. Part of the explanation for this lies in the limited nature of the Danish second-tier scheme. In Sweden and Finland, employers assume most of the costs for the statutory pensions. Finnish employers also pay a major part of the cost of the basic first-tier scheme. For this reason, their share of overall pension

Table 7.1/The Nordic Pension Mixes: Share of Total Pension Payments by Pension Type, 1960–1985 (percentages)

	PUBLIC (STATUTORY)		OCCUPATIONAL (NEGOTIATED)		INDIVIDUAL ANNUITIES (CONTRACTUAL)
	1st Tier [a]	*2d Tier*	*Public Sector*	*Private Sector*	
Denmark					
1961	78.8	—	11.6 [b]	3.8 [c]	6.0 [d]
1970	80.9	0.4	11.6 [b]	2.9 [c]	4.4 [d]
1980	79.3	2.0	11.1 [b]	2.8 [c]	4.8 [d]
1985	75.5	1.6	10.1 [b]	4.7 [c]	8.1 [d]
Finland					
1960	64.5	—	28.7	4.9 [f]	1.8 [g]
1970	53.3	10.8 [e]	29.7 [e]	4.7 [f]	1.6 [g]
1980	40.2	27.7 [e]	27.1 [e]	4.3 [f]	0.6 [g]
1985	39.2	30.9 [e]	25.2 [e]	4.2 [f]	0.5 [g]
Norway					
1960	62.5 [h]		32.5	3.3	1.8
1970	81.0		14.7	3.5	0.8
1980	87.0		9.5	2.9	0.6
1985	88.8		7.1	3.3	0.9
Sweden					
1960	70.9	—	16.1	4.0	8.9
1970	63.5	10.5	18.2	4.2	3.1
1980	52.5	33.6	8.8	3.0	2.0
1985	44.7	42.3	7.4	3.6	1.9

Sources: Henriksen et al. (note 39); Kangas (note 28); Hippe and Pedersen (note 30); and Ollie Kangas and Joachim Palme, "The Private–Public Mix in Pension Policy," in *Between Work and Social Citizenship*, ed. J. E. Kolberg (Armonk, N.Y.: Sharpe, 1988).

[a]The cost of non-second-tier early-retirement payments is included in the figures for first tier.

[b]Public-sector occupational pensions only include costs of civil servants' pensions. Occupational pension payments for other public-sector employees are included in figures for private sector.

[c]Including payments for non–civil servants from public sector. Figures that allow for a separation of occupational and individual annuity payments from insurance companies are not available. We estimate that half of insurance payments concern occupational arrangement. Hence, these figures constitute payments from pensions funds and half of payments from insurance companies.

[d]Figures constitute payments from banks and half of payments from insurance companies.

[e]From 1964 and 1966 municipal and state employees are covered by statutory compulsory second-tier schemes. Payments based on pension credits accrued from these dates therefore ought to be included in figures for statutory second-tier pension expenditures. However, the benefit formula in statutory schemes is significantly better for public-sector than for private-sector employees. While it takes the latter 40 years to obtain a replacement rate of 60% from age 65, the former may retire after 30 years with 66% of former pay from age 63. Hence, the positive differences in actual time, replacement rates, and retirement age must be categorized as occupational pension benefits and ought to constitute the recalculated figure for occupational pension payments for public-sector employees.

[f]Figures constitute payments from registered OCP schemes, pension funds, and pension foundations.

[g]Include payments from group life insurances.

[h]Time-series data that allow for a separation of first- and second-tier costs are not available. But if we assume that the distribution of cost was the same in 1984 as in 1985, first tier would have amounted to 64.3% and second tier to 24.5% of total pension payments.

Table 7.2/Distribution of Public Pension Expenditures in the Nordic Countries by Source of Finance, 1960–1984 (percentages)

	INSURED	EMPLOYERS	GENERAL REVENUE (STATE, REGIONAL, AND MUNICIPAL TAXES)
Denmark			
1960	12	1	87
1970	23	4	73
1981	4	18	78
1984	6	18	76
Finland			
1960	33	23	44
1970	13	66	21
1981	11	81	8
1984	10	80	10
Norway			
1960	39	25	36
1970	30	52	18
1981	29	52	19
1984	28	46	26
Sweden			
1960	34	16	50
1970	19	41	40
1981	2	82	16
1984	2	84	14

Source: Adapted from Kangas (see note 28).

expenditures has risen somewhat less than in Sweden where the employers' share has more than doubled since 1970. In the 1980s the emphasis on payroll taxes eased in Norway and Finland, whereas it rose in Sweden and remained constant in Denmark. Some of the conflicts over public pensions, naturally, focused on the distribution of costs.

The gross income or pretax replacement profiles of first- and second-tier provisions are illustrated and compared in Figure 7.1. The ceiling on pensionable earnings in the Swedish and Norwegian schemes, which makes for a certain degree of redistribution, accounts for the characteristic snap on the replacement curve. In the Finnish system there is no such ceiling. Consequently, replacement rates are constant for average and above-average incomes. Posttax figures would raise the replacement levels in the figure for Denmark without affecting the profile very much.

Contemporary posttax replacement rates for the sum of first- and second-

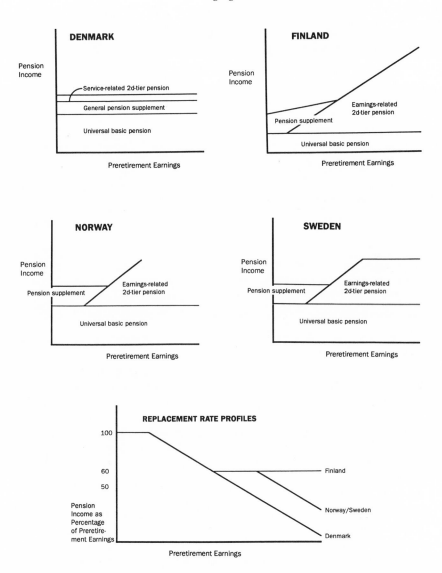

Figure 7.1 Earnings-replacement profiles of statutory pension packages in Denmark, Finland, Norway, and Sweden: an illustration. *Source:* Based on an idea from Ollie Kangas, *Agrarintressen och intagarintressen i pensionspolitiken* (Helsinki: Helsinki School of Economics, 1988), 66.

Table 7.3/Replacement Rates of First- and Second-Tier Pensions for Average Industrial Worker after Tax, 1984

	DENMARK	FINLAND	NORWAY	SWEDEN
Single man	51%	63%	73%	73%
Single woman	57	73	74	74
Pensioner couple with children	41	61	65	69

Source: Social Security in the Nordic Countries, 1984, 49.

Table 7.4/Occupational Pension Coverage

	DENMARK	FINLAND	NORWAY	SWEDEN
Total wage-earner coverage	34%	ca. 30%	54%	90%
Total public-sector coverage	51	100	ca. 90	100
Total private-sector coverage	22	10	40	ca. 85

Source: Social Security in the Nordic Countries, 1984, chart 2.

tier provisions are given in Table 7.3. Finnish and Norwegian figures will approach those of Sweden as their earnings-related systems mature.

It is often assumed that the role of private pensions in the pension mix is an inverse function of the adequacy of public provisions: The more pension needs are met by public schemes, the less room for occupational and individual plans, and vice versa. While this rule of thumb seems confirmed by the figures for individual pension contracts, it cannot account for the variations in payment from occupational plans in Scandinavia (see Table 7.4).

The minuscule role for individual pensions, and the moderate scope of private-sector occupational plans, in Finland may seem a logical function of the high and constant replacement levels in the second-tier scheme. But it would be difficult to explain the exceptionally high occupational pension coverage in Sweden in this way given the high quality of public pensions; or, for that matter, the large differences in coverage and share of payments between Sweden and Norway given that public pension provisions differ only slightly. Moreover, one would expect occupational and individual plans to have a far larger share in the total pension package in Denmark, since replacement rates in statutory plans are so poor.

The thesis should be modified to include the impact of taxation. Thus the demand for private pension provisions would be a function of both the accessibility and adequacy of public pensions across the income hierarchy *and* the degree to which pension purchasing power is enhanced by the system for financing public pensions and by tax subsidies for private pension savings. Yet, before 1983, there were only minor inter-Nordic differences in the tax treatment of nonstatutory pensions. Moreover, when taxes are taken into account, it is clear that the moderate flat-rate contributions to the Danish second-tier schemes have given private-sector employers and their employees much more room to establish occupational provisions than the *Allmnnetillggpensionen* (ATP)[8] scheme in Sweden. Despite the fact that there are both negative and positive incentives for greater occupational coverage in Denmark, the rate of coverage is little more than a third of that in Sweden.

The substitution thesis depends on market logic. It presumes that individuals are free to define and act on their own pension needs. Occupational pensions, however, are not bought under normal market conditions. Instead, they are a condition of employment and an integral element in the sale of labor power.[9] They are almost always collective in coverage and rarely optional. Employers usually control the establishment of schemes and can set limits on age, length of service, and possibly the health of the candidate as requirements for admittance. Hence occupational pensions are embedded in the logic of personnel management and industrial relations.[10] Organizational conditions in the labor market (i.e., patterns of unionization and employer association) are likely to be of greater importance for the prevalence and magnitude of occupational pension provisions than the needs and wants of the employed as individuals. Finally, in some countries, occupational pension funds act as a source of cheap finance for the employing company, which enhances their appeal for management.[11]

It would appear that the spread and growth of occupational pensions cannot be explained with reference to the tax–benefit design of public pensions and the tax rules about private pension savings. In order to understand the inter-Nordic variations in the role of occupational provisions we need to look also at the organization of the labor market and the nature of the bargaining system. More than anything, it has been the highly centralized system of wage bargaining in Sweden that has contributed to the expansion of occupational plans and produced the exceptionally high degree of coverage. Rates of unionization and employer association are lower and the industrial relations systems are less centralized in the other three countries.[12] Swedish unions have also taken a far more active interest in occupational pensions than have the union movements in the other countries.[13] A full explanation of the present mix of public, occupational, and individual provisions also requires a closer look at the historical circumstances that led to the specific designs of second-tier schemes.

The Second-Tier Settlements of the 1960s

While pension politics was relatively quiet in Finland, Norway, and Sweden in the 1980s, the growing importance of occupational provisions in Denmark caused a dramatic U-turn in political discourse. Debates about income conditions for pensioners escalated into intense strife about the future contours of the Danish political economy. Although no major changes occurred in statutory provisions, the Danish scenario of the 1980s was markedly different from developments in the other countries.

As elsewhere, the economic and political stability of public pension arrangements in the Nordic countries has been a function of their sensitivity to political change, of how well, in other words, they respond to and mediate between the conflicting needs of various interest groups. A major key to the differences between pension politics in Denmark and the other countries is to be found in the political implications of the design of second-tier, earnings-related, provisions. Struggles over earnings-related pensions produced different outcomes in the Nordic countries. Stable settlements were achieved everywhere but in Denmark, where the relationship between public and private pensions remained indeterminate, and reform proposals were left pending.

A review of the main characteristics of second-tier provisions in each of the four countries and the events that determined their configuration provide a basis for understanding inter-Nordic differences in the 1980s.

Sweden

In its pioneering efforts on behalf of public pensions, the Swedish labor movement had to overcome considerable resistance from the beneficiaries of the existing system of supplementary pensions. Among its initial enemies, the ATP could count the following: employers, who would have to finance the bulk of the scheme without a guarantee that benefit increases would be paid for through wage restraint and who stood to lose control over pensions as a means of regulating labor and a source of extra credit; the private pension savings industry (insurance companies, banks, and brokers), who would lose business and power; and bourgeois political parties, which opposed the idea of a publicly controlled pension fund and felt threatened by the labor movement's attempt to join forces with white-collar employees. In their opposition to the scheme, the bourgeois parties tried to enlist the support of other groups whose pension concerns were insufficiently acknowledged in the ATP formula: those who already had earnings-related coverage (public-sector employees and privileged white-collar employees in the private sector); those not fully included (the self-employed); those explicitly excluded (full-time homemakers and others outside the labor force); the retired, who would not benefit; and those who, because of age, would be unable to accrue sufficient credits for full benefits. Hence, for the labor movement, it was especially important to find ways to accommodate the interests of these groups.

Behind the scenes, *Sveriges Socialdemokratiska Arbetarparti* (SAP)[14] worked hard to appease the financial sector and reassure employers on the issues of control and investment of the pension funds.[15] The construction of the legal–institutional framework for the pension fund was left to a committee of experts that took great care to diffuse the potential power of fund boards and restrict the scope for investment.[16] On certain points, the design conflicted with the wishes of the *Landsorganisatione* (LO),[17] but SAP felt compelled to deideologize the question of fund control in order to keep the bourgeois parties from coalescing into a common block. Only a convincing separation of ATP from the ghost of creeping socialism could do the trick.

In a similar fashion, the Social Democrats sought to accommodate the pension interests of potential opponents. Transition rules for those who could not meet the twenty-year contribution requirement were built into the proposal. Improvements in the existing universal flat-rate pensions catered to the needs of the retired. The self-employed were invited to join on a voluntary basis. The occupational schemes for public-sector employees were to be integrated with ATP in such a way that the full value of accrued pension rights would be preserved through an additional third-tier pension on top of ATP. And a special clause reluctantly allowed for the contracting out of groups with adequate coverage in the private sector.

The passage of the ATP act, thanks to the abstention of one defecting Liberal,[18] was a dramatic event. It was the culmination of two general elections and a referendum, with years of intense political mobilization on the part of the LO. For the labor movement, this victory against formidable odds achieved the status of legend. In the heated aftermath of the passage, some bourgeois parties pledged themselves to overthrow the scheme. They urged the self-employed to boycott the scheme, and many employers vowed to contract out their plans.[19] The confederation of white-collar unions was split down the middle. The private-sector section, SIF, whose leadership was dominated by bourgeois party supporters, tended to side with the employers' position.[20] Yet it was precisely in the collective negotiations between these two parties that the key to a stabilization of ATP and a final settlement of a very important part of the conflicts would be found. On close scrutiny, the employers' association and the union of private-sector salaried employees came to agree that the benefits of "staying in" easily outweighed any to be derived from renouncing the state scheme.[21] Consequently, instead of taking alternative pension coverage to ATP, they adopted a system designed to pay for earnings above the ATP ceiling, which would also allow lower retirement ages. This structural complementarity with the state scheme secured a stable relation between public and occupational provisions in Sweden.[22] The statutory scheme provided the floor on which the negotiated plans could build. In this way, white-collar employees developed just as vested an interest in the upkeep of ATP benefit levels as manual workers. Furthermore, when successive collective agreements generalized occupational ITP[23] coverage to all white-collar employees in the private sector[24] and compensated those already covered for their partial loss of rights through substantial salary rises, the passage of ATP, in retrospect, became popular even with the traditionally privileged white-collar groups. In the subsequent elections, SAP's white-collar support grew markedly.[25] Thereafter, even the most recalcitrant bourgeois parties saw the light and announced their intent to accept the scheme. The self-employed also joined in large numbers, and when general supplements to pensioners with little or no ATP income were introduced in 1969, no group could claim to have been left out in the cold. All gainfully employed could benefit from ATP, and those outside the labor force were compensated.

The solution for private-sector white-collar employees created an important precedent. The generalization of ITP coverage motivated the LO to seek a modification of the new pension inequalities between blue- and white-collar employees through collective bargaining.[26] When LO in the early 1970s negotiated a general scheme of occupational coverage for their members, the relation between public and occupational pensions was reaffirmed as one between complementary tiers in a common structure. The resulting STP scheme was no equivalent of ITP, but it extended the principle of a third tier of occupational pension coverage to the rest of the labor market. Between 1959 and 1973, occupational pension coverage in Sweden grew from approximately 30 percent to more than 90 percent.[27] Paradoxically, this immense extension of nonstatutory pension provisions was neither perceived as, nor did it actually pose, a threat to the viability of ATP. On the contrary, the clear division of labor between second-tier ATP and third-tier occupational pensions meant that the position of the public scheme in the overall pension system was consolidated.

In the final analysis, collective agreements between white-collar unions and employers opposed to ATP, which established structural complementarity between occupational and statutory benefits in the private sector, may have been as instrumental in securing a stable solution to pension conflicts in Sweden as the famous political muscle and bargaining skill of the social democratic labor movement.

Finland

Both white- and blue-collar workers in the Finnish[28] private sector had never been satisfied with the universal scheme of basic pensions that the agrarians manipulated through parliament in 1956. Their contributions to the old actuarial scheme of 1937 had been expropriated when the fund was swallowed by the new scheme, and their income-replacement needs were ill served by the combination of a low flat-rate benefit and income-tested supplements.[29]

Demands for an earnings-related second tier originally came from the white-collar unions, which were soon joined by the federation of manual workers' unions. Initially, employers refused to consider proposals for a statutory, employer-financed scheme. But their resounding defeat in the struggle over statutory paid vacations, and the lessons from the Swedish showdown, convinced them that it would be wiser to try to influence the design of a second-tier scheme than resist it. A pension consultant from the Swedish employers' association also advised that the best tactic would be to minimize the damaging effects of the scheme. Decentralized administration by private pension insurance companies chosen by the employer and the possibility for enterprises to borrow from excess funds at low rates of interest were top priorities for the employers' association. Once these demands were met, employers were willing to accept the features that preoccupied unions so much.

Something along the lines of the Swedish centralized model had been discussed in the social democratic movement. But if anything like a single public scheme was established, it would be difficult to avoid allowing the existing national pension institute to administer it. The director of that institute was also leader of the Agrarian party, which was strongly opposed to an earnings-related system. The social democratic unions thus had little reason to entrust the administration of a new scheme to the national pension institute. Even if the Agrarian party members who dominated management did not wreck it, they could use it to fortify their already strong hold over important parts of the state apparatus. For this reason alone, the unions of wage and salary earners rejected a model with a single scheme under central state administration and were prepared to accept the idea of decentralized private-sector organization, if necessary.

Partly as a result of their rather precarious power position, Finnish Social Democrats were far more preoccupied with short-term goals than their strategically minded Swedish colleagues. Concern about benefit levels easily overshadowed concern about control of the fund. As long as the scheme would be statutory and financed exclusively by employer contributions, unions had no hesitation about accepting the terms of the employers. So a genuine compromise requiring few real concessions from either side was reached. Whereas Swedish employers fought against the introduction of the ATP system to the bitter end, Finnish employers and unions reached complete agreement at the committee stage and worked together for the realization of the scheme.

It was to be financed exclusively by a payroll tax and was to be partially funded. Employers would be able to retain contributions not needed for present pension payments as a low-interest, long-term loan. Administration would be left in the hands of the private insurance industry. The organizational structure would be decentralized. Employers were free to choose whether to insure their employees with insurance companies, pension funds, or pension foundations. A special institution with a governing board of union, employer, and state representatives was to coordinate pension claims.

An unholy alliance of Agrarians and the Democratic People's party (communist) at first tried to block the proposal. In their view, a new statutory scheme ought to be flat-rate, exclusively pay-as-you-go, and administered by the state together with existing pensions. But when the Social Democrats accepted a proposal from the Agrarian party for a separate, parallel scheme for previously excluded seasonal workers, the Agrarians agreed to support the plan, and it passed with a large majority. The model for statutory earnings-related pensions had now been established.

Separate schemes for municipal and state employees followed a few years later, and in 1969 special schemes for farmers and for the self-employed in urban trades were introduced. By 1970, all the gainfully employed were covered by a system of segregated but similar statutory second-tier schemes administered by private-sector insurance institutions. Benefits were closely tied to contributions, and redistribution was minimal. There was no ceiling on pensionable earnings. The replication of private-scheme features inside the public sector facilitated a permanent settlement of the relation between statutory and nonstatutory plans. There was no need for extra occupational provisions to compensate for the decline in replacement rates normally associated with rising incomes. Private occupational provisions had by no means been particularly widespread before the introduction of earnings-related statutory plans. Afterward, their numbers actually increased as employers offered benefits to older employees to bring their pension income up to the replacement maximum in statutory plans. But, once established, such occupational schemes are usually officially registered and administered together with the official second-tier scheme. Thus the majority of occupational pensions are not merely subordinate and complementary to the statutory ones. Their form of integration also makes them temporary. They are programmed to disappear as official second-tier provisions mature.

Norway
Initially, Norway[30] seemed headed for a Danish-style situation. When LO and the employers' association signed a general agreement about a service-related, flat-rate occupational pension in 1960, the Social Democratic party leader expressed the belief that the unions had found a solution to the pension problem and that Norway was therefore in no need of a public system along the lines of the Swedish ATP. The Norwegian Social Democrats would probably have stuck to this position if it had not been for a sudden change of events. In the 1961 election, the Norwegian labor party, DNA, lost the parliamentary majority it had enjoyed since the war. To stay in government, it now had to rely on support from the small People's Socialist party (PSP). When a mining accident in a poorly secured state pit in 1963 motivated the two PSP representatives to join the bourgeois opposition, the government fell.[31] Just as the new bourgeois coalition was to be confirmed in parliament, however, the Social

Democrats declared themselves in favor of a public scheme of earnings-related second-tier pensions. The idea was to drive a wedge between the Liberals and the other parties in the bourgeois coalition.[32] In the reconsidered opinion of the Det Norske Arbeiderparti (DNA) leadership,[33] the Swedish experience had demonstrated that second-tier pensions were an ideal tool for attracting white-collar support. A few weeks after their fall, the Social Democrats were back in power.

The bourgeois parties also had drawn lessons from the course of events in Sweden. They were not about to let the labor party split them apart and monopolize a seemingly popular issue. Instead of opposing an earnings-related scheme, they declared themselves in favor of it. It is unlikely that they would have come up with the proposal of their own accord. Yet as soon as DNA billed it as a major item in its program, the conflict turned into a race to see who would legislate it first. Since the left-wing majority disappeared in the 1965 election, it fell upon the first stable bourgeois coalition government in more than thirty years to draft the final proposal for a second-tier scheme as part of a general program of People's Social Security (*Folketrygden*), or FT, which was then passed with unanimous support in 1966. The self-employed were fully included from the start. Transitional rules allowed older cohorts to receive better second-tier pensions than their contribution records would normally allow. And in 1969 a first-tier pension supplement for those with few or no second-tier credits was established.

In spite of the many apparent similarities in terms of second-tier design, the Norwegian system was able to provide a stable settlement to conflicting pension interests for reasons that were very different from those in Sweden. First and foremost, the establishment of the scheme was supported by all parties in parliament. The curious consensus was the unforeseen outcome of tactical maneuvering that prevented second-tier pensions from developing into an issue of class. To all the significant actors, proposals for an earnings-related public pension had been entertained as a means to grander political goals, rather than an end in itself. Tactical maneuvering had motivated them to declare themselves so strongly in favor, however, that they were unable to back away. Moreover, a strong tradition of consensus in social policy, which had its roots in the bipartisan cooperation of the wartime Resistance, had developed in the postwar period. None of the major parties wanted to break from this tradition. In the political climate of the 1960s, the parties in the bourgeois coalition felt compelled to demonstrate they were as committed to social security as was labor. In the end, the labor movement was handed the scheme by the bourgeois coalition government without having to fight for it. The Norwegian LO had little if any hand in the invention and development of the earnings-related scheme. Similarly, DNA never had to wed its political fate to FT in the way SAP had with ATP. Consequently, the Norwegian labor movement has been less prone to view it as an irreplaceable element in its welfare-state edifice. In sum, the circumstances surrounding the establishment of FT implied that the parties were bound far more by the consensual character of the enactment than by any of the specific features in the design of the second-tier pension or its mode of financing.

When the Department of Social Security was asked to develop a proposal for a public scheme of second-tier pensions in 1963, the leadership of the labor movement had only a vague idea about the shape and design it wanted. It was left to sympathetic senior officials in the department to work out not only the details but also the overall configuration.[34] The department decided on an earnings-related second-tier pension integrated into a comprehensive program of "People's Social Security," composed of a first-tier universal flat-rate citizens' pension, the earnings-related second tier, and a scheme of sickness insurance. The entire system was to be financed by a combination of specially earmarked payroll taxes, income-related member contributions, and general tax revenues. These funds, however, were not kept separate. The costs of the various elements in the scheme were paid for through all three forms of taxation. In other words, whenever it was opportune, funds collected to cover future increases in demand for second-tier benefits might be used for unrelated purposes such as improvements to the first-tier scheme or the sick-pay scheme. This had far-reaching consequences. The result was that the fund buildup in the period before scheme maturation had the appearance of a genuine surplus. This surplus enabled governments to launch "free" improvements of coverage, access, or benefits in related programs. The temporary "excess" from payroll taxes and income-related member contributions also lent themselves to other purposes. In the 1970s, Social Democratic governments repeatedly lowered member contributions as part of income-policy settlements and differentiated the payroll taxes in order to promote investments and halt rising unemployment in peripheral regions.[35] Instead of raising the taxes necessary to pay for improvements and the alternative taxes to pay for depletion of revenues, successive governments used the temporary FT surplus to fund their "giveaways." One consequence was that the originally envisaged fund "buildup" never materialized. Since even the bourgeois center parties felt very uneasy about the idea of allowing the state to use pension funds for investment purposes, and since the Social Democrats never were particularly intrigued by the prospect[36], no one protested. All parties silently accepted the drain. As the money was used for necessary ends, it is hardly surprising. Nevertheless, the depletion of FT's money tank also had the rather convenient result that the issue of investment control of the fund evaporated.

Denmark

The Danish[37] second-tier scheme (ATP) was established as a result of government intervention in the national wage-bargaining rounds of 1963. Marked as it was by the peculiar circumstances of its conception, it remained a hybrid of occupational and statutory provisions. Though a committee appointed by LO and the employers' association (DA) had discussed and almost agreed on a scheme, it had not been included in the 1963 negotiations. The scheme eventually adopted did not build on or interfere with any existing schemes, nor was it ever intended to fulfil the functions of a genuine second-tier public scheme. It was merely introduced as compensation for compulsory wage restraint. Given this context, almost no debate about the merits of the design from a social-policy perspective occurred. As this was a piece of labor-market legislation, it seemed perfectly logical to exclude the self-employed. And since the main purpose of the exercise was to limit rising labor costs, member and employer contributions were fixed at very moderate levels. Stimulation of the savings rate was a secondary and subordinate aim.

Originally, LO had wanted a general occupational scheme for its members in order to reduce the inequalities in prospective pension coverage between salaried employees and civil servants with occupational schemes, and the great majority of wage and salary earners without them. Since government intervention in the wage-bargaining round affected the entire labor market, and the pension scheme was only one among many elements in the settlement, distinctions between groups with or without occupational pension coverage were not made. In the end, even civil servants managed to get themselves included.

At the committee stage, both LO and DA had rejected the idea of proportional or earnings-related contributions, albeit for different reasons. LO did not want a system that reproduced wage differentials in old age, and it reasoned that a moderate flat-rate benefit for a flat-rate contribution would give its low-income members the best deal. DA viewed proportionality in contributions as a form of automatic indexation through the back door. In order better to control costs, they preferred to have contributions defined as a fixed amount. LO had envisioned a mechanism for periodic adjustment of contribution levels, but DA refused to accept automatic indexation under any form. In DA's view, higher pension contributions should result only from concrete bargaining.

The act provided for the scheme and the pension fund to be managed by a board of representatives appointed by the national peak associations of employers and employees. This dual management and the careful legal restriction of the investment options open to the board removed any hesitations the employers and the bourgeois parties may have had about fund control and neutralized the issue. The public sector was represented in its capacity as employer. Though any changes eventually would have to be backed by legislation, only the board could decide on adjustments of contributions. Since LO and DA between them would appoint a solid majority of board members, changes really depended on agreement between these two interest organizations.

That the scheme contributes so little to the pension incomes of the currently retired is a product of the unrealistically low initial levels of benefits and the lack of adequate adjustment for developments in wages and prices. Since its introduction, contributions have been raised only three times. The two largest increases occurred in the early 1980s, and they just barely restored the original real value of contributions. Adjustments of ATP contributions have had a curiously low priority in the demands that Danish unions have brought to the bargaining table. The strange succession of events in the pension struggle over the next decade may provide elements of an explanation.

Neither LO nor the Social Democratic party (SD),[38] was particularly concerned about the limits of the scheme. ATP was viewed as merely a forerunner for a genuine second-tier public scheme. A commission charged with preparing a proposal for such a scheme—to cover all the employed—was appointed when ATP was passed. In the light of later events it is remarkable that the two big bourgeois parties initially subscribed to many of the same ideas about scheme design as did the Social Democrats. Unfortunately, this consensus evaporated under the strain of increasing ideological polarization over other matters. In the wake of the 1966 election, which produced the first-ever left-wing majority in a Danish parliament, the Social Democrats broke with their traditional coalition partner of the center and tried instead to rely on the support of the People's Socialist party. This *ouverture à la gauche* enraged and radicalized the bourgeois parties. They were accustomed to a high degree of courtship and accommodation from the Social Democrats, who had used consultation with the dual purpose of engineering broad majorities and keeping the bourgeois parties and private business from coalescing into a common front. In response to SD's move to the left, the bourgeois parties buried their disagreements with one another and united around a platform of antisocialism. Moreover, the blurred lines of contact between the right side of parliament and the private business community were patched up and strengthened. There were some similarities with the realignments in the Swedish ATP struggle. But in Denmark, the breakup of the old coalition was neither caused by proposals for, nor particularly conducive to, the passage of an earnings-related second-tier scheme.

When the minister for social policy in 1967 proposed a scheme largely identical to the Swedish ATP plan, it did not help much that the self-employed were to be included. Responses from employers, business associations, and the bourgeois parties were prompt, largely unanimous, and utterly negative. Private business objected to the replacement rates, the exclusive financing through payroll taxes, and the accumulation of large funds under political control. Liberals and Conservatives rejected the principles of earnings relation, claiming that the state should restrict itself to establishing a floor of basic universal protection on top of which people could provide for themselves.

Like the Swedish Social Democrats before them, SD tried to play down the issue of fund management and control. This was difficult, however, because the People's Socialists, while suspicious of earnings relation, naturally were intrigued by the macroeconomic policy potential of a megapension fund.

The minister for social policy was very aware that an earnings-related scheme was needed in order to moderate traditional lines of division between wage earners and to achieve an adequate degree of interest harmonization in a crucial area. If it was not passed, the growing white-collar workforce would be lost to the bourgeois parties and the pension needs of the weakest in the labor market would be left unaddressed. But few among the labor leadership were as visionary as this minister.

The union movement was unenthusiastic in its support for the scheme. The unskilled workers' unions would have preferred redistribution through higher flat-rate benefits. The metalworkers were generally in favor, but they struck a familiar chord in the labor movement when they voiced fears that the passage of a costly second-tier scheme would interfere with the realization of other priorities, such as the forty-hour week and longer paid vacations. They wanted to postpone its introduction until other goals had been achieved. To many in the labor movement, the need for a new pension scheme did not appear particularly pressing either. The ATP scheme was just three years old, and a plan for the gradual increase of basic pensions had recently been passed. Besides, unions were in the midst of negotiating a crucial reform of unemployment insurance. Keen on striking an accord with employers, they were reluctant to let a conflict over pensions rock the boat. What is more, social-policy experts in the party were opposed to the idea of a pension fund and feared that an earnings-related scheme would serve only to replicate existing income inequalities once workers became pensioners.

In a different situation, the SD probably could have maneuvered the proposal through parliament by dropping the notion of a fund and offering other concessions, such as a formal member contribution, but they were barely on speaking terms with the bourgeois parties. Even if the government and its left-wing majority had lasted for another couple of years, it is not certain that the proposed scheme eventually would have been enacted.

As it happened, the left-wing majority disappeared in an early election later the same year, and a bourgeois coalition government took over. The Social Democratic leadership had decided to call a general election ahead of time, after radical elements among the People's Socialists had refused to support its austerity measures. There had not been time for more than an initial skirmish over second-tier pensions, and though against a determined opposition, the Social Democrats had not conclusively been defeated. Strangely enough, however, the SD proposal simply vanished with the government. Apparently, SD hesitated to reintroduce the issue because of internal division and lack of active support from the union movement. The inability to overcome internal disagreement about scheme designs prevented the party from taking bold initiatives in pension policy for the next fifteen years. Other factors, though, contributed to the odd paralysis in this field of pension policy.

In 1970, the bourgeois government introduced a general surtax of 2 percent to be collected as part of the state income tax and paid into a fund supposedly to be used for second-tier pension reform in 1976. Again, immediate motivations were macroeconomic and had nothing to do with actual pension policy. In reality, the talk of pension reform was little more than a front for the introduction of a compulsory savings scheme. New commissions were appointed to consider all possibilities and implications once again. But when they reported, nothing happened. In 1976, decisions about a possible reform were postponed to 1979 because of the onset of the recession. In 1979, the recession was on the verge of developing into a real depression. Reform was put off indefinitely, while some of the earmarked tax revenues were used for improvements in basic pensions. Finally, in 1981, the earmarking of the surtax was dropped, while the 2 percent was included in the overall rate of taxation for general purposes. Although unions gave little consideration to pensions in all these years, there is some truth to their retrospective claim that the politicians had continued to give them the impression that a political solution to the second-tier problem was just a few years away.

The outcome of this long and complicated course of events was that Denmark was stuck with the coincidental product of a forced wage settlement as its only general second-tier scheme. Inasmuch as contributions and benefits were meager, flat rate, service related, and nonindexed, it was an entirely inadequate response to the need for income-replacing supplements emanating from the flat-rate character of first-tier pensions.

In the absence of an adequate public plan, the field was left to occupational and individual schemes. Yet this was an effect of neglect and indecision rather than the product of a conscious attempt to define a division of labor between public, occupational, and individual provisions. In other Scandinavian countries, earnings-related second-tier provisions had raised a foundation on which to build to substantially higher coverage levels. Aggregate replacement rates that could be bought for less than 8 percent of salary in Norway and Sweden required at least 15 percent in Denmark. This acted as a brake on the spread of occupational plans. Labor-market conditions, such as the fact that white-collar unions are spread among three national peak organizations and that negotiations are far more decentralized than in Sweden, had the same impeding effect. Nevertheless, though the growth in occupational pension coverage was by no means as impressive as in Sweden and Norway, it certainly did take place. But this was more as a product of the general expansion in white-collar and professional employment, areas that traditionally had enjoyed such privileges, than through incorporation of groups previously uncovered.[39] And whereas the growth of occupational provisions in Sweden never implied a challenge to the position of public pensions, the absence of a clear division of labor between public and private provisions in Denmark meant that coexistence became competitive and turned increasingly destructive as private pensions proliferated.

Ironically, substantial parts of the growth occurred as a function of the expansion of the welfare state. When the public sector in the late 1960s began to hire on contractual terms instead of granting new employees permanent status, public-sector unions won occupational pension coverage for their members as compensation. The majority of the new public-sector employees worked in the health, education, and social service sectors.

Over the two decades in which statutory pension policy remained a dead letter, occupational pensions developed from temporary substitutes into permanent alternatives to earnings-related public second-tier provision. Only at great political costs, if at all, could they be demoted to the status of providing additional coverage. The gap, in prospective pension coverage, between those with and those without occupational pensions grew far wider than in other Nordic countries. Schemes became entrenched, and members developed very definite interests in their preservation. Hence the institution of very significant permanent cleavages between employees with and without occupational coverage stands out as one of the lasting legacies of the Danish second-tier scheme from the 1960s. The bourgeois parties soon recognized the new trend in pension relations and did their best to widen and exploit the growing cleavages between different layers of wage earners.

Pension Politics in the 1980s

Sweden

The two major clashes over pension policy in Sweden in the past decade revolved around the bourgeois government's attempt in 1980 to reduce the indexation level of ATP benefits and the 1986 SAP proposal for taxation of excessive real rates of return from pension-fund investments.

The forty-four-year reign of the Social Democrats was temporarily broken in 1976 by a bourgeois coalition that managed to confirm its majority in the 1979 election. The coalition was a shaky alliance of parties and remained largely tied to the Social Democratic agenda. When the government in 1980 decided to lower ATP benefits through alterations in the indexing mechanism, it was not intended as a general assault on the scheme.[40] In the view of the premier, it amounted to a minor adjustment.

Awareness that the ATP scheme was maturing and benefit payments from now on would exceed contributions provided the impetus for change. A sudden upsurge in costs was connected with the fact that most of those who were retiring now had maximum pension credits.[41] The pay-as-you-go character of the plan meant that rising costs had to be met by increases in social security taxes. There was nothing new about that. But in a time of recession and wage restraint, employers objected to the rise in labor cost caused by taxation. In the 1960s, when wages grew faster than prices, the emphasis on price indexing had reduced the real value of benefits. By the 1980s, the scenario had been reversed for some time. Social security payroll taxes were raised in order to compensate pensioners for international energy price hikes and rising sales taxes, while the active labor force had to accept such increases in the cost of living without any compensation. Given this tradeoff, employers and the bourgeois parties thought that the electorate would approve cuts in future ATP benefits. Yet the move, which took rises in energy prices and indirect taxes out of the index and slowed down the rate of adjustment, was highly unpopular.

In the labor movement it was perceived as an affront to the old settlement. The Social Democrats were in no mood to allow the government the benefit of the doubt and chose to interpret the act as an attempt to dismantle of the entire welfare-state edifice. They vowed to repeal the act and restore benefits to their former value at the first opportunity. Thus SAP made the defense of ATP a major issue in the election of 1982, and it turned out to be a canny strategy. The new SAP government immediately proceeded to restore the index, except for the exclusion of indirect taxes. Though it failed to keep the promise of a full restoration, the party had issued such emphatic political guarantees for ATP that these in turn prevented it from considering a number of other adjustments that could have improved the finances of the scheme. By declaring the preservation of ATP at all costs a fundamental priority, LO and SAP had committed themselves to continuing tax hikes in order to fund the scheme. Thus they cut themselves off from one of the major advantages of a pay-as-you-go scheme: Adjustments to changes in the economic and demographic context can be made along the way.

The popularity and widespread support of ATP was confirmed. The Swedish labor movement can easily mobilize its strength in defense of fundamental aspects of the welfare state, and as its victory in the 1985 election reaffirmed, it is likely to beat any constellation of bourgeois forces in a showdown over an issue of this sort.[42] Popular confidence in the ATP scheme has been eroded somewhat, but it is still strong. In part, however, the stability of the scheme both depends on, and may be somewhat threatened by, the political dedication of the labor movement. If necessary minor adjustments in the benefit formula cannot be made for political reasons, the viability of the entire scheme may suffer.

When, in 1985, the Social Democratic minister of finance proposed the introduction of a tax on pension funds with aggregate real rates of return above 3–4 percent, it was with the explicit intention of finding new revenue sources that could ease some of the burdens levied on employers and wage earners through payroll and income taxes. Since taxes on earned and capital income were so high, it seemed plausible to assume that a majority of the electorate, and certainly everyone in the labor movement, would welcome a scheme to tax part of the enormous unearned income of private pension funds. While objections and opposition from certain quarters had been expected, the finance minister was shaken to see the white-collar unions (TCO) and at some points even the LO join the choir of protesting voices in the course of a year-long debate about the consequences, merits, and drawbacks of such a scheme. The minister and the government fought hard for the scheme, but in the end it had to be withdrawn. What killed it was not the predictable resolute opposition of the bourgeois parties and private business, but opposition from the labor movement. Particularly negative reactions from the national association of white-collar workers and serious criticisms from LO deprived the scheme of its natural allies. Even if LO might have conceded the necessity to legislate something similar, the TCO would have none of it. As the white-collar unions saw it, the tax would represent a confiscation of part of the deferred wages of their members, wages they had foregone because of their confidence in the rules of taxation that the Social Democrats themselves had been party to. Moreover, taxation would interfere with existing wage agreements, and unions would demand compensation. Finally, by wreaking considerable havoc on the pension expectations of ordinary people, taxation would destroy their motivation for saving and their belief in government guarantees. In this instance, the solid integration of white-collar unions in the labor movement—normally the strength of Swedish labor—turned out to be an impediment, though the LO certainly was not enthusiastic about the scheme either. The internal disagreement led to paralysis. The party was unable to engineer a compromise with the unions, and in the end the Social Democrats feared the proposal could turn into an electoral liability.

Swedish pension politics of the 1980s were circumscribed by the legacy of the 1960s. No changes at either end of the pension arrangement were to be tolerated. Statutory and occupational schemes had been braided into one entity, and wage and salary earners were ready to defend them both as natural rights whenever someone tried to infringe on them. Although private annuities have grown significantly in recent years, and the mix may be subtly changing,[43] this is largely a function of the search for tax shelters. As long as there is a political will to fund the ATP scheme, the Swedish pension arrangement will be stable. And its design greatly facilitates the construction of such a political will.

Finland
In contrast to the other Nordic countries, Finland actually experienced a substantial expansion of public pension provision in the 1980s. A major reform

of basic pensions in the first half of the decade limited the income test for the pension supplement to pension income and raised benefit levels markedly. There was common agreement on the need for reform, and the act was passed with wide support.

Generally, the 1980s were far easier on Finland than on the other three nations. Close trading ties with the Soviet Union cushioned the economy against the impact of the world recession.[44] In fact, the economy expanded throughout the period, and public finances were in good shape. The country did not have to endure the constant fiscal squeeze that made life so difficult for would-be reformers elsewhere. Moreover, Finland was spared a general swing to the right of the sort that marked politics in Denmark, Norway, and to some degree, Sweden. And, finally, the Finnish population is the youngest among the Nordic populations.

While the economic, political, and demographic context of pension policy thus was rather benevolent, stability and expansion in Finnish public pensions rest more on the compromises and accommodations embedded in the institutional design from the 1960s than on any prosperity-induced temporary consensus. The unique combination of high standard statutory pensions and decentralized private-sector administration largely defused the otherwise explosive issues of equality, adequacy, equity, and fund control.

Some issues were raised. In comparative international terms, Finnish employers' share of first-tier pension expenditures is exceptionally high. The employers' association has complained loudly about this tax burden, claiming that it interfered seriously with the international competitiveness of Finnish enterprises. Attempts to affect a cost shifting or a reduction of overall pension costs have been part of the employers' fairly low-key campaign to reduce their share.[45] In these efforts they have unsuccessfully tried to enlist the rhetoric of the new demographics. Warnings that Finland soon would be unable to afford such generous pensions have been ridiculed. Official figures demonstrate that, over the next two decades, dependency burdens will change only slightly, and Finnish pension expenditures as a share of GNP will remain below levels already reached in many OECD countries with similar demographic profiles. Likewise, complaints about the cost share have been countered with comparisons showing that the total sum of social security taxes levied on employers constitutes a smaller burden than the one placed on employers in many other West European countries. As well, social expenditures in Finland represent a lower share of GNP, and employers fund a smaller part of overall costs. Some cost shifting has occurred, albeit for slightly different reasons. In order to avoid adverse effects to employment of too high an emphasis on payroll taxes, an increasing part of the costs of the first-tier scheme have been financed from general revenues.

As for the fund question, original alliances and compromises have been confirmed. When the Center party (formerly the Agrarian party) proposed that the surplus in the second-tier funds be used for improvements in basic pensions for those without other sources of income, a united front of unions, the employers' association, and the insurance industry emphatically rejected the idea. According to the unions, the funds represented the deferred wages of employees, and as such they could not be used for general social-policy purposes. The employers supported this view, and both agreed that control over the funds should remain with the parties in the labor market. While the opposition may have been overpowering, the Center party did not push the issue particularly hard.

Despite some criticism of the ease with which employers may retract part of their pension contributions as loans, and programmatic demands for a democratization of the pension funds, union leaders have expressed general satisfaction with the way the funds are handled. Proposals to use some of the surplus for the benefit of the contributing workers have been discussed in the union movement, and the president of the trade-union confederation has proposed that workers be allowed to get mortgage loans from the funds. Yet no initiatives have been taken to turn this idea into a political or wage-bargaining priority.

The interest on pension-fund contribution credits to employers has slowly approached normal market rates for commercial loans, but it is still somewhat low. The amortization is only 7 percent, and the duration of the credit is almost indefinite. In exchange for an IOU to the pension fund, employers may retain as much as 65 percent of their contribution. As a result, a large portion of the second-tier pension fund has been on constant long-term loan. Hence it is hardly surprising that the employers' association has expressed great satisfaction with the system. As the schemes start to mature, however, and it becomes necessary to use the entire fund to cover pension payments, this attitude is bound to change. The otherwise so ingeniously stable Finnish pension design may be destined to unravel in the late 1990s.[46]

Norway

Once historically implanted, pension schemes, like other institutional designs, tend to take on a life of their own. In Norway, the inclusion of all the gainfully employed was intentional. It was the foundation of the original consensus, and it guaranteed broad support for the scheme over the years. In itself, the consensus was an unintended consequence of tactical maneuvering for government power. The lack of separation between the financial resources for the various schemes in the People's Social Security program (FT) had also come about by accident. In general, none of the significant actors seems to have wanted FT, nor did they pay any particular attention to it when the scheme was passed.[47] Whether intentional or accidental, these features were to influence Norwegian pension politics in significant ways in the 1980s. Scheme design and commitment to the consensual character of the original settlement largely seem to have defined the parameters of what could happen. In combination, they provide the essence of an explanation of the peculiar character of Norwegian pension politics over the past decade.

The 1969 enactment of a special pension supplement for those with very few or no second-tier pension credits did not prevent minimum pensioners from becoming a subproletariat among pensioners in the 1970s.[48] In its concern for distributional justice, the Social Democratic government commissioned a committee to investigate the problem. The 1978 report[49] confirmed the need for minimum pensions to be raised and proposed a 40 percent increase over the next five years. It was a perfectly sensible proposal, yet the government refrained from acting on it. The aggregate cost of N.kr. 2 billion was not prohibitive in itself, but FT finances had been strained by costly new programs and reductions in the earmarked social security taxes. Substantial increases in the "subsidy" from general tax revenues would be necessary in order to meet future demands from existing programs without any of the contemplated improvements in first-tier pension supplements. The pooling of funds in the FT caused the interests of minimum pensioners to be pitted against those of second-tier pensioners, and the former lost. If the other parties to the original consensus around FT had backed the proposal explicitly, the Labor government probably would have acted. At best they were lukewarm, however, and the whole thing was soon made even more implausible by a new political current. For the first time in more than a generation, the Conservative party soared in the opinion polls and appeared to find a quickly growing audience for their New Right rhetoric about the necessity to curb public expenditures and lower taxes.

Insufficient fund buildup was the logical consequence of the raiding of FT resources collected for the second-tier scheme. In turn this prepared the ground for a political discourse focused on "mounting deficits," "rising dependency rates," and "insufficient savings." As governments refrained from adjusting payroll and social security taxes in line with the growth in overall program expenditures, the contribution from general tax revenues had to be raised.[50] The intermingling of funds collected for the financing of various schemes had allowed politicians to act as if pension contributions intended to serve as equity actually represented a surplus, which could be used for unrelated purposes. When the fund was depleted and moneys had to be transferred from general revenues in order to top it up, this was portrayed by Conservatives as a mounting deficit. In their campaigns against the excesses of the welfare state at the beginning of the 1980s, the Conservatives claimed this "glaring" deficit made benefit reductions inescapable.[51]

Soon after they took over the executive in the aftermath of the 1981 election, the Conservatives established a parliamentary committee to review the financial situation of FT. The Willoch minority government appeared determined to affect "a balanced reduction of the role of the state in social security" and to improve incentives for growth in private pension provision. As expected, the 1984 committee report[52] confirmed that the sorry state of FT finances made certain retrenchments in the earnings-related scheme imperative. It was therefore surprising that these cuts failed to materialize. The will to administer the knife somehow disappeared. The Conservatives, who now headed a bourgeois, majority coalition government, were alone in their urge to renounce the postwar social-policy consensus. The other bourgeois parties in the coalition felt bound by this consensus and were not particularly eager to participate in the demolition of the welfare state. They represented a large section of FT's beneficiaries and were careful not to expose themselves to attacks from the Social Democrats. Even the Social Democrats were careful not to voice strong opinions on the report; possibly they realized that the FT finances would have to be balanced, and they had themselves been party to some of the problems. They might shortly have to face the same dilemma as a responsible government and would need the support of the center parties for adequate remedies. At any rate, for the next five years all actors kept remarkably quiet while watching for any moves from the others.

In 1987 the Social Democrats, who after the 1985 election formed a new minority government, managed to secure support from the center parties for measures to limit the tax subsidies to private pensions. As part of tax reform, the value of tax exemptions for private annuity savings was lowered, while the tax deductibility of contributions to occupational schemes was temporarily discontinued. The act represented the first substantial change in the framework of occupational and contractual pensions in twenty years.

After the private pensions regulatory act of 1968, no attempts had been made to interfere with the development of nonstatutory provisions. Yet in spite of substantial growth in the value and extension of occupational and individual annuity pensions, the FT second-tier scheme still accounted for the lion's share of pension payments. Until this point, the LO and the DNA had taken little notice of developments in the private pension field. But after the research unit of the union movement, FAFO, conducted a number of studies of private pensions and the relation between public and private welfare provisions[53], awareness of the issue rose considerably in the labor movement.[54] While occupational provisions had been expanding, the coverage and quality remained very uneven.[55] Though differences were more pronounced between sectors than between different positions in the wage and skill hierarchies, the growth had preserved and reinstituted some of the old demarcations between manual workers and white-collar employees.[56] While emphasizing their commitment to public-sector pensions, manual workers' unions were now contemplating whether they, like their Swedish colleagues, should attempt to even up the score through collective-bargaining arrangements.[57]

The return of the Social Democrats to government power, their new-found concern about the divisive aspects of private pensions, and the extent of nonpartisan support for curbs on tax expenditures for private pensions led observers to expect that public pensions might be insulated from cuts for a long time to come. When, in late 1988, the report on the financial state of FT from the Department of Social Security argued that moderate downward adjustments of the benefit formula would be the only alternative to heavy increases in social security taxes, even the experts presumed that the Social Democrats and the center parties would find ways to postpone a final decision on the suggestions. Hence the Social Policy Committee took everybody by surprise when it suddenly announced that it had arrived at broad political agreement on even larger cuts in the benefits of middle- to high-income earners than had been suggested by the Department of Social Security.

This sudden consensus about retrenchment derived, in a sense, from the political legacy of the establishment of the Norwegian second-tier scheme. All parties felt less bound by the details of design than by its consensual enactment. It was difficult for the parties to the original act to take the ultimate steps toward major improvements or significant retrenchment without the consent of the others. Alterations in the shape and design, even if they were crucial, were possible only if general accord could be reached. In the spring of 1989, the party representatives in the Social Policy Committee suddenly found that they all dared take a step forward at the same moment, and thus they were able to skip the usual endless procrastination and launch into a common agreement. There was little popular support for the cuts. Yet since all the major parties had found each other, there was only limited and ineffectual protest and opposition.

The committee argued that the economic and demographic prospects for Norway had forced them to lower the ceiling on pensionable earnings. From a Scandinavian perspective, this was indeed odd because Norway had fairly good prospects on both accounts. Despite some stagnation, North Sea oil had cushioned the impact from world recession, and economic prospects were far better than in the 1960s when the FT was established. The absence of a voluminous pension fund to meet the rising costs associated with maturation made demographic prospects seem particularly bleak. Though the proportion of the Norwegian population due to reach pension age over the next fifty years is smaller than in Sweden or Denmark, underfunding of the scheme made it easier to overestimate and exaggerate the magnitude of financial problems to come.

Insufficient funding also implies that the scheme is entirely without the benevolent impact on the economy associated with the Swedish and Finnish systems.[58] Therefore, it might also be argued that the only way to obtain the temporary macroeconomic benefits of funded pensions is to change the mix between public and private provision in favor of the latter, since private pensions usually have to be fully funded. At least this is the line of reasoning that the director of the national bank of Norway presented with some success in May 1989 when the cuts in FT were debated. Even the Labor party now felt obliged to bow to this argument: FT was to be preserved, but private pension savings would have to be increased considerably, and the lowering of the ceiling on pensionable earnings would no doubt contribute to this end.

Denmark
The Danish scenario of the 1980s confirms the counterfactuals implicit in the previous arguments about the importance of the sort of second-tier settlements reached in the other three countries. Whereas these settlements have tended to stabilize the mix between public and private pensions, to harmonize the pension interests of blue- and white-collar wage earners, and to reconcile them with those of the self-employed, the Danish second-tier scheme has exacerbated these divisions, made it easy to use the pension issue to pit various groups of wage earners against one another, and generally left the pension mix in a flux. Thus Danish pension politics can be said to have revolved around the absence of a general earnings-related scheme.

When a research unit under the labor movement published a white paper with the telling title "Private Pensions—Savings or Tax Shelter? A Study in Inequality," [59] the rhetorical question of the title largely summed up the negative attitude toward occupational and individual pensions in the LO and the Social Democratic party. The aggregate value of tax subsidies to private pensions had been estimated, and the general message was that the main part of the costs of those nest eggs accumulating in nonstatutory pension schemes was covered by the general taxpayer, who had to make up for revenues foregone through higher taxes. Since little additional saving of a genuinely private character was taking place, there was really no reason why the exchequer should undertake to subsidize the pension aspirations of an already privileged minority, particularly not given scarce resources and inadequate public pensions.

This position was reaffirmed when the Old Age Commission, appointed by the Social Democrats, reported in 1981. Basic first-tier pensions provided a level of income on the verge of poverty. The income drop at retirement was far too large. If the elderly were to live normal lives as active, independent citizens, the miserly level of the basic pension had to be improved substantially. Moreover, the commission calculated that if tax subsidies to nonstatutory pensions were discontinued, basic pensions could be raised by a third.[60] In this phase, political discourse about pensions focused on distributional justice and social needs. The dedication of labor to social-policy considerations and redistribution was further consolidated when the two main authors of the above-mentioned reports were appointed to government posts as minister of taxation and minister of social policy.

In the wake of the second oil crisis, interest rates on government bonds had soared to unheard-of levels of 22 percent. A majority of these bonds were held by pension-fund investors. It was hardly surprising that the new minister of taxation in 1981 began to design a scheme to tax the exorbitant real rates of return, which, if unchecked, would allow pension replacement rates to overtake wages.

The pension industry was bound to protest,[61] the Liberals and the Conservatives would object, the center parties would be reluctant, and no one expected the salaried white-collar unions to be jubilant. But the government was shocked by the vehemence of reactions. Public-sector unions joined in the coordinated campaign to block the scheme,[62] and some of them used their channels to the party and labor movement leadership to try to make the government drop the scheme.

The proposal for taxation of average real rates of return on pension-fund investments of more than 3.5 percent was an important element in the government's plans for curbing the state deficit. Realizing that the scheme would be defeated, the Social Democratic minority government took a radical step. In the early autumn of 1982, it decided to resign. The government had many problems apart from pensions, and the resignation was tactical in intention.[63] Yet, as it happened to open the way for the first stable bourgeois coalition government in more than a decade, and as it resulted in a realignment that ever since has managed to relegate the Social Democrats to an increasingly frustrating role as opposition, the pension issue has taken on an air of ominous importance in retrospect.

The Conservatives, who on this occasion gained the premiership for the first time since 1901, and their closest coalition partner, the Liberals, had learned the game of minority-government survival from years of being outwitted by the Social Democrats. Now it was their turn to prevent real alternatives from emerging by constantly pitting different groups of wage earners against each other and by separating the Social Democrats from the People's Socialists. In these endeavors, pensions often served as an excellent tool.

As it turned out, the opposition of the bourgeois parties to pension-fund taxation was quite soft. They were against it as long as the issue was instrumental in pitting white-collar against manual unions, thus splitting the labor movement. When the New Right–inspired government had consolidated itself, however, it took only a year before it legislated a similar scheme of pension-fund taxation with support from the Social Democrats. Faced with the same need to reduce the state deficit and direct money from passive to active investment to boost production and employment, the bourgeois government simply could not allow private pension schemes to collect tax-free real rates of return on their government bonds of 10–15 percent; active investments subject to tax brought 5–8 percent. The pension industry complained bitterly about the compromise with the Social Democrats, but private business and bourgeois opinion at large generally recognized that continuation of Conservative rule had to take priority over sectional interests. Minority union opposition of course carried no weight by this time.

That they themselves had to infringe on the tax privileges of private pensions did not stop the bourgeois parties in government from trying once again to exploit the divisive potential of occupational pensions. In the summer of 1984 prominent ministers suggested to the Metal Workers Union[64] that it opt for a funded occupational pension scheme for its members, instead of the thirty-five-hour week. LO, acting on behalf of all manual unions, was about to give the thirty-five-hour week top priority in the upcoming rounds of collective bargaining. The metalworkers were convinced; though they decided to stay in line in 1985, they gave LO an ultimatum: Either come up with a proposal for earnings-related supplementary pensions for all wage earners without coverage well before the 1987 national tariff rounds, or they, the metalworkers, would negotiate their own scheme.

More than anything before, these events convinced the Social Democratic party and union leadership that something had to be done to neutralize the divisive potential of the pension issue. To avoid further splits on fundamental issues and to escape the prospect of large income differences in old age between wage earners with and without adequate supplementary pension coverage, LO complied with the ultimatum. It came up with a proposal for a comprehensive reform of the Danish pension system that, to the pleasant surprise of the bourgeois parties and the pension industry and the anger of the left,[65] included a general scheme of mandatory occupational pensions. The three main elements of the proposal[66] were these:

1. The nominal value of basic pensions was to be raised so that the pensions could be made fully taxable and still retain their real value. On top of that, the amount was to be reduced for pensioners with extraordinarily high incomes, while the income test in the general supplement was to be liberalized to allow for moderate occupational pensions.
2. Contributions for the existing ATP scheme were to be doubled and wage indexation introduced.
3. An earnings-related occupational scheme was to be established for the two-thirds of wage earners currently without occupational coverage. This would be financed by employer and employee contributions to a central pension fund under union control.

In order not to jeopardize other union priorities, and in recognition that it would have to be paid for partly by wage restraint, the plan for the mandated occupational scheme was to be gradually introduced over a ten-year period.

After a twenty-year delay, the Danish LO had finally come to see the necessity of earnings-related pensions, only to discover that the labor movement was now unable to demote existing occupational schemes to a complementary role as a third tier on top of a general public scheme. The entrenchment of occupational pension interests forced the LO to conclude that earnings-related pensions in Denmark would have to take the form of occupational provisions. Unable to negate the privilege of a minority, LO tried instead to modify it by extending it to everyone in the labor market. A number of implications followed from this. LO would have to resign its long-time opposition to tax subsidies for private pensions. If occupational provisions were to be attractive to LO members, the tax deductibility of member and employer contributions would have to be preserved. Furthermore, in order for such provisions to result in additional pension income for workers with average incomes, income testing for supplements to the first-tier pension would have to be changed or abolished. As for the existing occupational schemes, they would be allowed to continue as before. Though the new scheme in time would modify some of the differences, those who were already covered would retain a substantial part of their initial advantage, and a significant measure of inequality would remain. Finally, to make sense of a general occupational scheme, LO would have to relegate basic first-tier pensions to a junior role in the overall pension system and reduce redistribution at one end while raising it at the other.

When the research unit of the labor movement presented the reform to union leaders, the cleverly devised multifunctional character of the package was emphasized. Some union leaders undoubtedly saw the occupational scheme as particularly attractive because a giant pension fund under union control[67] could be employed as a powerful tool in the struggle for economic democracy and worker coownership.[68] White-collar unions within the LO focused on the prospect of supplementary pensions for their members. The unskilled workers' unions, in contrast, remained skeptical. It would be difficult to ask the rank and file to forego part of their meager wages for supplementary pension credits. To them it was imperative that the occupational scheme be general and mandatory, and inseparable from the suggested adjustments to the basic pension and ATP. The package had been carefully constructed to serve as a common denominator for the various interests in the LO. At first sight it seemed to have succeeded. But agreement was conditional. It depended on the balance and connections between the elements in the package. If it became undone, sectional interests would erupt again.

The LO reform proposal was presented to the government and the employers' association as an alternative to incomes policy and compulsory savings measures in the autumn of 1985. The pension industry and the bourgeois parties complimented the LO for its policy reversal and welcomed the idea of vastly increased pension savings. But they were less enthusiastic about the format of the scheme, and they were skeptical about the proposed changes to the universal first-tier pension. Though certainly in need of a scheme to increase the national savings rate, the government fumed at the idea of building a central investment fund under union control[69] and refused to legislate a comprehensive mandatory scheme. Instead, ministers and leaders of the employers' association insisted that occupational pension coverage must result "voluntarily" from decentralized bargaining in the various parts of the labor market. The Liberals were far more emphatic in their refusal than the Conservatives, who were looking for areas where they could strike a grand stabilizing deal with the Social Democrats. But the fact remained that both bourgeois parties had little strategic interest in occupational pensions. And the employers' association was not inclined to help fund what, in its view, amounted to a general scheme of supplementary pensions. Much less were any of these two exponents of bourgeois opinion willing to allow the union movement control over the investment of the pension savings of their members in exchange for a little wage restraint and a larger rate of savings.

The government was, however, careful not to dismiss LO's proposal entirely. Ministers kept indicating that if a sufficient number of unions demonstrated their willingness to trade part of their wages for occupational pension credits at the bargaining table, the government would back the results by making occupational coverage of a certain standard mandatory.

Meanwhile, the plan came under increasing attack not just from the left but from within the social democratic labor movement. The association of retired union members, led by a former chairman of the LO, objected because the plan in its view neglected the needs of present pensioners and because macroeconomic goals took priority over social-policy concerns. The usual social-policy experts and welfare economists in the Social Democratic party, including the most recent minister for social policy and former head of the Old Age Commission, Bent Rold-Andersen, had not been asked for advice when the LO proposal was developed. As a fully funded, general occupational scheme ran against their fundamental beliefs about how a distributionally just and economically flexible pension system should be constructed, they could hardly be expected to applaud.[70] As soon as he had recovered from his initial surprise and learned that his position still had many supporters in the labor movement, Rold-Andersen decided to go public, denouncing the principle of funded private pensions and the idea of enlarging its role in pension policy.[71] He caught the imagination of the general public with the theme of generational conflict, which was picked up by the popular press. According to Rold-Andersen, Denmark's spoiled middle generation[72] was refusing to share with its parents and children. In the 1940s and 1950s, parents had refrained from consuming their surplus and from putting it away as savings for their old age in order to provide their children with security and free higher education. In the late 1960s and early 1970s, these children had entered a booming labor market and acquired secure and well-paid positions. Yet now they were refusing to pay for better public pensions for their parents. Instead, they used the resources, which they did not spend on extravagant leisure, on tax-exempt savings for occupational and private pensions for themselves, thus in effect not just neglecting the legitimate needs of their parents but also forcing their own kids to pay them exorbitant pensions when they retired.[73] They were breaking the contract between generations embedded in the public pension system by loading obligations on to their parents and children that they ought to pick up themselves. While Andersen was drawing great applause from pensioners and the little man in the street, he had violated the code of party discipline and was soon silenced by the LO.[74] The plan was adjusted in a few minor ways, and the Social Democratic leadership closed ranks behind the proposal.

More seriously, the national peak organization of middle-level white-collar employee unions, FTF, was entirely negative toward the proposal.[75] To the embarrassment of the LO and the Social Democrats, the FTF was demanding compensation for its members if the currently uncovered were given occupational coverage through statutory intervention, arguing that their members had paid for their pensions through wage restraint. The bourgeois government quickly picked up on this, reinforcing its demand that pensions should be paid through lower wages.

The largest opposition, however, came from the silent majority among the LO membership. In the spring of 1986, LO ran a campaign to convince people of the urgency and the ingenuity of the proposal. Yet subsequent surveys repeatedly demonstrated that the rank and file were anything but enthusiastic. Less than 20 percent were willing to forego part of their wages for better pensions in the future.

The negative attitudes of the FTF were to have even more dire consequences when the LO and the DA in the 1987 wage-bargaining round agreed to raise the level of contributions to the ATP scheme by 50 percent. Negotiations in the private sector had already been concluded when the minister of finance, negotiating for the public sector, suddenly accepted the request that public-sector employees with occupational coverage be allowed to contract out of the improvements in the ATP scheme. The result was that a new dual structure of coverage, which accentuated and consolidated interest cleavages between public and private employees, was established. Solidarity in a system where all wage earners shared the same conditions had been broken, and there was nothing the LO could do to prevent it.

Meanwhile, the two large unskilled workers' unions had calculated to what extent their members would benefit from a general occupational scheme. It turned out that, by and large, they could not expect forty years of savings in the occupational scheme to improve their aggregate pensions. In the present system of a universal pension with income-tested supplements, they were actually getting a posttax replacement rate that was slightly higher than the one they would obtain when occupational benefits were added. The simple reason was that their small occupational pensions would be "taxed" away under the current rules about combination of income from public and private pensions. Officials from unskilled workers' unions were now in agreement that these rules should be phased out as the general occupational scheme was introduced.

The government hinted that pension reform might follow if LO unions made it a priority goal in the wage-bargaining rounds of 1987, but they were still gambling for reform through parliament or as part of a forced settlement. Negotiations ended amiably, however, with employers conceding far larger pay raises than union leaders had expected. Thus reform did not materialize in 1987, and was put off until the 1989 collective-bargaining sessions. At the opening of parliament in the autumn of 1987, the prime minister declared pension reform a national priority in economic policy. A tripartite committee was set up under the auspices of the Department of Labor, to investigate various pension schemes, including the LO's proposal. A minor army of civil servants assisted experts from the unions and the employers' association in a hurried attempt to finish before the start of collective bargaining in January 1989. A ten-volume report, which met with reluctant approval from most quarters, was presented shortly before Christmas 1988. The public and certainly the unions now expected that negotiations about design and implementation would start. But Prime Minister Poul Schlüter stunned the entire nation—and even most of his inner cabinet—when, in his New Year's speech, he suddenly announced that pension reform had been dropped in favor of a 10 percent wage reduction for everybody. According to him, this would be of far greater benefit to the economy. Concern about pension reform was somewhat forgotten in the heated aftermath.

It appeared that the Liberals and a recalcitrant but very influential section of the DA had vetoed government negotiations with the unions about mandatory occupational pensions. The Liberals were bent on preventing the LO unions from gaining control of large pension funds.[76] In their view, private pensions were primarily interesting to the degree that they could be used as a strategy of popular capitalism. Only if occupational pensions were selective and only if the individual had some influence on the investment of contributions would he or she need to take some interest in the market performance of pension funds. Under collective control, occupational pensions would be nothing but a power tool in the hands of union bosses. No real dissemination of property rights would occur unless the influence on invested pension savings were individualized.

The Social Democrats had a hard time arguing for the necessity of a single fund. Under pressure from the Liberals and the private pension industry, they conceded that a number of separate schemes and funds would be possible as long as pension conditions were homogeneous and some redistribution in the contribution–benefit formula was retained. Fund boards could be elected by members instead of being appointed by unions. And if they could compete with union-operated pension institutes, the private pension industry would be allowed a share in running the schemes. These concessions had been meant to patch up the ailing, and odd, alliance between the LO leadership, the pension industry, and the financial sector at large. They had also been intended to help pacify the Liberals. Now it seemed that none of these effects was attained. Whenever the Social Democrats and the unions retreated, the Liberals seemed only to step up their attacks and augment their demands for concessions, while the private pension industry saw less and less reason to let the labor movement dictate the terms of their involvement in scheme management. The prime minister's abrupt about-face led the unions to lose faith in the government, but there were no other places they could turn if they still held hopes for even a watered-down version of their pension reform.

While they had been waiting for the new scheme, the Social Democrats and the unions had been anxious to develop an active and constructive investment policy for the two existing statutory pension funds, the ATP fund, where they have substantial influence, and the Wage Earners Indexation fund (LD), which is under exclusive union control. A demonstration of labor's capacity for efficient and profitable, yet socially responsible, investment management in the interest of national business and the Danish worker was supposed to convince the public of the beneficial potential of pensions funds under union–wage earner control and reassure the business community. The strategy was reasonably successful. The recent investment records of the two funds are good. In a number of dramatic interventions, the funds have prevented hostile foreign takeovers, rejuvenated large and ailing companies, and thus saved jobs while securing for the prospective pensioner a return easily comparable to that which the private pension industry could deliver. In a series of skirmishes with the Liberals, the Social Democrats succeeded in liberalizing the legal framework restraining the active investments of the ATP and the LD fund. But the Liberals immediately countered with demands that the statutory funds should operate under the same conditions as the private pension industry, in order not to distort competition. Thus they argued that public funds should allow their members the same right to withdraw their savings and place them in alternative pension schemes when dissatisfied. So far, their demands have not been met, but in public debates the Social Democrats have difficulty explaining why members should not have this kind of influence on their own savings. If union funds are so efficient and profitable, why then should individualization of property rights lead to their breakup?

Originally, the LO had produced the pension reform proposal to stop the Metal Workers Union from pursuing the struggle for occupational coverage alone. In the winter of 1990, the metalworkers declared that they were fed up waiting for a statutory scheme and would attempt to bargain a scheme for their members in the wage round of 1991. After almost half a decade of intense efforts to halt the drift toward a steadily increasing differentiation of wage-earner pension interests, the social democratic labor movement was not just back to square one. Since the 1985 reform proposal, the movement has also lost a very substantial part of the territory it formerly commanded. The five years have been a time of constant retreat in the vain hope of achieving internal unity and a grand compromise with labor's traditional opponents. Now, earnings-related pensions in Denmark seem destined to follow the British model with a myriad of different, negotiated occupational schemes and the attendant interest fragmentation.

In the 1980s, Danish political discourse about old-age pensions evolved from the Old Age Commission's demonstration of the inadequacy of state pensions in 1980 to the 1988 Labour Market Pension Commission's arguments about the necessity of substantial cuts in the basic first-tier pension, in order to motivate low-income wage earners to forego part of their wages for contributions to a system of funded occupational pensions. In just eight years, the debate was totally transformed. Focus shifted from public pensions for better living conditions and a fairer share for old people to occupational pensions for national economic recovery and a lighter burden on the future cohorts of the gainfully employed.

The social democratic labor movement shifted from an exclusive focus on adequacy to a growing concern about equity (i.e., on maintaining the link between contributions and benefits). But equity concerns grew like a cancer until they threatened to overshadow all sensible regard for redistribution and equality. The boomeranging implications of equity concerns became clear when the conclusion drawn from the conflict between the need for occupational pensions to increase national savings and wage earners' unwillingness to accept such a scheme appeared to be that government would have to scrap or significantly reduce basic public pension provisions. No longer is there concern about the "inadequacy" of first-tier pensions; the concern is with their "overadequacy." In government reports, first-tier pensions are now presented as disincentives to occupational pensions because the basic pension and income-tested supplement provide lower- to middle-income groups with a fair income-replacement rate. Private pension income is heavily taxed so that it makes more sense to spend wages before retirement rather than defer them for occupational pension income after retirement. In effect, the Labour Market Commission argued that the social pension system is simply too good to provide people with ordinary incomes with enough incentive to save. To induce low-income earners to save, they argue, the present basic benefit levels would have to be lowered. Soon, some politicians from the bourgeois coalition parties even felt brave enough to declare that the basic pension would have to go, partly because it was a disincentive to saving, and partly because demographic change would soon make the scheme far to costly.[77]

The long-frustrated need for earnings-related second-tier pension supplements have been made a vehicle for the competing strategic projects of economic democracy and popular capitalism. Promises of pensions some time in the future are the sugar that is supposed to make the bitter pill of compulsory savings acceptable to wage earners. Increased savings and wage restraint, instead of better pensions, are the dominant concerns of the center parties in the bourgeois government. The Liberals view a voluntary expansion of occupational pension provisions as one among other instruments in a move toward popular capitalism, while the labor movement has linked pension reform with its quest for economic democracy—or "fund socialism" as the bourgeois parties have labeled the project. Thus pension politics in Denmark has been turned into a struggle about the future contours of Danish political economy, and the protagonists seem to have lost sight of the original purpose of pension reform: provision for income in old age.

Conclusions

The fixing of a stable relationship between public and private pension provisions required accommodation. This involved structural complementarity, as in Sweden, or a blurring of the boundaries, as in Finland. In Sweden and Norway, occupational arrangements depend on public pensions because these provide the foundation on which they build.

Without pressure from the social democratic labor movements, adequate earnings-related public pensions would not have come about. But as I have taken great care to demonstrate, the establishment of stable pension systems always involved giving employers and the bourgeois parties a stake in the design of pension arrangements. The Nordic pension systems were not solely the products of the power and cunning of strategically minded labor movements, as some heroic interpretations of the Swedish experience would have us believe. In some instances, Scandinavian labor just scraped through and happened on formulas that would work. Furthermore, social-policy concerns have often been subordinate to macroeconomic and macropolitical aims and considerations.

In my explanation of the stability of pension arrangements and the relative tranquility of pension politics outside Denmark, I have pointed to the specifics of scheme design and to the political events that accompanied the establishment of earnings-related public schemes. But the dismal failure of Danish labor in the 1980s and the relative success of Swedish, Finnish, and Norwegian labor are also closely connected to the phenomenon of timing. The earnings-related second-tier systems in Sweden, Finland, and Norway succeeded because they were established in an expansionary period—at the start or in the middle of a boom period for the economy in general as well as for the welfare state—and before the enormous expansion in the white-collar and public-sector workforce. These workers had traditionally enjoyed the privilege of occupational pensions. Organized labor in Norway, Sweden, and Finland would probably have encountered difficulties very similar to those that have plagued the Danish labor movement in trying to establish general earnings-related second-tier pensions in the 1980s. Had the three countries also been without general systems until now, white-collar and civil servant second-tier privileges would have been equally entrenched, and universal solutions would have been impossible to launch. Once established, however, high-quality social security provisions that incorporate not just the middle-class elements of salaried white-collar workers but also the self-employed are indeed difficult to topple. The broadness of their social base is like a permanent comprehensive insurance cover.

As far as Scandinavia is concerned, pension politics in the 1980s was structured far more by the political legacy and institutional inertia of pension systems established in the 1960s than by economic problems or demographic predictions. In this sense, the 1980s were marked by continuity more than by a break with the past. With the exception of Denmark, the Nordic countries experienced a period of relative tranquality after a long burst of reforms. These reforms appear to have addressed pension needs successfully.

During the 1980s, the compromises and accommodations embedded in the basic design of public and occupational provisions withstood the pressure of changes in the economic and political context of pension policy. But, it should be added, by 1990 there were signs that change may be imminent.

In Sweden, the Social Democratic government is conducting a review of the entire social security system. Rumors of fundamental alterations and major retrenchments do not augur well for the future of the flagship among Nordic welfare states. In Denmark, the eventual legislation of a framework for negotiated and possibly statutory pension schemes is likely to involve cutbacks in the basic scheme. The Norwegians have already devised a solution to the financial problems of their second-tier scheme, whereas the Finns have not yet faced such difficulties. Until their schemes mature, and if their economy keeps humming along as before, they are in for a longer phase of tranquility, interrupted only by minor adjustments, similar to the ones that the Swedes and Norwegians experienced in the 1980s.

While larger changes in the age structure of Nordic populations are still far away, the increases in what we, for the lack of better words, may call the actual "socioeconomic dependency rates," caused by the trend toward earlier retirement, may start to make themselves felt. These will no longer be compensated for by growing female labor-force participation rates. Nevertheless, early retirement is just one among other important components in the socioeconomic dependency rate. If the high rates of unemployment in Denmark, for example, could be lowered to Swedish levels in the 1990s, this could easily offset the combined effects of aging and early retirement at present levels. The average age at which the young actually enter the labor force is another important element. The trend toward rising entry ages in the 1960s and 1970s seems to have been broken. Labor-market integration programs and educational reforms making for greater efficiency in higher education and vocational training may even contribute to a moderate reversal of the trend.

Although the rhetoric of the new demographics has gained little political currency so far, the Scandinavians, like everybody else, will have to adjust to demographic change. Yet adjustments can take many different forms. Current pension mixes may be preserved and the level of benefits may be upheld in the face of an aging population by three principal means: (1) increases in the labor-force participation rates of the nonretired; (2) reversal of the trend toward earlier retirement through the creation of jobs more suited to the work capacities and qualifications of the elderly, which will be easier if it is true that the objective physical and mental health of the elderly is improving; (3) increases in tax revenues. The less conflict-prone and more efficient ways of increasing tax revenues are those that widen the tax base and increase the efficiency of tax collection while distributing the burdens as widely and equally as possible.

The problems for the Scandinavian countries in relation to this catalogue of responses is that the main reservoirs of extra labor power already are pretty well drained, while taxes are broad based, high, and comparatively efficient. Whereas Norway and, to a lesser extent, Finland still have some room for the expansion of female labor-force participation and for higher taxes, the participation rates of those aged 20 to 54 in Denmark and Sweden have already climbed well above 80 percent, and taxes are substantially higher than in Finland and Norway. There are many proponents of changes in the tax system, but none of the political parties in these two countries believe that the aggregate tax burden can be raised. Yet, given traditions of close cooperation and mutual trust between unions and employers from the national level to the shop floor, the Nordic countries may be in comparatively better starting positions when it comes to restructuring jobs to fit the needs of the elderly.

Despite periods of recovery, the Nordic economies came under increasing strain in the 1980s. In Denmark, Sweden, and Norway, the bill from deficit-spending responses to the recessions of the late 1970s and early 1980s is just beginning to present itself. Distribution of the costs is bound to give rise to new conflicts and force a restructuring and retrenchment of public transfer and service programs. Compromises and coalitions that underlie the present pension systems may crumble, strife may erupt, and realignments may take place. The coalition, spanning both the collar line and the public–private divide, was always a precarious one. Though so far only Denmark is marked by pervasive dualism in pension provisions, the rest of Scandinavia is not entirely immune to British-style scenarios. Wage and salary earners in the better half of the labor market may yet align themselves with private business against adequate policies for low-income earners and the poor. This dualism can be avoided only so long as the labor movement can continue to devise policies that harmonize the different interests of the dependently employed, and can work out stable accords with private business and the bourgeois parties.

Notes

1. OECD, *Reforming Public Pensions* (Paris: OECD, 1988).

2. The words *Scandinavian* and *Nordic* are used interchangeably to refer to the four big countries in the Nordic Council: Denmark, Norway, Sweden, and Finland.

3. S. Marklund, *Paradise Lost? The Nordic Welfare States in the Recession, 1975–1985* (Lund: Arkiv, 1988); L. Mjset, ed., *Norden: Dagen Derp* (Oslo: Universitetsforlaget, 1986).

4. W. Korpi, *The Democratic Class Struggle* (London: Routledge & Kegan Paul, 1983); Gösta Esping-Andersen, *Politics against Markets* (Princeton: Princeton University Press, 1985).

5. Gösta Esping-Andersen and W. Korpi, "From Poor Relief to Institutional Welfare State: The Development of Scandinavian Social Policy," in *The Scandinavian Model*, ed. E. Erikson et al. (Armonk, N.Y.: M. E. Sharpe, 1987).

6. It may be measured as a share in the differentiated incomes of present and future cohorts of pensioners or as a share in present aggregate expenditure on pensions. Figures to support the first are not yet available, but data from the Luxembourg Income Study may eventually enable us to draw a comparative picture along these lines. One of the problems in constructing the aggregate measure is that the packages comprise both pay-as-you-go and funded schemes. What is more, a number of schemes are themselves a mix between these two forms of financing. One simple way to contain current and prospective elements in a single table is to list the costs of fully and partly funded systems as the difference between contributions and payments in a given year and thus give a picture of the distribution of present resources spent on pensions for current and future pensioners. This can be done, though comparable figures were not available to me. Ideally, however, we should compare both the value of pension credits accrued in each type of scheme over a year and the relative share of the different plans in present pension payments. While the former measurement is almost impossible to construct, the latter method is manageable.

7. G. Perrin, "Supplementary Pension Schemes in the Nordic Countries," *International Social Security Review* 25, no. 4 (1972): 357–75; OECD, *Reforming Public Pensions*, 85–101.

8. ATP is the standard abbreviation for the second-tier pension scheme in Sweden; it is also used in Denmark.

9. Fritz von Nordheim Nielsen, "Occupational Pensions in Northern Europe," Working Paper No. 1, Department of Sociology, University of Copenhagen, 1988, 29–31.

10. Fritz von Nordheim Nielsen, "Markeder og Statslige Politikker i Erhvervs-pensionernes vkst," Working Paper No. 4, Department of Sociology, University of Copenhagen, 1988, 12–17; Leslie Hannah, *Inventing Retirement* (Cambridge: Cambridge University Press, 1986), 21–29, 98–103.

11. Alicia Munnell, *The Economics of Private Pensions* (Washington, D.C.: Brookings Institution, 1982); Hannah, *Inventing Retirement*.

12. J. Visser, "The Position of Central Confederations in the National Union Movement," Working Paper No. 102, European University Institute, Florence, May 1984.

13. Fritz von Nordheim Nielsen, "Erhvervspension som Erstatning for Overenskomst-politik?" Working Paper No. 9, Department of Sociology, University of Copenhagen, 1987, 43–47.

14. SAP is the standard abbreviation for the Swedish Social Democratic Workers' party.

15. ATP was actually planned as a pay-as-you go scheme. The fund buildup resulted only from the collection of excess pension contributions in the twenty-year period until the scheme matured. And apart from a wish to establish a reserve from which to meet sudden increases in demand, the excess taxation was primarily motivated by a wish to maintain and possibly increase the aggregate level of savings. Otherwise, it was expected that the level would decline as a result of the expansion of public pension coverage. Jonas Pontusson, *Public Pension Funds and the Politics of Capital Formation in Sweden* (Stockholm: Arbetslivscentrum, 1984), 8–9.

16. ATP revenues were split into three separate funds managed by autonomous boards. The boards were to maximize the return on investments within the constraints of fiduciary responsibility, like ordinary insurance companies. But unlike these, they were barred from direct investments in the private sector. Primarily, they were to invest in bonds issued to the general public so that the lending decisions of fund boards could be isolated from the investment decisions of those who borrowed capital from the pension funds.

17. LO is the standard abbreviation for the national peak association of manual workers unions in Scandinavia.

18. Bjorn Molin, *Tjnstepensionsfrgan* (Goteborg: Scandinavian University Books, 1965), 113.

19. Ibid., 115.

20. Ibid., 135.

21. Jorgen Rasmussen, *Arbejderbevgelse og Penionssystem i Sverige, 1913–1983* (Copenhagen: University of Copenhagen, 1985), 71–73.

22. Michael O'Higgins, "Public/Private Interaction and Pension Provision," in *Public/Private Interplay in Social Protection*, ed. Martin Rein and Lee Rainwater (Armonk, N.Y.: M. E. Sharpe, 1986), 119, 123, 141.

23. The ITP scheme is administered by the SPP Mutual Insurance company,

which was established in cooperation with white-collar unions and the employers' association.

24. From the employers' point of view, the generalization of ITP coverage implied that ITP lost its fringe-benefit character within the white-collar group. An important distinction between employees and workers was retained, however, the ability of private-sector employers to compete with the public sector for qualified labor was improved, and the employers had the opportunity to borrow from pension contributions.

25. Molin, *Tjnstepensionsfrgan*, 120ff; Esping-Andersen, *Politics against Markets*, 162.

26. LO's success in negotiating an occupational plan has not, however, led to the disappearance of pension inequalities. In fact, in recent years a definite pattern of income differences between blue- and white-collar pensioners has reemerged, which must be attributed to the distinctions in occupational coverage. See Ann-Charlotte Stahlberg, *Public and Negotiated Pension Wealth in Sweden and Their Distributions* (Stockholm: Swedish Institute for Social Research, 1985; reprint, 1986), 18–31.

27. High degrees of unionization and the centralized system of industrial realizations facilitated the expansion and produced a very orderly system of occupational provisions dominated by four big national schemes: SKP (state employees), KKP (municipal and regional employees), ITP (private sector white-collar employees), and STP (private-sector workers).

28. The following paragraphs on Finland are based on Olli Kangas, *Politik och Ekonomi i Pensionsfrskringen*, 20–26, 31–40; idem, *Agrarintressen och lntagarintressen i pensionspolitiken* (Helsinki: Helsinki School of Economics, 1988); M. Alestalo and H. Uusitalo, "Finland," in *Growth to Limits: The Western European Welfare States since World War II*, vol. 1, *Sweden, Norway, Finland, Denmark*, ed. P. Flora (Berlin and New York: de Gruyter, 1986), 199–292. Personal communication from Kari Salminen and Olli Kangas of April 1989.

29. In 1960 the posttax maximum average production worker replacement rate was only 29 percent.

30. The following paragraphs on the establishment of statutory second-tier pensions in Norway are based on A. Seip, *Om velferdsstatens fremvekst* (Oslo: Universitetsforlaget, 1981), 57–60; Aksel Hatland, *Folketrygdens framtid* (Oslo: Universitetsforlaget, 1984), 46–48; S. Kuhnle and L. Solheim, *Velferdsstaten: Vekst og omstilling* (Kolbotn: Tano, 1986), 49–52; Stein Kuhnle, "Norway," in *Growth to Limits: The Western European Welfare State since World War II*, ed. Peter Flora (Berlin and New York: de Gruyter, 1986, 1987), 1:117–96, 4:65–122; K. Hagen and A. W. Pedersen, "Det Norske Pensionssystemet: En oversikt over de offentlige og private pensionsordninger" (Paper prepared for the seminar "Pensionssystem og pensionspolitikkens dilemmaer i Norden," Department of Sociology, University of Copenhagen, January 22–23, 1987); J. M. Hippe and A. W. Pedersen, *For lang og tro tjeneste? Pensioner i Arbeidsmarkedet*, FAFO report No. 84 (Oslo: FAFO, 1988), 33–36, 63–74; personal communication with Einar Verbye of April 21, 1988; lecture by Einar Skaug, former top official in the Department of Social Policy, to the 1989 Norwegian Social Policy Seminar, Folket Hus, Oslo, December 6, 1989.

31. The incident is known as the King's Bay Crisis.

32. Except for the Liberal party, none of the bourgeois parties wanted earnings-

related public pensions. The Agrarian party preferred flat-rate schemes and the Conservatives saw occupational and individual annuity pensions as the natural complements to the basic public pension.

33. DNA is the standard abbreviation for the Norwegian (social democratic) Workers' party.

34. In 1966 the bourgeois coalition government simply presented the proposal inherited from its labor predecessor, which had been developed by the Department of Social Security.

35. J. E. Kolberg, *Farvel til velferdsstaten?* (Oslo: J. W. Cappelen, 1983), 78–88.

36. While they recognized that a certain fund buildup might be necessary to counteract a possible decline in private savings rates, they believed firmly in the pay-as-you-go principle of financing. Furthermore, unlike the visionaries in the Swedish labor movement, they were not fascinated by the capital formation and investment-steering potential of a huge pension fund under public control. In retrospect, however, they probably underestimated the potential of such a fund in more conventional strategies of macroeconomic stabilization through the raising of savings rates, etc.

37. The following paragraphs on the establishment of statutory second-tier pensions in Denmark are based on G. R. Nelson, *ATP's Historie 1964–83 i Hovedtrk* (Hillerd, Denmark: ATP, 1984), 20–149; C. Vester Jensen, *Det Tvedelte Pensionssystem*, Report No. 1 (Roskilde, Denmark: Roskilde University Centre, Institut for Samfundskonomi og Planlgning, 1984), 126–53, 155–63; Nielsen, "Erhvervspension som Erstatning for Overenskomst-politik?" 57–62; J. Henriksen, P. Kampmann, and J. Rasmussen, *Fordelingen af Private Pensioner i Danmark* (Copenhagen: Department of Sociology, University of Copenhagen, 1987), 162–67; idem, "Danmark," draft chapter for *Pensionssystemer og Pensionspolitiske Dilemmaer i Norden*, ed. J. Henriksen et al. (Lund: Arkiv, forthcoming), 8–17.

38. SD (Socialdemokratiet) is the standard abbreviation for the Danish Social Democratic party.

39. J. Henriksen, P. Kampmann, and J. Rasmussen, *Fordelingen af Private Pensioner* (Copenhagen: Forlaget Sociologi, 1988).

40. When the 1968 commission to investigate the capital market finally reported its evaluation of the system of ATP pension-fund management in 1978, the bourgeois parties did not seize this opportunity to alter the legal–institutional framework of the funds. The government merely passed the commission's proposals for minor revisions on to parliament. That they refrained testifies to the fact that the exiting rules effectively prevented the politicalization of investment issues and that the framework largely functioned to the satisfaction of the financial sector. Pontusson, *Public Pension Funds and the Politics of Capital Formation in Sweden*, 19.

41. T. E. Eriksen, "Some Reflections on the Role of the National Supplementary Pension Scheme in the Swedish Pensions System," *International Social Security Review* 34, no. 4 (1981): 410–26.

42. Deane Sainsbury, "Welfare State Variations, Women, and Equality: On Varieties of the Welfare State and Their Implications for Women" (Paper presented at ECRP Workshop "Equality Principles and Gender Politics," Paris, April 1989).

43. K. Hort, "Vlfrdsstat och marknadsekonomi," in *Zenit Vintern, 1986/87*, no. 94 (Lund, Sweden: Arkiv), 25–35.

44. Mjset, *Norden: Dagen Derp*.
45. Kangas, *Politik och Ekonomi i Pensionsfrskringen*, 53–56.
46. Ibid., 43.
47. Lecture by Einar Skaug, Dec. 6, 1989.
48. The group, which consisted primarily of former full-time homemakers who had survived their husbands, had to subsist on pension incomes that barely kept them out of poverty.
49. Norges Offentlige Utredninger, 1978, 12, *Pensjonsutredningen* (Oslo: Universitetsforlaget, 1978).
50. J. E. Kolberg, *Farvel til velferdsstaten?* (Oslo: J. W. Cappelen, 1983), 78–95.
51. The contribution from general revenues had risen only from 15 to 20 percent of overall cost from 1975 to 1980. Considering that FT also encompassed a general health insurance and a universal citizens' pension, the contribution from general revenues was in reality very moderate by international standards. Nevertheless, prospects were that the contribution from general revenues would have to be doubled over the next decade unless benefits were cut or member and payroll taxes raised. See Kolberg, *Farvel til velferdsstaten?* 78–79, 187.
52. Norges Offentlige Utredninger 1984, 10, *Trydgefiansiering* (Oslo: Universitetsforlaget, 1978).
53. J. M. Hippe and A. W. Pedersen, *Velferd til Salgs*, FAFO report No. 65 (Oslo: FAFO, 1986); J. M. Hippe and A. W. Pedersen, "Nr markedet slr tilbake. Arbeidsmar-kedspensjon og velferdsstat i Norge," in *Offentlig eller privat?* ed. P. Bogen and M. Langeland, FAFO report No. 78 (Oslo: FAFO, 1988), 345–75; Hippe and Pedersen, *For lang og tro tjeneste?*
54. "LO-kongressen nsket nye pensjonsreformer," *Trygghet*, no. 4 (1989): 1.
55. Hippe and Pedersen, *For lang og tro tjeneste?*
56. Ibid.
57. Paradoxically, it seemed that some employers might share their concern about general schemes. In a situation with few general collective agreements about occupational pensions, the private insurance industry had exploited individual employer's ignorance about the complexities of pension schemes and their fears about losing in the competition for scarce, high-quality labor and had managed to saddle them with pension schemes that are far too costly or ill suited to the needs of their particular mix of employees. See lecture by the chief pension consultant of the Norwegian employers' association to the 1989 Norwegian Social Policy Seminar, Folkets Hus, Oslo, December 7, 1989.
58. In increases in savings, capital formation, and long-term investments, and the resulting general macroeconomic stabilization effects.
59. Arbejderbevgelsens Erhvervsrd, *Private Pensioner* (Copenhagen, 1978).
60. Bent Rold-Andersen, "Hvordan vil det offentlige pensionssystem udvikle sig fremover," *Konomi og Politik* 55, no. 4 (1982): 366–77.
61. See, for example, Forsikringsoplysningen, *Private pensioner: Ogs i fremtiden* (Copenhagen: Forsikringsoplysningen, 1982).
62. See, for example, Pensionskasserdet, *Pensioner og Beskatning* (Copenhagen: Pensionskasserdet, 1982).
63. Bitter rivalries between the seven parties that compete for the bourgeois vote

had for long prevented them from turning their collective majority into government power. Bourgeois politicians were planning a five-party coalition government. Still, it would have to rely on support from the notoriously unpredictable Progress party. Hence the Social Democrats were confident that, if it could be formed at all, the alternative government would soon come apart.

64. The metalworkers union had voiced grave doubts about the wisdom and realism of the thirty-five-hour-week demand and some interest in occupational pensions for their members, though it was more concerned with the prospect of controlling a major pension fund. As the manual union with the best bargaining position in the labor market, it was very likely to obtain occupational pensions if it decided to include them in its demands. With its right-wing social democratic leanings, its commitment to cooperation with employers, and its belief in the blessings of rapid technological change, it presented an obvious target for a government campaign about selective occupational pensions.

65. For examples of left-wing reactions to the scheme, see J. Henriksen, P. Kampmann, and J. Rasmussen, "Et Solidarisk Privillegiesystem?" *Information* 7, no. 2 (1986); Socialarbejdernes Fllesudvalg, *Pension: Privat eller Solidaritet* (Copenhagen, 1985); Socialistiske konomer, "Pensionsreform: Strre lighed? get opsparing? Tikkende bombe?" *Konomisk Bulletin*, no. 8 (December 1985).

66. LO's Pensionsreformudvalg, *Forslag til en samlet pensionsreform* (Copenhagen: Landsorganisationen i Danmark, Okt, 1985).

67. Leaders of the Danish LO unions had no hesitation about the idea of exclusive union control of the ensuing megafund because some of the largest existing occupational schemes were managed and controlled entirely by the unions that had negotiated them for their members. A comparative international survey of union influence on occupational pension funds would have taught them to be more careful. The present situation is more of a coincidence than a rule in Denmark. Prior to the expansion of the public sector and the change from permanent to contractual employment, a few large multiemployer schemes under dual management dominated the field. Schemes under exclusive union management are found solely in the private sector and have resulted only because the public sector neglected its interests as employer.

68. Since the onset of the recession in the mid 1970s, the SD and LO had tried in vain to trade a general long-term agreement about wage restraint for a moderate scheme of collective profit sharing or wage-earner funds. This was to be a general mandatory scheme where profit shares would be collected in funds under union control and reinvested in order to preserve and increase employment and secure a gradual democratization of property relations. Employers had flatly refused to accept a general scheme, and the main bourgeois parties would not hear of anything legislated or mandatory.

69. Collective savings on that scale invariably touches on a fundamental power question in bourgeois society, since capital control and capital power are the prerogative of the bourgeoisie. With compulsory occupational pensions as a collective savings device, within a decade wage earners can turn their numerical power into a major source of capital power that could dwarf any congregation of corporate power in its own field. Thus occupational pensions may invoke the pipedream of labor movements and the nightmare of employers and bourgeois parties.

70. According to the "orthodoxy" to which they and the labor movement at large

hitherto had subscribed, funded, selective, and earnings-related pension designs were to be avoided. Such designs would only contribute to present patterns of inequality in old age. Their proclaimed beneficial effect on the economy was entirely fictitious. To the extent they contributed to the raising of savings rates, it was only a temporary phenomenon. When schemes matured, they would give rise to strong trends of dissavings and inflation, and thus disrupt the economy and provide intense intergenerational struggles about the distribution of the social product. In the interest not just of distributional justice and adequacy but also of economic flexibility and generational harmony, pensions ought to be universal with income-tested supplements and funded on a pay-as-you-go basis.

71. Thus avoiding a frontal attack on the LO proposal.

72. Often disdainfully referred to as the "generation of '68," that is, the generation most intimately associated with the student and youth rebellion.

73. That is, consumption for retired parents can be paid only out of present production, which means that their children would have a judicial owners' claim to future production.

74. In turn they even managed to convince the majority of Danish welfare economists that whatever the merits of the proposal in relation to old-age provision, the general economic predicament of Denmark made it necessary in order to boost the savings rates, even if only in the middle–long term, and to increase long-term investment.

75. Since the overwhelming majority of its members had occupational coverage of good quality, the tacit support of FTF was particularly crucial to the fate of LO's proposal. The committee that developed the LO proposal had briefed the FTF when the proposal was still on the drawing board and had received an obliging response. When the plan was presented to the public, however, the FTF reacted with irritation. This expression of interunion rivalry and demonstration of total lack of coordination was particularly unlucky because of the issue at stake. While a simple concern about preservation of wage and fringe-benefit differentials should not be discounted, part of the friction stemmed from general developments in the labor market. The LO had always played a hegemonic role among wage-earners' organizations. Its sheer size had secured that what LO did and thought influenced relations for all other groups of wage earners in the labor market. Yet, class structural developments had boosted the membership of the other peak organizations, and they were getting tired of playing second fiddle. By demanding a single scheme for all wage earners without coverage, the LO was also infringing on the turf of the FTF, which felt entirely able to handle the pension interests of its own members and certainly did not want to see them included in a megascheme dominated by LO unions.

76. The LO had somewhat naively used the present exclusive control of public-sector unions over their pension funds as a model. The argument that pension funds represented the savings of wage earners, over which they should not have to share influence with employers, was only being developed. The Liberals immediately countered references to the situation of public-sector unions, however, with demands that they also be put under dual management as part of a reform of the legal framework of pension funds. And it did not stop at demands for employer influence. Like the British Thacherites, the Liberals envision individual control over individual shares of pension savings as the ideal.

77. In this way, the search for solutions to the dilemma of how to make it pay—

or how to make entry into an occupational scheme meaningful for the large group of low-paid unskilled workers—had helped revive the political currency of the traditional conservative view that social security provisions removed the incentive for people to provide for themselves, thus creating collective irresponsibility. This is the infamous Feldstein argument.

8/Aging under State Socialism: The Case of Poland

Ewa Morawska

To the dismay of social scientists trying to predict the course of human affairs, history seems never to tire of surprises—this time, in Eastern Europe. As the world moves into the last decade of the twentieth century, 1989 may prove to have been a watershed in the dismantling of the political–economic order in that region known as state socialism. Or perhaps not, should current developments be frozen or even reversed (*vide* China). For now, however, the Soviet, Hungarian, and Polish *perestroikas*, which until recently appeared no more than another round of cosmetic correctives issued from above, are reaching ever deeper and activating increasingly radical transformations.

In Poland in particular, the six months following the relegalization of Solidarity in April 1989 and the agreement by the Communist party to open up the political process to other groups witnessed accelerated developments beyond the wildest expectations of Poles and Western observers alike. Candidates backed by Solidarity and the Catholic church won a spectacular victory in semifree elections to parliament in June, and a few months later, the first non-Communist-led government since the 1940s was formed, with half the posts filled by Solidarity members or open sympathizers. Amid an economic crisis of unprecedented scale and urgency, the task of bringing Poland "back to normalcy" (the current Polish shorthand phrase for overhauling the country's inoperative political and economic structures) will be formidable. Nevertheless, the vast entrenched state apparatus along with its policies and procedures, the central planning and other administrative offices, including social-welfare

---

EDITORS' NOTE: To make our coverage of old-age policy as comprehensive as possible, we here include a study of aging in an Eastern bloc country. This chapter was written in fall 1989 and therefore does not take into account the most recent events in Poland.

programs, the economic monopolies in production and distribution, and tens of thousands of Communist *nomenclatura* at middle and lower management levels are still in place, even though threatened by a genuinely new political configuration. And these structures and policies, formed in the course of the past four decades, together with dramatically deteriorating economic conditions, primarily determine the position of Poland's elderly.

The English-language literature on the functioning of welfare systems in state socialist societies has been scarce and fragmentary, and even scantier on the situation of the aged. Most of it has been limited to sketches of legal and institutional frameworks and reports on current provisions, without linking these structures and policies to economic circumstances and political configurations within and around particular countries as they changed over the years.[1] In three chronological sections, and in the context of broader economic and sociopolitical conditions shaping the Polish welfare system, domestic and international, this chapter presents the origins and evolution of Poland's old-age provisions and, data permitting, the life situations of the elderly through the 1980s. Having demonstrated the multiple malaises that afflict Poland's socialist welfare forty years after its introduction, in conclusion I look at the grave dilemmas facing the present reformers.

The Origins

Having regained sovereignty in 1918 after almost two hundred years of foreign domination by Russia, Germany, and Austria, for the next twenty years Poland was ruled by a series of fiercely nationalist but politically stalemated governments, and despite some industrial development, the country remained predominantly agrarian, split by deep-seated social divisions. On the eve of World War II, nearly two-thirds of the population still resided in the countryside; most were either landless and working for subsistence wages or owners of small, poor holdings. In the cities, the ratio of incomes was about 200:1. The average income of manual urban workers was five times lower than that of nonmanual workers, and apart from a small elite stratum of skilled labor concentrated in a few industrial centers, most lived in economic insecurity.[2]

Traditional church and private charities for the poor and the destitute were supplemented by social benefits and services for (urban) working people and their families by two self-governing institutions organized and supervised by the state (Ministry of Work and Social Welfare): the Bureau of Social Security, which administered unemployment benefits, old-age, disability, and survivor pensions (for salaried employees since 1927, and for wage earners since 1933); and Insurance Health Centers that provided medical services (there were fewer than three hundred such centers at the end of the 1930s, all of them in the cities). All state programs were financed by contributions from employers and employees. Old-age pensions were wage linked, and nonmanual workers received about six times more than manual ones. Civil employees and the military had a separate pension program funded by the state treasury. At the outbreak of World War II, the overall proportion of the adult Polish population participating in all these benefits and service programs combined was less than 15 percent.[3]

As a result of the Yalta and Potsdam agreements between the USSR and the Western Allies, in 1945 Poland and the rest of Eastern Europe were placed under Soviet domination. The Soviet model was used to organize the new state administration. Assisted by Soviet political and military advisers, a small cadre of the Polish Communist party took control of the bureaucracy to enforce a program of economic and social policies based on Marxist–Leninist prescriptions for transforming an economically backward and socially unjust society into a developed and just socialist one.

According to these prescriptions, political determination of economic and social priorities in the newly established state was to, and did, occur at the top of the power hierarchy in the Polish United Workers' party (PUWP) central committee. In what Marxist–Leninists call *democratic centralism,* decisions were transmitted down, to the Commission of Economic Planning, the parliament, to the government and its regional agencies, the state (party)-controlled labor unions and other central organizations, to the provincial and municipal party committees, and lower yet to the party cells and management collectives in individual factories, service establishments, and social institutions. This massive etatization, accomplished, in Wlodzimierz Brus's words, "in a concentrated form, almost at a single stroke"[4] prompted rapid growth in the bureaucracy of planners, managers, and controllers. Starting in 1945 with a force of twenty thousand, by Stalin's death (1953) the political rulers, including the ubiquitous security forces, party members in supervisory positions, and others in the *nomenclatura* numbered close to half a million people.

After the nationalization (or *etatization,* rather) of production and distribution in 1945 as the first step toward the socialist transformation of society, the party-state adopted accelerated industrialization as its overriding political priority. This program, instituted in the first two *trzy-* and *pieciolatki* (three- and five-year central economic plans), required mass mobilization of labor, to be drawn largely from the overpopulated countryside by relocating millions of people to the cities and into the factories. This mass labor demand, combined with the new regime's need for political legitimation and with ideological considerations requiring the socialist state to eliminate social inequalities, led to the legislated creation (from 1945 to 1949–1950) of a broad welfare system in which the state assumed social responsibilities in a large number of areas.

In the dominant, socialized sector of the economy, these provisions encompassed—in addition to guaranteed employment at a minimum wage with paid holiday—social security programs (based on the contributions of state-owned enterprises, wage-linked retirement, survivor, and disability pensions, sickness insurance, and maternity benefits), free medical service and child-care centers, and material and institutional assistance to the (justifiably) needy. For all citizens, regardless of employment, the state also guaranteed free public education (compulsory first for eight, then for ten years), subsidized low-rent urban housing, and offered basic consumer (food) items at cheap and stable prices. All these measures were hailed by the regime's ideologues as a dem-onstration of the new party-state's munificence: "It was suggested . . . that not only was the new system superior to the old one, but also that it was unneces-sary to organize [social] interest groups from 'below,' since everything was being taken care of from 'above.' Moreover, it was made clear that [socialist welfare benefits and services] were not based on individual or citizen's rights, but, rather, were the 'gift' of the state." [5]

In this Stalinist phase of revolutionary transformation (1945 to the mid 1950s), the socialist state gave priority to its function as employer over that as provider of social services. In central and local administrative decisions concerning economic planning and the allocation of funds, as well as in the party-state's propaganda aimed at sustained mobilization of the workforce, welfare programs were subordinate to production goals, and the "needs of the country" (i.e., rapid industrialization and urbanization) took precedence over the consumption needs of citizens.

Enforcement of these economic priorities was facilitated by society's weak bargaining position in a general climate of intense political intimidation that enfeebled major social groups, preventing them from exerting pressure on the state bureaucracy to reassert their own or broader social needs. Prewar political parties were disbanded or, like the Polish Socialist party, absorbed into the PUWP. In the old middle class, prewar owners of the means of pro-duction were dispossessed, and members of the intelligentsia were treated as ideologically suspect and often politically persecuted unless they joined the party-state apparatus, which only a small minority did. The industrial worker, the presumptive social base of the new socialist state, was only in the making, its mass composed of peasants newly arrived in the cities, whose accustomed standard of living and material expectations were modest, and whose collective political aspirations were as yet undeveloped. In the rural areas, the peasants, even those forced into agricultural collectives, were seen as "reactionary," as actual or potential *kulaks* to be resocialized into the new socialist soci-ety. (Poland diverged from the standard Soviet model in that even during the Stalinist period a majority of small farmers remained on their land.)

The only group capable of collectively securing its needs against those of "the country" (or, more accurately, identifying one with the other and using its power to translate this equation into practical profits) were the members of the higher echelons of the state *apparat:* officials of the central administration and military and public security forces. Under the Soviet-modeled policy of *uravnilovka* (forced social equalization), the incomes of nonmanual and manual workers employed in state enterprises differed by less than 10 percent in 1950, but the salaries of government and security officers exceeded those of the workers eightfold, and they enjoyed access to special shops with merchandise unavailable to the public, restricted health and vacation resorts, and the like.[6]

Except for general statistical data published by the state censuses and summary reports of the Bureau of Social Security (ZUS), not much is known about the actual living conditions of people beyond "productive age" (7 percent of a population of 25 million in 1950) in this first phase of the socialist welfare state in Poland. Given pervasive postwar austerity, further aggravated by the party-state's policies of accelerated industrialization and forced "social equalization," the elderly's overall economic situation seems not to have been much worse than that of the rest of the population. Most existed on meager incomes and in substandard living conditions.

Legislated in 1946, old-age and survivor pensions (together with sick leave and maternity benefits) accounted in 1950 for 13 percent of state expenditures (3 percent of GNP), and covered 47 percent of the population— only those employed in state-owned enterprises. In addition to low-rent urban housing and low-priced food staples subsidized by the state and equally available to the gainfully employed population, retirees from the socialized economic sector and their families were also entitled to free medical care, senior citizen rates in public transportation, and, upon request and subject to a means test, to services such as nursing homes, social workers' assistance, and material help. All these welfare provisions excluded the self-employed (petty artisans and repairmen, and institutionally unaffiliated artists—a numerically insignificant group, which did, however, profit from state-subsidized urban housing and basic food items) and the whole class of peasants living from their own land.[7] As instituted in 1949–1950 after initial modifications, the old-age and survivor pensions program in the socialized sector of the economy was, and has remained, what the party-state ideologues and officials have called "noncontributory," to emphasize the contrast with Poland's prewar social security and with the Western capitalist system. In fact, it has been based on payments made by individual enterprises from their gross wage funds (15 percent in 1950) directly to the central Bureau of Social Security, but never marked as deductions on employees' paychecks. To qualify, a worker has to have been employed for a prescribed length of time: twenty years for women (retirement age of 60) and twenty-five years for men (65). This measure was meant to keep active the large workforce needed for the labor-intensive program of economic development, and the party-state propaganda in the period explicitly discouraged the elderly from retiring at the officially permitted age by frequent appeals to their sense of socialist responsibility for the development of the country. In fact, in the 1950s, nearly 50 percent of the total population of "postproductive age" continued working (in the countryside, this proportion was 75 percent).

The social security act defined the minimum old-age pension as 80 percent of the minimum wage and linked retirement income to earnings. Pensions were to be calculated from average monthly earnings during the last twelve months of employment or the best two years of the last twelve years; earnings below the amount of the average national wage in the socialized sector were replaced at 80 percent, plus 25 percent of the remainder over this sum.[8]

Although meager, social security benefits and free medical care constituted guaranteed entitlements available to all who qualified and, given low and stable consumer prices, offered the insured elderly a modicum of economic and psychological security. The second tier of old-age public welfare, *opieka spoleczna* (social assistance), was not included among the entitlements. It was administered as charity-like handouts by local administrators, who closely scrutinized the candidates' social provenance and economic means, looking for relatives who might be able to support the claimants. In contrast to social security programs, which constituted a permanent element of the state budget, social assistance was funded with surpluses available from other expenditures. As a result, few new nursing, retirement, or old-age day-care facilities were built, leaving only what was left undestroyed by the 1939–1945 war. Equally insufficient was the staffing of these services, since labor (mostly female in this case) was first and foremost directed into industrial production, and the Catholic church, openly persecuted during the Stalinist period as a "class enemy," was not permitted to continue its prewar social charity services (nursing nuns and volunteer social workers were removed from the hospitals, old-age homes, and Red Cross centers).[9] In this situation, assistance to the elderly was delivered primarily within families, and this form of primary old-age care was actually promoted in the party-state media as a "natural obligation." [10]

"Mature Socialism": The 1960s and 1970s

The basic structure of the welfare system instituted in the first phase of state socialism in Poland remained in place in the post-Stalinist period and through the 1970s. But shifts in international and domestic political configurations, changes in economic conditions, and internal societal transformations made for important modifications of the state's social policies. Among the major factors was the loosening in the second half of the 1950s of direct Soviet intervention in the domestic matters of member countries of the bloc, including Poland, permitting somewhat more independent economic and social policies as "national ways to socialism." This in turn opened the way to more political maneuvering inside the Polish party-state *apparat,* which was now firmly established in power and had grown increasingly complex as various central and regional administrative and managerial groupings took shape.

With the initial phase of accelerated industrialization accomplished, by the 1960s the absolute priority of production goals was less binding. Modernization, economic efficiency, and good management became part of the official vocabulary in pronouncements concerning the country's further development. Increased trade with the West, particularly multimillion-dollar credits contracted by the state during the 1970s for modernization, allowed the state to direct more funds to domestic consumer and social needs. The Polish economy was tied to the international one, while the general standard of living and material aspirations of the population rose.

Revamped by mass urbanization and industrialization and the wide avenues for social mobility provided by free education and the expansion of factory and white-collar jobs in the socialized sector of the economy, Polish society became increasingly internally stratified. Stablilization of economic growth and the resulting slowing of social mobility hardened the vertical structure of society; by the mid 1970s, the average "hereditary" component of the major strata (the proportion of intergenerational retention of socioeconomic positions) was 75 percent. By the 1960s, income differentials between occupational strata reached 10:1, and more than double that ratio (22:1) in the 1970s.[11] New social groups were acquiring firm boundaries and a sense of collective interests and identity. In particular, a large working class, created, as it were, by a socialist state that presumed to rule in the name of the proletariat while depriving workers of political influence, began to express its discontent and to assert its rights through repeated strikes and street demonstrations. In 1956, workers protested en masse against totalitarian Stalinist rule; in 1970 and 1976, their protest reversed the party-state's announcements of substantial across-the-board price increases. Other social groups actively joined these actions (1956) or applauded them from the sidelines (1970, 1976). Continued authoritarian control of political and cultural life by the party-state evoked repeated public opposition from the intelligentsia, supported by the Catholic church (1964, 1966, 1968, 1972); this opposition took permanent organizational form following brutal repressions launched against the workers involved in the 1976 protests (KOR—Workers' Defense Committee; ROP-CIO—Movement for the Defense of Human and Civil Rights; TKN—Society for Educational Courses). Depending on the economic situation and state policies concerning wages, supply of goods, and prices, and on the tightening or loosening of repressive measures of political control, civil society, increasingly less intimidated by the regime, accorded the party-state varying degrees of legitimacy, but with each subsequent outbreak of unrest it became more tenuous.[12]

The state's welfare policies were influenced from within the party-state apparatus by the interests of various administrative and managerial groupings, and from without by the Polish economy's growing dependence on Western credits and the protests of civil society, particularly among the working class.

By 1975, the proportion of the population of retirement age had expanded to 12 percent (of a total of 32.5 million), an increase of 135 percent since 1950 (from 1.7 million to over 4 million). The number of those employed in the socialized sector covered by social security increased by 65 percent, while that of those receiving old-age and survivor pensions more than doubled, from about 1 million in the 1950s to 2.2 million by the mid 1970s. This increase in the elderly population entitled to benefits required considerable expansion of the social security fund; between the 1950s and the 1970s, contributions from state-owned firms increased from 15 to 25 percent of the enterprises' gross wage fund.[13] During the same period, employees in industrial branches considered of special importance to the state economy (coal mining, iron and steel, railroad transportation)—hotbeds, it should be noted, of repeated "worker disturbances"—were granted special retirement and pension programs with the backing of local party officials and managers whose position within the *apparat* depended on the fulfillment of economic plans and the quiescence of the labor force. *Dodatki preferencyjne* (preferential supplements) to pensions were also given to employees on two important ideological fronts—journalism and education—and to those awarded high-level decorations for service to the state. As before, civil servants, the military, and members of the security forces had a special retirement program and fringe benefits in shopping, housing, allocation of cars, and vacation resorts.[14]

As more budgetary leeway became available after completion of the primary phase of industrialization, especially after Western credits started flowing to Poland in the 1970s, social security was incrementally extended to groups employed in the private sector. Official pronouncements accompanying these entitlements described them as a sign of the party-state's protective benevolence toward all citizens of the now-mature socialist society. The unspoken purpose was to assert the regime's shaky legitimacy among groups thus far excluded from its social patronage. In 1965, the owners and employees of small handicraft and service establishments (about 3 percent of the labor force) received separate social security coverage, as did the clergy and self-employed artists (less than 1 percent) in 1972–1974. Finally, private farmers, who made up 38 percent of the population, were granted free medical care in 1972 and old-age retirement and survivor pensions in 1978. They cultivated 86 percent of the land after collective farms were disbanded after 1956, but had remained subject to particularly obstinate bureaucratic harassment by the party-state authorities, who never reconciled themselves ideologically to the existence of private holdings. This official reluctance surfaced in the social security program for this group, which calculated private farmers' pensions on the minimum wage in the socialized sector, not on their actual income; supplements were added for the sale of agricultural produce to state-owned enterprises and for the sale of the farm to the state.

As a result of these extensions, by 1980 99.7 percent of the Polish population was covered by social security programs. Global expenditures on social security (including, in addition to old-age and survivor pensions, which made up about 65 percent of the total, sick and maternity benefits) increased by 353 percent between 1970 and 1980. In 1980, they constituted 19 percent of current state expenditures and 11 percent of GNP (an increase by 6 percent and 8 percent respectively since 1950).[15]

Wage-linked retirement pensions reproduced a growing income disparity in the general population, created by the state's redistributive policies rather than the actual needs of the recipients—as the socialist ideology of the original social security act had proclaimed. Preferential programs for selected branches of employment further accentuated these differences.[16]

In the two decades following Stalin's death, Poland's economic growth was relatively stable. In the second half of the 1970s, however, the cumulative effects of the structural inefficiencies of a centrally planned economy combined with the party-state bureaucracy's massive mismanagement of Western credits and the impact of international stagflation came visibly to affect the economic situation. Although the government's attempts at across-the-board price hikes failed, creeping increases caused the cost of living to grow by 39 percent between 1975 and 1980, shortages of consumer goods became more widespread, and the construction and renovation of houses and public facilities slowed. Unchanged since the introduction of social security in the period of low and stable prices, the method of calculating pensions failed to account for the rise in the cost of living, and current wage increases did not affect benefits granted at an earlier date.

Recurrent reports in the media and in OBOP (National Opinion Research Center) studies, which indicated that the economic situation of the elderly dependent on *stary portfel* (old portfolio benefits) was rapidly deteriorating, were taken up by the PUWP as an issue of "ideological principle and social urgency." As a result, from 1975 to 1977 the old-age and survivor benefits system (in the socialized sector) was modified by increasing both minimum benefits (to 90 percent of the minimum wage) and the base rate for calculating pensions. Computed, as before, as an average of monthly earnings during the last year of employment or the best two of twelve years, pensions were not to replace 100 percent of a wage lower than two-thirds of the national average in 1975, and 55 percent of the remainder exceeding this sum. This reform, however, was unsuccessful either in increasing social security pensions in relation to the steadily growing wages of the population or even in maintaining the existing ratio (51 percent in 1970, which dropped to 46 percent by 1980). Even though old-age pensions in the socialized sector grew an average of 28 percent between 1975 and 1980, this increase continued to lag behind the cost of living (39 percent) in the same period.[17]

Despite the expansion of social security insurance to provide universal coverage, and a manifold increase of state expenditures on old-age benefits, even the minimum program of the socialist welfare state—adequate material protection of the weak—remained unfulfilled. As prices rose and the general economic situation deteriorated, a growing number of the elderly found their material existence increasingly insecure. According to a national study (1980) of urban household budgets, close to half of all elderly households (nearly 75 percent of whom were dependent on social security) subsisted on incomes below or around the so-called social minimum. Particularly disadvantaged were households of elderly widowed women (constituting three-quarters of survivor pensioners), whose pensions averaged 65 percent of the average retirement income. In another study conducted at the same time, 26 percent of the total number of urban elderly reported they held full- or part-time jobs; over two-thirds of these individuals stated that economic necessity was their main reason for working.[18]

More vulnerable yet were the rural elderly, who depended on the social security program for private farmers (nearly 70 percent of them women); their average pension was only 60 percent of that received in the cities. Data on the continuation of employment beyond retirement age reflect the inadequacy of old-age coverage for the rural population. While the overall proportion of the gainfully employed among persons over 60 (women) and 65 (men) decreased from 44 to 28 percent between 1960 and 1980, in the countryside it remained almost unchanged at over 70 percent. (The rural elderly's proclivity to continue working has also been in part a result of their reluctance to sell their farms to the state and, it appears, of peasant culture's traditional condemnation of idleness.)[19]

Even less adequate than old-age benefits was social assistance, which continued to be neglected in the state's welfare fiscal allocations and to be treated as "charity" rather than part of entitlements. In 1980, only 1.5 percent of the country's elderly, less than half of the qualified applicants, were in nursing and retirement centers (three-quarters of these facilities were in prewar buildings in need of restoration). From 1970 to 1980 alone, the number on the waiting list for these centers increased by over 500 percent, while the total of available places grew only by one-fourth. And although the number of social workers increased fivefold in the same period, their ranks were able to cover only half the recorded need, and in rural areas they were scarcely to be found at all.

Those elderly who resided with their children or with other relatives—over 40 percent in 1980—could count more readily on family assistance, although the living conditions of a large number were far from comfortable. According to a study conducted in the late 1970s among the elderly in several cities, nearly half lived in overcrowded apartments, one-fourth slept in the kitchen, and one-third shared a room with another person (other than spouse). The situation of those in separate households (single or in a couple) has been even worse. A national survey of the living conditions of elderly households (including urban and rural areas) conducted at the same time revealed their disadvantage compared to the general population. The absence of bathroom facilities was reported in 45 percent of elderly households studied (71 percent in the countryside), compared to 30 percent for the general population; of gas in 45 percent (75 percent) versus 33 percent; of central heating in 60 percent (76 percent) versus 45 percent; of telephones in 85 percent (96 percent) versus 80 percent. In the cities, nearly half the apartments inhabited by the elderly required renovation, and among the 40 percent who lived on higher floors of multistorey buildings, only 1 percent had access to an elevator.[20]

Cul-de-Sac: The 1980s

The situation of the elderly and of old-age policies in Poland in the 1980s has reflected the ability—or inability—of the party-state to reconcile multiple and contradictory economic and political pressures exerted from within and without its institutional network. I first outline this context and then look at the current benefits and public assistance programs available to the elderly, and their general welfare. In the conclusion of the chapter, I briefly outline the dilemmas facing Poland as it tries to move away from a single-party statism toward democratic pluralism and market economy under a new leadership.

As the 1970s turned into the 1980s, the precipitous decline of Poland's overcentralized and overendebted economy turned into a macrocrisis unparalleled in any of the Soviet-bloc countries in the region. At the beginning of the decade, a "great reform" was announced by the party-state leadership, which aimed to restore the country's faltering economy through decentralizing planning and management; expanding private ownership of small enterprises; and introducing features of a market economy by eliminating inefficient firms, tying wages to productivity, and aligning prices with supply and demand. Nevertheless, although hundreds of new rules and regulations have been issued, creating an immense bureaucratic chaos and making the economy even more inefficient, "reform" has not eliminated the dominant monocentric economic structures and the ubiquitous old-style management.

Instead, the 1980s have witnessed galloping inflation (resulting from partial freeing of prices and spiraling wage raises), which by the summer of 1989 exceeded 300 percent; skyrocketing budget deficits (doubling between 1988 and 1989); persistent shortages of basic consumer goods (made more widespread as state funds are redirected to service Poland's enormous foreign debt—nearly $40 billion); and the increasing pauperization of society.[21] Average household expenditures on food—a sensitive indicator of general material welfare—increased from 34 percent in 1981 to 44 percent in 1988. In that same year, 57 percent of respondents interviewed in a national survey of family budgets reported they had no savings whatsoever.[22] Even more recently, in the spring of 1989, over 60 percent of Polish households polled by the National Opinion Research Center reported their monthly incomes sufficed to meet only basic needs; 33 percent stated that even by drawing on savings they could not afford large household purchases; and 24 percent were found to subsist on the cheapest food and clothing. Public expectations about the near future appeared even bleaker. The same survey revealed that over 60 percent of respondents felt their standard of living would continue to deteriorate, and nearly 75 percent feared the next couple of years would be even worse.[23]

Accompanying the profound economic crisis has been an equally dramatic breakdown of the regime's political legitimacy, including within the party-state *apparat*. The spectacular rise in 1980 of the nationwide Solidarity union (it held the allegiance of nearly 75 percent of the 12.5 million employed in the socialized sector) in protest against the arbitrary and inept rule of the party-state profoundly shook the ruling bureaucracy.[24] The imposition of martial law and the delegalization of Solidarity in 1981 left civil society momentarily subdued, but resentful and restless. A special commission of PUWP charged with inquiring into the causes of the repeated social upheavals that have convulsed Poland during forty years of Communist rule reported one of the main reasons as "the power organs' ignoring popular opinion and discouraging local initiatives for independent action and reform."[25] Soon after martial law was lifted, a host of officially sponsored advisory bodies were set up to represent the interests of different social groups and act toward "national reconciliation" and "socialist pluralism" (these included PRON—the Patriotic Front for National Renewal, *Rada Konsultacyjna*—the Consultative Council, and new state-controlled labor and professional unions). In addition, a revamped National Opinion Research Center, which previously steered away from politically sensitive issues, was commissioned to conduct and publicize regular surveys of public opinion on current economic and social issues; the state-sponsored media, though censored as before and used primarily to present the official standpoint, were nevertheless given increased freedom of expression. Although these institutions never gained wider credibility, they have had a voice in the institutional decision-making process.

The conspicuous downfall of Poland's socialist economy and the crushing of Solidarity had a demoralizing effect on a large number of party-state functionaries: nearly one-third of PUWP members belonged to Solidarity, and about that number left the party following the union's delegalization. The reforms of the system toward "market socialism" attempted by the party-state since 1981–1982 have split its *apparat* into conflicting factions pushing for, or obstructing, particular economic and social policies. Concentrated mostly at the top of its power structure, in the PUWP Central Committee and the government, and encouraged by Gorbachev's *perestroika* in the Soviet Union, advocates of market socialism have been battling with hard-line conservatives ensconced in provincial administrative centers who oppose the reform and accuse its proponents of betraying the true idea of socialism. Criss-crossing these divisions have been the entrenched interests of the central planners and managers of powerful industrial monopolies, posed against those of smaller and more dispersed industries, and, at the grass-roots level, party cells in the local enterprises confronted daily with the severe discontent of the workers.[26]

Aside from the party-state bureaucracy, the most direct influence on social-policy decisions during the 1980s has been exerted by the restless working class, particularly its most self-confident component in the largest industrial centers, who have repeatedly gone on strike or taken to the streets in protest against deteriorating living conditions, authoritarian treatment by managers, and the lack of independent unions. Until its inclusion into the institutional-political process as a result of developments in the spring–summer of 1989, an indirect outside impact on state social policies had also been exerted by the so-called *Polska rownolegla* (Parallel Poland), consisting of the powerful Polish Roman Catholic church, the unofficial central council and locals of the banned Solidarity union, widespread "second circuit" (underground) publishing and educational networks, and, mostly among the intelligentsia, political groupings with different economic and social programs. By their very existence, these bodies acted as an alternative to the party-state structures.[27]

Confronted with these profound economic and legitimacy crises, Poland's party-state found itself gripped by disabling contradictory pressures. According to Marxist–Leninist prescriptions for an affluent and socially just society, it took upon itself the all-in-one role as central administrator, employer, and distributor and provider of social services. For several decades, it presented itself to its citizens as *the* agency responsible for society's welfare. And, in fact, the modest but reliable welfare benefits of real socialism—guaranteed employment (with low wages as a tradeoff for job security, and a relatively slow work tempo), state-provided education, medical care, and social security insurance, and low consumer prices subsidized by the state—had over the years been the foundation of an enduring if tenuous popular acquiescence to Communist party rule. As resources diminished during the 1980s, and the economy plunged into deeper and deeper disarray, the party-state desperately tried to reconcile all these multiple functions at once, and simultaneously faced its own disaffected ranks and a resentful civil society posing demands as employees, as consumers, and as social-welfare recipients. The result has been a growing bureaucratic boondoggle, fiscal chaos, and general social malaise.

Even experts seem unable to find their way through the scores of central, regional, and branch-industrial acts and regulations concerning social welfare enacted in recent years. The media, including *Nowe Drogi* (New Roads), the organ of PUWP, have repeatedly deplored the state administration's "arbitrary, *ad hoc* social policy interventions," "the undertaking of fragmentary, incoherent and temporary steps instead of a complex approach," "a lack of the clear conception of welfare policy resulting in disjointed decisions that reflect uninstitutionalized pressures of various employee groups, and of the different segments of the political and managerial *apparat*." [28]

According to reports in the media and consultative economic bodies on the intensified shortages of given consumer articles, central or regional authorities have been redirecting emergency funds from one deficient branch of production to another. In a similar fashion, now one, now another group of basic articles whose prices were deregulated (and thus skyrocketing) would be taken back under state control (at present, prescription drugs and clothing for small children). In addition to increases in the minimum wage, which have been repeated several times over in the past few years to protect the general standard of living from progressively falling because of racing inflation, under the pressure of various lobbies within the *apparat* and its auxiliaries, different groups received special state patronage, which was subsequently revoked and bestowed on others. For example, between 1984 and 1988, workers in the industrial branches most crucial to the domestic economy were first granted extra income compensation, then employees of enterprises with the highest production for export, families with many children, farmers, young couples setting up households, and finally war invalids. Simultaneously, pressure from employees in particular enterprises (exerted through strike threats, actual work stoppages, or via internal negotiations) eventuated in temporary benefits, income supplements, and various "shielding" compensations added to the basic wages.

As a result of all these protective interventions, wages have not been tied to increased productivity. In fact, whatever weak relationship there was between the two, it has been further loosened over the past few years. Remuneration for work, which in 1985 constituted about 70 percent of the monthly paychecks received by employees in the socialized sector of the economy, by the end of 1988 made up only 53 percent; the rest consisted of various welfare benefits, which changed with current policies.

Despite this huge expansion in state welfare expenditures from 1981 to

1985, the value of social protection benefits in the state's expenditures rose from 20 to 30 percent (13 and 12 percent of GNP, respectively), the pauperization of society continued. During the same period, the proportion of the population below the social minimum (poverty) level increased from 17 to 27 percent, and the estimates for 1988 placed it at over 30 percent.[29]

In comparison with other groups, the elderly have been even more severely affected by the macroeconomic crisis and state social policies aimed at the ad hoc alleviation of current crises rather than the long-term, systematic satisfaction of needs. In 1985, close to 5 million people of retirement age (12.5 percent of a population of 37.4 million) were receiving old-age and survivor pensions, about 83 percent of all those in the 60+ (women) and 65+ (men) age category.[30] Like the rest of the state social policies during the 1980s, old-age legislation has been undergoing continuous changes and modifications conducted in an arbitrary, scattershot fashion without a systematic plan.

The PUWP Plenary Conference in 1981 appropriated the demands of Solidarity and announced a reform of the old-age and survivor security pensions. In 1982–1983 the "old portfolio" pensions were liquidated, and benefits in all existing programs were recalculated from an increased minimum base, adding the percentage of the increase of the average nominal wage during the period from the year in which the pension was granted until 1981. Since increases in wages and cost of living continuously create new "old portfolios," the same operation was repeated again in 1985–1986, and again in the summer of 1989 when a one-time "emergency" across-the-board 120 percent increase of social security pensions was instituted. To offset the effects of spiraling inflation, in 1982 annual valorization was introduced, to be applied to all social security benefits. Modified in 1986, benefits adjustments were for the next three years calculated as a percentage of average monthly wage increases in the socialized sector and were added to pensions at the end of each year. But this method of adjustment payments did not protect pensioners from the many price increases occurring throughout the year. In the summer of 1989 a new, more frequent quarterly valorization of all state-provided incomes, including old-age payments, has been introduced at .8 percent of current average inflation rates. Thus far, however, none of the above measures has enhanced the elderly's economic security. The newly elected parliament's instant deregulation of food prices as a first step toward real marketization of the economy pushes prices higher almost every day, and the notorious inefficiency of the ZUS bureaucracy delays adjustments far longer than prescribed by the new regulations.

In 1982, in expectation of considerable temporary unemployment following the PUWP's announcement of economic reform, the early-retirement act was passed, allowing women to withdraw from employment at the age of 50, and men at 55. A complementary act instituted partly paid leave of three years for mothers of young children. As a result, nearly a million persons quit work and were added to the social security rolls. But since the planned market restructuring has not taken place, nor has unemployment appeared (in fact, the departure of so many workers created a severe labor shortage), the early-retirement legislation was withdrawn the following year. To ease the pensioners' economic situation, they were allowed (1985) to earn a limited amount from gainful employment without affecting security benefits. This has since been adjusted several times by ad hoc regulations permitting retirees to take different jobs (in food or newspaper stands, in the post office, in repair shops, in kindergartens, after hours in particular industrial enterprises), depending on workforce and production shortages.[31]

Between 1980 and 1985, the number of social security recipients grew by over 50 percent (due to the natural increase in the population of retirement age and the addition of beneficiaries from the early-retirement act). This growth, and the increments in pension benefits, led to a 480 percent increase in the old-age and survivor payments made by the ZUS, while contributions to the ZUS fund by employers and the self-employed in the nonsocialized sector rose from 15 percent to 25–33 percent, and of the enterprises in the socialized sector from 25 to 43 percent of the gross wage fund. In 1988, however, in order to direct more funds into falling reinvestment, a central administrative decision reduced social security contributions from state-owned enterprises to 38 percent.[32]

As a result of increments introduced between 1980 and 1985, average social security pensions increased 3.5 times; in 1989 alone, they increased by nearly 2.5 times over the previous year. Yet they continue to lag considerably behind wages, which are rising at a much faster rate. In 1980, the ratio of the average old-age and survivor pensions to the average wage in the socialized sector was 46 percent; it increased to 50 percent in 1982 and then dropped to 49 percent in 1985; in 1988, it grew once more to 53 percent, only to fall again to 48 percent in 1989. Inefficient as wage substitution, social security also performs badly as poverty relief. Among the 27 percent of all Polish households subsisting in 1985 on incomes below the social minimum, over one-fifth were households of old-age and survivor benefits recipients; and by the beginning of 1989, nearly 50 percent of Polish pensioners' households received payments lower than the current social minimum.[33]

As before, social security benefits remain linked to wages, reflecting not the actual material situation of recipients but income differentiation in the general population. The previously privileged groups, covered by special retirement programs, have likewise retained their economic advantage. Data published for the first time following the entry of Solidarity representatives into the country's legislative and executive bodies in the summer of 1989 reveal that in addition to various indirect financial benefits (in free medication obtained through well-supplied drug centers closed to the general public, lower housing rents, and subsidized vacation resorts and sanatoria), the 100 percent-indexed old-age pensions received by party-state functionaries, the military, and internal security forces average well over three times the mean paid to retirees from the socialized sector. As for others with special coverage, ZUS records show their old-age and survivor pensions to have been nearly twice the average received by regular retirees. At the other extreme, as before, elderly women survivors and individual farmer retirees (nearly three-quarters of them female) continue to receive the lowest benefits. Even though the nominal value of average survivor benefits increased more than retirement pensions (4 times vs. 3.5 times), they were only 65 percent of the average retirement pensions in 1980 and 72 percent in 1988. In the latter year, 75 percent of survivor pensions, as compared to 40 percent of retirement ones, were below the social minimum. Farmers, who from 1980 to 1982 were the object of benevolent attention from state social policymakers because of a particularly acute food shortage, received retirement benefits first at 73 percent (1980), then at 80 percent (1982) of average pensions in the socialized sector. But as the food crisis abated and state emergency allocations were directed elsewhere, this ratio dropped back to 70 percent in 1983, and to 61 percent in 1984, only to increase again to 66 percent in 1985, following renewed public discontent with the food supply and a flow of negative reports to the government on the situation in agriculture. Still, according to a sociological study of the life situations of the rural elderly conducted in 1985, 80 percent of social security recipients in the countryside subsisted on incomes below the social minimum. The inadequacy of social benefits for the rural elderly continues to be reflected, even more dramatically than before, in a very high proportion of rural persons of retirement age who continue working. While in the general elderly population, labor-force participation declined from 27 percent to 24 percent between 1980 and 1985, in the countryside it actually increased, from 75 percent to 95 percent. Recent media reports also indicate that in the last few years the urban elderly have been working more; between 1986 and 1988, the average share of employment earnings in their total incomes (often from the "second economy" and therefore unrecorded in official statistics) grew from 10 to 12 percent.[34]

During the 1980s, the deteriorating situation of the "productive" population was surveyed with very close attention by the welfare state administration because of its potential to generate social unrest, but repeated signals that the retirees' plight was even worse prompted the Central Statistical Office to commission in 1980, and again in 1985, the first two nationwide studies of the economic and social situation of the elderly. The 1985 report showed that 20 percent of the elderly lived alone, 40 percent with a spouse, and 40 percent in households shared with children or relatives. About 75 percent of the elderly population depended for their livelihood on social security, 5 percent were supported by children, and 20 percent relied on wages (of these, half were employed part-time). About 48 percent of the total incomes in the households studied were below the poverty level; about 13 percent were at poverty level. The economic situation of the elderly dependent on social security was worse than that of those supported by wages; among retirees, 44 percent had total monthly incomes below, and 25 percent at the social minimum; among survivor pensioners, 73 percent and 24 percent respectively; these proportions among the gainfully employed were 33 percent and 14 percent. Living alone or with a spouse, instead of sharing a household with children or relatives, also meant economic deprivation; total incomes below and around the social minimum were found in 54 percent and 13 percent of households among the former, and in 43 percent and 21 percent among the latter. More than a third of the total number of elderly in the study stated their incomes permitted only a "very modest livelihood," a similar proportion said they could afford only the cheapest food and hardly any clothing, whereas 5 percent admitted their income was insufficient even for food bills. Again, the deprivation of the elderly in independent households (alone or with spouse)was considerably greater than that of those sharing households with children or relatives. Answers similar to those above were given by nearly nine-tenths of respondents in the former group (28, 47, and 14 percent respectively), and by 56 percent in the latter (35, 16, and 5 percent).[35]

Assistance from the family, a very important element in the welfare of the elderly since the institution of state socialism (but after the initial, austere phase of "socialist reconstruction" seldom officially acknowledged), has become even more crucial in the 1980s, as the economic crisis has deepened and the general standard of living has fallen rapidly. Public assistance, underfunded from the beginning and treated as "charity," not as entitlement, has in the 1980s received even fewer funds than in the previous period. While the share of social security benefits in state welfare expenditures increased from 26 to 37 percent between 1980 and 1987, that of funds for medical care and social assistance declined from 22 to 17 percent.

According to the 1985 report on the elderly mentioned above, only 10 percent of the whole population studied received any assistance from "institutions and organizations," and of this number, 70 percent received it from religious and other private organizations. No new nursing or retirement homes have been built since 1980, and the list of qualified persons waiting for admission has increased (several thousand disabled elderly in need of daily care are kept in hospitals that substitute for nursing homes). The small number of mostly female and poorly paid social workers, affiliated with state medical and public assistance institutions, has actually decreased in recent years. The inadequate infrastructure in existence can barely serve the most destitute, and even the elderly capable of paying for assistance have great difficulty finding it, since the awaited market reform of services connected with economic reform has not produced private assistance agencies.[36]

In this situation, realistic if discontented elderly persons have been turning for help to their children and relatives, or to neighbors and friends. A large proportion (40 percent) of those who share households with their families have ready access to assistance. Among those who reside alone or with spouse, the majority live close to their children or relatives. The 1985 national study of the elderly revealed that 50 percent in this group lived a half hour's distance or less from their families, 15 percent lived an hour or less away, and only 35 percent lived at a distance greater than one hour. More than half declared receiving regular or occasional assistance from children, either in household tasks, personal care, and shopping (32 percent) or through financial or in-kind aid (20 percent). Nearly two-thirds receive assistance in sickness from children or relatives. In the earlier (1980) national study, to the question "Who would help the elderly in financial need?" nearly 60 percent pointed to children, only 2 percent referred to public institutions, and 29 percent said they would have nowhere to turn. In exchange, it may be added, 70 percent of the elderly assist their children, mostly in caring for grandchildren and shopping (the latter no small matter in today's Poland).[37]

Close cooperation between the elderly and their children eases the difficulties of the elderly in crisis-ridden and public-welfare-deficient Poland, but a sense of deep-seated insecurity remains: "Everybody . . . now is simply afraid to go on retirement if not forced to do it by bad health, because no one knows what he will live on tomorrow, when he'll be left alone, say, if the children emigrate." (Since 1980, nearly a million people have left Poland, 70 percent of them less than 35 years old; in September 1989 alone, the waiting list for visa applications at the American embassy in Warsaw numbered nearly 50,000).[38]

Conclusion: Into the 1990s

After four decades of state socialism in Poland, not even its minimum goals have been fulfilled. There is neither social equality (the original socialist ideal) nor modest but continual improvement in the standard of living—the regime's major claim to legitimacy in the phase of "mature" socialist development. And, in recent years, as Marxist–Leninist prescriptions for economic development have proven to be a spectacular failure, even protection against poverty—the state's ultimate claim to superiority over the capitalist welfare state [39]—has been beyond reach.

With the national economy nearing collapse, and faced with a civil society profoundly resentful and "mobilized" in various forms of protest, the PUWP leadership has finally resolved to cede the responsibilities it usurped as the central decision maker, employer, distributor of goods, and provider of services. Relegalization of the independent Solidarity union, followed by partially free elections to parliament (completely open ones are to take place in 1992) and the formation of a non-Communist-led government with PUWP members in the minority, have by the last quarter of 1989 created a new political situation and thus a chance, it is hoped, to lead Poland out of its cul de sac.

The problems are immense, however. With Mikhail Gorbachev at the helm in Moscow, there seems for the nearest future to be no grounds to fear adverse Soviet intervention in Poland's internal matters, as long as the process of change does not threaten either the solidity of the Warsaw Pact or the security of the Soviet Union. Yet there appears to be no realistic expectation of badly needed, substantial economic assistance from the West to support Poland's restructuring as a market society and stabilize its fledgling democracy. Without it, as the new Polish leaders openly admit, chances of success in either of these difficult tasks will be significantly diminished. The West, having seen millions of dollars of credits poured into Poland during the 1970s, to be squandered by its managers, remains cautious, maintaining a wait-and-see posture. Instead of the $10 billion in combined debt postponements, concessionary lending, credits, and business investments to be provided over a period of three years that Solidarity chief Lech Walesa requested during his meetings with Western leaders (summer–fall 1989), the European Community and the United States have thus far offered about $400 million, most of it in emergency food aid. The International Monetary Fund (IMF) is similarly reluctant to commit funds ($1–2 billion in long-term loans have been requested) until Poland actually implements the harsh austerity measures needed to trigger economic recovery.[40]

As it looks at present, left largely to their own devices by East and West, Polish reformers will have to rely first and foremost on domestic resources. The difficulties at home are staggering, as those emerging from new developments are superimposed on old problems embedded in the structures and routines formed during the past forty-five years. The task of resolving them appears no less difficult than attempting to square a circle.

In his inaugural speech to parliament, the new prime minister called "rescuing of the national economy . . . the matter of utmost priority for the country." [41] Two major directions for the rescue operation were announced, to be implemented as soon as experts complete their work on the economic program. On the one hand, the state economic monopoly in production, distribution, and services will be smashed by applying strong doses of capitalism, mainly through privatization of enterprises and free markets. On the other hand, a wide range of austerity measures consisting of drastic cuts in government spending, abolition of guaranteed employment (by eliminating inefficient enterprises), and full deregulation of price controls will be implemented. Since Poland's economic condition requires quick and decisive action, leaving no time for working out details and coordinating steps to be taken, it seems unavoidable that such a program will leave several important points unspecified. To judge from public pronouncements and discussions by experts involved in the preparation of the new government's program, this lack of concreteness and coordination affects, in particular, such issues of great practical consequence as how to "capitalize" the economy and which forms of state participation to retain, and what exactly, how much, and from whom sacrifices are expected. There is a danger that, insufficiently elaborated, when put into practice these restoration programs will exacerbate rather than eliminate existing problems.[42]

Both political pluralization and the impending deetatization of the economy are opposed, especially at middle and lower levels, by a considerable number of state bureaucrats with vested interests in the status quo: "Prime Minister yours, ours the *apparat*" came a muted reply to the PUWP's parliamentary and cabinet concessions from several local power centers. This resistance, even if only passive, is capable of significantly thwarting the "new course." More vocal in their resentment are activists of the *Centrala* and locals of the government-sponsored unions created after the suppression of Solidarity in 1981. Unsaddled by recent political developments, in an effort to retain influence they are using increasingly radical populist slogans against the marketization–austerity program of the new administration as harmful to the people, especially the working class.[43] This agitation, if it gathers sufficient following, may water down the "rescue operation" into inconsequential half or quarter measures that will not do the job of salvaging the failing economy and thus will undermine the new administration.

It is evident that the projected combination of Western-style free competitive markets with austerity measures (in particular, the slashing of funds slated for the state's protective functions) will threaten one necessary condition for the enduring legitimacy of the new political arrangement and therefore for societal cooperation: preventing, or at least minimizing, the further pauperization of large segments of an already struggling society.

Issues of legitimacy and cooperation will unavoidably present the present legislators (formerly in opposition) and government members with an intractable problem: In order to accomplish the long-term restructuring for which the labor union Solidarity vested them with authority, they now have to implement measures directed against the immediate interests of their electorate. Eager for the benefits of a market economy, this electorate, by and large, has little understanding of the actual workings of that system, especially of its cost side, and the mostly abstract nature of current public discussions on the marketization of the Polish economy has not been instructive in this regard. Further, inasmuch as they would like to see the inefficient state-socialist structures finally disappear, as recent national opinion polls indicate, a majority of Poles—and most of the working class—take for granted public responsibility for citizens' social welfare.[44] Yet in this area—on the issue of which *oslony spoleczne,* or "social safeguards," will be retained (or remade) in the course of economic restructuring—the proposals of the rescue program seem particularly vague, and the public policy debate pallid.

If implemented as planned, "capitalization" (marketization) of the Polish economy will bring, as experts now estimate, about 20 percent unemployment to the country. That would be a radically new phenomenon after forty-five years of job security (and a potential source of social unrest), and a whole system of "social safeguards," enormously costly considering the large numbers predicted, will have to be created very soon to assist these people: financial and material benefits, aid in relocation (a tremendous problem because of the acute housing shortage), retraining programs. Not surprisingly, the employed and potentially unemployed concentrate the attention (and worry) of regional and local Solidarity cells; likewise, their needs dominate the limited public debate on the tasks of the welfare system in the new situation.[45] And the "productive" population—the base of the economy and the bulk of the electorate of the recently installed government—has the potential power to exert pressure on administrative decisions and can be expected to use it to try to secure its interests in the allocation of limited public-welfare funds.

In comparison, as an economic and political group, the elderly are powerless. Although "retirees' sections" or "labor veterans' associations" appeared in some enterprises following the relegalization of Solidarity, these are numerically small and dispersed, and their voice and cause are hardly heard in public forums, whether within Solidarity, in the new parliament, or in the media (the sociologists, it may be noted, remain silent as well). Reviewing the Polish press, I counted passing references in general economic debates to "the very difficult existence of the pensioners" and "our common obligation to defend their dignity of life," and occasional desperate letters from retirees expressing a profound fear of the future and complaining about a lack of public interest in their situation, but no more than a few articles were devoted specifically to the issue of old-age welfare provisions in the changing system.[46]

There is no way to predict at this point what shape Polish welfare policies regarding the elderly will eventually take, for these policies will be influenced by the overall size of the deficient state budget (and whether it is enhanced or not by Western assistance), by allocations from it assigned to or won by force by more powerful groups, and by the (expected) appearance and practical functioning of private or collectively managed benefits–insurance agencies. On the basis of the preceding analysis, as well as on this brief overview of the current situation in Poland as it begins the march toward economic recovery, there are reasons to fear that the position of the growing population of the elderly—expected to reach 13 percent of the total population by 1992—will remain vulnerable, perhaps even more vulnerable than before.

A new adjustment of the old-age benefits currently under consideration projects a monthly (instead of a quarterly) valorization, according to the percentage of average wage (not price) increases. While this adjustment, if implemented, would slow down the rapid rate of diminution of retirees' incomes, most of them will still be inadequately low for a materially secure existence. Among more far-reaching projects for reshaping the inefficient social security system is a proposal that employees take control of their wage contributions to the ZUS fund and make the ZUS reinvest these monies in the market so that they bring profit and provide resources for increased benefits in the future. A similar idea is contained in a project for the marketization of medical care, until now "free" (i.e., financed by the state budget), through the introduction of Western-style insurance companies operating as profit-making organizations, possibly under the (financial) umbrella of the Medical Insurance Bank created for this purpose. The elderly would contribute according to their means, and those unable to do so would qualify for help from the ZUS. How exactly "inability to pay" should be defined, and what would be the level of assistance, remains unclear. Finally, in the area of social assistance, the expectation is that the practically nonexistent state network—and, given all other needs pressing on the state budget, the odds for its upkeep, let alone expansion, do not look good—will be supplemented or replaced by market-based private agencies that would provide services paid in full by the elderly in higher-income groups; progressive state reimbursements would be available for those more economically disadvantaged. These projects at present represent wishful thinking rather than feasible reality.[47] Most likely, social aid to the elderly will continue to be provided, first and foremost, by private networks of family assistance that have been filling in when state welfare programs fail. But the children of the elderly, who themselves will be affected by the combination of marketization with austerity, and who may soon be unemployed or forced to change residence, will manage to help only so much, and possibly less than before. Old-age and survivor benefits are part of the budgets of over 30 percent of Polish families, and this sharing may emerge as a substitute of sorts for the absence of an "elderly lobby" as Poland reshapes its economic and social policies. This, however, requires that "productive" groups integrate on a permanent basis the retirees' needs into their own agenda (something they have not done so far). Otherwise, in the enormously difficult period awaiting Poland, the situation of the elderly, who lack the strength to defend their interests, will hang in large part on policymakers' sense of moral responsibility and on the compassion of their compatriots. Both are powerful but frightfully fragile ropes.

Addendum

This chapter was completed in the early fall of 1989, after the first noncommunist government was formed in postwar Poland. Soon after that, state socialist regimes throughout Eastern Europe began to collapse, and it now appears that the USSR will not survive much longer either. Thus the picture of the region is very different from what it was at the time of writing; the situation, still unstable, can be described as "postcommunist transition," backward or forward (depending on the world views of critics and advocates) to Western-style liberal democracy and free-market capitalist economy. Poland seems to have decided to traverse this route by the most radical steps, particularly in regard to the national economy. Amid a multitude of government programs and parliamentary regulations issued during the past year and aimed at "recapitalization" of the country, however, the nature and extent of public responsibilities toward society's weak and helpless have not been decided. Aside from ad hoc interventions, mostly to increase insufficient pensions, no coherent program regarding the elderly has been formulated, and their situation and prospects, if not worse than described at the conclusion of this chapter, are certainly no better.

Notes

Acknowledgments: I wish to thank, first and foremost, Grazyna Kacprowicz from the Institute of Sociology at Warsaw University for her patient cooperation in locating, selecting, and mailing—along with valuable comments—the often obscure materials related to the subject of this chapter as they kept surfacing in the course of my research. Margaret Weir kindly assisted in directing me to the relevant literature in the English language and then helpfully commented on the manuscript I produced, as did Jill Quadagno and John Myles.

1. Somewhat surprisingly, considering a present upsurge in Western social science of historical-comparative interest in the states as strongly capable and potentially autonomous interveners in economy and society, and the attention in so informed studies to the "powerful" behavior of states in Third World countries, despite the availability of the English-language studies of this issue in the Soviet bloc, with the exception of a few "global surveys" with brief, descriptive chapters on individual East European countries, recent investigations of modern welfare-state systems by Western historical comparatists do not include those of the Soviet type. For chapters on Yugoslavia, Hungary and Poland, see Robert Friedmann et al., eds., *Modern Welfare States: A Comparative View of Trends and Prospects* (Brighton: Wheatsheaf Books, 1987); Adalbert Evers et al., eds., *The Changing Face of Welfare* (New York: Gower, 1987); Else Oyen, ed., *Comparing Welfare States and Their Futures* (New York: Gower, 1986). In the specialized East European and Soviet studies, analyses of the socialist welfare system can be found in A. McAuley, *Economic Welfare in the Soviet Union* (London:

Allen and Unwin, 1979); Vic George and Nick Manning, *Socialism, Social Welfare and the Soviet Union* (London: Routledge and Kegan Paul, 1980); Zsuzsa Ferge, *A Society in the Making: Hungarian Social and Societal Policy 1945–1975* (White Plains, N.Y.: M. E. Sharpe, 1979); David Lane, *The End of Inequality? Class, Status and Power under State Socialism* (London: Allen and Unwin, 1982); Walter Connor, *Socialism's Dilemmas: State and Society in the Soviet Bloc* (New York: Columbia University Press, 1988). To my knowledge, the only comprehensive comparative analyses of the state socialist and capitalist welfare systems remain Gaston Rimlinger's classic, *Welfare Policy and Industrialisation in Europe, America and Russia* (New York: Wiley, 1971), followed by his more recent article, "The Historical Analysis of National Welfare Systems," in *Explorations in the New Economic History*, ed. R. I. Ransom et al. (New York: Academic Press, 1983), 149–67, and Julian Le Grand and Wlodzimierz Okrasa's *Social Welfare in Britain and Poland* (London: Suntry-Toyota International Centre for Economic and Related Disciplines, 1987). Frank Parkin's *Class Inequality and Political Order: Social Stratification in Capitalist and Communist Societies* (London: MacGibbon and Kee, 1971) contains some discussion of the two types of welfare systems, but is principally devoted to other issues.

2. Wlodzimierz Wesolowski, "Changes in the Class Structure in Poland," in *Empirical Sociology in Poland*, ed. Jan Szczepanski (Warsaw: Panstwowe Wydawnictwo Naukowe, 1966), 7–25; Lane, *End of Inequality?* 61.

3. *Rocznik Statystyczny Ubezpieczen Spolecznych, 1946–1985* (Warsaw: Zaklad Ubezpieczen Spolecznych, 1987), xviii–xix, 170–76.

4. Wlodzimierz Brus, "Stalinism and the 'People's Democracies,' " in *Stalinism: Essays in Historical Interpretation*, ed. Robert Tucker (New York: Norton, 1977), 239.

5. This quotation from a description of the first postwar years of the welfare system's operation in Hungary is equally applicable to Poland. Cited in Zsuzsa Ferge, "The Changing Hungarian Social Policy," in Oyen, *Comparing Welfare States*, 155.

6. Wesolowski, "Changes in the Class Structure in Poland," 27; Jozef Swiatlo, *Za Kulisami Bezpieki i Partii* (Munich: Free Europe Committee, 1954), 5, 26.

7. *Rocznik Statystyczny*, xi–xv, 3, 58; *The Cost of Social Security* (Geneva: International Labour Office, 1985), tables 2, 8; Jerzy Piotrowski, ed., *Miejsce Czlowieka Starego w Rodzinie i Spoleczenstwie* (Warsaw: Panstwowe Wydawnictwo Naukowe, 1973), 7; Barbara Tryfan, "Specyfika Wiejskiej Starosci," *Wies i Rolnictwo* 2 (1986): 125–42; Lech Ostrowski, "Polityka Socjalna w Stosunku do Wsi a Swiadczenia Spoleczne Ludnosci Chlopskiej," *Wies i Rolnictwo* 1 (1988): 148–49; Michal Wisniewski, "Miejsce Sfery Socjalnej w Polityce Panstwa Socjalistycznego," in *Funkcje Opiekuncze Panstwa Socjalistycznego* (Wroclaw: Zaklad Narodowy im. Ossolinskich, 1986), 33–40; Grazyna Szpor, "Regulacje Prawne Funkcji Socjalnych Panstwa," in *Funkcje Opiekuncze*, 287–89.

8. *Rocznik Statystyczny*, x–xix, 5, 83; *Ludzie Starsi w Polsce—Ich Warunki i Potrzeby* (Warsaw: Instytut Pracy i Spraw Socjalnych. Studia i Materialy, 1982), Z.16, 28–32; Szpor, "Regulacje Prawne Funkcji Socjalnych Panstwa," 287–93.

9. Barbara Balcerowska-Ryzy, "Z Problematyki Badan Spolecznych: Ludzie Starsi," *Wiadomosci Statystyczne* 12 (1987): 2–4; Leon Grela, "Czlowiek Stary a Pomoc Spoleczna," *Studia i Materialy IPSS* 5 (1982): 19; Mieczyslaw Izdebski,

"Pomoc Spoleczna i Zintegrowany Program Dzialania na Rzecz Ludzi Starszych i Niepelnosprawnych," in *Ludzie Starsi*, 20–21; Lucyna Frackiewicz, "Sfery Niedostatku a Funkcje Opiekuncze Panstwa," in *Funkcje Opiekuncze*, 143–45. See also Zsuzsa Ferge, "The Impact of the Present Economic Crisis on Social Policy from a Comparative European Perspective," in Evers, *The Changing Face of Welfare*, 84–85.

10. Danuta Kozinska, "Czynnosci Domowe i Stosunki z Rodzina," in Piotrowski, *Miejsce Czlowieka Starego*, 302–11.

11. Walter Connor, *Socialism, Politics and Equality* (New York: Columbia University Press, 1979); Wesolowski, "Changes in the Class Structure of Poland." On the increasing socioeconomic stratification of Polish society in the 1960s and 1970s, see Wlodzimierz Wesolowski et al., eds., *Investigations on Class Structure and Social Stratification in Poland, 1945–1975* (Warsaw: Instytut Socjologii UW, 1977); Kazimierz Slomczynski and Wlodzimierz Wesolowski, eds., *Struktura i Ruchliwosc Spoleczna* (Wroclaw: Zaklad Narodowy im. Ossolinskich, 1973); Michal Pohoski, "Ruchliwosc Spoleczna a Nierownosci Spoleczne," *Kultura i Spoleczenstwo* 4 (1983): 133–64; Janusz Meller, *Zroznicowanie Plac w Polsce* (Warsaw: Panstwowe Wydawnictwo Ekonomiczne, 1988). See also Frank Parkin, "Class Stratification in Socialist Societies," *British Journal of Sociology* 4 (1969): 355–74; Connor, *Socialism's Dilemmas*, chaps. 7–8.

12. On the repeated social upheavals in Poland, see Zygmunt Bauman, "Social Dissent in the East European Political System," *Archives Europeennes de Sociologie*, nos. 1–2 (1971): 25–51; Jakub Karpinski, *Countdown: The Polish Upheavals of 1956, 1968, 1970, 1976, 1980* (New York: Karz-Cohl, 1982).

13. *Rocznik Statystyczny*, 3, 9, 30, 36–37; Zbigniew Januszek, "Charakterystyka Systemu Emerytalno-Rentowego Jako Zrodla Dochodow Osob w Wieku Emerytalnym," in *Ludzie Starsi*, 6–9; Miroslaw Ksiezopolski, "Polish Social Policy in a Situation of Economic Crisis—Is There a Choice of Alternatives?" in *The Changing Face of Welfare*, 98.

14. Frackiewicz, "Sfery Niedostatku a Funkcje Opiekuncze Panstwa," in *Funkcje Opiekuncze*, 139–40; *Rocznik Statystyczny*, xiv–xv, 34, 52, 59; Mervyn Matthews, *Privilege in the Soviet Union: A Study of Elite Life Styles under Communism* (London: Allen and Unwin, 1978), 171.

15. *Rocznik Statystyczny*, xii–xv, 3–4, 8, 30–32; Ostrowski, "Polityka Socjalna w Stosunku do Wsi," 188; Januszek, "Charakterystyka Systemu Emerytalno-Rentowego," in *Ludzie Starsi*, 9.

16. *Rocznik Statystyczny*, 143–44; Joanna Starega-Piasek, "Skutki Polityki Spolecznej Wobec Ludzi Starych," in *Ludzie Starsi*, 9; Balcerowska-Ryzy, "Z Problematyki Badan Spolecznych," 3.

17. Januszek, "Charakterystyka Systemu Emerytalno-Rentowego," in *Ludzie Starsi*, 7, 12; Starega-Piasek, "Skutki Polityki Spolecznej," 29; *Rocznik Statystyczny*, 83; *Social Security Programs throughout the World* (Washington, D.C.: U.S. Department of Health and Human Services, Social Security Administration, 1987), 200–201. According to this legislation, a person retiring in 1980 whose average monthly earnings the previous year were, for instance, 5,000 zlp, would receive a pension of 3,000 (100 percent replacement of two-thirds the average national wage in 1975) plus 1,100 (55 percent of the remainder), or a total of 4,100 zlp.

18. *Sytuacja Zyciowa Osob Starszych* (Warsaw: Glowny Urzad Statystyczny, Prace Zakladu Badan Statystyczno-Ekonomicznych, 1982), Z.127, 56–57, 132–41; *Ludzie Starsi w Polsce*, 8, 28–29. See also *Rocznik Statystyczny*, 4–5, 34–35, 59; Marlena Kuciarska-Ciesielska, "O Ludziach Starszych w Roku Im Poswieconym (I)," *Wiadomosci Statystyczne* 6 (1982): 4–5; Brunon Synak, "Kierunki Badan i Stan Gerontologii Spolecznej w Polsce," in *Postepy Gerontologii*, ed. Brunon Synak and Tadeusz Wroblewski (Warsaw: Panstwowy Zaklad Wydawnictw Lekarskich, 1988), 21–26.

19. Andrzej Tymowski, *Minimum Socjalne* (Warsaw: Panstwowe Wydawnictwo Naukowe, 1973); *Rocznik Statystyczny*, 5, 35, 42–43, 65; Tryfan, "Specyfika Wiejskiej Starosci," 127–40; Kuciarska-Ciesielska, "O Ludziach Starszych," 4–5; Starega-Piasek, "Skutki Polityki Spolecznej," 32; *Sytuacja Zyciowa Osob Starszych*, 49.

20. Marlena Kuciarska-Ciesielska, "O Ludziach Starszych w Roku Im Poswieconym (II)," *Wiadomosci Statystyczne* 7 (1982): 8; Izdebski, "Pomoc Spoleczna," 20–21; Starega-Piasek, "Skutki Polityki Spolecznej," 30–31; Danuta Kozinska, "Sytuacja i Potrzeby Mieszkaniowe Ludzi Starszych," in Evers, *Miejsce Czlowieka Starego*, 285–300; Slawomir Szwedowski, "Wplyw Postepu Technicznego na Rozwoj Funkcji Spolecznych Panstwa," in *Funkcje Opiekuncze*, 102; Malgorzata Dziubinska-Michalewicz, "Analiza Wydatkow Panstwa i Przedsiebiorstw na Cele Spoleczne w Polsce," in *Funkcje Opiekuncze*, 124–36. *Sytuacja Bytowa Ludzi Starszych* (Warsaw: Glowny Urzad Statystyczny, Materialy Statystyczne, 1985), Z.36, 95–103, 112–24.

21. On the deepening economic crisis in Poland, see Ernest Skalski, "Rownowazyc czy Reformowac?" *Tygodnik Powszechny*, March 20, 1988, 1–2; Alexander Paszynski, "Drogi i Bezdroza Reformy," *Tygodnik Powszechny*, December 11, 1988, 1–7; Ryszrad Bugaj, "Ksztalt i Warunki Polskiej Przebudowy," *Tygodnik Powszechny*, November 13, 1988, 1–7; Abraham Brumberg, "Poland: State and/or Society," *Dissent*, Winter 1989, 47–48; "Z Materialow GUS," *Zycie Gospodarcze*, August 20, 1989, 11; Tomasz Jezioranski, "Latanie Budzetu," *Zycie Gospodarcze*, August 13, 1989, 2; idem, "Na Horyzoncie Zapasc," *Zycie Gospodarcze*, May 28, 1989, 1–4; Krzysztof Hagmajer and Stefan Malecki, "Koncentracja, Monopol, Konsumpcja," *Zycie Gospodarcze*, August 13, 1989, 7.

22. Joanna Solska, "Nasza Stopa," *Polityka*, August 20, 1988, 106; Grazyna Smulska, "Konsumpcja," *Zycie Gospodarcze*, October 30, 1988, 4; Marek Henzler, "Ile Potrzeba na Zycie," *Polityka*, March 26, 1988, 1–10; Dziubinska-Michalewicz, "Analiza Wydatkow Panstwa," 129–30; Bugaj, "Funkcje Opiekuncze Panstwa," 278; Jerzy Baczynski, "Ile Sa Warte Pieniadze?" *Polityka*, September 9, 1989, 4; Halina Sterczynska, "Oszczednosci i Praca," *Zycie Gospodarcze*, August 6, 1989, 3.

23. Marek Henzler, "Poczucie Chaosu," *Polityka*, December 24, 1988, 3. On a widespread sense of increasing "economic insecurity and pessimism" among Poles (as reflected in the national opinion polls), see also Stanislaw Kwiatkowski, "Na Recznym Hamulcu," *Polityka*, March 21, 1987, 3; idem, "Obawa Przed Monopolem," *Polityka*, June 3, 1989, 7; *Spoleczenstwo Polskie Drugiej Polowy Lat Osiemdziesiatych, Proba Diagnozy Stanu Swiadmosci Spolecznej* (Warsaw: Polish Sociological Society, 1988); Miroslawa Marody, "Awans i Krach," *Polityka*, April 30, 1988, 1–10.

24. On the emergence, the sixteen months of existence, and the crushing of the Solidarity Union, see Jadwiga Staniszkis, *Poland's Self-Limiting Revolution* (Princeton: Princeton University Press, 1984).

25. "The Kubiak Report: The Causes of Political Crises in Poland," *Survey* 26 (1986): 87–108.

26. There is no systematic information on these internal divisions within the party-state *apparat*, but the frequent polemics in the party media between spokesmen of particular factions permit a rough reconstruction of the major camps. On opposition to the economic reform by the entrenched bureaucracy in the manufacturing and planning establishments, see Jerzy Kleer, "Gospodarka Nie Jest z Plasteliny," *Polityka*, November 21, 1987, 4; idem, "Czas Nadzwyczajny," *Polityka*, May 21, 1988, 4. On the split within the party administration, Hieronim Kubiak, former Politburo member (1980–1981), in "Udawanie to Bardzo Kiepska Polityka," *Polityka*, December 5, 1987, 3.

27. On the workers' protests and the activities of *Parallel Poland* in the 1980s, see T. J., "Rozmowa z Wojciechem Gielzynskim," *Kultura* (Paris) 11 (1988): 79–87; Alexander Smolar, "The Polish Opposition Since December 1981," *Wilson Center's Occasional Paper* 14 (1988); *Poland Watch Quarterly*'s reports, 1981–1989; current reviews of the "second circuit" press in Poland by the Polish Section, Radio Free Europe; Brumberg, "Poland: State and/or Society," 49–54.

28. Barbara Brach, "Nowej Uchwaly Nie Bedzie," *Zycie Gospodarcze*, June 5, 1988, 2; S. C., "Uczucie Niedosytu," *Zycie Gospodarcze*, July 3, 1988, 16; Bugaj, "Funkcje Opiekuncze Panstwa," 281–82. See also Ryszard Bugaj, "Spoleczne Uwarunkowania Realizacji Polityki Gospodarczej," *Studia Ekonomiczne* 6 (1984): 133–57; Magdalena Wojciechowska, "Bledne Kolo Roszczen," *Polityka*, January 21, 1989, 1–6; Ksiezopolski, "Polish Social Policy in a Situation of Economic Crisis," 96–98, 101; Andrzej Tymowski, "Dylematy Wspolczesnej Polityki Spolecznej w Polsce," *Ruch Pracowniczy, Ekonomiczny, i Socjologiczny* 4 (1984): 294–307. Similar discontents with the operation of the socialist welfare state are also voiced in other Soviet-bloc countries; see, for example, Horst Herlemann, ed., *Quality of Life in the Soviet Union* (Boulder, Colo.: Westview Press, 1987); Mervyn Matthews, *Poverty in the Soviet Union: The Life-Styles of the Underpriviledged in Recent Years* (Cambridge and New York: Cambridge University Press, 1986); Ferge, "Changing Hungarian Social Policy," 152–63; idem, "The Impact of the Present Economic Crisis on Social Policy," 71–91; Ivan Szeleny, "Social Inequalities in State Socialist Redistributive Economies: Dilemmas for Social Policies in Contemporary Socialist Societies of Eastern Europe," *International Journal of Comparative Sociology*, nos. 1–2 (1985): 63–87; Connor, *Socialism's Dilemmas*, esp. chap. 6.

29. Helena Goralska, *Dochody i Konsumpcja Ludnosci Zyjacej w Niedostatku* (Warsaw: Instytut Pracy i Spraw Socjalnych, 1985); Dziubinska-Michalewicz, "Analiza Wydatkow Panstwa i Przedsiebiorstw," 114–16, 129; Bugaj, "Funkcje Opiekuncze Panstwa," 278; Solska, "Nasza Stopa," 1–6; Smulska, "Konsumpcja," 4; Wojciechowska, "Bledne Kolo Roszczen," 1–6; *Rocznik Statystyczny*, 32 and Appendix.

30. *Rocznik Statystyczny*, 31–36, 52, 59; Januszek, "Charakterystyka Systemu Emerytalno-Rentowego," 7–9; Starega-Piasek, "Skutki Polityki Spolecznej," 29; Dziubinska-Michalewicz, "Analiza Wydatkow Panstwa i Przedsiebiorstw," 112; "Z Kraju," *Polityka*, June 17, 1989, 2.

31. Solska, "Nasza Stopa," 1–6; Bugaj, "Funkcje Opiekuncze," 266–85; Synak, "Kierunki Badan i Stan Gerontologii," 19; Ksiezopolski, "Polish Social Policy in a

Situation of Economic Crisis," 94–96; Berna Bakowska, "Najpierw Place—Potem Swiadczenia," *Zycie Warszawy*, November 24, 1988, 3; idem, "Emerytury i Renty Po Nowemu," *Zycie Warszawy*, December 20, 1988, 3; Dziubinska-Michalewicz, "Analiza Wydatkow Panstwa i Przedsiebiorstw," 112–14; "Komunikat GUS," *Zycie Warszawy*, July 25, 1989, 2; Ryszard Bugaj, "Indeksacja, Watpliwosci, Zagrozenia," *Tygodnik Solidarnosc*, August 18, 1989, 5; "Z Materialow GUS," *Zycie Gospodarcze*, July 30, 1989, 2; Jerzy Baczynski, "Poczatek Licytacji," *Polityka*, August 13, 1989, 4.

32. *Rocznik Statystyczny*, 15, 20–21, 30–43, 50–51, 64–65; Dziubinska-Michalewicz, "Analiza Wydatkow Panstwa i Przedsiebiorstw," 112–16; Ksiezopolski, "Polish Social Policy in a Situation of Economic Crisis," 98–99.

33. *Rocznik Statystyczny*, 34–37, 63–64, 83; Dziubinska-Michalewicz, "Analiza Wydatkow Panstwa i Przedsiebiorstw," 119; Balcerowska-Ryzy, "Z Problematyki Badan Spolecznych," 2–7; Henzler, "Ile Potrzeba Na Zycie," 1–10; Solska, "Nasza Stopa," 1–6; "Komunikat GUS," 2; "Z Materialow GUS," 2; Jezioranski, "Latanie Budzetu," 2; Baczynski, "Ile Sa Warte Pieniadze?" 4.

34. *Rocznik Statystyczny*, 5, 35, 38–39, 42–43, 50–51, 63–65, 71–77; Kuciarska-Ciesielska, "O Ludziach Starsszych w Roku im Poswieconym (I)," 4–5; idem, "O Ludziach Starszych w Roku im Poswieconym (II)," 10; Henzler, "Ile Potrzeba na Zycie," 1–10; Wojeciechowska, "Bledne Kolo Roszczen," 1–6; M. K., "Indeksacja—Dziecko Inflacji," *Zycie Gospodarcze*, August 6, 1989, 5; Sterczynska, "Oszczednoscia i Praca," 3; Jozef Lewandowski, "Ludowe Wojsko Polskie," *Zeszyty Historyczne* (Paris) 89 (1989): 3–22; Wojciech Markiewicz, "Kask z Przylbica Czyli Budzet MSW," *Polityka*, September 9, 1989, 3; Barbara Tryfan, "Starosc na Wsi—Kwestia Spoleczna," *Wies Wspolczesna* 6 (1987): 60–67; idem, "Badanie Warunkow Bytu Ludnosci Wiejskiej," *Wies i Rolnictwo* 1 (1988): 130–46; Jan Lopato, "Dochody Emerytow Wiejskich w Latach Osiemdziesiatych," *Wies Wspolczesna* 11 (1987): 72–79.

35. The studies were based on 9,500 samples representative of the Polish elderly population, excluding those (1 to 1.5 percent) in public institutions: *Sytuacja Zyciowa Osob Starszych* (Warsaw: Glowny Urzad Statystyczny, Zaklad Badan Statystyczno-Ekonomicznych, 1982), Z.127; and *Sytuacja Bytowa Ludzi Starszych w 1985 R* (Warsaw: Glowny Urzad Statystyczny, Materialy Statystyczne, 1985), Z.36. The data are from the latter study, xi–xii, xvii–xviii, tables 9–10, 52–53, 57. A review of the existing limited research on the elderly in Poland is in Synak, "Kierunki i Stan Gerontologii Spolecznej w Polsce," 20–28. (It may be of interest to note that although the Polish Gerontological Society has among its members a number of sociologists, there is no gerontology section in the Polish Sociological Association.)

36. *Sytuacja Zyciowa Osob Starszych*, tables 6–9, 138–41; *Sytuacja Bytowa Ludzi Starszych w 1985 R*, xx–xxi, tables 83–89; Izdebski, "Pomoc Spoleczna i Zintegrowany Program Dzialania," 18–21; Starega-Piasek, "Skutki Polityki Spolecznej," 33–34; Leon Grela, *Ludzie Starzy a Pomoc Spoleczna* (Warsaw: Instytut Pracy i Spraw Socjalnych, Studia i Materialy, 1982), Z.5, 19; Dziubinska-Michalewicz, "Analiza Wydatkow Panstwa i Przedsiebiorstw," 108–12, 124; Frackiewicz, "Sfery Niedostatku a Funkcje Opiekuncze Panstwa," 143; Ruta Pragier, "Panstwo Finansuje Zaslugi Lub Biede. Lobby Przyszlych Staruszkow," *Polityka*, July 9, 1988, 5; personal communications from Poland, summer 1989.

37. *Sytuacja Zyciowa Osob Starszych*, 137; *Sytuacja Bytowa Ludzi Starszych w*

1985 R, xviii–xix, tables 41–43, 69–74; Bugaj, "Funkcje Opiekuncze Panstwa," 276–77.

38. Quoted after Bakowska, "Emerytury i Renty po Nowemu," 3. On the pervasive insecurity among the elderly, see also Solska, "Nasza Stopa," 1–6; and Bugaj, "Funkcje Opiekuncze Panstwa," 266–85. "They don't dare to think about the future, everything's so uncertain, changing from one moment to the next." Personal communication from Poland, summer 1989. The data on recent emmigration from Poland is in Jacek Mach, "Czas Polonii," *Glos Wybrzeza*, February 21, 1988, 29; Dariusz Szymczycha, "Ocean i Sprawa Polska," *Sztandar Mlodych*, February 25, 1988, 5; personal communication from Warsaw, September 1989.

39. Widespread poverty, especially among the elderly—"the shame of socialism"—has also been recently discovered (i.e., made public) in the USSR and Hungary. See Esther Fein, "Soviet Openness Brings Poverty Out of the Shadows," *New York Times*, January 29, 1989, K1–9; Henry Kamm, "Hungarians Shocked by News of Vast Poverty in Their Midst," *New York Times*, February 6, 1989, A3.

40. Warsaw-based Solidarity daily *Gazeta Wyborcza* published (September 29, 1989) the text of a confidential document, confirmed by PUWP officials, indicating that in August the hard-line Rumanian government appealed for Warsaw Pact intervention in Poland to prevent the ceding of power to non-Communists; reportedly, the Soviet Union rejected the idea (after the information in "2,500 East Germans Still Camp Outside Embassy in Prague," *New York Times*, September 30, 1989, A4).

41. Tadeusz Mazowiecki's inaugural speech in parliament; quote after "Rzad Naprawy Gospodarki," *Zycie Gospodarcze*, September 3, 1989, 12.

42. Karol Szwarc, "Radykalnie Czy na Oslep?" *Zycie Gospodarcze*, September 10, 1989, 1–2; Stanislaw Gomulka, "Uwaga: Krokodyle!" *Zycie Gospodarcze*, September 10, 1989, 1–4; Daniel Passent, "Wstrzymany Oddech," *Polityka*, September 16, 1989, 16; Andrzej Tymowski, "Wydatki z Cienkiego Portfela," *Polityka*, September 9, 1989, 5; Jerzy Szperkowicz, "Na Kim Zacisnac Ten Pas," *Gazeta Wyborcza*, September 6, 1989, 3; Ernest Skalski, "Nedza? Bezrobocie? Zniesienie Swiadczen? Koszty Realne," *Gazeta Wyborcza*, September 5, 1989, 3; "Ministrowie w Komisjach," *Zycie Gospodarcze*, September 17, 1989, 6–8.

43. Michal Walewski, "W Bastionie Betonu," *Polityka*, August 12, 1989, 5; Jane Curry and Jacek Wasilewski, "Nomenklatura o Sobie," *Polityka*, September 16, 1989, 3; "Two Sides in Warsaw," *New York Times*, September 4, 1989, A2. On the other hand, Polish media increasingly often report cases of what has been termed *uwlaszczenie nomenklatury* (*en*propriation—as an antonym of *ex*propriation—of the *nomenklatura*): the acquisition, under new laws, as individual or group property, of state enterprises by local party bosses, the very same ones who mismanaged them for years (e.g., K. S., "Robotnicy Wobec Reformy," *Zycie Gospodarcze*, July 30, 1989, 12; B. K., "Jaka Wlasnosc?" *Zycie Gospodarcze*, August 13, 1989, 1–6.

On the strongly "populist" pronouncements of the OPZZ, the former government-sponsored unions, Janusz Ostaszewski, "Koniec Miodowego Miesiaca," *Zycie Gospodarcze*, September 17, 1989, 3.

44. Stanislaw Kwiatkowski, "W Obawie przed Monopolem," *Polityka*, June 3, 1989, 7; Stefan Cichowicz and Witold Morawski, "Co to Znaczy Sprawiedliwie?" *Zycie Gospodarcze*, June 25, 1989, 5; K. S., "Robotnicy Wobec Reformy," *Zycie*

Gospodarcze, July 30, 1989, 12. These widespread attitudes among Poles, in spite of state socialism's ever-worsening ill delivery of expected services, have been noted in several sociological studies conducted during the 1980s. See Stefan Nowak, "Values and Attitudes of Polish People," *Scientific American* 245 (1981): 45–53; David Mason, *Public Opinion and Political Change in Poland, 1980–1982* (Cambridge and New York: Cambridge University Press, 1985), 41, 56–58, 62–66; Lena Kolarska and Andrzej Rychard, "Visions of Social Order," in *Crises and Conflicts: The Case of Poland, 1980–1981* (Warsaw: Sisyphus Social Studies, 1982); Miroslawa Marody, *Spoleczenstwo Polskie Drugiej Polowy Lat 80-tych. Proba Diagnozy Stanu Swiadomosci Spolecznej* (Warsaw: Polskie Towarzystwo Socjologiczne, 1987).

45. Gomulka, "Uwaga: Krokodyle!," 1–4. As planned, unemployment benefits will amount to 70 percent of the last paycheck for the first three months, 50 percent for the next six, and 40 percent after nine months of unemployment (quote after H. S., "Zatrudnienie po Nowemu," *Zycie Gospodarcze*, June 4, 1989, 15).

46. This conclusion based on content analysis of *Polityka*, *Zycie Gospodarcze*, *Tygodnik Powszechny*, *Tygodnik Solidarnosc*, *Gazeta Wyborcza*, and *Zycie Warszawy* from June to September 1989. Quotations from *Kontrontacje*, June 1989, 9.

47. Personal communication from Grazyna Kacprowicz, Warsaw, September 30, 1989; Bakowska, "Emerytury i Renty po Nowemu," 3; idem, "Najpierw Place—Potem Swiadczenia," 3; Pragier, "Lobby Przyszlych Staruszkow," 5; Wojciechowska, "Bledne Kolo Roszczen," 1–6; Krzysztof Lozinski, "Emeryt Tez Czlowiek," *Gazeta Wyborcza*, September 6, 1989, 3.

The Restructuring of Old Age: Older Workers in the Economy

9/International Perspectives on Early Withdrawal from the Labor Force

Anne-Marie Guillemard

Since the mid 1970s, the labor-force participation of persons 55 to 64 years old has been decreasing rapidly in most developed industrial societies. This trend began among those aged 60–64 and then swept over the 55–59 age group. Significant changes have affected the timing of withdrawal from the labor force. In this chapter, international comparisons of the ways older people stop working are used to shed light on the social meaning of this rerouting of the pathways leading from work to retirement.

Early Retirement: A Change in Timing or a Transformation of the Life Course?

This study is undertaken from the perspective of the social organization of the life course. In the construction of the modern life course, the point at which people exit from the labor force has acquired particular significance. Besides revealing the changing social organization of the later stages of the life course, a study of trends in the timing of permanent labor-market withdrawal can shed light on how the whole life course is being reorganized.

Changes affecting labor-force exit can be analyzed at three levels. First, the *timing* may change, advancing or delaying the date of passage toward economic inactivity. Second, the *form* of the transition may be altered so that this turning point becomes a period of gradual passage or a cutoff line marking an abrupt entry into another stage of life. In both instances, the individual's control over the process must be taken into account when assessing its significance. Third, the *reference marks* that society uses to signal the boundaries between ages in the life course may change. In developed industrial societies, these marks, to a large extent, have been incorporated in the arrangements, rules, and eligibility requirements adopted by private and public welfare systems, which thus become involved in constructing the stages of life and setting the boundaries between them. In these societies, welfare systems and social policies have been powerful forces in shaping the tripartite division of the modern life course into a period of education (youth), work (adulthood), and retirement (old age). Both private and public old-age funds have shaped the order and hierarchy among these stages.

In industrial societies, then, there is a close relationship between the social organization of the life course and the structure of the welfare system. In sociological writings, however, these two aspects have typically been analyzed independently of each other. Analysis of social policy and the welfare state, a well-developed field of sociological inquiry, takes little account of studies of the life course and the stages of life. Similarly, life-course studies, now undergoing a revival, seldom take questions of social policy into account. My intention here is to build a bridge between these two separate fields of sociological inquiry by analyzing, together, the transformation of welfare systems and the reorganization of the life course. Do the recent changes in patterns of permanent labor-force withdrawal reflect new linkages between the welfare system and the social organization of the life course? From this perspective, I endeavor to reexamine the function of retirement within the structure of the life course.

Before the establishment of pension funds, the social content of old age and its very definition varied from one social group to another. Traditionally, the only criterion used to identify old age was the loss of functional aptitudes. Aged French workers at the turn of the century received relief payments; they were thus classified as "old" only when they were no longer able to work and provide for their needs.[1] Retirement systems have singled out the last stage in the life course and have conferred a common trait—economic inactivity with a pension—on social groups differing from each other in almost every respect except chronological age. Old age has gradually been redefined as retirement. As retirement has expanded, a new life-course model has prevailed that combines old age and retirement. It should be pointed out that this model is of rather recent origin, and only since the 1970s has it become virtually universal.

Besides being the principal cause of a new division between stages of the life course and their social content, retirement has helped redefine the transition from adulthood to old age. This transition is regulated by formal requirements (chronological age, number of years worked) rather than functional aptitudes. Retirement has thus been a powerful factor in the "chronologization" of the life course. Since the beginning of this century, the principal reference marks signaling the passage from one stage of life to another have been chronological (i.e., calendar or age based). As a consequence, the life course has been "standardized," becoming much the same for all individuals and social groups: starting school, finding a first job, marrying, and retiring. All these events occur following a stable, homogeneous, and predictable timetable.

One interpretation of the rapid lowering of the age of labor-force exit is that it is merely an acceleration of the trend toward earlier withdrawal from the labor force resulting from the generalization of pension coverage. As a result, the period of retirement has been extended but without effecting any fundamental change in the tripartite organization of the life course. As with the rising age of entry into the labor market, early exit merely means that the time spent working is concentrated in a shorter period. The major social determinant of the life course is, therefore, still work. Though fluctuating, the chronological boundaries separating the three stages of life are still set by entry into and exit from the labor force. It follows that the meanings of work and its counterpart, retirement, have not altered. In brief, modifications in the passage out of the labor force are but changes in the retirement calendar, with all else remaining the same.

In contrast, I attempt to show that the changes under way are signs that the threefold life-course model is being deinstitutionalized. The boundaries between economic activity and inactivity are shifting not merely as a consequence of applying the retirement logic to younger age groups but as a result of a fundamental transformation in the linkage between the welfare system and the life course. The result, I argue, is to undermine the threefold model in which *retirement* and *old age* have become almost synonymous.

Throughout the following discussion, it should be kept in mind that *retirement* is used in a strict sense to refer *only* to exits from the labor force accompanied by entry into a pension system. Many aging wage earners stop working without becoming retired (i.e., acquiring old-age pension entitlements). Until they are eligible for such entitlements, they may rely on a great variety of arrangements to survive: live with kin, draw unemployment or disability benefits, and so forth.

After examining trends in labor-force participation by 55–64 year olds in a number of OECD countries, I compare the institutional arrangements used to handle early exits. It is the variations in these arrangements that underlie differences in participation rates. In general, any definitive exit automatically entails an entry into some social program—what I call a welfare subsystem—whether private or public. I describe these subsystems and their conditions of entitlement in order to highlight the principles that are redefining the boundaries of old age and modifying the pathways that lead out of the labor market. I show that the process of permanent labor-force exit is being regulated by a wide range of public welfare subsystems (not only by the traditional private or public retirement funds). As a result, we are witnessing a major transformation of the end of the life course; the chronological bounds between ages are being systematically torn up. The power of retirement systems to regulate definitive withdrawal is being undermined, and conventional conceptions of "old age as retirement" and an "intergenerational contract" are being dissolved.

The Rising Tide of Early Labor-Force Withdrawal

Since the early 1970s, OECD statistics on the labor-force participation rates of men and women aged 55–64 show a massive downward trend (table 9.1). Table 9.2[2] shows that from 1970 to 1988, the rates for men fell from 75 percent to 47 percent in France, 81 percent to 38 percent in the Netherlands, 82 percent to 56 percent in West Germany, 91 percent to 68 percent in Great Britain, and 81 percent to 66 percent in the United States. Since those who are unemployed but are looking for work are included in the definition of "labor force," the actual decrease is even sharper than depicted by these figures. Actual employment rates are approximately 10 percent lower than the labor-force participation rates shown in Table 9.1. If we consider actual employment rates, Great Britain joins the list of countries with a steep downturn. Only Sweden and Japan have not been swept up by this trend.

Cross-sectional data on the changing labor-force participation of women 55–59 are not particularly useful because large numbers of women have been entering the labor market during the years in question. Nevertheless, cohort analysis shows that the trend toward early exit has affected them as well. For older women, as for older men, participation rates have fallen considerably since the early 1970s. But since available statistics are more readily interpretable for men, the following observations focus mainly on the early-exit patterns among males in the five countries where the trend has been especially pronounced. West Germany, the Netherlands, the United Kingdom, the United States, and France stand at the head of the early-withdrawal list. By way of contrast, Sweden, where the boundaries between work and retirement have shifted little, if at all, is also included.

After an evolution that took nearly half a century to set the retirement age at 65 (the most common age of entitlement to a full old-age pension), the chronological bounds used to determine personal identities throughout the life course and organize the end of it have changed radically. Since the early 1970s, the age when persons stop working has fallen significantly. This change first affected 60–64 year olds, whose labor-force participation rates plummeted. For men, the rate fell by about 40 percent from 1965 to 1985 (see Table 9.1). In the early 1980s in most countries, except in Sweden and Japan, 55–59 year olds were affected as well, as the male activity rate fell by 10 to 20 percent.

These data highlight the massive trends affecting the exit of older workers from the labor force. To interpret them, however, it is necessary to examine the institutional arrangements underlying this shift of boundaries.

Table 9.1/Labor-Force Participation Rates of Older Men and Women: An International Comparison, Selected Years, 1965–1988

	1965	1970	1975	1980	1985	1986	1987	1988
Men aged 55–59								
France	82.9	82.9	83.3	80.9	67.8	69.4	67.3	67.3
Germany	90.5	88.4	84.5	80.0	76.2	75.7	76.3	76.6
Japan	90.0	91.2	92.2	91.2	90.3	90.5	91.0	91.3
Netherlands	—	—	78.9	74.8	64.8	63.2	61.3	60.0
Sweden	92.8	90.8	89.7	87.7	87.6	86.4	85.9	85.9
U.K.	95.7	95.3	93.0	90.1	81.8	80.9	81.0	81.6
U.S.	85.7	88.3	83.3	80.9	78.9	78.4	79.1	78.7
Men aged 60–64								
France	68.8	68.0	56.7	47.6	30.8	27.4	25.7	25.4
Germany	78.1	71.8	56.2	42.5	32.4	32.3	31.4	31.5
Japan	82.8	81.5	79.4	77.8	72.5	72.5	71.7	71.1
Netherlands	—	—	64.9	48.8	27.8	23.4	19.0	14.6
Sweden	83.0	79.5	74.0	69.0	65.1	65.2	64.2	64.1
U.K.	89.2	86.7	82.3	71.2	54.5	52.2	53.3	55.1
U.S.	79.2	71.7	64.5	59.8	55.1	54.3	54.3	53.8
Women aged 55–59								
France	41.2	46.0	43.5	47.3	42.8	43.1	44.6	45.3
Germany	36.3	36.4	37.9	37.4	35.9	36.8	38.0	38.5
Japan	49.8	48.7	48.8	50.5	51.0	49.9	50.8	50.9
Netherlands	—	—	17.5	18.5	18.3	17.8	17.2	16.7
Sweden	46.6	52.8	60.8	68.8	74.5	76.3	78.9	79.6
U.K.	44.5	50.1	52.4	53.6	51.6	52.1	53.5	54.8
U.S.	44.9	48.8	47.5	48.1	50.1	51.1	51.9	53.0
Women aged 60–64								
France	31.7	34.3	29.8	27.3	18.9	18.4	18.0	17.3
Germany	23.3	20.4	15.5	12.0	10.1	10.2	10.6	10.8
Japan	39.8	39.1	38.0	38.8	38.5	38.6	32.5	38.6
Netherlands	—	—	10.8	9.5	6.3	4.9	3.4	1.9
Sweden	30.9	35.8	38.3	41.0	46.6	47.6	50.1	50.5
U.K.	25.8	27.9	28.6	22.4	18.6	18.3	18.2	19.3
U.S.	34.5	34.8	33.2	32.9	33.2	33.0	32.9	33.6

Source: Compiled by A.-M. Guillemard.

Table 9.2/Labor-Force Participation, Unemployment, and Employment Activity Rates: An International Comparison, Selected Years, 1970–1988

	1970	1975	1980	1985	1986	1987	1988
Labor-force participation rates: men aged 55–64							
Canada	84.2	79.4	76.2	70.2	68.5	66.4	66.6
U.S.	80.7	74.6	71.2	67.3	66.7	67.0	66.4
Japan	86.6	86.0	85.4	83.0	82.9	82.6	82.3
France	75.4	68.9	68.5	50.1	49.5	47.6	47.3
Germany	82.2	68.1	65.5	57.0	55.7	56.3	56.5
Netherlands	—	72.2	63.2	47.0	44.3	41.3	38.5
Sweden	85.4	82.0	78.7	76.0	75.5	74.9	74.9
U.K.	91.3	87.8	81.8	68.2	66.5	67.1	68.4
Unemployment rates: men aged 55–64							
Canada	5.8	3.9	4.3	8.4	7.3	6.8	6.2
U.S.	2.8	4.3	3.4	4.3	4.3	3.7	3.5
Japan	2.1	3.2	3.7	5.0	5.2	5.4	4.4
France	1.9	2.6	4.7	6.7	7.6	7.7	7.5
Germany	0.9	3.9	4.3	10.1	8.5	9.4	10.2
Netherlands	—	3.1	3.3	6.0	6.4	7.5	8.1
Sweden	1.5	1.6	1.6	3.5	3.0	2.0	1.6
U.K.	5.0	6.3	9.5	13.4	14.9	14.0	11.4
Employment activity rates: men aged 55–64							
Canada	79.3	76.3	72.7	64.3	63.5	61.9	62.5
U.S.	78.4	71.4	68.3	64.4	63.8	64.5	64.0
Japan	84.8	83.2	82.2	78.9	78.7	78.2	78.6
France	74.0	67.1	65.3	46.7	45.7	43.9	43.7
Germany	81.5	65.4	62.7	51.2	51.9	54.9	54.5
Netherlands	—	70.7	60.9	44.2	41.5	38.3	35.4
Sweden	84.1	80.7	77.4	73.3	73.3	73.4	73.7
U.K.	86.7	82.3	74.0	58.7	56.6	57.7	60.5

Source: Compiled by A.-M. Guillemard.

A Comparative Analysis of Early-Withdrawal Arrangements

In industrial societies, labor-force withdrawal has become a major criterion for socially defining entry into old age. By examining the institutional arrangements for early withdrawal, we can see how stages in the life course have been turned into social categories and how, as a consequence, old age is being redefined. The rules and eligibility requirements of these new arrangements show how the transition toward economic inactivity is being socially reconstructed. They also shed light on the principles governing the distribution of work and free time in the later years of life.

The complicated institutional arrangements to be taken under consideration must be explored country by country so as to identify the principal passages leading out of the labor force. To concentrate exclusively on one arrangement, such as preretirement programs, would be inadequate. For each of the six countries under study here, the most frequently used passages for early exit have been examined, as well as the institutional arrangements that have been combined to open them. In the sections that follow, the main results of this empirical investigation are presented with the goal of highlighting cross-national similarities in the operation of these arrangements. These points of convergence show how national welfare systems are being reorganized along with the life course.

Two general conclusions can be drawn from a systematic examination of these convergences. First, retirement systems are less and less often the main institutional form regulating exit from the labor force. In all six countries, a significant number of people leave the labor market long before they start receiving pensions from public old-age funds. Labor-market exit no longer leads directly and systematically into the retirement system. Aging workers who give up their jobs and go directly to retirement in France, West Germany, and the Netherlands are in a minority. Second, and as a consequence, the new institutional arrangements for regulating definitive withdrawal bring other public welfare subsystems into play. They are connected so as to create unanticipated and unstable passages out of the labor market before the age of entitlement to a pension. These arrangements, their rules and requirements, govern the transition toward inactivity and set the bounds of old age as a period of life after work.

The Retirement System's Loss of Power to Regulate Exit
The decline of labor-force participation among those over 55 is not merely a product of the expansion of public retirement systems to cover people at younger ages. Instead, it is the result of intermediate arrangements, unrelated to the old-age funds, that were erected to bridge the period between exit from the labor force and entry into retirement. Consequently, the conventional social model of the transition toward economic inactivity has been overturned. Until recently, exit from work was made possible by entitlement to an old-age pension. These two events now have been separated; the period of inactivity often starts before the receipt of a pension. Among the six countries under study, only the Swedish retirement system has been able to maintain its power of regulating definitive exit, thanks to the development of programs for part-time retirement for those over 60. Elsewhere, labor-force withdrawal no longer

Table 9.3/Distribution of Retirees, Early Retirees, and Preretirees in France in 1981

	MEN	WOMEN	TOTAL
Retirees at 65 with full pensions	17.3%	18.4%	17.7%
Early retirees with full or reduced pension			
(World War II prisoners, disabled, etc.)	15.6	12.4	14.5
Preretirees under:			
The special National Employment Fund program	15.6	12.8	14.7
The 1972 guaranteed-income dismissal scheme	17.1	16.9	17.1
The 1977 guaranteed-income resignation scheme	26.7	32.1	28.4
Company-sponsored early-exit programs	7.7	7.4	7.6

Source: Ministry of Labor Survey (Paris, 1981).

regularly coincides with admission to a public retirement system. A minority of older wage earners in France, West Germany, and the Netherlands now pass directly from the labor force to retirement. The conditions of eligibility for retirement (age and years spent working) no longer serve to set the boundaries between economic activity and inactivity.

In Great Britain in 1983, 700,000 men aged 60 to 64 no longer worked but could not benefit from public retirement pensions, which are paid out only at the age of 65. Of the 700,000, 32 percent were on unemployment, 28 percent were receiving disability benefits, 12 percent were covered by the Job Release Scheme, 6 percent were on welfare, 17 percent had pensions from occupational retirement funds, and 5 percent had found other solutions.[3]

In the United States, eligibility for a social security old-age pension begins at age 62. Many older persons who stop working earlier must wait for retirement, relying on company programs combined with limited coverage under unemployment compensation or disability insurance. The major incentive for early withdrawal has been sizable bonuses paid by employers along with early allocations from company retirement funds. In this way, many older jobless workers are able to wait for retirement.

In the French private sector, according to a 1981 survey by the Ministry of Labor, a minority of older wage earners went directly from work into retirement. Table 9.3, taken from this survey, shows that less than 18 percent had retired at the normal age of 65. An additional 14 percent retired early with full or reduced pensions. In contrast, nearly two-thirds (68 percent) were "preretirees," those who stopped working before retirement under intermediate arrangements related to welfare subsystems other than the old-age fund: 8 percent under company-sponsored programs and 60 percent under arrangements managed by the Unemployment Compensation Fund.[4]

France is the only country that has actually lowered the official age of

Table 9.4/Admissions into Retirement for Men, West Germany, 1980–1987

Men who took retirement between 1980 and 1987 in the following proportions, previously had been:

	COVERED BY DISABILITY INSURANCE	COVERED BY LONG UNEM- PLOYMENT (52 WEEKS)	DECLARED UNFIT FOR WORK, HENCE ELIGIBLE TO RETIRE AT 60	WORKING AND ELIGIBLE FOR FLEXIBLE RETIREMENT AT 63	WORKING AND ELIGIBLE FOR NORMAL RETIREMENT AT 65
1980	48.3%	7.6%	16.2%	13.1%	14.6%
1981	50.3	8.5	17.7	11.7	11.8
1982	48.3	10.5	17.1	14.4	9.7
1983	47.7	9.4	15.4	18.2	9.3
1984	47.4	10.8	12.8	16.6	12.4
1985	42.9	11.4	12.4	16.1	17.0
1986	40.8	11.0	13.0	16.4	18.8
1987	40.1	10.8	12.9	16.4	19.8

Source: K. Jacobs, M. Kohli, and M. Rein, "Early Exit from the Labor Force in Germany," in *Time for Retirement*, ed. M. Kohli, M. Rein, A.-M. Guillemard, and H. Van Gunsteren (Cambridge: Cambridge University Press, forthcoming). Reprinted by permission of Cambridge University Press.

retirement. Since 1982, workers can retire at 60 rather than 65. One might conclude from this that the retirement system was restored to its function of regulating definitive withdrawal. But such a conclusion could be drawn only by ignoring the extension of "preretirement" under unemployment compensation to 55–59 year olds. Although some of these arrangements have subsequently been terminated or made less attractive, the employment rates of persons over 55 have continued falling since 1985 (Table 9.2). These persons, in ever-growing numbers, depend on ordinary unemployment compensation, particularly special long-term benefits. In this way, they manage, once ejected from the labor force, to wait for retirement.

West German data on people who have just entered the pension system (Table 9.4) also show that a minority of workers now pass directly from the labor force to retirement. In 1987, 40 percent of new pension beneficiaries earlier had been receiving disability benefits and about 10 percent had been on unemployment benefits. Direct admissions to normal retirement at 65, or "flexible" retirement at 63, accounted for 23 to 36 percent of new pensioners between 1980 to 1987; in the 1960s, these "normal retirees" accounted for over 50 percent of new pensioners.

Despite the lack of comparable survey data for the Netherlands, it can be pointed out that 43 percent of those receiving disability benefits and 10 percent of those on unemployment benefits in 1985 were in the 60–64 age group. Eligibility for retirement in Holland, whether public or private, is at age 65. Inactive men, who represented about 70 percent of all males 60–64, in 1985, were covered as follows: preretirement programs (VUT) under collective agreements, 21 percent in 1983 and 32 percent in 1985; disability insurance, 58 percent in 1983 and 51 percent in 1985; unemployment, 11 percent in 1983 and 9 percent in 1985.[5]

Public old-age pension funds have provided the institutional foundation of the tripartite model of the life course. And, as Kohli[6] argues, retirement has become a central element in the "moral economy" of industrial societies. Give the retirement system's importance in constructing the life course, what are the consequences of its loss of power over definitive exit? Is the tripartite model of the life course coming undone? It is clear that recent trends represent more than a mere modification of the retirement calendar. But to understand the implications of this, it is necessary to examine the new institutional arrangements for early exit in more detail.

New Institutional Arrangements and Their Implications
The principal subsystems increasingly used to manage the transition from work to retirement are unemployment compensation and disability insurance. This holds not only for France, the Netherlands, and West Germany but also to some extent for Sweden and Great Britain. In the United States, public programs have had little effect on early labor-force exit, but many companies have set up their own programs, particularly as a result of the Early Retirement Incentive Program (ERIP), which has spread widely since the early 1980s. Let us look at the two principal welfare subsystems handling early withdrawal and examine their implications.

DISABILITY INSURANCE
Disability insurance is now a major pathway out of the labor force in the Netherlands, West Germany, Sweden, and Great Britain. In some instances it has been linked to other arrangements, particularly unemployment compensation, to bridge the period until normal retirement. This has usually entailed broadening eligibility requirements for disability benefits.

In the Netherlands, entry into the disability insurance system was the most common form of early exit until the late 1970s and is still a well-trodden path. The number of disability beneficiaries increased 130 percent from 1973 to 1979, a year when nearly 60 percent of persons receiving such benefits were over 50 years old. Under this arrangement, health insurance covers a first stretch of fifty-two weeks; then, if total disability is recognized, disability insurance takes over. This arrangement was increasingly used after 1973 when eligibility requirements were broadened so that partial, even minimal, disabilities could be reclassified as total disability if applicants were unable to find jobs adapted to their qualifications and their handicaps in the local labor market. According to Van den Bosch and Petersen,[7] one-third of these beneficiaries in 1978 could be described as having a purely "economic disability"; it had no medical basis. After 1980, two other arrangements were introduced. First, collective agreements incorporated early-retirement provisions (VUT) that initially were subsidized by the government. Government saw the VUT as a means of transferring the costs of early withdrawal from public funds (disability insurance) to the private sector. The VUT provisions have had a limited scope, however, mainly affecting 60–64 year olds. A second arrangement, related to unemployment compensation, has developed since 1975 and now covers a significant proportion of 55–59 year olds. Its success signals the failure of the government's effort to transfer the costs of early exit to corporations.

Since 1976, disability insurance has also become the major path for early exit in the Federal Republic of Germany. By 1984, 48 percent of new admissions to the retirement system were people previously receiving disability benefits (Table 9.4). As in the Netherlands, this arrangement's success has come from broadening eligibility requirements beyond strictly medical criteria so as to take into account factors related to the labor market. Since 1976, partially disabled persons have been able to receive full disability benefits if there are no suitable part-time jobs available for them. This arrangement has been widely used by 55–59 year olds, an age group that cannot enter the retirement system and whose position in the labor market is precarious. Although the tightening of eligibility requirements since 1985 has somewhat limited this option, it is still often taken, despite passage of a May 1984 act about pre-retirement contracts intended to transfer some of the costs of early exit to the private sector. In 1987, about 30 percent of new old-age pensioners exited from the labor force through disability insurance before retiring.

In Sweden and Great Britain, the role of disability insurance has also been expanded. Swedish eligibility requirements for disability insurance were loosened to assist aging jobless persons so that "employability" as well as medical criteria are used to establish eligibility. Since 1976, jobless persons over 60 have been able to claim disability benefits till normal retirement at 65 if they cannot find employment. Companies have not missed the opportunity to work this arrangement into their personnel policies. It allows them to shed workers often seen as less productive and who have the best legal protection against dismissal. Despite an active public policy of keeping aging employees at work, Sweden has opened a breach in this protection by broadening the definition of disability, allowing a new form of early exit to come into competition with the part-time retirement program. Since it was set up in 1976, this program makes it possible to adjust work schedules so that older workers can combine part-time jobs with part-time retirement. By authorizing total early withdrawal, the arrangements under disability insurance have opened a route for getting around this policy. For the time being, however, the linkage between the life course and the welfare system has changed little. What still characterizes Sweden is both the relative stability of labor-force participation rates for persons over 55 and the maintenance of the retirement system's power over definitive withdrawal.

In Great Britain, more and more workers have been withdrawing early under disability insurance, even though the system has not been reorganized nor have its eligibility requirements been broadened. Piachaud[8] has found a strong correlation between the number of persons receiving disability benefits and the jobless rate. In effect, physicians, who in Britain are solely responsible for judging whether people are fit for work, apparently take into account conditions in the labor market. Nonetheless, only a small proportion of aging wage earners (mainly manual workers over 60) have been able to negotiate this sort of coverage.

As these cases show, disability insurance has become a major mechanism for early withdrawal in countries where eligibility requirements have included, besides medical criteria, the "employability" of aging workers. Disability has thus been redefined in terms that are more economic than medical. The result is that age discrimination by employers is now often euphemistically called "worker disability."

The shift from the pension system to disability insurance as a way of exiting the labor force means that criteria for definitive withdrawal have been redefined. A functional criterion—disability, or the inability to work—is replacing the age criterion for determining labor-force exits. Disability benefits have nothing to do with chronological age; the condition for receiving them is to be "unfit" for work. This change can be interpreted as a new way of marking the end of the life course with functional labels rather than chronological milestones. It reflects a "dechronologization" of the life course, a process that inevitably involves "destandardizing" it. Since people's ability to keep working as they grow older depends on their social group, functional criteria lead to major differences among individuals with regard to the timing of the passages between stages of the life course. Furthermore, a new social construction of old age and its relation to work is emerging. Older workers are no longer simply said to be close to the age of entitlement to rest with a pension; instead, they are labeled unfit for the labor market. This is a new development, especially in France, Germany, and the Netherlands where, unlike in the United States, there has traditionally been no requirement actually to leave the labor market to be eligible for a pension; the sole criterion has been chronological age. When, as in West Germany or the Netherlands, nearly half of those who reach retirement age have previously passed through the disability insurance system, economic inactivity no longer means the right to rest. It means being unfit for work.

UNEMPLOYMENT COMPENSATION

Unemployment compensation is the second welfare subsystem being used with great regularity to manage the transition into old age. In the mid 1970s, special procedures were adopted almost everywhere in Europe—including France, the Netherlands, West Germany, and Sweden—for compensating older workers for lost jobs.

In France,[9] arrangements under unemployment compensation were a principal means of managing the massive early-withdrawal trend (Table 9.3). A guaranteed-income scheme was set up in 1972 for persons over 60 years old who had been dismissed from their jobs. It was extended in 1977 to those who had resigned. In 1982, other measures further extended these schemes to 55–59 year olds. Under agreements between the government and firms, wage earners aged 56 years and 2 months (and sometimes earlier) could be dismissed with the National Employment Fund paying them special benefits until normal retirement, which, since 1983, is age 60 for persons having contributed to the old-age fund for 37½ years. More recently, government attempts to block preretirement arrangements, because of their heavy costs, have caused a groundswell in the ranks of older long-term jobless workers who receive ordinary unemployment benefits.

The Netherlands adopted new rules in 1975 stipulating that anyone between 60 and 64 years of age who received unemployment benefits could continue to do so until the legal retirement age of 65. Under these rules, people can stop working at age 57½. Unemployment insurance and then welfare assistance bridge the period until age 65.

West Germany has gradually loosened conditions for providing unemployment benefits to the jobless over age 54. Since 1987, persons aged 57 years and 4 months dismissed from their jobs can receive unemployment benefits until age 60, the age when the "long-term unemployed" become eligible for a normal retirement pension. Hence, the "59 rule," which has worked as a means of early withdrawal for many years, but especially since 1975, has become a "57 rule." In 1986, 11 percent of new retirees had previously been on unemployment compensation (Table 9.4).

In Sweden, arrangements under the unemployment and disability insurance funds have been combined to open a pathway to definitive withdrawal as early as age 58 (with unemployment benefits till 60, then disability benefits till 65, the normal retirement age). In comparison with the five other countries however, this pathway is seldom followed.

In Great Britain, no special protection has been offered to the aging jobless. But unemployment compensation for cases of long joblessness is often provided to supplement the incomes of "discouraged" older workers[10] who have stopped working because of partial disability or the early receipt of occupational old-age pensions. Occupational pension funds are a major means of early labor-force exit in Britain.

In all six countries, the consequences are similar. Making it easier for older workers to receive unemployment compensation also makes it easier for companies to dismiss older workers. Firms can thus get rid of such workers at the least economic and social costs. Adopting measures that compensate older workers for lost jobs reinforces age discrimination, especially in periods of economic downturn.

The growing importance of unemployment compensation, disability insurance, or both as a means of regulating labor-force exit has considerable significance. First, the boundaries between economic activity and inactivity are set as a function of the labor market. Even though it may be optional, as in the now-terminated French guaranteed-income scheme, early withdrawal under unemployment compensation depends mainly on the employer and his power to dismiss, not on employees and their claim to rest and a pension. Second, the right to receive social-transfer payments, whether disability or unemployment benefits, entails surrendering the right to a job. In contrast, the practice in most countries (except for the United States and the United Kingdom) has been to separate the right to employment from the right to a pension. In most countries, one does not have to give up working in order to receive a public old-age pension. Using unemployment compensation or disability insurance to manage labor-force exit considerably weakens the older wage earner's right to a job. Third, with respect to the life course, replacing the retirement income system with disability insurance or unemployment compensation has opened a gap between the second and third stages in the life course. Wage earners lose control over the later years of their lives. Age specialization is emphasized. After the working years comes a time when one is denied the right to a job and is forced to stop working. In fact, working in the later years of life is frowned upon. At the same time, one can no longer clearly anticipate the transition to the last stage in the life course. The chronological reference marks of retirement have been swept away and, with them, any principle providing for an orderly transition out of the labor market. While there is more flexibility in organizing the end of the life course, the exit process is increasingly regulated by the labor market and by companies' employment policies. The unemployment and disability systems regulating this process are extremely flexible;[11] they are constantly reworked as a function of the labor market.

THE DECLINE OF "PRERETIREMENT" PROGRAMS

A description of the institutional mechanisms used to manage early withdrawal would not be complete without mention of "preretirement" programs, the third principal pathway out of the labor force. These include solidarity preretirement contracts in France, the Preretirement Act in West Germany, the Job Release Scheme in Great Britain, and the VUT in the Netherlands. Essentially, such programs are intended to improve the situation in the labor market by proposing voluntary early withdrawal to aging wage earners and requiring that these departures entail the hiring of young people. Whether part of public policy or of collective agreements, they tend to manage labor-force exits in the same way as retirement systems: Age remains the essential eligibility requirement, and the choice of whether to go on preretirement is left up to the worker. Although eligibility requirements fluctuate depending on conditions in the labor market, preretirement provides for a regulated transition out of the workforce without placing beneficiaries in the precarious position of relying on unemployment compensation and disability benefits.

Significantly, however, most preretirement schemes have been either abandoned (in France in 1986 and West Germany in 1988) or cut back (the British Job Release Scheme). Only the Dutch VUT program is still in effect, and it too is being called into question. The decline of preretirement programs corroborates my general interpretation of the early-exit trend, which is not just a result of lowering the age of retirement. The end of these preretirement schemes can be interpreted as a symptom of the general decline of the retirement system both as a mechanism for regulating labor-force exit and as an indicator of the dechronologizing of the life course.

The Deinstitutionalization of the Life Course

This comparative analysis shows the scope of the changes under way. Although, at first glance, we might think that they amount to little more than an adjustment to the retirement timetable, on closer inspection they turn out to be signals of a thoroughgoing reorganization of the life course. The retirement system's loss of power to regulate definitive exit is evidence that the linkage between the life course and welfare subsystems is being reworked.

The Swedish case illustrates, *a contrario*, the maintenance of a tight linkage between the retirement system and the institutionalization of the threefold life-course model. Whenever the public retirement system maintains its power over labor-force withdrawal, the social organization of the end of the life course stays much the same. The thresholds of entry into old age do not change much, nor do the boundaries that mark them.

In all other countries under study, much more than the timing of retirement has come into question; the very ways in which people make the transition from one age to another, as well as the boundaries marking these thresholds, have been deeply affected by the changes analyzed here.

The welfare subsystems (principally unemployment compensation and disability insurance) that have taken the place of retirement bring their own logic for regulating the transition from work to nonwork. As a result, the chronological milestones used to mark the life course are becoming less visible; and functional criteria are becoming more important in organizing the later years of life.

This change is especially noticeable when disability insurance replaces retirement, but there are other indications of this trend. The 1986 U.S. law against age discrimination in employment, for instance, can be interpreted as indicating a different organization of the life course. While placing less importance on chronological age, it lays greater stress on functional criteria based on the individual's capabilities and effectiveness in the workplace, since only these criteria can be legally used by employers to dismiss or retire employees.

This "dechronologization" entails a "destandardization" of the life course. Since the chronological markers are becoming less visible, the end of the life course has been blurred. The tripartite model, which places everyone in a continuous, foreseeable trajectory of successive stages, statuses, and roles, is coming apart. The life course is becoming variable, imprecise, and contingent. As a result, workers can no longer predict at what age and under what conditions they will exit from work. Retirement as a social situation and a system of transfers no longer constitutes the horizon where everyone sees the pathway he or she will one day take out of the labor force toward old age.

Although the end of the life course is now flexible, it can hardly be said to be individualized. This destandardization does not reflect greater decision making by individuals. The large majority of early withdrawals are not voluntary.[12] Instead, the early-exit trend reflects conditions in the labor market and companies' strategies.

The fundamental changes affecting the end of the life course can also be detected in reports of those affected by these developments. Retirement is no longer a unifying principle that gives a meaning to a third stage of life, starting with exit from the labor force. For example, very few of the "young old"— those 55–65 who no longer work—identify themselves as retired. One-quarter of the jobless British population between the ages of 60 and 64, and only 12 percent between 55 and 59, classify themselves as retired; the rest say they are unemployed or "discouraged" workers no longer looking for a job. Much the same is true in France.[13] These results provide a measure of the impact of early-withdrawal arrangements on the organization of the life course.

In sum, the social construction (closely associating old age and retirement) of the third stage of life is coming apart. Old age, retirement, and labor-force withdrawal no longer coincide. Occupational old age starts well before retirement. Doing away with retirement as the means of determining the meaning of the last phase of life has overturned the tripartite life-course model. The boundaries are becoming less clear, the thresholds between ages less visible.

The magnitude of the changes under way makes it difficult for us to imagine a return to the previous situation, even if, as some anticipate, there is a marked increase in labor-market demand for older workers in the future. Even though many of these new arrangements were intended to be temporary, a certain conception of the life course, as well as a certain social construction of old age, seems to have come undone.

Besides keeping people from forming a continuous image of how their lives will evolve, the tendency to deinstitutionalize the end of the life course upsets the system of reciprocity between generations. Doubt is being cast not only on retirement but also on the underlying long-term contract of commitments binding the generations together. What are the prospects of this long-term contract, which involves several *successive* generations? The reciprocity of commitments between generations is no longer reliable in a society where time is speeded up and the life course is no longer organized around fixed chronological markers. Those now in the labor force are beginning to doubt whether the next generation will pay for their pensions as willingly as they are paying for those of current retirees. The temporal strategy underlying this transfer implies delaying compensation for the alienation of work in exchange for the right to rest at the end of life. But the values underlying this strategy are weakening because the life course no longer provides individuals with a predictable future.

The passage from a society of "managed time" [14] to one that refuses time can help us understand the changes that are now altering the tripartite life-course model. This institution no longer places people in a series of uniform, successive, and predictable phases so that they play their parts in industrial society. In the new social context, this institution must, on the contrary, prepare people for an evolving world. Perhaps the meaning of the changing life course is related to the new requirements that an ephemeral society imposes for socializing individuals.

Notes

Acknowledgment: Translated from French by Noal Mellott, CNRS, Paris.

1. A.-M. Guillemard, *La vieillesse et l'état* (Paris: Presses Universitaires de France, 1980), chap. 1.

2. The statistics used here were gathered by an international research group (Martin Kohli, Martin Rein, Anne-Marie Guillemard, and Herman Van Gunsteren) that has worked on six countries (United States, Netherlands, France, West Germany, Sweden, and Great Britain) in collaboration with F. Laczko and C. Phillipson (for Great Britain), Harold Sheppard (for the United States), and E. Wadensjo (for Sweden). The information thus gathered is the basis of a personal interpretation of observed trends. The results of this collective undertaking are in *Time for Retirement*, ed. M. Kohli, M. Rein, A.-M. Guillemard, and H. Van Gunsteren (Cambridge: Cambridge University Press, forthcoming).

3. F. Laczko and C. Phillipson, in Kohli et al., *Time for Retirement*.

4. A.-M. Guillemard, *Le déclin du social: Formation et crise des politiques de la vieillesse* (Paris: Presses Universitaires de France, 1986); idem, "Formation et crise d'une politique sociale: Le cas de la politique de la vieillesse," in *Sociologie du Travail* 2 (1986): 156–72.

5. B. de Vroom and M. Blomsma, "The Netherlands: An Extreme Case," in Kohli et al., *Time for Retirement*.

6. M. Kohli, "Retirement and the Moral Economy: An Historical Interpretation of the German Case," *Journal of Aging Studies*, nos. 1–2 (1987): 125–44.

7. Quoted by B. de Vroom and M. Blomsma, "The Netherlands."

8. D. Piachaud, "Disability, Retirement and Unemployment of Older Men," *Journal of Social Policy* 15, no. 2 (1986): 145–62.

9. See note 4.

10. F. Laczko, "Older Workers, Unemployment and the Discouraged Worker Effect," in *Social Gerontology: New Directions*, ed. S. di Gregorio (London: Croom Helm, 1987), 239–51.

11. B. Casey, "Early Retirement: The Problems of Instrument Substitution and Cost-Shifting, and Their Implications for Restructuring the Process of Retirement," *International Social Security Review* 4 (1987).

12. B. Casey and F. Laczko, "Recent Trends in Labor Force Participation of Older Men in Great Britain and Their Implications for the Future" (Paper presented at the Colloquium Futuribles devoted to the theme "Demographic Ageing in Europe," held in Paris, October 4 and 5, 1988). See also note 4.

13. See note 4.

14. L. Roussel and A. Girard, "Régimes démographiques et Ages de la vie," in *Les Ages de la Vie* (Paris: Presses Universitaires de France, 1982), 1:15–23.

10/The Demographics of Age in Labor-Market Management

Gösta Esping-Andersen and Harald Sonnberger

According to conventional wisdom, labor markets "clear" in a way analogous to how prices influence supply and demand. The exit of older workers is a principal element in the clearing process because it opens the gates for younger cohorts, allows firms to shed presumably less productive manpower, and generates flexibility and dynamism in the economy. Yet, standard textbook economics have considerable difficulty in fitting exit through retirement to the strict logic of prices. Retirement is an institution created by politics, not by autonomous markets.

In the early stages of capitalism, it was unusual for workers to retire. Some older workers died or continued with diminished capacity; many others were simply asked to leave and fend for themselves through the aid of family or poor relief. During the first phases of welfare-state construction, programs emerged for the protection of impaired aged workers, but benefits offered little more than a minimum for survival. Under none of these conditions could mass retirement occur. The principle of retirement, as several writers have suggested, emerged only when pension levels reached a de facto adequate wage. And this is something that happened only with the consolidation of the postwar welfare state.[1]

An adequate retirement wage alters the parameters of the labor-market clearing mechanism; the labor-supply decisions of older workers are shaped by an incentive system exogenous to the market. In this sense, the demographics of age enter into the regulation of labor markets.

It may be that pension reforms have historically been designed with the intent of either raising productivity or creating new jobs for the young. One can easily find examples of industrialists advocating pensions with an eye to the former, and unions and labor parties demanding pension reform with full-employment objectives in mind. But, until recently, coverage, benefits, and eligibility rules were such that a typical older worker's welfare tradeoff would favor continued employment.

Over the past few decades, this has changed. Liberalized eligibility and high benefit standards now offer workers a genuine choice. Moreover, with early-retirement reforms, the traditional flow of labor-market exit has changed fundamentally. If, in the 1960s, people normally retired at 65–70 years of age, today the rule is anywhere between the ages of 55 and 65, depending on the nation. It may be that these reforms were designed for purely welfare reasons, in order to allow older and often disabled workers a deserved rest after decades of toil. But, for whichever reasons, pensions have also come to serve as perhaps *the* major vehicle with which governments try to manage unemployment, deindustrialization, and far-reaching economic transformation.

The new prominence of pensions as a tool for labor-market management may be explained by a lack of policy alternatives. With mounting unemployment, the erosion of the Keynesian consensus, and the adoption of restrictive anti-inflationary policies, aggregate employment-stimulation policies were more or less ruled out. Hence it became tempting to reduce the labor supply. But the objectives of major interest groups also conspired to catapult pensions into prominence in the field of labor-market-management policies. Employers, imprisoned by job rights, found in early retirement a means to enhance productivity and undertake desperately needed rationalization; trade unions, similarly restricted by seniority rights, embraced early retirement as an acceptable means of enhancing job opportunities for youth; and governments, having to deliver on full-employment promises, found in early retirement a convenient helping hand. Into this triad of implicit consensus entered the aged worker, more often than not tied to a tiring and incapacitating industrial job, whose welfare would clearly improve by moving into an acceptably remunerated pension.

Two facts are indisputable. First, the trend toward early labor-force withdrawal of aged male workers is universal among the advanced countries. In almost all countries, the trend accelerated in the 1970s. The second fact is that the rate of early retirement among males varies dramatically among nations. Germany and France represent a group of countries in which participation rates among males aged 55–65 has plummeted. Indeed, France has officially lowered normal retirement age to 60. Across the board, early-retirement schemes and a variety of "social pacts" have made labor-market withdrawal a normal occurrence for males in their late 50s. It is among this group that labor-market problems most clearly found a solution in retirement schemes. At the other extreme, the decline has been small indeed in such countries as Sweden and Norway. In between lie the United States and Great Britain.

West Germany, Sweden, and the United States exemplify the international

Table 10.1/Participation and Retirement Rates for Men, 55–64, in Germany, Sweden, and the United States, 1965–1985

	GERMANY	SWEDEN	UNITED STATES
Participation rates			
1965	86.7	87.6	84.2
1975	72.0	80.9	75.6
1985	57.5	76.0	67.9
Average annual percentage change	−1.5	−0.7	−0.7
Percentage of population, 55–64, in retirement			
Disability, 1975	6.4	7.0	4.5
Disability, 1985	8.7	7.2	3.3
Other, 1975	18.3	3.1	18.3
Other, 1985	27.6	11.0	23.2

Source: WEEP data files (see note 2).

variation very well, and these countries constitute the empirical test cases in our study (see Table 10.1).[2] As we can see in the table, cross-national diversity is a recent phenomenon. In 1965, participation rates were virtually identical in all three countries; by 1985, they were ten percentage points lower in Germany than in Sweden.[3]

The data illustrate a second important point: The decline in labor-force participation is almost exclusively an effect of early retirement; the disability pension rate has remained essentially constant. Since access to nonmedical early retirement has undergone substantial improvements in terms of both eligibility and benefits in all three countries, it is probably no longer true that disability programs contain other than genuinely disabled workers. If this is the case, it would appear that almost the entire increase in retirement is caused by factors unrelated to the health of workers. Hence, our aggregate participation rates should measure a trend that is more or less *net* of the health, or disablement, effect.

These facts speak to the longstanding debate on whether declining participation among the aged is a phenomenon compelled by adverse economic conditions (e.g., recessions, high unemployment, industrial rationalization) or induced by the financial attractions and leisure opportunities afforded by improved pension arrangements.

Empirically, there is no doubt that governments have taken deliberate legislative action to accommodate pension schemes to economic objectives by, for example, lowering retirement age, liberalizing eligibility, or offering various incentives. Nonetheless, most early-retirement reforms were initially introduced for social-policy reasons and then, more or less inadvertently, employed for labor-market goals.[4] As Jacobs and Rein (see Chapter 11) note, in West Germany key court decisions as well as government legislation pertinent to early retirement emerged in the era of buoyant economic growth and labor shortages. But as economic conditions worsened in the 1970s, the social security schemes were admirably suited to the needs of German industry to shed itself of excess (elderly) manpower in its struggle to rationalize and restructure. And many countries found new ways to extend eligibility and encourage early retirement as unemployment rates soared in the late 1970s and 1980s.

That early retirement has been accelerated by pension reforms in tandem with slack labor markets is indisputable. But it remains unclear how the two factors interrelate. The tendency toward increasingly early labor-market exit is, at least for males, a long-term phenomenon that predates the 1973 and 1979 oil shocks, rising unemployment, and widespread industrial rationalization. In Germany, there was a noticeable increase in the rate of older male (55–64) exit during the 1970s and 1980s, but in both Sweden and the United States, the annual rate of decline in participation for the same group has remained essentially constant since the early 1960s.

On a broader scale of comparison, international differences in early retirement are much more extreme than variations in pension systems or the severity of economic crisis warrant (see Table 10.1). The annual rate of early exit in Germany is twice as high as in Sweden, even if (as we discuss below) Swedish pension benefits are clearly more attractive; and the rate of industrial job loss has been similar in the two countries. In contrast, the American rates of early exit are similar to the Swedish, even if benefits in the United States are dramatically lower. Clearly, benefit incentives alone cannot explain much of the international variance. Unemployment and job losses in manufacturing are not, per se, convincing causes. In Sweden, it is true, unemployment rates have remained extraordinarily low; but they were high in the United States throughout the 1970s and most of the 1980s; and in Germany, since the mid 1970s.

Early retirement is predominantly a masculine affair. This is to an extent logical when we consider the historically low and typically interrupted participation profiles of women. In very few countries, and then only recently, have women's labor-force-participation profiles come to parallel those of men. Women typically left the labor market at child-bearing age, and even if they later returned, they would normally not have accumulated adequate pension rights for a full pension, let alone early retirement. Furthermore, be it for "push" or "pull" reasons, men are more likely than women to participate in early-retirement schemes. On the push side, unemployment-prone unskilled jobs in smokestack industries are more likely to be filled by men. On the pull side, older men are for the same reasons more likely to be physically or otherwise impaired and are, as mentioned, more likely in possession of adequate pension rights.

In this study, we explore the interplay of social policies and labor-market conditions in the formation of early retirement among male workers. We begin with the classical debate on whether early retirement is induced by attractive benefits and "negative" work incentives (the pull argument) or whether it is primarily compelled by adverse economic conditions, unemployment, and industrial restructuration strategies (the push argument). Whereas most studies generalize from single-nation analyses, our approach is comparative and longitudinal. We have selected Sweden, Germany, and the United States not only because they represent three diverse early-exit trajectories but also because each represents a unique welfare-state regime type.[5]

Sweden typifies the Scandinavian social democratic model of universalist, egalitarian, and "institutional" social policy; in Sweden, the decline in older male participation has been internationally modest. Germany represents the typical European welfare state with an emphasis on occupationally differentiated programs, relatively high benefit inequalities, and somewhat narrowly defined government responsibilities in the labor market; in Germany, the rates of early male retirement have been extraordinarily high. The United States illustrates the typical "residualist" welfare-state regime with its modest public welfare responsibilities and powerful bias in favor of private-sector solutions. The American rates of early male retirement fall in the middle category.

In most studies, the social-policy "pull effect" has been examined fairly narrowly in terms of pension entitlements. With the concept of welfare-state regimes, our analyses are pitched at a more macro level of comparison. We do not just mean that pension benefits or legislation pertaining to early retirement vary significantly. Rather, our countries represent three internationally distinct welfare-state clusters in terms of underlying institutional principles, among which the relationship between work and welfare, labor market and social policy, is one of the most crucial factors. So, while pension policies are crucial, they by no means exhaust the analytically relevant package of policies. We must take into consideration also the integration of active employment policies and, more generally, the ways in which citizens face a menu of choices between working and retiring.

Choice and Circumstance in Early-Retirement Decisions

The bulk of existing research has been conducted by American economists concerned with the issue of work–leisure tradeoffs.[6] The issue has been typically studied at the micro level because only at the level of the individual is it possible to distinguish push and pull factors in retirement decisions. We need to know which conditions—such as layoffs, unemployment duration, health, or expected retirement benefits—are most decisive in the actual tradeoff situation. Also, in the microeconomics of early retirement, the actuarial approach is dominant; that is, estimating retirement decisions on the basis of actuarial accounting principles.

By and large, what we have available for theoretical generalizations are studies based on American data. The ethnocentric bias of existing research makes it impossible to evaluate how different kinds of welfare states and different kinds of labor markets affect elderly male labor-force participation. Very few studies have directly addressed the push–pull debate on the basis of comparative, macrodata-based research.[7]

The empirical case for a negative work-incentive effect (the pull thesis) appears to have weakened considerably in recent research. Early econometric studies, such as those by Feldstein, Boskin and Hurd, Leonard, and Parsons,[8] found strong evidence supporting the argument that workers leave the labor market primarily because of attractive benefits. Leonard, indeed, claimed that pension-benefit increases alone explain 40 percent of the decline in participation.

A principal weakness of this early literature is its narrow actuarialism and its frequent neglect of competing variables. To begin with the actuarialism problem, it may be pointed out that there are alternative interpretations of the correlation between benefit improvements and exit. If, for example, we took workers' health conditions into account, it may very well be that there always existed a large pool of partially disabled workers ready to embrace early retirement once adequate provisions were granted.

Second, when research began to control for competing variables, the negative-incentive thesis suffered. Thus, Pampel and Weiss found that economic development was the strongest explanation for early retirement; Haveman et al. showed that unemployment experience among older workers was the chief cause behind the retirement decision; and Diamond and Hausman, as well as Burtless and Moffitt, found that the importance of incentive effects relative to alternative variables, such as unemployment, health, and education, varies between labor-force groups.[9]

Jacobs, Kohli, and Rein offer one interesting first attempt to test the push thesis by examining industry bias in early retirement.[10] If early retirement were a function of industrial decline, one would expect that the rates of early exit would be higher in nations or industries in which declining employment is most dramatic. Yet, when they compared high-, low-, and medium-level exit countries across sixteen industrial sectors, they failed to find significant "industry" effects. Indirectly, then, they lend some support to the pull thesis.

It is clear that existing research fails to add up to any single, unambiguous conclusion. To an extent, this is to be expected given sharply different methodological approaches. The real problem may lie in the specification of the problem. The perspective offered by the standard "American" approach may be too narrowly focused on individual work–leisure choices. As such, it often fails to see the forest for the trees. Without a comparative design, its results are difficult to generalize; with its microperspective, the larger logic of welfare-state and labor-market dynamics is lost.

In this study we offer an alternative, macrolevel approach. First, we attempt to highlight welfare-state differences within Sweden, West Germany, and the United States. Concomitantly, we employ a time-series design to capture important legislative changes over the past decades. In this sense, our analyses on declining participation rates of older males are couched in identified structural contexts.

Second, we examine the relative influence of economic push variables at the macro level: unemployment rates among the relevant age groups and then levels of job losses (or gains) in the manufacturing sector. All three nations in our study have experienced significant job losses and unemployment levels in the manufacturing sector over the past fifteen years.[11] These events, however, have not translated into similar trends in early exit. Hence our design allows us to identify the relative influence of the welfare state on labor-force exit under fairly similar economic circumstances. It is important to note that ours is not a study of work–leisure tradeoffs per se. Its aim is to show how, under fairly comparable economic constraints, the nature of welfare-state regimes comes to be decisive for the process of labor-market clearing; that is, certain welfare states are much more likely than others to use demographic instruments in labor-market management.

The Three Welfare-State Regimes

The welfare-state's impact on retirement behavior depends on a complex set of variables, of which the pension system is but one. On one side, we must consider the interaction between income-maintenance programs: Older workers can retire, but often they can choose to apply for unemployment or sickness benefits as an alternative. And sick or unemployed workers may choose the retirement option if it exists. Accordingly, we must examine the menu of alternative income-maintenance choices. On the other side, the choice between income-maintenance programs depends also on the labor market and overall employment policy. With active manpower programs, retraining, and employment expansionary policies, for example, the potential retiree is also offered greater opportunities to remain in the labor force. Our three nations differ considerably in the configuration of these variables. For this study, the relevant approach is to examine the three welfare-state regimes from the vantage point of a male worker in the 55–64 age range.

During the 1970s, all three countries extended access to early retirement. Apart from disability pensions, there are special early-retirement options. In the United States, actuarially discounted social security benefits can be drawn at age 62. Benefits have improved significantly, especially since 1972–1973, and for a "primary"-sector worker, we must bear in mind the likelihood that he will complement the social security pension with occupational pension benefits. Employers may even offer these at an earlier date to induce retirement. But, overall, the financial attraction of early retirement in the United States would appear, all other factors held constant, quite modest. From the point of view of a pure leisure–work maximization tradeoff, a healthy, employed American worker would be better off delaying retirement. The incentive to retire early, in other words, would be most likely to operate when a worker faces unemployment or ill health. In the latter situation, however, the disability insurance program offers superior benefits. The usually modest unemployment benefits are quickly exhausted, even when entitlements are prolonged, and the United States offers no sickness-benefit insurance.

Hence, for redundant American aged workers, early retirement is often the only really viable option, especially when we consider the labor-market side of the American welfare-state regime. First, the experience of layoffs and unemployment in the United States tends to be very concentrated, industry-wide and regionally; this implies that the probability of finding alternative employment for an older worker is small. Second, there are no organized manpower programs that help the redundant older worker relocate or retrain. Third, government employment stimulus generally and the provision of sheltered employment specifically are essentially nonexistent. In brief, our understanding of the American welfare state would seem to exclude a significant pull effect.

If, then, the push effect is likely to dominate in the United States, its effect may not be that powerful. Deindustrialization with its concomitant job losses in manufacturing began in earnest only in the 1980s (until 1980, manufacturing continued to grow in absolute number of jobs) and was heavily concentrated in the old primary sector, unionized industries with strong seniority rights. Indeed, average unemployment rates among older men have been relatively low in the United States.

In contrast to the United States, the German system is one in which early-retirement programs were deliberately employed as the basic means to accelerate industrial restructuration and combat rising unemployment. With the reform in 1972, a person was eligible for a full pension at age 63 (with thirty-five years' contribution). But more important was the emergence of "social plans," agreements between unions and employers (and, implicitly, the government) that allowed for de facto retirement at age 58. In return for trade-union concessions on job security, employers could dismiss older workers by topping up unemployment pay (or discounted retirement benefits) until they reached full pension age. This practice was made possible by a legislative act permitting early retirement before age 63 for workers with one year's unemployment experience. An even more recent (1984) law permits early retirement at age 55. In Germany, active manpower programs and employment-stimulation policies are, in comparison to Scandinavia, underdeveloped, especially for older workers. The German welfare-state regime is peculiar in its heavy transfer bias. This means that services in the government are underdeveloped and that the state will fail to compensate significantly for private-sector employment stagnation. This inability is strengthened by the unusually restrictive economic policies pursued by German authorities over the past decade. Put differently, with overall high unemployment, a rising female labor supply, and large new cohorts entering the labor market, government's chief means to clear labor markets are to reduce the labor supply via early retirement.

Hence, for Germany, we are likely to explain the extraordinarily rapid rise in early retirement best as a combined function of heavy job losses with unemployment, and the liberalization of early-retirement provisions.[12] Since pension-benefit levels have been left unchanged over the past two decades, it is not possible that rising retirement rates are caused by a purely pecuniary inducement.

In Sweden, it is unlikely that growing early retirement is directly related to push factors such as unemployment and industry job losses. Although Swedish industry has been shedding jobs at a very rapid rate, it does not automatically translate into unemployment because of Sweden's active manpower-policy system. The manpower programs offer financially attractive support for relocation, retraining, or sheltered reemployment. On the pull side, eligibility and benefit rules offer considerable incentives (offering probably the highest pension benefits in the world), but usually not of such magnitude that they overpower the incentive to remain in the labor force. Beginning in 1963, a Swedish worker could retire at age 60, but with a reduced pension. Workers could also claim a full disability pension after 1970 for "labor market reasons," meaning that they face difficulties in finding jobs. Access to early retirement at age 60 with a full pension was liberalized in 1972, but only under conditions of previous unemployment. For the average older Swedish worker, however, the likelihood of unemployment has remained minuscule, in part because of job-security provisions and in part because of manpower policies and general employment expansionary programs of the government. In the mid 1970s, the Swedish government introduced partial pensions, a scheme designed to allow older workers to remain in the labor force on a part-time basis while drawing a corresponding fraction of their pensions. While this program never grew to huge proportions, it forms part of the menu of alternatives to early retirement open to older workers.

In Sweden, the trend toward early retirement is much lower than in either Germany or the United States, clearly not because the Swedish pension system offers inferior incentives—on the contrary—but because the overall package of social policy is designed to inhibit the emergence of those push factors that induce early retirement. It virtually guarantees an older worker the possibility of remaining in the labor force, and with government's success in averting unemployment and simultaneously expanding (social service) jobs for new job seekers (mainly women), the system is not under pressure, as in Germany, to clear the labor market of older workers.

Explaining Comparative Early-Retirement Profiles

What we must examine, then, is an over-time and comparative variation in early retirement, measured as a percentage of labor-force participation among men aged 55 to 64. Although we must rely on assumptions derived from aggregate data, we can pretty well assume that changes over time *and* variations across countries are not caused by differences in the health status of workers. This in turn implies that the push effects will primarily be related to labor-market conditions, while the pull effects primarily reflect the marginal incentive of retirement programs.

In what follows, we present a similar time-series econometric model for the three countries in which we attempt to explain changes in the participation rates of older men by two key labor-market variables: (1) the rate of unemployment among men in the 55–64 age range, and (2) the annual number of jobs (net) lost in manufacturing and mining industries. As noted, we choose to exclude annual GDP growth as a variable in the model.

To capture the role of pull effects, we included initially two variables. First was pension benefits as a percentage of average worker earnings. This variable, however, has been omitted because in all three cases its explanatory power (either alone or with the other variables) remained consistently nil. Indeed, this is hardly surprising, since the relative pension benefit has remained unchanged in both Sweden and Germany and has changed only marginally in the United States. Second, to identify changing incentives of retirement programs, we introduce a social-policy dummy variable in which the years after a significant liberalization–benefit increase are scored 1; the years before, zero. Thus, following our discussion of legislative reforms above, for Germany the social security variable is scored zero for 1966–1971 and 1 for 1972–1986; for Sweden, zero for 1964–1975 and 1 for 1976–1987; and for the United States, zero for 1961–1972 and 1 for 1973–1986. The dummy-variable approach was chosen because it best fits with the actual evolution of early-retirement policy. In all three countries, early-retirement provisions have remained very stable except for a one-shot major reform.

The time series for the three countries differs according to the availability of data. For the United States, the series covers 1961 to 1986; for Germany, 1966 to 1986; and for Sweden, 1964 to 1987. In all three cases, the data cover periods of full employment with rapid growth (up to at least 1973–1974), and periods of high unemployment and stagnation.[13]

Our interpretations of the relative causal importance of pull and push factors cannot be based solely on the relative explanatory power of discrete social-policy, or labor-market, variables, but must in the end take into account the regime within which these variables operate. Our analysis tests over-time models for each country individually; comparative conclusions are derived from a confrontation of the three countries' parameter structure.

How, in the light of our welfare-state-regime discussion, are we likely to explain the trends in each country and the differences between them?[14] The Swedish case is perhaps the simplest. We have already argued why we should not expect to find a strong push effect. This is supported by the unusually low unemployment rates among older workers (.9 percent in 1965, 1.6 percent in 1975, and 3.5 percent in 1985). In Sweden, the eligibility rules and benefits would seem to offer positive incentives to retire. First, with a combination of the flat-rate, universal people's pension and the earnings-related second-tier pension, the average employee facing retirement can expect to receive 75 to 85 percent of his previous earnings. The benefit spread is quite small, and a program of pension supplements for those not eligible for the second-tier pension ensure that very few, indeed, would expect to receive less than 70 percent of an average wage. In comparison to our two other countries, the Swedish system probably offers the superior incentives. Nevertheless, within the structure of Sweden, these are likely to be outweighed by the incentives to stay in the labor force. Hence, we would in the final analysis expect that neither pull nor push factors, as identified here, will explain the decline in participation among older men. Instead, we would anticipate a fairly large residual of unexplained variance that, most probably, can be ascribed to individual attributes or random factors.

In the United States, the push effect is likely to be somewhat stronger than in Sweden. In the absence of active manpower programs, and with a comparably weak unemployment insurance scheme, laid off or unemployed older workers have little recourse other than early retirement or finding a new job. We must note that labor-market conditions have not been extremely adverse to older workers, at least not in the primary sector. Indeed, unemployment rates among men in the 55–64 age group reflect its rather sheltered position: 3.3 percent in 1965, 4.3 percent in 1975, and 4.1 percent in 1985. For general labor-market-management reasons also, government has not faced serious pressures to soak up excess supply via retirement. The extraordinarily dynamic growth of service employment at both the bottom and top ends of the labor market has allowed both large youth cohorts and the female labor supply to be absorbed, even in the absence of any job expansion in the public sector.

Comparatively speaking, the pull effect in the United States is expected to be modest. First, we recall that the minimum age for eligibility to early retirement is 62. Second, although eligibility is liberal in terms of contribution requirements, the benefit structure harbors many disincentives. The pension is actuarially reduced, and the normal social security benefit is hardly more than 50–55 percent of an average worker's earnings, implying a steep income decline for a large portion of the labor force. The primary-sector workforce will usually have occupational pension rights, which may add another 20 percent to the total retirement income package. Still, unless the employer chooses to induce early retirement with a special premium, most American wage earners would clearly have a marginal financial advantage in delaying early retirement if they could. Hence, although for different reasons, the United States is likely to share with Sweden any strong push *or* pull effect—with the modification that the American push effect ought to be somewhat stronger than the Swedish.

Germany is likely to deviate sharply from the other two countries, both on the push and pull side. Of the three cases, German industrial job losses have been proportionally the heaviest, with consequent high unemployment rates among elderly workers. For 55–64 year olds, the percentage of unemployment jumped from .8 in 1965 to 3.7 in 1975 and to 9.9 in 1985. Indeed, in Germany, the elderly are more likely to experience (long-term) unemployment than other groups, although here we must recall that unemployment among 58–59 year olds is often early retirement in disguise. Still, in the 60–64 age group, unemployment rates were about 10 percent in 1981 and 6.4 percent in 1985. Furthermore, the framework of such unemployment and job loss in Germany is such that it adds considerably to the overall push effect. Among our three countries, Germany is the only one in which policymakers and trade unionists identify the situation as a genuine tradeoff between young and old in the competition for scarce jobs.[15]

On the pull side, the German system offers incentives that are not as generous as the Swedish but that may easily appear attractive when we consider the lack of employment alternatives. Except for the comparatively steep thirty-five-year contribution requirement for a full pension, the pension system offers considerable attractions. An average worker can expect 70 percent of normal earnings in benefits (net), and although private occupational schemes are of marginal importance, the "social plan" implies that employers will top-up any income loss resulting from early retirement. In Germany, conditions are lined up so that the incentive *and* compulsion to retire early are powerful.

Table 10.2/Push and Pull Factors in the Long-Run Trend toward Labor-Market Withdrawal of Men, 55–64, in Germany, Sweden, and the United States: Model 1

	GERMANY (1966–1986)	SWEDEN (1964–1987)	UNITED STATES (1961–1986)
		(t statistics in parentheses)	
Constant	87.214	88.025	85.949
	(95.36)	(62.11)	(39.45)
Unemployment	−2.215	−1.373	−0.492
	(−11.16)	(−2.11)	(−0.85)
Industrial job losses	−0.005	−0.021	0
	(−2.83)	(−1.14)	(0.06)
Legislation dummy	−8.310	−9.236	−11.886
	(−6.64)	(−8.03)	(−9.84)
R squared (adjusted)	0.949	0.799	0.809
Durbin–Watson	1.400	1.105	0.563
N	21	24	26

Source: WEEP data files.

Combining the essential push and pull variables, the basic model (Model *Y*, Table 10.2) to be tested for the three countries can be written in the following way:[16]

$$Yt = B(c) + B(Ut) + B(Zt) + B(Xt) + e, \tag{10.1}$$

where
Y is male (aged 55–64) participation rates for the years $t = 1, n$;
U is male (aged 55–64) unemployment rates for the years $t = 1, n$;
Z is number of net jobs lost/gained in each year $t = 1, n$;
X is a social security legislation dummy with scores of zero for years before (and including) major reform, and scores of 1 for years thereafter.

The job-loss and unemployment-rate variables both capture the major push effects identified in the literature. We have included both because they need not be substitutable. Job losses in industry may not automatically translate into mass unemployment if alternative employment growth is strong, active manpower policies are applied to elderly workers, or both. Indeed, the zero-order correlation between the two variables is quite low in all three countries: in the United States, −.353; in Germany, −.138; and in Sweden, −.036. The social security dummy has already been explained.

Model 2, tested in Table 10.3, elaborates on the basic model by includ-

Table 10.3/Push and Pull Factors and Their Interaction in the Long-Run Trend toward Early Exit among Men, 55–64, in Germany, Sweden, and the United States: Model 2

	GERMANY (1966–1986)	SWEDEN (1964–1987)	UNITED STATES (1961–1986)
		(t statistics in parentheses)	
Constant	83.468	87.144	81.362
	(46.37)	(30.54)	(35.77)
Unemployment	0.241	−0.897	0.933
	(0.23)	(−0.60)	(1.45)
Job loss	−0.003	−0.019	0
	(−1.82)	(−0.91)	(0.66)
Legislation dummy	−3.836	−7.969	−0.907
	(−1.73)	(−2.14)	(−0.26)
Interaction of unemployment	−2.550	−0.616	−3.057
and legislation	(−2.33)	(−0.36)	(−3.32)
R squared (adjusted)	0.959	.790	0.869
Durbin–Watson	1.438	1.032	0.772
N	21	24	26

Source: WEEP data files.

ing an interaction term of unemployment and the social-legislation dummy. This serves to capture the possibility that exit behavior is not just additively the result of either push or pull effects but results when the two combine in a particular way. In essence, this model tests for whether legislation is an active midwife in the management of unemployment. This particular situation is, in our view, most likely to obtain for Germany. Model 2 can be written as follows:

$$Yt = B(c) + B(Ut) + B(Zt) + B(Xt) + B(Ut \times Xt) + e. \qquad (10.2)$$

Finally, in Model 3 (Table 10.4), we insert the one-year-lagged dependent variable (participation rate of males 55–64) as an explanatory variable. By including the (lagged) dependent variable as an explanatory variable, the model soaks up the heavy autocorrelation. Its theoretical rationale is that we can in this way identify the possible existence of a trend that is independent of push and pull forces. In essence, what it captures is the probability that increasingly early retirement is a self-generated, or self-inspired, trend with its own momentum. The lagged participation variable will clearly explain much of the trend in all three countries, especially since it is realistic to expect that a large

Table 10.4/Push and Pull Factors in the Long-Run Trend toward Early Exit among Men, 55–64, in Germany, Sweden, and the United States: Model 3

	GERMANY (1966–1986)	SWEDEN (1964–1987)	UNITED STATES (1961–1986)
		(t statistics in parentheses)	
Constant	27.166	9.780	4.264
	(2.05)	(0.96)	(1.18)
Unemployment	−0.800	0.151	−0.047
	(−2.35)	(0.37)	(−0.37)
Job loss	0.001	−0.008	0
	(0.29)	(−0.79)	(−0.05)
Legislation dummy	−2.245	−1.322	−0.976
	(−1.41)	(−1.02)	(−1.93)
Participation rates, lagged $(t - 1)$	0.681	0.874	0.944
	(4.53)	(6.87)	(22.97)
R squared (adjusted)	0.974	0.939	0.993
Durbin–Watson	1.524	2.217	1.565
N	20	23	25

Source: WEEP data files.

percentage of older workers chose to retire for an array of personal or random reasons related neither to the labor market nor to the lure of a pension benefit. But to the extent that this lagged variable absorbs the explanatory power of the alternative independent variables, we may conclude that the early-retirement trend is caused by *neither* push nor pull factors. We expect this situation to dominate in Sweden. Model 3 can be written as follows:

$$Yt = B(c) + B(Yt - 1) + B(Ut) + B(Zt) + B(Xt) + e. \tag{10.3}$$

The "basic" model (Table 10.2) does not perform very well, except perhaps for Germany, where autocorrelation is modest, where heteroscedasticity is not a problem, and where the main explanatory variables are strongly significant. For Germany, unemployment is by far the strongest determinant of exit, accounting for 55 percent of the total variance (the legislation dummy accounts for 33 percent).[17] This supports our argument that, in Germany, the pull effects and, especially, the push effects are crucial. For Sweden and the United States, the basic model is essentially misspecified. The only variable of real significance is the legislation dummy, which in Sweden explains 72 percent of the variance and in the United States a full 91 percent. But, in both cases, the model is heavily autocorrelated.

In Table 10.3, we test the interactive Model 2. The question is whether the combined, multiplicative effect of unemployment and the legislation dummy captures better the trend in declining participation. This is what we would expect to happen for Germany, since it is in this regime, we argue, that labor-market push effects and legislation went hand in hand to clear labor markets of older workers. Our case would be especially strong were it to emerge that the inclusion of the interaction variable does *not* annul the independent effect of unemployment. For the two other countries, there is no reason to believe that the interaction term will fundamentally alter the previous model.

For Sweden and the United States, the inclusion of the interaction term does not improve on the initial model. In both cases, the model fit is considerably worsened, as indicated by the poor performance of the Durbin–Watson statistic. But, for Germany, the interaction model gives support to our hypothesis. The model fit has improved, and the interaction variable is significant. But, contrary to expectations, the independent effect of unemployment disappears. In brief, the exit of older men in Germany appears to be a function of push and pull factors operating in synchrony.

Table 10.4 presents a test of Model 3. The inclusion of the $(t - 1)$ lagged dependent variable on the right-hand side serves to identify the degree to which the trend in early retirement is, so to speak, autonomously driven. If we find strong significant effects of the lagged participation variable, and if it obliterates the independent effect of the alternative push and pull variables, our conclusion would have to be that early exit is a trend autonomous from either labor-market or legislative forces. This is especially what we would anticipate to be true for Sweden and (to a lesser degree, and for different reasons) the United States. For Germany, our thesis would be seriously weakened if the lagged participation variable cancels out the independent effect of the push and pull variables, the former in particular.

Examining Table 10.4, it is, of course, no great surprise that we eliminate previous autocorrelation problems with the inclusion of the lagged dependent variable. In this model also, all three nation tests are free of heteroscedasticity problems. What is considerably more interesting is the effects on the overall parameter structure. For Germany, Model 3 essentially confirms our argument. Although the lagged participation variable of course is significant (as one would expect), the independent effect of unemployment remains strong and significant; the legislation variable is close to significance. For Germany, then, the push effect dominates, but the pull effect cannot be disregarded. Alone, the unemployment variable now accounts for 24 percent of the total variance explained; the legislation dummy, 11 percent.

The results are also consistent with our argument for Sweden. Early retirement there is driven neither by push nor pull effects; the strong and significant effect of the lagged participation variable suggests that, in Sweden, early retirement is an independently generated trend. Finally, for the United States, the story parallels the Swedish. Alone, the lagged participation variable accounts for 92 percent of the total variance explained; unemployment plays no role whatsoever, and only the legislation dummy approaches statistical significance. This contradicts our expectations, since we would have anticipated that unemployment (push) should have been stronger than legislation (pull). It is evident that American early retirement has been driven by neither labor-market reasons nor by the lure of pension benefits. The push effect that we anticipated to have some influence in the United States does not exist, at least at the level of aggregate trends.

So far, our analyses confirm the presence of basic structural differences in the three nations' early-retirement behavior. Only in Germany do we detect a clear push effect, mediated by legislation. We should, however, note that our time series bridges two distinct epochs: the pre-1970s period of dynamic growth, full employment, and labor shortages; and the post-1973 period of stagnation and unemployment. By chance, our legislation dummies tend to coincide with the division of these epochs; in all three countries, the major early-retirement reforms or improvements occurred from 1972 to 1975. In this sense, the previously found effects of the legislation dummy variable may, in fact, also have been picking up a break in economic performance.

It is clearly vital to distinguish between the precrisis and postcrisis epochs, especially if we wish to isolate the push effect. It is not very likely that the economies, that of Germany included, exerted much of a push to rid themselves of older workers during a full-employment boom.

To identify more directly whether different causal logics operate in the former, as opposed to the latter, period, we have tested for structural breaks in the data, using the CUSUM test for regression constancy. For Germany, there is a clear structural break beginning around 1974, indicating the presence of two distinct regimes: 1965–1972 and 1975–1986, with the years 1972–1973 acting as transition years. For the United States and Sweden, we can similarly identify structural breaks; in Sweden, the two regimes are 1964–1975 and 1975–1987; in the United States, 1961 and 1972–1973, and 1973–1986. For all purposes, the CUSUM test has identified the shift from economic growth to stagnation very well.

Table 10.5 presents analyses on the basis of Model 3 for the separated periods (designated P1 and P2). We omit the social-legislation-dummy variable due to its coincidence with the regime changes. What we expect, of course, is that the push effects should operate much more powerfully in the second period, since it is here that the countries experienced rising unemployment, stagnation, and major industrial rationalization. Concisely, we expect that the push effect emerges more powerfully for Germany, that it remains insignificant for Sweden, and that it plays a modest but significant role in the United States.

Our conclusions regarding the first time period must be considerably

Table 10.5/Early Exit in the Period of Growth (P1) and the Period of Economic Decline (P2): Germany, Sweden, and the United States

	GERMANY		SWEDEN		UNITED STATES	
	P1	P2	P1	P2	P1	P2
			(*t statistics in parentheses*)			
Constant	2.560	28.900	6.056	−1.750	−22.170	−5.525
	(0.21)	(1.91)	(0.37)	(0.10)	(1.86)	(1.30)
Unemployment	0.544	−0.973	−0.647	0.372	−0.387	−0.090
	(0.58)	(−2.46)	(−0.64)	(0.68)	(−1.75)	(−0.46)
Industry job loss	0.001	0.003	−0.021	0.013	0	0
	(0.37)	(1.24)	(−1.36)	(0.73)	(0.96)	(0.17)
Participation ($t - 1$)	0.944	0.641	0.935	1.005	1.270	0.916
	(6.06)	(3.31)	(4.91)	(4.47)	(8.69)	(17.95)
R squared (adjusted)	0.897	0.968	0.694	0.802	0.914	0.977
Durbin–Watson	3.004	2.066	2.024	2.363	2.470	1.776

Source: WEEP data files.

hedged given that we have so few degrees of freedom. Beginning with Germany, we see from the table that the model for the growth period (P1, 1966–1972) performs poorly with regard to autocorrelation, but this aside, it indicates a complete absence of push factors in early-retirement behavior. In this pre-crisis period, Germany more or less behaves like Sweden. It is clearly in the post-1973 period (P2) that push factors come to the fore. The unemployment variable is significant, and the job loss variable, albeit insignificant, has become stronger. The model for the post-1973 period provides a very good fit, as indicated by the increased variance explained and the complete absence of autocorrelation or heterescedasticity problems.

For Sweden, the model is robust for both periods, but it is also evident that the underlying logic does not change at all from P1 to P2. The only variable with explanatory power is the lagged participation rate. Hence, we may fairly safely conclude that even during the more troublesome period of economic crisis, early retirement in Sweden was not moved by push factors.

The results for the United States come as somewhat of a surprise. The model is robust for both periods and in both cases shows results parallel to the Swedish case, that is, early retirement is largely a self-generated autonomous process happening independently of labor-market constraints. The effect of unemployment is insignificant in both periods. Hence the early-retirement trend after 1973 appears to have nothing to do with the deterioration of the economy.

Table 10.6/Age Structure of Men in Manufacturing Industries in Germany, Sweden, and the United States: Percentage Point Over- or Underrepresentation Relative to Proportion in Total Population

	GERMANY		SWEDEN		UNITED STATES	
	15–24	*55–64*	*15–24*	*55–64*	*15–24*	*55–64*
1970	+2.8	+4.0	+0.9	+6.5	+3.9	+5.1
1980s	+2.8	−1.1	+1.9	+3.1	+3.8	+3.1
Change	0.0	−5.1	+1.0	−3.4	−0.1	−2.0

Industrial Restructuration and Early Retirement

If, indeed, early retirement has been the midwife of industrial rationalization and restructuration, be it via push or pull mechanisms, it should be evident in the age composition of the industrial labor force. There are two scenarios possible. First, in the optimistic version usually espoused by trade unions, the mass exit of older workers should open the gates for youth entry. In this scenario, we should find that the proportion of young workers has increased while that of older workers has decreased. In the second, more cynical scenario, companies had set their eyes solely on slimming their workforce of the less productive (and generally more costly) older workers. In this case, the gates were not opened to youth, and the result should be that the proportion of aged workers declines with no increase among the young. The cynical scenario comes closest to what we would expect in Germany.

One can approach the question in a number of ways. Clearly the most appropriate test would be to analyze over-time data at the micro level of firms. A second approach is that of Jacobs, Kohli, and Rein.[18] In the present study, we offer only suggestive data on the changing age distribution in manufacturing industries.

In Table 10.6, we present data on the age structuration of manufacturing industries in the three countries for 1970, that is, prior to the period of economic upheaval and accelerated early retirement, and for the latest year available (1980 for Sweden, 1985 for the United States, and 1986 for Germany). As an index of age-specific over or underrepresentation, we give the percentage point deviation for each age group relative to its proportion in the total working-age population.

Table 10.6 helps elucidate two important questions. First, it illustrates the degree to which trends in early retirement of older workers have gone hand in hand with recasting the age profile of the (male) industrial workforce. It is clear that manufacturing used to be markedly overrepresented by elderly workers, and this has declined. That manufacturing has been biased in favor of older men is no surprise. By and large, these are industries that emerged and grew in the immediate postwar years and that recruited a labor force that, by the 1970s, would tend to be elderly.

As would have been expected, the decline in aged male overrepresentation is most dramatic in Germany where, indeed, older males now are relatively underrepresented. The decline in Sweden and the United States is far less marked.

The second lesson from Table 10.6 is that the reduction in numbers of older workers hardly produces a major influx of youth. Hence, using early retirement as a strategy for generating youth jobs has not been very rewarding, as most experience also has shown. Instead, it seems evident that where early retirement has been utilized for economic reasons, the aim—and the result— has primarily been to slim the existing workforce at the cost of its oldest and least productive manpower.

Conclusion

This study has sought to examine how demographically specific age groups have become tools for labor-market management during the past twenty years. All three countries have passed legislation to help facilitate early retirement. Our objective has been to identify the conditions under which such programs played the role of active instruments in clearing labor markets and accelerating industrial rationalization.

In addressing the existing literature on the subject, we have argued that the trend toward early labor-market withdrawal must be understood in the nexus of welfare-state policies and labor markets. Hence, we arrived at three divergent hypotheses to explain the trend in Germany, Sweden, and the United States.

Our econometric analyses tend to confirm our expectations for the three cases. In Germany, social legislation made early retirement both feasible and attractive in its own right. But what was decisive for Germany was the concomitant lack of employment growth and the absence of public programs to provide alternative employment possibilities for elderly workers. In this context, early retirement emerged as one of the few means of managing both labor markets and industrial renewal. Our interaction model and the separate analyses of the post-1973 period confirm this argument strongly.

In Sweden, too, social legislation made early retirement an attractive option; yet the insertion of the welfare state in the Swedish labor market is such that the individual prospective early retiree faces more options, among which the ability to remain employed is the most important. In this context, we may understand the very modest Swedish trend toward early retirement and, above all, the absence of any push factors.

Finally, in the United States, social legislation has offered what are, comparatively speaking, the least attractive incentives to choose early retirement. We believed, however, that the absence of Swedish-style welfare-state alternatives would mean that older workers would choose early retirement when push factors such as unemployment and industrial job losses emerged. Yet this scenario does not fit well with the American experience. It is, instead, overwhelmingly true that early labor-market exit in the United States parallels the Swedish profile; that is, it is a largely self-generated process, not observably related to either push or pull effects. This somewhat unanticipated result can certainly not be explained by active government intervention, but must be traced to a double circumstance. First, a strong Keynesian growth effect in the American economy went in tandem with the process of industrial rationalization in the 1980s; hence, the United States remained capable of an immense job growth, if, perhaps, predominantly in poorly paid jobs. Second, job security in the primary sector of the U.S. economy is pervasive and strong, meaning that the layoff or unemployment risk for large segments of the elderly male labor force is lessened. Our analyses suggest that the older worker has not borne the brunt of economic restructuration in the United States. It is possible that other demographic groups have.

Appendix: Table 10.7/Summary Statistics for Variables Included in the Study

	MEAN	STANDARD DEVIATION	MAXIMUM VALUE	MINIMUM VALUE
Germany (1966–1986)				
Participation	72.8	9.1	86.7	57.5
Unemployment	4.1	2.8	9.9	0.8
Job loss/gain	−117.4	287.3	407.0	−768.0
Sweden (1964–1987)				
Participation	80.6	5.6	89.2	73.1
Unemployment	2.2	0.9	4.2	0.9
Job loss/gain	−8.5	28.8	58.0	−53.0
United States (1961–1986)				
Participation	77.8	6.7	87.3	66.5
Unemployment	3.6	1.1	6.1	1.8
Job loss/gain	275.8	908.2	1639.0	−1933.0

Source: WEEP data files.

Note: Participation and unemployment data refer to men aged 55 to 64. Job losses or gains are annual totals (in thousands).

Notes

1. See, especially, W. Graebner, *A History of Retirement* (New Haven: Yale University Press, 1980); Anne-Marie Guillemard, *La vieillesse et l'état* (Paris: Presses Universitaires de France, 1980); J. Myles, *Old Age in the Welfare State* (Boston: Little, Brown, 1984); and J. Quadagno, *The Transformation of Old Age Security* (Chicago: University of Chicago Press, 1988).

2. The WEEP (Welfare State Entry–Exit Project) data files, which provide the source for all tables in this chapter, are the result of a cross-national research program housed in Scandinavia, at the Science Center in Berlin, and at the European University Institute in Firenze. It would fill a book to list the individual data sources. Aside from standard statistical sources on labor markets (both international and national), much of the data derive from labor-market surveys (e.g., the AKU in Sweden and the Mikro-census in Germany).

3. More or less the same picture obtains for women. If we confine ourselves to women aged 60–64, we find that their participation rates actually rose in Sweden, were more or less stagnant in the United States, and declined sharply in Germany.

4. In Germany, the first major liberalization of early-retirement provisions occurred in 1972 (i.e., before the OPEC oil crisis and recession). In the United States, the principal reform dates back to 1961 and can indeed be regarded as more directly motivated by labor-market concerns; it emerged with the relatively deep recession of 1959. Note, however, that major benefit improvements occurred from 1971 to 1973. In Sweden, the first provision for early retirement came in 1963 and was extended in 1970 and again in 1975. See also B. Casey and G. Bruche, *Work or Retirement?* (Aldershot: Gower, 1983); OECD, *Employment Outlook* (Paris: OECD, 1988); and Chapter 11.

5. For a detailed discussion and empirical treatment of the concept of welfare-state regimes, see G. Esping-Andersen, *The Three Worlds of Welfare Capitalism* (Cambridge and Princeton, N.J.: Polity Press and Princeton University Press, 1990).

6. For representative examples, see M. Feldstein, "Social Security, Induced Retirement, and Aggregate Capital Formation," *Journal of Political Economy* 82 (1974); I. Leonard, "The Social Security Disability Program and Labor Force Participation," NBER Working Paper no. 392, Cambridge, Mass., 1979): M. Boskin and M. Hurd, "The Effect of Social Security on Early Retirement," *Journal of Political Economy* 10 (1978); M. Hurd and M. Boskin, "The Effect of Social Security on Early Retirement in the Early 1970s," NBER Working Paper no. 659, 1981; D. Parsons, "The Decline in Male Labor Force Participation," *Journal of Political Economy* 88 (1980). For an overview of the debates, see H. Aaron and G. Burtless, eds., *Retirement and Economic Behavior* (Washington, D.C.: Brookings Institution 1984).

7. Among the few exceptions are J. Pechman, H. Aaron, and M. Taussig, *Social Security: Perspectives for Reform* (Washington D.C.: Brookings Institution, 1968); F. Pampel and I. Weiss, "Economic Development, Pension Policies, and the Labor Force Participation of Aged Males," *American Journal of Sociology* 89 (1983); and K. Jacobs, M. Kohli, and M. Rein, "Testing the Industry-Mix Hypothesis of Early Retirement" (Paper presented at the University of Bergen, Norway, June 1987).

8. See note 6.

9. Pampel and Weiss, "Economic Development." See also R. Haveman et al., "Disability Transfers, Early Retirement, and Retrenchment"; P. Diamond and J. Hausman, "The Retirement and Unemployment Behavior of Older Men"; and G. Burtless and R. Moffitt, "The Effect of Social Security Benefits on the Labor Supply of the Aged"; all in Aaron and Burtless, *Retirement and Economic Behavior*.

10. Jacobs, Kohli, and Rein, "Testing the Industry-Mix Hypothesis."

11. Since economists routinely use GDP growth variables in their models, we ran all the subsequent statistical models with a (one-year-lagged) real annual rate of GDP growth variable, substituting for the industry job-loss variable. The argument in favor of the GDP variable is that it captures overall macroeconomic performance, hence including also its expected effects on the labor market overall. This variable, however, proved to be systematically uncorrelated with participation trends and, moreover, seems to us to be vaguer and less directly relevant for the testing of the "push" effect. In the estimations to follow, we have thus omitted the GDP variable entirely.

12. A special problem we confront in analyzing the German data is that some early retirement is disguised as unemployment; a significant proportion of the unemployed males aged 58–59 are *de facto* retired.

13. Summary statistics of the main variables included are provided in the appendix.

14. Much of the data on which the subsequent discussion is based derive from G. Esping-Andersen, M. Rein, and L. Rainwater, "Institutional and Political Factors Affecting the Well-Being of the Elderly," in *The Vulnerable*, ed. J. Palmer et al. (Washington, D.C.: Urban Institute, 1988).

15. In this light we can also understand why German trade unions, the I. G. Metall in particular, have been such forceful advocates of a policy of reduced working time, the objective of which is to redistribute more fairly the stagnant pool of jobs. Indeed, the Swedish trade unions are unequivocally against such a strategy, not merely because the net new employment dividend is questionable but also (and principally) because their main strategy is to expand jobs.

16. For all estimations, we have used the IAS system developed at the Institute for Advanced Studies in Vienna. This package is especially rich in econometric tests and diagnostic checks not widely available in other econometric packages. We have applied tests designed to detect irregularities in the deterministic part of the model (e.g., incorrect functional form, structural breaks, and errors in variables). For an introduction to the modeling approach used, see W. Kraemer et al., "Diagnostic Checking in Practice," *Review of Economics and Statistics*, 1985. For a synthetic overview of the diagnostic procedures used in this study, see W. Kraemer and H. Sonnberger, *The Linear Regression Model under Test* (Heidelberg and Wien: Physica Verlag, 1986).

17. The IAS program routinely provides the standardized beta coefficient. For space reasons, these were omitted from the tables.

18. Jacobs, Kohli, and Rein, "Testing the Industry-Mix Hypothesis."

11/The Future of Early Retirement: The Federal Republic of Germany

Klaus Jacobs and Martin Rein

Since the early 1970s, there is clear evidence that individuals are leaving work at an earlier age. This chapter documents the trend to early retirement in Germany, offers an interpretation of the processes that created it, and reviews changing conditions that might reverse the pattern in the future.

Early exit from paid employment has an obvious meaning for the changing structure of the labor market and for the organization of the individual life course. Both aspects have been analyzed in great detail. A widely neglected subject, in the context of early exit, has been the conceptualization of the welfare state, the variety of welfare-state concepts across countries, and conceptual changes over time. The subject of early exit from the labor market offers a window for understanding not only the social policy of the state but also the interplay between that social policy and private firms. Therefore, the social policy of the firm, its main objectives and (direct and indirect) instruments of promoting early exit while passing the costs along to the state, is a central topic of this chapter.

Documenting the Trend to Early Retirement

Although the general pattern is clear, detailed empirical evidence is elusive because the statistics available are organized to reflect institutional realities that obscure the full extent of the process of early exit. There are two approaches to documenting trends: entry into the statutory pension system of retirement and general disability and exit from the labor force of paid employment. Each approach encounters measurement and conceptual difficulties; therefore, no single statistic can provide an adequate summary of the trend.

Although the age of receipt of a statutory pension is a limited measure, the figures are nevertheless so striking that they are worth reporting. If we take the cohort born in 1913, we find that 23 percent of the men and 39 percent of the women were drawing pensions at age 60. But when we examine the pattern for the cohort born ten years later (1923), we find that this proportion has risen to 51 percent for men and 66 percent for women.[1] Thus we can conclude that 65 is no longer the normal age of retirement and that, for younger cohorts at least, half the men and two-thirds of the women are receiving a public pension at age 60. In fact, the average age of receipt of a statutory pension is now 59 years for men. This measure is inadequate because the exit from paid employment also takes place outside the pension system.

Many people who have effectively left the labor market are not included in the pension system but receive their benefits through other programs, such as unemployment insurance or sick pay or the preretirement program or private pensions financed by firms. Workers 58 years of age and older who receive unemployment benefits are unlikely in a slack labor market to return to work after an extended period of unemployment. These unemployed nonpensioners are *de facto* retired, in the sense that they have permanently exited from the labor market without entering into the pension system. We therefore need to distinguish between exit from the labor market and the receipt of a pension, which signals formal retirement. We do not have an adequate social category to describe this transitional group, whose identity is shaped by the classification system created by the welfare state and not by their objective situation.

In the German preretirement program the individual continues to be paid directly by the firm, and if the preretired worker is replaced by an unemployed worker, the firm is partially reimbursed by the state. Because the firm is paying the individuals, they are not enrolled in the public pension system until they reach age 63 (age 60 for women and the severely handicapped).

Finally, a person can receive a private pension. Although almost 50 percent of workers are covered by private schemes, these programs are insufficient to serve as the primary source of income. By themselves, they are not an important route into retirement. But, as we later see, private arrangements are often used to "top up" public unemployment programs, leaving workers almost as well off in retirement as when at work.

Measures of labor-force participation, in part, correct the major weakness of the statutory pension approach to measuring early retirement because they measure the proportion of persons employed and unemployed as a proportion of different age groups.[2] Based on these rates, we see a decline in male labor-force rates and a stable picture for female rates. To illustrate the trend we cite some selected figures. In 1972, the participation rate for 64-year-old men was 60 percent; by 1986, the proportion had declined sharply to only 18 percent. For men 60 years of age, the rate was only 51 percent in 1986, down from 77 percent in 1972.

When participation rates are seen from a cohort perspective, we get a rather different picture of gender differences. For male cohorts born between 1907 and 1922 (see Figure 11.1), we find that the participation rates of 55 year olds in all cohorts was around 90 percent. The younger the cohort, the earlier and sharper the decline in labor-force participation. At age 61, 46.5 percent of the youngest cohort (1922) were in the labor force, compared to over 80 percent for the oldest cohort (1907). The situation for women is quite different (see Figure 11.2). Up to the age of 59, the labor-force participation of younger cohorts is higher than that of older cohorts. This is simply another way of saying that two different trends are occurring at the same time. More women, at younger ages, are entering the labor force at the same time that older women (over age 60) are exiting. These overlapping trends cancel each other out when cross-sectional data are used.

The labor-force participation measure is inadequate because it includes older unemployed workers whose probability of reentering work is virtually nil. There are numerous problems surrounding the definition of unemployment that make it difficult simply to exclude the unemployed. An official indication of this difficulty is that the maximum period of receipt of unemployment benefits was extended to thirty-two months for individuals over 54 years of age. Most countries have two definitions of unemployed: those officially registered as unemployed, which is necessary to receive unemployment benefits or fulfill requirements for specific pensions after unemployment; and those who self-report their unemployment status in interview surveys. In 1985 in Germany, 37,000 men aged 59 were officially registered as unemployed, compared to only 23,000 self-reported unemployed (i.e., those not working in the survey week and looking for a job). Which is the appropriate statistic to measure un-employment among older workers? To complicate the situation further, since 1986 unemployed persons 58 years and older can receive unemployment bene-fits but do not need to register for work. These individuals have a right to unemployment compensation, but they are no longer included in the figures for unemployment released by the federal agency for employment. By the end of September 1986, there were 40 percent fewer registered unemployed 59-year-old men than in the previous year. These workers now are not in the statistics either of the pension system or of the labor market. Looking at trends in employment by age by subtracting the unemployed from the total labor force can be very misleading if one does not pay attention to rule changes and competing ways of estimating the unemployed.

Persons who participate in the preretirement program sometimes are treated in the labor-force statistics as employed because they continue to re-ceive a salary from a firm and have to pay income taxes and social contributions based on this salary.

Employment activity rates correct some of these problems. The level of early exit appears even larger because the unemployed are excluded from these

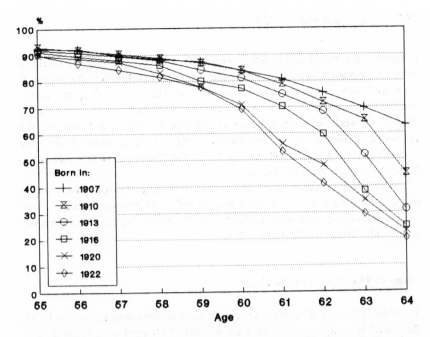

Figure 11.1 Labor-force participation rates of male birth cohorts by age in Germany. *Source:* Mikrozensus, EC Labor Force Survey, 1983–1984, in *Time for Retirement: Comparative Studies of the Decreasing Age of Exit from the Labor Force*, ed. M. Kohli et al. (Cambridge: Cambridge University Press, forthcoming).

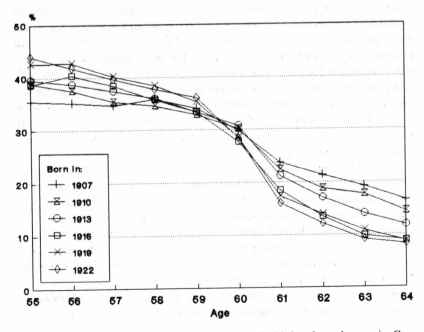

Figure 11.2 Labor-force participation rates of female birth cohorts by age in Germany. *Source:* Mikrozensus, EC Labor Force Survey.

statistics. Nevertheless, the employment rates still underestimate the extent of early exit because some individuals are being paid and therefore counted as employed even though they are not at work and will never work again. This is true for many sick workers, who continue to receive their regular wages during the first six weeks of sickness before getting sick pay from the statutory health insurance. If long-term sickness leads directly to general disability, then the disability pension replaces the sick pay, and the absence from work proves to be not temporary but permanent.

Our interpretation of the processes that created early exit in Germany is that although there was no explicit societal policy to achieve this aim, nevertheless early retirement occurred because of an informal agreement among key actors. The details of this story follow.

Stage 1: The State and the Court

The state set the stage by introducing a series of reforms designed to strengthen the social security system. The main legislative changes were introduced in 1957 and 1973 in a period of economic vitality when there was very little evidence of growing unemployment or a weakening of labor-market conditions. In 1957, the Conservative party (CDU/CSU) and the Liberal party (FDP) were in power; however, there was a broad political consensus among all political parties about the principles on which the social security system should be established. At this time, a statutory rule was introduced that made it possible for an individual to draw pension benefits at age 60, provided that during the previous one-and-a-half years the recipient had been unemployed for at least one year. When this rule was introduced, it was designed to be an exception in recognition of the fact that some individuals had been victimized by the war and had suffered in the hard circumstances immediately following the postwar period. These "exhausted" workers had limited capacity to adjust to the labor market, and if they became unemployed, they should be entitled to an early entry into the pension system.

When the Social Democrats were in power together with the Liberals in 1973, they introduced a series of liberalizing social reforms designed to make the social security system more flexible and more humane. Specifically, they introduced a law that made it possible to retire at age 63. This legislation was referred to as "flexible retirement." The theory that inspired this reform was that not all people of a certain age face the same personal situation. A uniform age of retirement fails to take into account special individual situations. The flexible retirement age was primarily designed to introduce elements of choice into a uniform system of retirement; the labor-market dimensions of such a policy were seen as subordinate. But flexible retirement was immediately accepted by most male workers and became the new standardized norm for retirement. Since 1973, severely handicapped persons have been eligible for a public pension at age 62, one year earlier than the flexible retirement age.

In 1969, the Federal Social Court made a far-reaching decision that came to be known as the "concrete method of interpretation of disability." It established the principle that labor-market conditions could play an important role in the disability system. Previously, only medical criteria were taken into account in setting the level of benefits received by the disabled who could work. A partially disabled person could receive only a reduced disability pension because it was assumed that such an individual would work part-time. After the economic downturn in 1966–1967, the court recognized that part-time jobs might not be available in sufficient numbers, so it ruled that a partially disabled person should be entitled to a full disability pension if no part-time jobs were available. In the 1969 decision, the court assumed that general standards could be developed for determining part-time-job availability in local labor markets. It turned out, however, that such information was not readily available, and this led to a new decision. In 1976, the court decided that if an individual was not able to work full-time and could not find a part-time job within one year, then this individual would be regarded as permanently disabled and therefore entitled to receive a full disability pension. For administrative reasons, the court decision was even further simplified: The insurance board decided that the partially disabled over 50 years of age would automatically receive a full disability pension because the probability that older disabled workers could find part-time work was virtually zero.[3]

The disability system is one of the major routes to early retirement. In the early 1980s, of all new entrants into the pension system, more than 50 percent entered via the disability route. The court decision further increased the significant role that disability had always played in early retirement. For example, the number of 55–59-year-old new male entries into the disability system more than doubled from 26,000 in 1975 to 56,000 in 1984, while the population of this age group increased by less than two-thirds. (But in the mid 1980s this situation changed, as discussed later in this chapter.)

How shall we interpret the court decisions? The years 1966–1967 brought the first recession Germany experienced after World War II. It is also true that labor-market conditions by the mid 1970s had begun to worsen in the aftermath of the oil crisis. But the court did not intend to use the disability system as an instrument to adjust the size of employment in the labor market. Instead, its main focus was to fill a hole in the network of social security that affected partially disabled workers. The court rulings are therefore part of the infrastructure created by the state during the "stage-setting" process.

In summary, then, the state and the court "set the stage" that led to the practice of early exit from the labor market. They did this by introducing programs that created the institutional basis actors later could make use of. The four main programs were early retirement for unemployed older workers at age 60 (introduced in 1957); flexible retirement at age 63 (introduced in 1973); early retirement for the severly handicapped (introduced in 1973 at age 62 and gradually lowered to age 60 in 1980); and the introduction by the court of the "concrete method of interpretation of disability." Taken together, all these reforms were designed to improve the social security system and were neither intended as a strategy to promote early retirement nor primarily a response to labor-market conditions of high unemployment, a situation that emerged only in the later 1970s. The existence of this legislation, however, provided the social infrastructure that, in a later period of weak labor markets and high unemployment, was used by firms to forge a policy of early retirement.

Stage 2: The Period of Social Consensus

The growing exit from employment by older workers since the early 1970s is the outcome of converging interests among key actors in the retirement process. Early exit from the labor force is initiated by the social policy of the firm and not by an explicit social policy of the state to promote early retirement. It is difficult to imagine that a divided society could create such a dramatic transformation of the labor force and a redefinition of the boundaries of the life cycle. The consensus was not arrived at spontaneously. According to some theories, the driving force was the change of work value of individuals made possible by the growth of per capita income and high-pension replacement rates. In other theories, it was the efforts of unions that were important. They initiated work-sharing programs in the hope that the early exit of incumbent workers would make room for the younger unemployed. Theories of the individual retirement decision or theories in which the firm yields to union pressure are incomplete. In our view, early retirement is driven by the interest of the firms, using the social infrastructure originally created by the state and the court for other purposes, making it possible to pass on costs to the state and making early retirement financially attractive to workers.

Firms are the central actors in a discourse with the state, unions, and individuals. A better understanding of the social policy of the firm is essential in order to grasp the early-exit process in Germany. Firms are economic institutions expected to pursue policies that have an economic rationale constrained by certain social norms. Economy is embedded in society by a set of norms that change over time through conflict and agreement and vary across countries.

The development of norms of seniority was an outcome of struggle between unions and firms. By contrast, the principle of "make room for the young" was a more consensual process. Interestingly enough, the seniority norm is reinforced by legislation, whereas the new norm of early exit is inforced by practice. American norms permit firms flexibly to adapt their personnel needs by layoffs and firings provided that they do not discriminate by sex, age, or race. European norms and contracts make dismissal, especially of the elderly, more difficult. But the process of early exit could take place even in the European context because of changes in social norms and practice.

German firms pursue a "proactive social policy." They use the social-policy instruments and regulations of the state to realize their economic aims. This does not imply that firms take no action of their own, but whatever action they take is shaped by the rules and financial resources provided by the state. This has led to the development of a social invention we call "pathway of early exit." It is a strategy to combine programs and regulations that make it possible, through public and private resources, to encourage workers to exit from work before the formal retirement age. A pathway is more than a single program—it is a cluster of interrelated programs used by firms in collaboration with individual workers, unions, and the state to create the possibility of early retirement. The firms created pathways to early exit by combining and partially supplementing different instruments of social security to make early exit both attractive to individuals and, by stressing the economic rationale underlying this process, acceptable to unions and the state.

The proactive social policy of the firm in Germany contrasts with the practice in the Netherlands and the United States where firms pursue an "active social policy." In the Netherlands, trade unions organized on an industry basis and the association of firms implement much of the social policy authorized and financed by the state. In the absence of a national earnings-related pension scheme, life insurance, firm pensions, and industrial-sector pensions developed. In this context, the early-retirement program known as VUT was bargained and implemented at the sectoral and firm level. The state does not contribute funds to this program, which in the mid 1980s was the most important program of early exit. In the United States, the public infrastructure is weak. Unemployment insurance lasts only twenty-six weeks and provides no formal linkage into the retirement scheme; actuarially reduced pensions are available at age 62, and access to the disability system is difficult. Thus firms are forced to create their own active social policy if they wish to encourage early retirement.

There are two examples of the proactive social policy of the firm in Germany. The first is known as the "59 rule," a pathway that makes it possible to combine unemployment benefits with pensions for older workers. The rule allowing workers to receive a pension at age 60 after one year of unemployment was converted into a pathway when firms used the "59 rule" to shed workers entitled to seniority rights whom the firm wished to get rid of. The firms offered these workers severance pay as well as topping up unemployment compensation to a level virtually equal to their former net wages. At age 60, they qualify for a public pension. Most of the cost of shedding these older workers was passed on to the unemployment and pension insurance systems. Some of these practices were only quasi legal because in this period an older worker was required by law to be actively looking for a job in order to receive unemployment insurance benefits. But such rules have been flexibly interpreted by the unemployment insurance board in response to the weak labor-market conditions prevailing since the mid 1970s.

The second example of a proactive policy of the firm is the use of disability as a pathway to early exit. A survey of firms in the private sector carried out in 1988 shows that the use of the disability system is very sensitive to whether a firm has a stable, expanding, or declining workforce. Declining firms have higher uses of disability claims than expanding firms.[4] If we assume that health status should not be influenced by the changing personnel requirements of the firm, then we might conclude that at least some of the disability claims are not initiated directly by the individuals affected.

We offer an interpretation of why firms pursue a proactive early-exit policy. The early exit of older workers is a very attractive instrument when a firm wishes to change the quantity or quality of its workforce. Such a practice can contribute to the rationalization of production (producing the same product, but with fewer people) or to the development of product differentiation (changing the workforce and producing new products). There are two reasons why early exit is especially appealing to firms: It is socially acceptable; and it provides firms with a way of partially shifting costs to the public sector through existing and new pathways.

During the first series of external shocks following the rise in oil costs in 1973 and in the aftermath of the high unemployment that followed, German firms began to make extensive use of programs to encourage early retirement. Labor-market conditions were, without doubt, the driving force in the growing use of early retirement by the firms. In this loose labor market, the distribution of jobs became a critical policy question. How should the available hours be distributed among those seeking work and holding jobs? From a societal point of view, early retirement seems an attractive approach. It is based on the deep cultural belief that young people should not be deprived of an opportunity to enter the labor force. As a contribution to the societal good, older workers should retreat from employment and make room for the young. Given the appeal of early retirement to the individual and to the firm, it is difficult to distinguish between workers' free choice to retire and a firm's policy to expel workers. But we believe that the retirement decision is initiated by the firm and made financially attractive to the individual.

While labor-market conditions were certainly critical in the development of pathways of early exit, the process soon became generalized. Many firms that are not in economic difficulties also appear to have used existing and new regulations as a way of changing their workforce, with the result that, over time, the pattern of exit from the labor force appears to have extended to growing industries as well as to those in decline, although at a lower rate.[5]

A study of sixteen industrial groups in three different countries between the early 1970s and the early 1980s shows that, even in growing industries, there is a declining employment share of older workers. In the public-service sector where there are special regulations to permit early exit, we see a similar pattern of decline. We conclude, therefore, that early retirement is a general, rather than an industry-specific, trend. It takes place almost everywhere—in both growing and declining industries—although not to the same degree. This pattern of more-or-less uniform exit is found in Germany and in the Netherlands, countries with very different industrial mixes. By contrast, in Sweden there is an increasing share of older persons in some branches of industry (transportation, telecommunication, public administration, and business services).[6]

After a lifetime of hard work, many older workers feel that they have earned the right to retire.[7] The seniority system also gives older workers the right to stay on their jobs if they so choose, so they cannot easily be laid off for refusing to change jobs. Investment in the reskilling of older workers is too costly to firms, since workers will not remain at work for many years longer. The easy availability of skilled young workers makes the retraining of older workers even less attractive. In the absence of a tradition of lifetime retraining, many workers do not want to be retrained and prefer to retain the job they already have. This is especially true when a significant change in skill level is required.

This situation is similar to that in the United States. A report to Congress notes that exit practice is "particularly tempting when firms employ older, comparatively expensive workers with obsolescent skills, while new production systems place a premium on credentials and basic skills that these older workers may lack. It is difficult to justify retraining when workers with adequate training are looking for work, and when the costs of training can be lost if an employee leaves a job to work elsewhere."[8]

If a firm can pass on the cost of early retirement to the state, if the wage bill is higher for older workers without any productivity gains, if retraining is too costly given the ample supply of skilled young workers, and if older workers accept as morally legitimate a claim for retirement, then it is not difficult to see why early retirement seemed attractive to all actors.

The firms' interest in rationalization is undoubtedly an even more important determinant of early exit. Piore and Sabel have promoted the idea that "flexible specialization" is the production system of the future, replacing mass production. "In this system of production, technological dynamism is achieved through continual innovation in product design, and resources are made as general as possible so they can shift from one product to another in response both to the market changes and design innovation."[9] In such a system, employment security is critical. We argue that the age composition of the secure workforce is equally important, since general skills in flexible specialization are better performed by younger workers than older workers. The age transformation of the labor market in the firm is an essential precondition for the introduction of these new production regimes. Early retirement as a social policy of the firm serves as a handmaiden in shifting the production regimes. It is part of a broader strategy of rationalization by the firm.

The political and economic consequences of the early-retirement profile have raised considerable anxiety about the long-term feasibility of such a shortening of the working-life cycle. There are now governmental efforts in Germany to make access to early retirement more difficult or less attractive in order to reverse the trend of early exit. These initiatives have failed so far because they do not take into account pathway substitution and the more fundamental problem of the limited willingness and capability of firms to reemploy or retain older workers. This effort to reverse the early-retirement movement is likely to be the center of political debate for some time to come.

Stage 3: The State in an Active, Ambivalent Mode

When the state began to see how the firms had accommodated to the existing social infrastructure created by the state in the stage-setting phase in the evolution of social policy, it actively attempted to undo what it had created.

One of the more effective means the state used to discourage early retirement was by making it more difficult to get access to the disability system. In 1984, it introduced a rule that required a person to have worked in three of the preceding five years to be eligible for disability benefits. This new rule particularly affected women with little recent labor-market attachment. The result of the rule change was dramatic: The share of female entries into the pension system via disability dropped sharply from 52 percent in 1983 to 48 percent in 1984, 30 percent in 1985, and less than 20 percent in 1986. This raised the average age of entry of women into the pension system from 59.6 in 1983 to 61.4 in 1986.

The state was ambivalent—torn between conflicting short- and long-term goals, the goals of expansion and retrenchment of early exit. In the long run the projected labor shortage must lead to a decline of early retirement. In the short run, however, the desire to lower unemployment would lead to an increase of early retirement. In order to reduce unemployment the state broadened early retirement by liberalizing the early reforms introduced in the stage-setting period. It did this by periodically extending the period of unemployment coverage for workers over age 54 from twelve to thirty-two months. The pathway originally known as the "59 rule" can now begin at 57 years and 4 months.

Another attempt to adjust to labor-market conditions was by lowering the retirement age for the severely handicapped to 61 in 1979 and then to 60 in 1980. We might expect that a program for the severely handicapped would have only a very small impact. In fact, changes in the age limit affected a substantial number of persons. In 1980, the share of male entries into the pension system via this program was over 16 percent, compared to 1978 when it was less than 4 percent. The absolute number increased from 10,000 men in 1978 to 46,000 in 1980.

Below we focus on the main retrenchment efforts developed by the state during the period from 1980 to the present and explain why this initiative faltered.

In 1982 and again in 1984, the state imposed a set of reimbursement obligations on the firms. These rules called for a reimbursement by firms for benefit money paid out as a result of the "59 rule"; however, from the beginning, certain firms and branches were exempt from the ruling. Later, the firms brought the state decision to the courts on the grounds that this constituted a violation of the equal-treatment amendment to the constitution. The issue is now under legal consideration, and until a final ruling by the Federal Court for Constitutional Affairs is handed down, the reimbursement clause *de facto* has been suspended. As a result, the state's effort to halt the cost shifting of early retirement failed. There is no evidence for any diminution in the significance of the "59 rule" as a form of exit from paid employment.

The state actively continued its efforts to reverse the social policy of the firms. It did so by the introduction in May 1984 of the Preretirement Act, a temporary act that was to last four and a half years. The introduction of the act was part of a continued strategy by the state to get the firms to pay for a larger part of the cost of early retirement. Preretirement could begin at age 58 and continue until the earliest possible age for drawing pension benefits (i.e., 60 for the severely handicapped and most women and 63 for other workers). During this phase, the employer paid a "preretirement sum" amounting to at least 65 percent of the previous gross income. If the position vacated was filled by an unemployed person, then the federal agency for employment took over a share of 35 percent of the costs incurred by the firm. For most active male workers, then, the firm was required to pay the preretirement income of individuals between the ages of 58 and 63, at which time the state would take over responsibility for a statutory pension. By the end of 1987, there were about 140,000 cases of preretirement since the program began in May 1984. This figure was considerably lower than original expectations. The firms obviously preferred to follow the "59 rule" where the unemployment and pension insurance funds paid for the basic benefit and the firm topped up only part of that cost. Firms prefer the "59 rule" for two reasons: It permits them to shift costs to the state, and it leaves management with the sole decision over which workers should retire early. Moreover, the "59 rule" was made even more attractive when the extent of unemployment was extended to thirty-two months instead of the original year and a half. Moreover, all these individuals are entitled to receive a pension at age 60, instead of at age 63, as required at the Preretirement Act.

In summary, in this stage the state shifts toward an active mode, seeking to undo the policies created in the stage-setting process. It is effective in reducing the importance of the disability pathway as an exit strategy. But its efforts to reduce the importance of the "59 rule" as an exit route fails. Perversely, this pathway becomes even more important, as the possible age of exit in this route declines to 57 years and 4 months.

In the next section we briefly discuss the new active position of the state in reversing the trend of early exit. The state has two reasons for its position, and both are driven by changing demography. The first is protecting the financial solvency of social security, and the second is anticipating a future situation of severe labor scarcity that involves a reversal of the present high unemployment. In this stage, the state is seeking to develop a more consistent and coherent position, in contrast to the ambivalent period described above.

Stage 4: The State Tries Again

We are now entering a new state initiative designed to slow down or reverse the trend to early exit. The state's rationale for the case against early retirement seems to be based largely on arguments about cost. The state is concerned about how declining fertility, rising life expectancy, and the changing demographic profile (the ration between dependent and active population) will threaten the long-range fiscal solvency of the social security system.

In the context of this debate, "can't afford" arguments play a large role. This position is designed to show that the social security system is financially instable. The evidence cited in the German case includes the considerable shift in the age structure. Between 1970 and 1985, the number of persons under 20 years of age declined from 18.2 million to 14.4 million. In the meantime, the number of persons over 60 increased from 11.6 million to 12.4 million, while the total population remained roughly constant. Demographic projections from 1985 to the year 2030 show that the total population will decline by 15 million. More important than this change is the shifting age structure, as reflected in the old-age dependency ratio. In 1985, there were 36 persons age 60 and over for every 100 between the ages of 20 and 60. The projected change of this ratio to 74 per 100 in 2030 would imply that if no other actions were taken, within the present pay-as-you-go system of old-age security the contribution rate would have to be roughly doubled. Given that the actual contribution rate is already 18.7 percent of gross income, a drastic increase in this rate is unrealistic. Therefore, some action has to be taken, and extending the average age of entry into retirement is one plausible, even if partial, remedy.

The first action that the state took in this period was the decision in January 1988 not to renew the preretirement legislation. The basic argument was that labor-market conditions will change in the future and there will be a need for more older workers because of a projected shortage of younger workers by the turn of the century. A continuation of the Preretirement Act as one pathway to early exit would send a wrong signal to the actors involved.

In the fall of 1989, the state took the second action when a substantial reform of the public pension system was passed by legislation. A central part of this reform is the gradual increase of the age limits of all types of pensions up to age 65, with the exception of the pension for the severely handicapped at age 60 and the age-free disability pension. Beginning in the year 2001, the age limits of the pension for women and the pension after long-term unemployment, today both at age 60, will be increased gradually until they reach age 65 in the year 2012. The "flexible retirement" at age 63 will be completely abandoned by the year 2006.

The receipt of a public pension prior to age 65 (aside from disability and pensions for severely handicapped) will still be possible (up to a maximum of three years), but only with financial penalties in the form of actuarial deductions, which have been unknown in the German pension system so far.

Another part of pension reform is the introduction of partial pensions, which could raise the retirement age by encouraging part-time employment among older workers, if those who may have fully retired remain at least partially in employment. Of course, a partial pension can also further increase the cost of early retirement if the program recruits those who would have remained in full-time employment.

In either event, such a program is not likely to affect the labor-force behavior of a large number of workers for two reasons. First, there is already a shortage of part-time jobs for older workers, as demonstrated by the inability of the partially disabled to acquire part-time jobs. This experience led the court to redefine all such individuals as fully disabled. Second, such programs have failed in all countries where they were introduced with the exception of Sweden.[10] They failed for a variety of reasons, mostly because full early exit is more attractive both for the employer and the older worker. In Germany, one clear alternative is the "59 rule." Unless the state is prepared to eliminate this alternative or make access to it more difficult or less attractive, then the partial-pension program is unlikely to become an effective alternative.

Why does the state promote such legislation? We believe that the importance of this legislation does not lie in its potential effectiveness as an alternative to early retirement but as a symbol of the state's determination to reverse the social norms that legitimate early exit. How far it will succeed is unclear. Much depends on how serious the state really is and how the other actors will respond to the message. The dialogue between "the message as intended" and "the message as received" is part of the political process of resetting the social norms about early exit.

If the state is not able to alter the behavior of the firm to create part-time job opportunities for older workers as an alternative to full retirement, the state might shift strategies and attempt to change the incentive structure of individuals. One such effort is the introduction of an actuarial method for calculating the benefit value of statutory pensions. At present, the German social security system takes into account only the number of contribution years in determining the individual pension level, not the number of expected benefit years. By this formula, a pension received at age 60 is only marginally lower than one received at age 63 or 65. But an actuarial method that takes into account the extended years of benefit coverage due to early retirement would substantially lower the replacement rate and create a clear individual disincentive to exit early.[11] But since the driving force for early retirement is the firm, a change in the individual incentive structure would not alter the pattern of early exit but would make it more costly to the individual. Maybe, in this way, the state hopes to make the individual an ally in its struggle with the firm to redefine the social norms.

The era of consensus and converging interests is now changing. The state in an active mode is seeking to reverse an established pattern. This cannot be done easily if the other actors strongly object. How will the firms respond to the efforts of the state to create a new agenda? This is the next stage of the political discourse.

Stage 5: How Will Firms Adapt to the New Political Environment?

There are at least two possible responses. First, firms can change their position and decide that the shedding of older workers has gone too far and that they now need to retain older workers because they are a valuable asset to the production system. In this view, the firm accomodates to the new environment, accepting the new agenda of the state and restoring the era of converging interests. Alternatively, the firms continue their goal of retrenchment of older workers. Should they need additional personnel in the predicted tight labor market in the future, they will turn to the recruitment of better-educated women and more highly qualified foreign workers. In this situation, the firm and the state are engaged in a conflict of objectives.

Some observers point out that the firms' interest in the future might be to follow the first response and retain its older workers. The experience of British Petroleum is often cited as an example. When Germany introduced unleaded gas for environmental reasons, they needed to change the system of distributing gas at local gas stations. British Petroleum then discovered that it had fired all the older workers who had the know-how for producing such a change. As a result, it had to rehire older workers in order to produce the change needed at the local gas stations. At Audi Automobiles, there is increased discussion of the fact that the firm needs not only technical knowledge, which younger workers might have, but also social competence, which older workers are more likely to have. As a result, they have embarked on a policy of retaining older workers. Moreover, the older cohorts of tomorrow will have better qualifications and more social competence and the ability to adapt to new situations. The continued process of retraining is a familiar part of their work career. If the production regimes of the future require more teamwork, then social maturity will become more important than concrete knowledge. In this environment, older workers become a more valuable asset to the firm.

Others believe that firms will continue to reduce the proportion of older workers as the most efficient way of achieving their economic objectives. They do not want social norms redefined; instead, they seek to retain a policy of early retirement as an "unbloody way" of retrenchment. Although in this scenario the firms and the state have clashing goals, this does not mean that the firms would oppose every action taken by the state. The firms did not actively oppose the state's decision to abolish preretirement because this program, from their perspective, was an unattractive pathway of early exit. While firms hope that by abolishing this program, a more favorable pathway can be found, the state hopes that its action will be received as a signal to reverse the general trend to early exit.

Given the firms' continuous commitment to early exit, there are two strategies they may follow in this new environment. First, they can form coalitions with new allies in an effort to prevent the state from realizing its new objectives. To the extent that early retirement is now widely accepted among workers as part of the moral economy, the unions form an obvious ally. If the firms fail in this effort and still retain their conviction that early retirement is necessary, then they may be forced to shift to an active social policy. Firms may still find it to their advantage to move in the Dutch and American direction of introducing private early-retirement schemes. That there is scope to move in such a direction is provided in a study by the European Communities on the structure of labor costs in 1975. It shows that in firms employing ten or more individuals in the manufacturing sector, the contractual or voluntary costs in Germany as a percentage of total labor costs was only 1.6 percent, compared to over 6 percent in the Netherlands.[12]

Conclusion

We believe that we are entering a new era in social policy, one dominated by a contest between the social policy of the firm and the social policy of the state. The view that the firm will increasingly need older workers because of the changing skill mix required in the production process is important. If this view is correct, then firms will indeed accommodate to the state's active mode of seeking a new social norm to reverse the pattern of early retirement. We believe that this scenario is plausible and will certainly take place in some limited sectors of the economy. But the belief that this scenario represents a general trend for the economy as a whole is much too optimistic. We conclude, therefore, that if firms continue to reduce the number of personnel, shedding older workers is still the most socially acceptable way. Early exit is also attractive to firms that have no interest in shedding workers. As we have shown, early exit is a general trend that helps firms to alter the skill mix of their personnel and perhaps the impact of the age–wage profile on the total wage bill. We conclude, therefore, that firms will want to continue early exit in the future. We are entering an era of political debate about cost sharing and cost shifting because the interests of the state and the firms are increasingly diverging. If no successful accommodation can be reached between these key actors, then there is likely to be a shift in the costs of early retirement to the individual in the form of lower benefit levels. Again, this suggests not a reversing of the trend of early retirement but a shifting of the distribution of costs. But in this case, cost shifting is not only limited to the firms and the state but is extended to the individual, and the trend to early retirement will not be reversed.

Notes

1. Cohort data on entry into the pension system are given by A. Reimann, "Trend zur Frühverrentung noch ungebrochen," *Die Angestelltenversicherung* 32 (1985): 406–13.

2. The decline in participations rates of older workers in Western industrialized countries is documented in detail for five-year age groups, single years of age, and birth cohorts in K. Jacobs, M. Kohli, M. Rein, "The Evolution of Early Exit: A Comparative Analysis of the Labor Force Participation of the Elderly," in *Time for Retirement: Comparative Studies of the Decreasing Age of Exit from the Labor Force*, ed. M. Kohli et al. (Cambridge: Cambridge University Press, forthcoming).

3. The pension insurance board for white-collar workers (BfA) found out in a sample that for 1,100 concrete requests for part-time jobs, the employment agency could offer only five jobs, of which three were on a temporary base. See H. Kaltenbach, "Probleme der Rentenversicherung bei den BU/EU-Renten einschließlich der Zukunftsperspektiven," *Die Angestelltenversicherung* 33 (1986): 358.

4. G. Wagner, E. Kirner, J. Schupp, *Verteilungs-, sozial- und arbeits-marktpolitische Bedeutung eines Teilrentensystems*, DIW-Gutachten im Auftrage des Ministers für Arbeit, Gesundheit und Soziales des Landes Nordrhein-Westfalen ("Stufenweise in den Ruhestand?") (Berlin, May 1988), table 5.1.

5. K. Jacobs, M. Kohli, M. Rein, "Testing the Industry-Mix Hypothesis of Early Exit." WZB discussion paper IIVG/dp87-229, Science Center, Berlin, 1987.

6. Ibid.

7. Cf. M. Kohli, "Retirement and the Moral Economy: An Historical Interpretation of the German Case," *Journal of Aging Studies* 1 (1987): 125–44.

8. U.S. Congress, Office of Technology Assessment, *Technology and the American Economic Transition: Choices for the Future* (Washington, D.C.: Government Printing Office, May 1988), 38.

9. M. Piore and C. Sabel, "Work, Labor and Action: Work Experience in a System of Flexible Production," ms., July 1987.

10. For a comparison of partial pension systems in Denmark, Finland, France, Germany, Sweden, and the United Kingdom, cf. K. Jacobs, "Teilrentenmodelle: Erfahrungen im In- und Ausland," *Internationale Chronik zur Arbeitsmarktpolitik* 32 (April 1988): 1–9.

11. If the replacement rate declines below the two-thirds average rate that now prevails, then in many cases the basic pension will come very close to the standard of means-tested social help. The effort to ease the fiscal crisis might simply shift it from the pension insurance system to financing the cost by general taxation through an increase in the use of social help. If this were to occur, then the total level of spending might not change very much, only the source of financing. Avoiding the downstream effect of such a reform will be difficult.

12. European Communities, *The Structure of Labor Costs* (Luxembourg, 1975), table 72.

12/Retirement in Japan

Toshi Kii

Although the population of Japan is relatively young among the industrialized nations—the proportion of people aged 65 and over reached 10.1 percent in 1985—it is aging more rapidly than other nations. It took Sweden 85 years to double its population of aged from 7 percent to 14 percent. For France, the figure was 115 years. For England and West Germany, the figure was 45 years. The United States is projected to have 14 percent of its population 65 and over by the year 2020, which means the aged population will have taken 75 years to double. Japan, in contrast, will have 14 percent aged in the population in 1996, which means that it will have taken only 26 years for this proportion to double.[1] Indeed, Japan is projected to have the most aged population in the world in 2043, at which time the proportion of the aged will be 22.2 percent.

While the degree of population aging in Japan is at present relatively low, its longevity is the highest in the world today. Life expectancies of males and females at birth were 74.5 years and 80.2 years respectively in 1984. The rapid decline in the fertility rate is the cause of the aging of the population. In 1930, the average number of children a woman bore was 4.7. This figure declined to 2 in 1963 and to 1.8 in 1983.[2] These demographic data suggest that increased pressures will be placed on Japan's retirement system in the future.

Origins of the Retirement System

The retirement system can be traced back to the feudal era. In those days, as a paternalistic gesture, it was customary for an employer to give money as a gift to a worker at the end of his term of service. During the early stage of industrialization (around the turn of the twentieth century), this custom was systematized by industries in order to attract workers. Unions demanded that the system be reestablished and negotiated with management regarding how it was to be run.

268

The circumstances surrounding the origin of the retirement system are vague at best, but it can be noted that the Japan Mail Steamship Company had an employment regulation in 1902 according to which workers were to be relieved of duty at the age of 55.[3] The record of a board meeting of the company in that year stated that it was necessary to establish and implement a policy that allowed the dismissal of old workers if the company was to maintain a healthy and effective business environment.[4]

The idea gained impetus from a more practical consideration—the post–World War I recession, which provided large industries with a legitimate basis on which to dismiss workers. In 1919, for example, the largest iron factory set up a policy of dismissing operatives at the age of 55. It was estimated that by the mid 1920s over 50 percent of the factories in Japan had some form of mandatory retirement policy for skilled and semiskilled workers. In relation to the total labor force, relatively few workers were affected by the new retirement policy as the majority of workers were self-employed in primary industries as well as in small-scale, often family-type manufacturing industries in which retirement systems did not exist.

Labor unions worked for the establishment of the retirement money system and for increases in the amount of retirement money paid as compensation. The government also enacted retirement compensation legislation in 1937 in which it was stipulated that, in companies with more than fifty employees, the employer and employee had to reserve one-fiftieth of the employee's monthly salary for retirement compensation. In other words, the retirement money system that had originated in the private domain became legislated by public policy. When the Welfare Annuity Insurance Act (equivalent to U.S. social security) was established in 1944, the Retirement Compensation Act was abolished, and the retirement money system returned to the private domain of industries.

After World War II, as the power of labor unions increased, management's discretion regarding the retirement money system eroded, making it increasingly difficult for employers to dismiss workers. Many large and medium-sized industries established a mandatory retirement age at which the labor contract was dissolved automatically so that workers could be replaced legitimately. The abundance of young men in the labor force who had returned from the war aided the diffusion of such retirement regulations.

The interpretation of "retirement money" has become a crucial issue in negotiations between management and labor unions. There are three interpretations of retirement money. The first is that retirement money is a reward given at the conclusion of a worker's service to the company. This interpretation emphasizes the origin of the system. Retirement money does in fact carry this flavor of how the amount is determined and how it is given. The amount is determined by length of work and degree of contribution. But it also depends on the reasons for retirement (retirement age, personal reasons, or reasons of management). Retirement money is usually given in a lump sum at the time of retirement. It is a paternalistic gesture on the part of management—at least according to management's interpretation, which distinguishes between retirement money and wages, seeing only the latter as linked directly to the value of labor.

The second interpretation is that retirement money is a deferred payment of wages, a part of the surplus value of labor performed that is returned at the time of retirement. This is the view taken by labor unions, whose position is that a worker has a right to this money. This interpretation enables labor unions to negotiate the amount of retirement money with management, since it is a part of the wage. But dealing with two kinds of earnings—monthly wages and retirement money—creates problems for unions, making them sometimes less successful in their negotiations with management because of the clouding of the issue. Today, fewer unions press for this interpretation.

The third interpretation of retirement money is that it is a supplement to the welfare pension. According to this view, the amount of retirement money is calculated on the basis of living costs after retirement. For example, when a man retires at 55, his own and his wife's expected remaining years are obtained from the life table, and a total expected living cost is calculated on this basis. The required amount of retirement money is the total expected living cost minus welfare pension payments. A man receives welfare pension benefits beginning at age 60, and his wife receives them following his death. In fact, the iron and steelworkers' union demanded an increase in the retirement money based on this reasoning in 1973 negotiations with management.[5] The amount of retirement money calculated in this manner far exceeds the amount currently offered by management.

According to a report published by the Japan Federation of Employers Association in 1974, the retirement money policy should be reevaluated because of the general increase in wages, the recent increase in the welfare pension, and the fact that work is available after retirement. In other words, management also interprets retirement money as a supplement to the welfare pension. Its contention is that, in the past, when the welfare pension was almost nonexistent, retirement money was the only source of income; now that the welfare pension system has been expanded and the extension of the retirement age would increase financial security, the amount of retirement money should at least have a ceiling, if not be reduced.

The problem in interpreting retirement money as a supplement to the welfare pension is that it is usually discharged through a lump-sum payment. The majority of companies discharge retirement money in a lump sum at the time of retirement, although the use of a method combining a lump sum and a pension system has been increased recently among larger companies.[6] In this method, part of the money is paid at the time of retirement and the rest is paid over five, ten, or fifteen years. The majority of the retired do not want a pension system. Because lump-sum retirement money has been such an integral part of retirement in Japan, it would undoubtedly be difficult to change to a complete pension system with no lump-sum payment. There are practical reasons for which the retired prefer a lump-sum payment of their retirement money. First, the lump-sum retirement payment carries a tax advantage. Second, it is more profitable and secure in an inflationary economy, at least until and unless the pension system adopts a sliding scale that takes inflation into account. And third, in view of the rather early retirement age, it is more attractive to have a lump sum of money and continue to work for a different company.

The methods by which the amount of retirement money is calculated vary considerably from one company to another and from one industry to another. Nevertheless, the major factors determining the amount and the relationship among and between them are as follows:

1. The longer the period of employment, the larger the amount of retirement money. Roughly, the retired worker will receive three to five times as much money after thirty years of employment as he would after fifteen years of employment.
2. Larger companies generally pay more than smaller companies. But the size of the company has less effect when the number of employment years is small. This factor takes effect after around fifteen years of employment.
3. The more education one has, the greater the amount of his retirement money. But education is a less important factor in smaller companies. After thirty years of work, a person with a senior high school education will receive roughly 70 percent as much as a college graduate, and a person with a junior high school education will receive 50 percent as much.
4. More is paid for mandatory retirement than for retirement for personal reasons.

According to a survey done by the Ministry of Labor on model retirement money schedules of industries in 1981, the average amount of retirement money after thirty years of employment is equivalent to about forty-three times the monthly salary at the time of retirement in large companies (with more than 1,000 employees) and twenty-eight to thirty-three months' worth of this salary in small companies (with fewer than 100 employees). The model retirement money schedule is the anticipated amount of lump-sum money the retired worker will receive according to the factors mentioned above.

It would appear that the amounts of retirement money being paid are barely enough to support the retired between the ages of 55 and 60, or until the welfare pension becomes available. But even this is not the situation of the contemporary retired. First, the contemporary retired worked, on the average, only twenty years in one company before their retirement. This reflects the industrial expansion after World War II, when many of the middle-aged were newly employed. The amount of retirement money for those with a high school education after twenty years of work is less than half of what they would receive after thirty years of employment. In addition, the welfare pension provides less than the average living cost for two. In short, a substantial number of the contemporary retired are unable to be financially independent with only their retirement money and welfare pension.

Lifetime Employment and the Seniority System

Today, most Japanese industries have retirement regulations, but they vary considerably depending on the type and size of the industry or company. It has been erroneously suggested that retirement at the age of 55 meant lifetime employment because the life expectancy of the Japanese at the turn of the century was around 44 years. The fact was that those who were 55 had about fifteen more years to live on the average in those days. This so-called lifetime-employment idea, and the seniority system, both of which are prevalent in industries today, are important factors in the evolution of the retirement system in Japan. These two systems are often considered to be unique features of Japanese employment practices and labor policies that are not found in any other industrialized nation. For this reason, it is worthwhile at the outset to delineate them.

The Lifetime-Employment System
The literal translation of *Shushin Koyo Seido* is lifetime-employment system, but it does not imply that workers continue to be employed in a given organization until their death or even until the time they wish to retire. It simply means that workers are not dismissed under normal conditions until designated retirement ages. Abnormal conditions include labor disputes, severe economic downswings, and workers' absolute incompetency. The designated retirement age varies depending on the industry, the size of the organization, and the status of workers in the organization. No legal agreements exist that bind employers and employees to the system. Nevertheless, it definitely is carried out as an honor system between the two parties. Since this is an honor system, it has been suggested that the Japanese work organization is like a family in which the authority exercises paternalism and the subordinate returns loyalty. There is some truth in this analysis. For example, a company, particularly a large, financially secure, and stable company, does not dismiss workers who are seemingly less competent than expected and who may be easily replaced by newer recruits. Their promotion may be curtailed, or they may even be re-

located, but dismissal because of apparent incompetency is rare. But, it is also quite true that such workers may feel psychologically pressured to leave the company because of their strained relationships with other workers. Even in periods of economic downswing, many large manufacturing companies have opted for shortened work hours for their laborers rather than resort to the dismissal of a short-term surplus of labor.

Two industrial structures appear to influence such behaviors. One is the inflexible movement of workers between industries and between companies. Except for workers who are in small service and retail businesses and unskilled or semiskilled workers in small manufacturing industries, most workers employed in medium- and large-scale industries do not change jobs. One reason for this is that a company seldom recruits workers from other companies, particularly if they are over 30 or 35 years old. One does not often find in Japan people who make a so-called midcareer move. This relates to the second industrial structure, namely, the recruitment system.

The industrial recruitment system is closely tied to the education system in Japan. New graduates, both from colleges and from high schools, are recruited by industries during a designated period, usually late winter and early spring. Instead of each new graduate independently seeking a prospective employer, industries seek new graduates from schools that they consider acceptable. The relation between industries and schools, then, is quite important in terms of the possibility of new graduates launching careers in a given industry. A good example of this is that a large company seeks new graduates only from a small number of top-level schools, not necessarily because it has open positions to fill, but because it is attempting to secure the best available prospects of a year in the hope that some of them will contribute to the company in the long run. Indeed, it is customary for companies to sift new graduates for employment through vigorous written and oral examinations at the time of recruitment. From the standpoint of industry, this recruitment procedure is considered an important investment in human resources for the future of the industry. From the standpoint of the new recruits, this system gives them a sense of security and loyalty toward the company because they are accepted only after surviving such difficult screening processes. There exists an approximate fit between the size of the industry and the ranking of the schools from which companies recruit new graduates. In other words, there is a tendency for large industries to recruit only from among the graduates of those schools that the general public considers the highest-quality institutions. It appears that large industries render their commitment to their employees because through their recruitment procedures they procure only the best available prospects. It also appears that the quality of an industry's commitment to its workers is reflected in the public appraisal of the industry as a socially responsible institution. For these reasons, a company seldom seeks workers from other companies.

The Seniority System

The *Nenko Joretsu Seido,* or seniority system, means that workers' salaries or wage increases are based on a designated scale according to the length of the worker's contribution to the company. Since a major criterion on which to determine the pay scale is the length of employment, rather than the worker's perceived as well as measured qualitative contribution to the company, the pay scale at the time of the employee's entry into the company becomes a major determining factor in the amount of monetary reward the worker receives in any given year. The pay scale at entry varies depending on the industry, the size of the company, the educational attainment of the employee, the type of work—generally white collar or blue collar—and the sex of the worker. This does not mean that two workers who have the same background and work in the same company receive the same monetary reward because they have worked the same number of years. Obviously, some workers attain more responsible positions in a company, and they would be rewarded differently from those who do not achieve such managerial status. But the differential is not significant because that would be considered disruptive of the interrelationship among workers in a work environment. Indeed, in the Japanese work organization, status differentiation is for the most part based on seniority. It is rare that younger employees are promoted over older ones before they reach 40 or 45 years old, as the company considers the worker's all-round experience in the company the most important determinant of leadership potential. Clearly, though, the worker's ability and personality are considered important with regard to leadership. But these are considered minimum requirements, and the emphasis is placed on the worker's loyalty to the company and his capability to gain the confidence of his coworkers, which may come only from many years' experience in a company.

One important result of these two systems is that they create a need among industries for a legitimate basis for discharging workers because any organization must continuously renew its workforce for competitive survival. While it is necessary for any industry to secure competent workers continuously over a long period of time, it becomes expensive to maintain the workers acquired under these systems. So the traditional 55-year-old retirement age became a legitimate means by which industries could save labor costs.

Changing Patterns of Labor-Force Participation of Older Workers

Small-scale manufacturing industries have over the years played an important role in the industrialization of Japan in that they have been subcontractors for larger manufacturing industries. As much as the small businesses accommodated urbanization, the layers of small manufacturing industries provided the

Table 12.1/Percentage of Labor-Force Participation of Selected Age Groups by Sex, 1984

	AGE GROUP			
	15 and Over	*50–54*	*55–64*	*65 and Over*
Male				
Employed	76.5	93.3	78.4	36.5
Unemployed[a]	2.1	2.3	2.5	1.1
Nonemployed[b]	21.4	4.4	19.1	62.4
Total (male)	100.0	100.0	100.0	100.0
Female				
Employed	47.4	59.5	43.9	15.7
Unemployed[a]	1.3	1.7	0.6	0.2
Nonemployed[b]	51.3	38.8	55.5	84.1
Total (female)	100.0	100.0	100.0	100.0

Sources: Ministry of Labor, *Rodoryoku Chosa* (Tokyo: Government Printing Office, 1984); Somu-cho Tokei-kyoku, *Rodoryoku Chosa Nenpo* (Tokyo: Government Printing Office, 1985); Somu-cho Tokei-kyoku, *Suikei Jinko* (Tokyo: Government Printing Office, 1985).

[a]The unemployed are classified as part of the labor force since they were seeking some type of employment at the time of the survey.

[b]The nonemployed, such as housewives, students, and the retired, are not considered part of the labor force because they are not actively seeking employment.

means to successful industrialization. In 1981, over 85 percent of all manufacturing industries were small-scale factories with fewer than twenty employees.[7] This structure has been termed the dual structure of Japan's economy to indicate that, over the years, the profit arising out of the structure has been far greater in the larger industries and that the benefits accorded workers have also been far better in these larger industries. The continued existence of small-scale industries is an indication that large industries benefit from the dual structure of Japan's economic system. The contemporary elderly have shared in this economic phenomenon. It is precisely this structure that enables the elderly to continue to work beyond the customary age of retirement. As Table 12.1 shows, 36.5 percent of men over age 65 and 78.4 of men 55–64 were still employed in 1984. Among the employed aged 60 and over are those retired from larger enterprises that have some kind of retirement system— mandatory or customary—who have been reemployed in small enterprises. The small size of the industries is almost a prerequisite for the elderly to continue working. Yet the fact remains that the proportion of the elderly who are working has declined over the years.

The decline in the working elderly may be attributable to the occupational

Table 12.2/Percentage of Workers in Selected Age Groups by Industry and Sex, 1984

INDUSTRY TYPE	15 AND OVER	50–54	55–64	65 AND OVER
Male				
Primary	7.6	10.2	17.4	33.3
Secondary	38.0	40.2	33.9	21.1
Tertiary	53.9	49.6	48.4	45.6
Nonclassifiable	0.5	0	0.3	0
Total (male)	100.0	100.0	100.0	100.0
Female				
Primary	10.8	16.7	27.1	36.0
Secondary	28.4	30.3	21.8	14.4
Tertiary	60.6	53.0	51.1	49.5
Nonclassifiable	0.2	0	0	0.1
Total (female)	100.0	100.0	100.0	100.0

Source: Somu-cho Tokei-kyoku, *Rodoryoku Chosa Nenpo.*

diversification brought on by industrialization. When we look at the elderly who were working in the three major industrial categories in 1940 and in 1984, certain changes can be discerned. Among working elderly men, 71.8 percent were in primary industries and 27.2 percent in secondary and tertiary industries in 1940, whereas in 1984, 33.3 percent were in primary industries and 66.7 percent in secondary and tertiary industries (Table 12.2). Similar patterns could also be seen for females, but the proportion of females remaining in the primary industries was slightly larger than that of males.

The contemporary elderly, the majority of whom are second and higher-order sons in the case of males, have contributed to interindustrial movement as the nation has industrialized. They were born into a society in which the main economic activities were agricultural. As wage earners, they were able to become independent of their family of origin and establish their own families in cities. The expansion in secondary and tertiary industries over the years is reflected in the increase in the proportion of the working elderly in these industries. The majority of the contemporary elderly moved out of the primary industries when they were younger and contributed to the expansion of secondary and tertiary industries.

Nevertheless, the extent to which the expansion of secondary and tertiary industries brings about regulation of the age of retirement is also a factor. Considering that 24.3 percent of males aged 65 and over (66.7 percent of all working elderly) were still working in these industries in 1984, there seems to be something unique about the secondary and tertiary industries of Japan.

In 1984, 26 percent of all workers were either self-employed or working in the family business.[8] Also, the higher the age, the higher the proportion of self-employed workers. About half of the working elderly over 60 were estimated to be self-employed in that year. Although it is understandable that the great majority of primary industries consist of small-scale family enterprises, such characteristics are also found to a lesser degree in the secondary and tertiary industries of Japan. A proliferation of small retail shops, wholesale businesses, and manufacturing enterprises run by members of a single family has been an integral part of urbanization and industrialization. Small retail–wholesale businesses are an integral part of city life in Japan. Daily necessities are obtained at the shop closest to home, since it is customary in Japan to shop for them daily. Small, independent shops, such as vegetable shops, fish shops, meat shops, bakeries, and drugstores, are always found nearby. In fact, urbanization has been possible in Japan only with the proliferation of small, independent shops.

It has been noted that workers retire at an earlier age (55 years) in Japan than in other industrialized nations.[9] According to a 1973 survey by the Ministry of Labor, about one-third of companies of various sizes did not have mandatory retirement systems. Retirement at 55 was the rule, however, in more than half the companies that had mandatory retirement systems.[10]

Since then, there has been a discernible change in the mandatory retirement age. A 1984 survey by the Ministry of Labor showed 48 percent of the companies that had mandatory retirement systems set 60 years old as their retirement age, while only 30 percent had 55 years old.[11] Industries have been under considerable pressure, both from the government and from labor unions, to extend their retirement age to at least 60 years, particularly those large industries that had the traditional retirement age of 55. The government's concerns are based on three major points. First, there has been a substantial increase in the older labor force that may be utilized in less stressful fields of work because of technological development. Second, because there is a five-year gap between the age at which the public pension becomes available and the traditional retirement age of 55, workers must often continue to find work after retirement. Third, given a rapidly aging population, conditions must be created that will foster effective use of an older labor force from the standpoint of the nation's overall economy.

The pressure from labor unions is also based on the five-year gap between ages 55 and 60, at which time the government's old-age pension becomes available. The unions' basic theme has been that the lump sum paid employees on retirement in lieu of a private pension is too little to maintain a livelihood, both as sole support before age 60 and as a supplement to the old-age pension beyond 60, and that many of the retired must find supplementary work. The length of time an individual has worked has a direct effect on the amount of the lump-sum retirement money. The unions' goal is to secure for workers the wages they can accrue by working at least until the age of 60 and a larger amount of retirement money as well, based on the added working years, since they consider present lump sums small.

It appears that industries are accepting these challenges from the government and labor unions without a legislative mandate. But the industries must compensate somehow for the increasing cost of retaining older workers for longer periods of time under the seniority system.

Type of Retirement-Age Determination

There are four major retirement systems in contemporary industries according to which the retirement age is determined: (1) uniform systems in which all employees retire at a specified age; (2) systems that differentiate between men and women; (3) systems that differentiate among types of work; and (4) systems that differentiate among positions in the company. All these systems apply to employees, but usually not to directors or officers in the executive branch of the company. Civil service employees are not covered by a mandatory retirement system, except for those in certain positions, such as judges, attorneys, and instructors at national universities. Civil service workers are affected by a so-called customary retirement age (generally 60) when they are advised to retire. And most do retire.

According to a survey by the Ministry of Labor in 1984, over 87 percent of all companies had some kind of retirement system. Almost 80 percent of those with retirement systems had uniform systems, and approximately 17 percent had systems that differentiated between men and women with respect to retirement age (Table 12.3).

Table 12.3 also shows that the size of the company and the type of industry are factors in the retirement system established. Nevertheless, it should be recognized that in the past the movement has been toward establishing a uniform system of retirement in all industries regardless of company size. In 1973, for example, only about two-thirds of all companies had some kind of retirement system, and the larger the company, the more likely it was to have a mandatory retirement system.[12] Almost all companies with more than 1,000 employees had retirement systems, compared to only about half the companies with fewer than 100 employees in 1973. Of those having retirement systems, the majority (66 percent) had uniform systems, and 30 percent had systems that differentiated between men and women in that year.

As for the setting of the age of retirement, again, company size and industry type are factors (Table 12.4). Here, too, there has been a movement

Table 12.3/Percentage of Companies and Selected Industries Having Various Mandatory Retirement Systems, 1984

	Manda- tory Retire- ment System	No Manda- tory Retire- ment System	TOTAL	Uni- form Sys- tem	Sepa- rate Men/ Women	Sepa- rate Types of Work	Others	TOTAL
				Mandatory Retirement System by Type				
Size of company (number of employees)								
30–99	83.9	16.1	100.0	80.3	16.1	3.0	0.6	100.0
100–299	94.8	5.2	100.0	76.6	18.7	3.7	1.0	100.0
300–999	98.9	1.1	100.0	78.1	17.4	2.9	1.5	100.0
1,000–4,999	99.5	0.5	100.0	80.4	15.1	3.1	1.4	100.0
5,000 and over	99.6	0.4	100.0	86.1	5.7	3.2	5.0	100.0
Total	87.4	12.6	100.0	79.3	16.7	3.2	0.8	100.0
Selected industries								
Mining	76.5	23.5	100.0	77.8	14.4	7.8	—	100.0
Construction	74.1	25.9	100.0	75.0	17.8	4.8	2.4	100.0
Manufacturing	89.9	10.1	100.0	74.5	23.6	1.5	0.4	100.0
Wholesale/retail	89.6	10.4	100.0	85.8	10.8	2.9	0.6	100.0
Insurance/finance	97.4	2.6	100.0	84.7	9.4	2.5	3.4	100.0
Real estate	90.4	9.6	100.0	91.8	5.1	2.0	1.1	100.0
Transportation/ communication	93.1	6.9	100.0	83.7	5.0	11.1	0.2	100.0
Electric/gas/water	98.3	1.7	100.0	91.4	5.2	3.4	—	100.0
Service	86.2	13.8	100.0	85.2	12.4	1.0	1.4	100.0

Source: Ministry of Labor, "Koyo Kanri Chosa, 1984," in Somu-cho Tokei-kyoku, *Nippon no Tokei* (Tokyo: Government Printing Office, 1985), 35.

toward setting 60 years as the retirement age under a uniform system. This is most conspicuous in large companies with more than 1,000 employees. In 1973, only 11 percent of companies with more than 5,000 employees and 19 percent of companies with 1,000 to 4,999 employees had 60 years as their retirement age, while 38 percent of the former and 43 percent of the latter had 55 years as the retirement age.[13] In 1984, almost 59 percent of the companies with more than 5,000 employees and over 44 percent of companies with 1,000 to 4,999 employees had 60 years as the retirement age, while only 9 percent of the former and 22 percent of the latter had 55 years. It seems clear, then, that the extension of the retirement age has been proceeding steadily, led by the large companies and promoted by the government.

One impetus for large industries to extend the retirement age to 60 was the

Table 12.4/Mandatory Retirement Age under Uniform System, by Size of Company and Selected Industries, 1984 (in percentages)

	UNDER 55	55	56–59	60	61–64	65 65	66 AND OVER	TOTAL
Size of company (number of employees)								
30–99	—	28.6	15.1	52.1	1.3	2.3	0.7	100.1
100–299	0.3	33.6	23.1	39.6	1.9	1.2	0.2	99.9
300–999	0.2	29.9	30.0	38.4	0.2	1.3	—	100.0
1,000–4,999	—	21.9	32.4	44.3	1.0	0.4	—	100.0
5,000 and over	—	8.7	33.5	57.9	—	—	—	100.1
Total	0.1	29.6	18.3	48.3	1.3	2.0	0.5	100.1
Selected industries								
Mining	—	39.5	13.3	47.1	—	—	—	99.9
Construction	—	14.9	9.6	69.9	2.4	2.7	0.4	99.9
Manufacturing	—	31.9	18.2	47.8	0.2	1.6	0.2	99.9
Wholesale/retail	0.3	37.3	18.7	39.6	2.2	1.3	0.8	99.9
Insurance/finance	—	35.2	22.8	38.3	1.6	2.1	—	99.9
Real estate	—	20.3	22.8	40.0	7.1	9.7	—	99.9
Transportation/ communication	—	27.7	26.7	45.6	—	0	—	100.0
Electric/gas/water	—	17.0	51.0	31.1	0.9	—	—	100.0
Service	0.1	22.3	18.1	49.4	3.1	5.5	1.6	100.1

Source: Ministry of Labor, "Koyo Kanri Chosa, 1984," 35.
Note: Totals vary from 100 because of rounding.

success of labor unions in the iron industry in negotiating with management over extension of the retirement age in 1979. The negotiations ended with an agreement that the industry would extend the retirement age gradually from 55 to 60 years between 1981 and 1984. But the unions accepted management proposals that workers' wage hikes stop at age 50 and that the lump-sum retirement money be calculated at age 55, but not awarded until age 60.[14] Other unions and their respective industries appear to have followed the precedent set in the iron industry. Even though there has been a movement in all industries to extend the retirement age, however, there has not been a straight extension of the retirement age. Under the seniority system, straight extension of the retirement age would be too costly to industry. Thus, certain mechanisms have been deployed to offset the increasing cost of retaining workers, as exemplified in the labor–management agreement mentioned above. On the other hand, the majority of Japanese industries have for a long time utilized two systems of prolonging the working life of workers beyond the customary retirement age. These are the reemployment system and the extension of employment system.

Reemployment System

Under the reemployment system, management retires workers who have reached the retirement age and rewards them with lump-sum retirement money, then rehires them, generally in lower positions and at lower salaries. One survey showed that over 50 percent of those reemployed were earning less than half the income they had earned before retirement, and only 2.5 percent were earning more.[15] Of the companies having retirement systems, over 50 percent had reemployment systems in 1982.[16] It appears that large companies are more likely to resort to this system of retaining workers when they are faced with a labor shortage. Management has more or less absolute control over the selection of retirees for reemployment. Most often, these retirees are reemployed in a smaller company, usually a subsidiary or branch company, through mediation carried out by the company they have worked for. In a sense, this is a paternalistic gesture on the part of management. Larger companies have affiliated subsidiary companies whose economic existence is controlled by the parent companies. Taking advantage of this relationship, large companies provide desirable and selected retirees with new jobs. This is popularly referred to as "coming from above," particularly when the retirees have held high positions in the large company.

Extension-of-Employment System

The extension-of-employment system enables certain workers who have reached retirement age to continue to work without formally retiring. Only about 28 percent of companies utilized this system in 1982.[17] As with the reemployment system, the majority of companies using the system allow only those workers approved by management to continue to work. Their positions and salaries are often reduced, although not as severely as under the reemployment system. The extension-of-employment system is more often used among medium- and small-size companies than among larger companies. One possible reason is that smaller companies often find themselves in need of experienced and competent workers who may not be available among the younger cohorts in the company, whereas large companies can find replacements from within with less difficulty.

Approximately 18 percent of companies use both systems, depending on the health and ability of the workers and, most important, on the company's need to fill certain positions. It appears that workers are treated more favorably under the extension-of-employment system than under the reemployment system. One example is the method of supplying the lump-sum retirement money.

Under the reemployment system, workers usually receive a lump sum at first retirement, based on the preretirement years, but nothing at all following the reemployment period, whereas extended-employment workers' lump sums are generally calculated taking the extended years into account. For both systems, however, there is considerable variation in how retirement money is handled from one company to another and from one industry to another.[18]

As the above explanations show, Japanese industries have long utilized experienced workers beyond the customary retirement age when they are needed. But since it would be too costly to retain these workers under a straight seniority system, the industries have invented these other systems to deflect the cost. A significant aspect of these systems is that industries have complete control over the selection of older workers for extended working years.

Why, then, has there been a movement toward extension of the retirement age by industries when most of them already have incorporated the reemployment system or the extension-of-employment system or both? According to a 1982 survey on this issue, the majority of companies, regardless of size, indicated that societal demand was the most important reason for extension of the retirement age, with larger companies voicing this opinion more strongly than smaller companies.[19] Indeed, over four-fifths of the large companies (with more than 5,000 employees) agreed with this statement, although these were the companies that had maintained the traditional mandatory retirement age of 55. The same survey showed two other reasons to be important: demand by labor unions and the enhancement of workers' morale. Again, large companies cited these reasons more frequently than smaller companies, particularly labor unions' demands. Thus, as noted previously, the government's promotion and the strong demand by the unions to extend the retirement age have influenced industry's movement in this direction, particularly among large companies. It appears that large companies have accepted the challenges from the government and labor unions not only because of the strong tie between the government and large industry, as well as strong, visible union activities, but also because they are evaluated by society in general based on how responsible and progressively they deal with the aging population.

But certainly the reemployment system and the extension-of-employment system operate as deterrents to straight extension of retirement ages. Indeed, many companies that say they have extended their retirement age actually use these two systems and other innovative methods during part of the extended period to reduce the cost from that of a straight extension of the retirement age. In fact, it is rare to find companies that have instituted a straight extension of the retirement age. For example, a company may extend its retirement age from 55 years to 60 years, but its labor agreement may state the following: (1) The retirement age is 60; (2) the day of retirement is the last day of the month of the sixtieth birthday; (3) beyond age 57, management examines the individual's labor contract on a yearly basis; (4) upon this examination, if the labor contract is difficult to renew due to health or other problems, the employee may be retired with the consent of the labor union; (5) the amount of retirement money is calculated when the employee is 57 years old; (6) the payment of retirement money is carried out on the employee's request after his fifty-seventh birthday; and (7) there are to be no pay hikes after age 57.[20]

In this example, the actual straight extension of the retirement age is two years with essentially three years of reemployment added on. But the fact that management requires the labor union's consent to retire the worker makes the worker's status considerably more secure than it is under the reemployment system or the extension-of-employment system. At the same time, the company is able to reduce the cost of keeping the worker.

Flexible Retirement

Recently, many innovative retirement systems have been implemented by industries in addition to uniform systems in which all employees retire at one specified age. One such system is called the voluntary retirement system. Under this system, employees over a certain age who have more than the designated length of contribution to the company and who wish to retire before reaching the specified retirement age are treated as regular retirees, which enables them to receive lump-sum retirement money and other benefits equivalent to those they would have been given if they had worked until the retirement age. Companies with this system also provide those early retirees with special bonuses calculated on the basis of their length of contribution to the company. Under the traditional retirement system, workers leaving the company voluntarily before reaching retirement age incurred substantial reductions in their lump-sum retirement money. The voluntary retirement system is an effective method of enticing workers to retire before reaching retirement age to avoid the increasing cost of retaining them.

One well-known company proceeded to establish this system when it extended the retirement age from 55 to 60 in 1978. Interestingly, after the company extended the retirement age, employees asked that an early-retirement system be implemented without too much penalty so that those who wished to move into different areas of work would be able to do so more favorably before the age of 60. The company complied and implemented a voluntary retirement system under which employees who were 50 years old and over and wished to retire before age 60 received lump-sum retirement money calculated on the basis of involuntary retirement, which provided 30 percent more than they would have received on the basis of traditional voluntary separation from the company. There are numerous variations in terms of length of contribution, age, rank, and even the worker's new company that affect the application of the system. Regardless of these variations, it is clear that Japanese companies are faced with a challenge of how to economize personnel costs while extending the retirement age.

But when an economic recession took place, industries set up mandatory retirement systems to cope with the excess labor force.

Retirement System Differentiating between Men and Women
Although the majority of companies with retirement systems used the uniform system, almost 17 percent had a system that differentiated on the basis of sex in 1984 (Table 12.2). There has been a discernible movement toward equality between the sexes on this issue, since in 1973 approximately 30 percent of the companies had systems that differentiated between the sexes.[21] Still, this is one of the problems facing industries attempting to reform their retirement systems. Under systems differentiating between men and women today, over 96 percent of companies set their retirement ages for men between 55 and 60 with 60 years old increasingly being the accepted retirement age. But, for women, over 75 percent of companies have set retirement ages between 50 and 55.[22] Indeed, less than 4 percent of companies had 60 years old as their retirement age for women. This form of discrimination increases as the size of the company becomes smaller. Certainly women have not historically been allowed to enter career work paths, and have been able to work only in less-prestigious occupations where workers can easily be replaced. They are expected to leave work when they reach their mid 20s for marriage, and even when they return to work at middle age, they can get only jobs that do not require any skills. Moreover, women's work is simply looked on as a means of supplementing household income, and industries have not considered women's work worthy of serious consideration. Also, since women are able to receive social security benefits at age 55, companies feel justified in their sex discrimination.

Smaller companies with less favorable economic situations have taken advantage of women's willingness to work under adverse conditions. Not only is the average salary of women about half that of men (although there are substantial variations among industries), but also there is no realistic avenue for their advancement in the company. Although larger companies are less likely to use a sex-differentiated retirement system, their workers do not fare better regarding salaries, wages, or promotions. In 1981, one company using this form of retirement system was judged irresponsible, though not in violation of the law, under the civil code by the Supreme Court. The Ministry of Labor has attempted to eliminate sex-based retirement systems, and indeed there has been a decline in the number of companies instituting this system over the years. But it appears that the problems surrounding women's status in Japan are too institutionalized at present for retirement systems to be easily remedied.

Government Programs for the Elderly

The government first developed pension systems for civil service employees in 1923, then for employees in private industries in 1954, and finally for self-employed workers, including farmers, in 1959.[23] There are now eight independent public pension programs, categorized according to occupational groups: (1) employees in the private sector; (2) national government employees; (3) local government employees; (4) public utility workers; (5) private school teachers; (6) agricultural and fishery employees; (7) seamen; and (8) self-employed workers. All these programs are financed by employees, employers, and the government.

These eight programs may be classified under four pension systems that differ with respect to government contribution, age at which people receive the pension, and period of membership required for eligibility. They are (1) the welfare pension system, which applies to employees in the private sector; (2) the national pension system, which applies to the self-employed and some employees; (3) seamen's insurance; and (4) the mutual relief association pension, which applies to those in the other five programs. Also, various provisions have been added since 1959 to include persons who do not work outside the house, housewives, as well as those who were not able to participate in any of the pension programs. Under the national pension program, these people are eligible for a pension if certain conditions are met. Thus, theoretically, all the elderly can be said to be covered by a public pension program today.

The basic eligibility requirement for all four major public pension systems is twenty years of membership in any one program (twenty-five years in the case of the national pension programs). Those who have not fulfilled this requirement in one program may draw a substantially reduced pension if their years in a combination of any of the eight programs add up to the required number. In 1982, over 15 million of the 16 million persons aged 60 and over received one or another form of public pension, with national pension recipients predominating. Since almost 90 percent of the retired who receive public pensions come under the welfare pension or the national pension system, only these are explained here.

The Welfare Pension System
The so-called laborer's annuity insurance plan, conceived as a source of military funding in 1942, became the welfare pension program in 1954.[24] This is a mandatory program for workers employed by private firms with five or more employees. The program is equivalent to the U.S. social security system in its structure. Receipt of a welfare pension begins at age 60 for those who are not working (55 for women and mine workers) after twenty years of enrollment in the program (fifteen years for mine workers). For those still working beyond

the age of 60, the pension benefit starts at the age of 65 at a reduced amount. Certain concessions to the newness of the program are in effect, however, which provide benefits for those who had already begun their working careers when the program began, although at a reduced rate. For example, persons aged 40 at the time the program became available are eligible after fifteen years of membership in it. In 1983, 4.1 million of the 16.5 million persons aged 60 and over received welfare pension payments.

The National Pension System

There are two programs under this system: one based on premiums paid by the members and one called the old-age welfare pension program, which does not require a premium. The first program applies to workers in firms with fewer than five employees, self-employed workers, and nonemployees such as housewives and students over 20 years of age, who participate by paying a monthly contribution. But it is not mandatory for the spouse of a worker who participates in any of the other pension programs or for students.

Eligibility for the national pension requires at least twenty-five years of membership in the program. It is paid beginning at age 65 for both men and women. The government pays one-third of the pension, the rest coming from the pension fund. Because the program is relatively new (in effect since 1959), special provisions such as ten-year and five-year programs with reduced pension amounts have been made. In 1982, 6.9 million of the 11.6 million persons aged 65 and over received this form of pension.

The second program under this system, the old-age welfare pension, is intended to compensate for the immaturity of the system for those who have not been able to participate in any pension programs. To receive the old-age welfare pension, a person must be at least 70 years old and must not be receiving any other form of public pension. The pension is provided entirely by the government. There are restrictions on the pension amount under the old-age welfare pension program depending on the level of a person's income from private sources. As of 1983, 2.4 million persons aged 70 and over received this form of pension. Since the old-age welfare pension is intended to compensate for the immaturity of both the national pension system and the welfare pension system, it is expected to be inapplicable to anyone within a few decades.

Work after "Retirement"

Japan's retirement system has two significant effects on the retired with respect to their economic condition in the later years: (1) relatively early retirement ages from their career jobs at between 55 and 60 years old; and (2) a lump-sum retirement payment that is substantial, but not sufficient for the retired to be economically independent. And indeed, the majority of those who retire from their career jobs continue to work either in the same companies through the systems of reemployment and extension of employment or in other companies through the mediation of the companies they have worked for. According to a 1983 survey by the Ministry of Labor of people who had retired from career jobs, over 77 percent of men (54 percent of women) indicated they had continued to work, and of those working, about 80 percent indicated economic necessity as the most important reason for continuing to work after retirement.[25] Other reasons were given, such as to supplement family income, to earn extra money, to stay in good health, to participate in society, and to use abilities, though these reasons were stated much less frequently, and older workers over 65 were more inclined to give these reasons than younger workers aged 55 to 59.

Income during the extended work period is generally lower, although approximately 10 percent of those who worked after retirement earned more than before retirement.[26] Over half of those workers receive less than 70 percent of what they used to earn before retirement, and over 20 percent receive less than half their previous earnings. Although about 40 percent of those working indicate satisfaction with the jobs they have, lower salaries and wages are overwhelmingly the most frequently mentioned reason for expressed dissatisfaction with the job. And this is particularly so for those aged 55 to 60. Other reasons for dissatisfaction with work are unstable status and labor conditions, such as worsened working hours and days, but these reasons are less frequently mentioned. About 60 percent of workers indicated that their income had to be supplemented by using the lump-sum retirement money and savings, and one-third of workers indicated that another member of the family had to work to supplement their income.[27]

It appears that attitudes toward the continuation of work are related to the life cycle, the type of work before retirement, the age at which the public pension is available, living arrangements, and health status. Although at any age the majority express a desire to continue working, reasons for wanting to work vary depending on the life-cycle stage the old workers find themselves in. In this regard, up to 60 years old, many workers are heads of household who have more than one dependent to support, often including their youngest child. Their health status is excellent overall, and economic issues are the primary concern. When they reach age 60, the welfare pension becomes available, and the last child has become independent. Even though their health is still good, work becomes less attractive because of worsened work conditions. But they still have a desire to work, many do find work, and such reasons as "making extra income," "good for health," and "social participation" become more visible. When they reach age 70, they still indicate a desire to work, but their health status becomes an important factor in determining whether they actually can work. Indeed, roughly one-quarter of this group indicates impossibility to work due to health reasons even if they wanted to work. At the same time, they are more likely to be living with married offspring, and their children are for all practical purposes heads of household. Also, at age 65 the national pension becomes available, however meager it might be, and indeed available jobs, which are quite scarce, are so unattractive that true retirement becomes the only realistic option. Certainly this is an oversimplified view of the life cycle of the older worker, but it shows that work after retirement from a career job is very much related to the economic conditions the older worker faces.

Notes

1. Somu-cho, *Chunenso no Ryoshin Fuyo ni Kansuru Chosa* (Tokyo: Government Printing Office, 1983).

2. Ibid.

3. T. Tsukamoto, *Rogo Mondai Jiten* (Tokyo: Domesu Shuppan, 1973).

4. S. Matsushima, *Koreika Shakai no Rodo-sha* (Tokyo: University of Tokyo Press, 1983).

5. K. Murakami and C. Yamazaki, *Korekara no Nenkin, Nenkin Seido* (Tokyo: Nihon Seisansei Honbu, 1975).

6. Somu-cho Tokei-kyoku, *Nippon no Tokei* (Tokyo: Government Printing Office, 1985).

7. W. Lockwood, *The Economic Development of Japan* (Princeton: Princeton University Press, 1954).

8. Somu-cho Tokei-kyoku, *Nippon no Tokei*.

9. T. Kii, "Recent Extension of Retirement Age in Japan," *Gerontologist* 19, no. 5 (1979): 481–86.

10. G. Kato, *Taishokukin, Nenkin no Tebiki* (Tokyo: Rodo Horei Kyokai, 1975).

11. M. Ogihara, *Teinen-sei Taisaku* (Tokyo: Chuo Keizai-sha, 1985).

12. Kii, "Recent Extension of Retirement Age."

13. Ibid.

14. Matsushima, *Koreika Shakai*.

15. Kii, "Recent Extension of Retirement Age."

16. Matsushima, *Koreika Shakai*.

17. Ibid.

18. A. Kurozimi, "Teinen to Shotoku Hosho," in *Rojin no Fukushi to Shakai Hosho*, ed. S. Okamura and F. Miura (Tokyo: Kakiuchi Shuppen, 1974).

19. Ministry of Labor, *Koenenrei-sha Shuqyo Jittai Chosa* (Tokyo: Government Printing Office, 1983).

20. Nihon Rodo Kyokai, *Teinen, Taishokukin, Nenkin Romu Sodan* (Tokyo: Nihon Rodo Kyokai, 1973).

21. Ministry of Labor, *Koyo Kanri Chosa* (Tokyo: Government Printing Office, 1973).

22. Ministry of Labor, *Koenenrei-sha Shuqyo Jittai Chosa*.

23. Sorifu Kohoshitsu, *Shakai Hosho Tokei Nenkan* (Tokyo: Office of the Prime Minister, 1984).

24. A. Kurozimi, M. Chubachi, and K. Matsumoto, *Rorei Hosho-ron* (Tokyo: Yuhikaku, 1975).

25. Ibid.

26. Ibid.

27. Ministry of Labor, *Koenenrei-sha Shuqyo Jittai Chosa*.

13/Early Retirement: Questions and Speculations

Harold L. Sheppard

This chapter raises questions and issues that require resolution, or more definitive knowledge, before we can talk confidently about the future of "early retirement" (i.e., before the age of 62, the earliest American workers can leave the labor force with a social security retirement benefit). Among them are external, especially international economy, trends; productivity; labor-market policies; political–economic bases for changes in social security and tax-related incentives or disincentives to exit early; and the leisure versus work tradeoff.

Any discussion about early retirement in the future must include a consideration of factors that are external to the individual and his or her place of employment, which are too frequently ignored in research and analyses of this phenomenon. I refer here, for example, to the emergence of global or multinational economies. If the competitive position of the United States is weakened, to what extent will the American economy be able to afford pensions for growing numbers of nonworkers at levels deemed by them to be adequate?

A more dramatic dimension of this process, called to my attention by Xavier Gaullier, Centre National de la Recherche Scientifique, Paris, calls for a crucial modification of an argument, now gaining popularity, that the expected decline in the numbers of young persons available for future American labor forces will compel employers to reexamine their policies toward middle-aged and older workers, thus leading to later retirement ages. But Gaullier points to the employment impact of international communication systems (e.g., satellites). It is now possible to "transport" by satellite all kinds of computer-based paperwork (recordkeeping, invoices, etc.) to countries where there is a plentiful supply of young, computer-competent workers willing and able to be employed at relatively lower wages than those paid in the so-called developed countries. A global economy, in other words, does not simply involve the transfer of goods and technology among different nations or the migration of "cheap labor."

In the example suggested by Gaullier, a youth shortage in one country need not be alleviated through immigration or through improved programs for middle-aged and older workers in the host nation. Depending on the nature of the industry and the technology associated with that industry, it is apparently becoming increasingly possible to export the work to be done elsewhere and then to return the product to the originating country, all electronically. Earlier examples include the more primitive practice of exporting raw materials (or incomplete ones) to be finished by workers in the country with more plentiful and less costly labor and then returned to the originating country. A case in point is the apparel industry.

Another caveat concerning labor shortages relates to the *productivity* question. It is possible, though not inevitable, that American productivity might progress to such an extent that we may need no increase in the proportion of Americans engaged in remunerative labor, which ostensibly forms the basis for supporting nonworkers. For some time in the United States (and elsewhere), productivity gains have been distributed through a combination of higher purchasing power (including fringe benefits), longer vacations, shorter workweeks or hours, *and* reduced retirement ages. How these choices have been allocated, and for and by whom, is not the pertinent issue here. What is important is that productivity increases have been one ingredient in the retirement-age phenomenon. Whether we can expect further progress is still unresolved. The future of investments in research and development aimed at productivity improvements is at stake here.

Other factors also influence the early-retirement phenomenon, for example, national employment (or labor-market) policies. Insights into this element can be gained by cross-national comparisons of labor-force participation by older persons. To illustrate, consider that in noncommunist Europe, the labor-force participation rate of men 55–64 years old is as high as 76 percent in Sweden, but as low as 50 percent in France (as of 1985). A discrepancy of such magnitude cannot adequately be explained as a function of contrasting technologies, occupation–industry structures, or per capita gross national product. One explanation, it seems to me, lies in the two countries' contrasting labor-market policies. Such policies reflect different sets of values, too. Unlike France (and many if not most European and North American industrialized societies), Sweden has long had a "positive" labor-market policy.

Values regarding work versus leisure may be at play here. But it may be difficult to take that explanation too seriously when we consider that in 1970, the 55–64 male participation rate in France was 75 percent, while in Sweden it was 85 percent. A drop from 75 to 50 percent in France cannot easily be explained by citing an absence of the frequently invoked Protestant work ethic. The fact that the French rate declined so sharply, from 75 percent in 1970 to 69 percent only five years later, cannot reflect a sudden emergence of "Latin" values about leisure over work.

Furthermore, it should be noted that in Sweden, over the same five-year period, the corresponding participation rate declined only from 85 to 82 percent. This comparison points up, once again, how two different societies responded in contrasting ways to the OPEC-induced recession that took place from 1970 to 1975.

Sweden's labor-market policy, comparatively speaking, has meant that early retirement (i.e., earlier exit or increases in the numbers exiting the labor force at current "early" ages) has not been used in that country as a *first resort* for meeting unemployment problems. A robust, continuous training policy, along with such other policies as flexible public service and public works employment programs, have helped keep Swedish jobless rates low *and* older men's activity rates high. The same cannot be said for France, which still has a high jobless rate and a low activity rate for men 55–64 years old. The most recent data indicate the same relative positions of Sweden and France.

The future of early retirement also is intertwined with political issues. Before the early 1980s, mandatory or compulsory retirement age was a controversial political matter in the United States. That issue has been succeeded by debates over how far we can go in lowering the pensionable age, or at least over how many more workers can leave the labor force at what is *now* defined as an early age. No longer can age 62 be accepted as the cutoff point. In the 1950s, we typically used the labor-force participation of persons 60–64 as a category of early exit. By the 1960s, we discerned participation rates declining sharply in the 55–59 category, and by the late 1980s, there were even signs of a decline in the 50–54 age category, especially of men.

Even with such offsets as the high and increasing participation rates of women 55 and younger, the overall decline in the rate of the 55-plus group has begun to raise questions that cannot remain unaffected by the political realm. At least at the governmental level (as distinct from the private level), there is some degree of conscious effort to stem the flow of early retirements from the labor force. The most notable of the political decisions were those resulting in these 1983 amendments to the Social Security Act:

1. Taxation of some part of retired-worker benefits.
2. Delaying by six months payment of indexed-for-inflation benefit increases.
3. The gradual raising of the full-pension-benefit age from 65 to 67.
4. Increasing the "bonus" for continuing to work after age 65.

5. Lowering the penalty for continuing to work while in receipt of a "retired" benefit.

The first three of these changes constitute financial disincentives to retire early, while the other two are financial incentives to *remain* in the paid labor force. At least, they are or were so intended.

After 1983, there was another level of political decision making that has not been widely recognized by gerontologists. According to Sheila Zedlweski,[1] the 1986 tax-reform legislation resulted in higher taxes for the aged while reducing them for the nonaged. Zedlewski also points to the increasing costs of Medicare paid by the aged. All these developments have produced an increasing fiscal burden on the elderly. This is a point totally ignored by the New Agists, who have been painting portraits of the American elderly as greedy and undeservedly growing in economic affluence.

The primary point is that these changes, which have resulted in greater costs for being old and retired in America, should, according to the doctrine of *homo economicus,* put a brake on, or produce a reversal of, early-retirement trends. But other influences may be at play, some of them economic, others of a sociopsychological nature. Among the economic factors is the unresolved question of the future of private pensions. For one thing, will private-employer pensions correspondingly align themselves with the direction of the 1983 social security amendments or with the drift of the 1986 tax reforms that consisted of penalties for the aged? To what extent will the proportion of workers effectively covered by pension plans grow, decline, or remain steady? And apart from the question of coverage is the issue of pension-income *adequacy.* We no longer can be complacent about these questions.

In the opinion of Rachel Boaz,[2] as long as the current pattern of early-retirement provisions in the private pension realm remains untouched, the 1983 changes in social security will probably have little upward effect on age at retirement. If Boaz is correct, such financial incentives will make little difference as far as the early-retirement phenomenon is concerned.

To repeat, we cannot be too certain about the impact of the 1983 social security amendments and other legislative and regulatory developments, the effects of which ostensibly could put a brake on the American early-retirement trend. Is it possible to be more certain about a shift in the work versus leisure tradeoff, toward the leisure side of the equation, among older workers of the near future? Short of truly drastic economic penalties for retiring while still healthy, we seem to be witnessing an *institutionalization* of retirement as young as 60 as virtually a cultural norm. There is also the growth of private-enterprise interests that are advertising *retirement lifestyles* in the American mass media and that have a serious stake in the growth of a 55-plus retiree population. Retirement may increasingly become a valued end in itself, a life goal. Large numbers of adult Americans appear to be working *in order to retire,* as soon as possible, with resources that will allow them to enjoy a satisfying nonwork lifestyle.[3]

This observation does not mean that we will have solved the problem of poverty or that persons retiring early with adequate living standards will not, over time, move into poverty. It does mean that despite such risks, we may be witnessing the emergence of a new and large "leisure" class, in the literal sense of that term—*non*work on a full-time basis—*within* the American aged population. These are men and women who retire despite good health and despite the fact that they *could* continue to work after age 60. They choose leisure over work. They retire, among other reasons, because they simply do not want to work any longer, and they are able to retire because they have the financial resources (private pensions, savings, and investments) to make it possible to realize their nonwork wishes. Attractive financial resources are not the *cause* of early retirement (or retirement at any age); they are *conditions* making it possible to leave the world of work if individuals want to do so.

In this connection, it should not be surprising to learn that "tired of working" or "wanting to retire" outstripped all other retirement reasons among the full-time retirees interviewed in the 1982 *New Beneficiary Survey* of the Social Security Administration.[4] The availability of other than social security pensions increased the probability of retiring *before* age 62 among workers retiring primarily because of "work tiredness" or "wanting to retire." This kind of research points to the *joint* interaction of *motives* and *conditions* (work tiredness and pension opportunity), leading to the possible emergence of a young, healthy leisure class of American retirees.

Notes

1. Sheila Zedlewski, "The Increasing Fiscal Burden on the Elderly," in *Social Security and Economic Well-Being Across Generations*, ed. J. R. Guest (Washington, D.C.: Public Policy Institute, American Association of Retired Persons, 1988), 13–66.

2. Rachael Floursheim Boaz, "The 1983 Amendments to the Social Security Act: Will They Delay Retirement? A Summary of the Evidence," *Gerontologist*, April 1987, 151–55.

3. Meredith Minkler, "Gold in Gray: Business' Discovery of the Death Market," *Gerontologist*, February 1989, 17–23.

4. Harold L. Sheppard, *The Early-Retirement Issue in the United States* (Tampa: International Exchange Center on Gerontology, University of South Florida, 1988); Michael Packard and V. Reno, "A Look at Very Early Retirees," in *Issues in Contemporary Retirement*, ed. R. Ricardo Campbell and E. P. Lazear (Stanford, Calif.: Hoover Institution Press, 1988), 243–72.

14/Epilogue:
The "Buffer Years": Market Incentives and Evolving Retirement Policies

James H. Schulz

Today, more than ever, political systems are embracing the incentive–control mechanisms of markets and, in the process, exposing themselves to all the economic insecurity that goes with them.[1] We see, for example, growing market interdependence among countries, the rising popularity of "privatization," and the establishment of a new and expanded "free trade" zone in Europe and between the United States and Canada.

Competitive markets—reacting to technological change, shifts in consumer preferences, new sources of productive inputs, and so forth—threaten workers' jobs and firms' profits if the demands of new economic production possibilities and output "needs" are ignored. With market incentives that promote efficiency, innovation, and growth also come unemployment, bankruptcy, social disruption, and inequality.

The contemporary economic and political commentator James Fallows has expressed it well: "Capitalism is one of the world's more disruptive forces. It can call [through market forces] every social arrangement into question, make cities and skills and ranks merely temporary. To buy into it is to make a commitment to permanent revolution that few political creeds can match."[2]

But it is not just the so-called capitalist countries that have embraced the power of market mechanisms. China under Deng Xiaoping has tried to move away from complete dependence on central planning and has allowed markets to operate, especially in agriculture.[3] And the Soviet Union (along with various Eastern European regimes), reacting to *perestroika,* has begun to experiment with the economic potentials and problems arising from markets.

Markets and Retirement Policies

The story of tradeoffs between efficiency and social stability has been told many times over the years.[4] What has not been given sufficient attention is the extent to which manpower policies for older workers have been shaped by more general issues of economic policy. Historically, the problems arising from markets have had a powerful impact on evolving pension—retirement policies in industrialized countries.[5] We need to see clearly that "aging policies" have been strongly influenced by the evolving political–economic situation in various countries. Retirement policies, for example, continue to be shaped by the constant need for micro and macro labor-force adjustments necessitated by the ever-changing nature of productive processes.

Welfare states in many European countries are associated with highly interventionist government action and a large amount of coordination between business, labor, and individuals disadvantaged by market forces. Even in modern Japan, where the traditional welfare-state apparatus has lagged behind other countries, state intervention, coordination, and cooperation between business, workers, and government are seen by many as a major part of the Japanese miracle.[6]

Goran Therborn's major study of unemployment in market-oriented countries during the postwar period seeks to understand *Why Some Peoples Are More Unemployed Than Others*.[7] As he points out, the economic crises of the 1970s and early 1980s were accompanied in 1984, for example, by nearly 32 million unemployed workers (8.2 percent of the labor force) in the OECD countries.[8] But unemployment rates in the various OECD countries have been substantially different, with five countries (Austria, Japan, Norway, Sweden, and Switzerland) able to keep their unemployment below 5 percent.

Therborn's econometric, historical, and political research leads him to conclude that the traditional explanations for these differences leave much of the variation unexplained. Only partially satisfactory explanations are these:

- Differences in economic growth and labor supply
- Differences in currency–exchange-rate policies, world market dependence, and/or general economic structure
- Differences in wage restraint and the costs of labor
- Differences in inflation rates
- Differences in tax policy, social expenditures, and/or levels of unemployment compensation
- Differences in profit rates or trends in profit rates

Instead, Therborn points to the importance of "the existence or nonexistence of an institutionalized commitment to full employment." In addition, low-unemployment countries have exercised effective control over one or more strategic economic market variables (e.g., labor supply, labor demand, investment, or price–cost structures) and have followed more compatible macroeconomic policies.[9]

But not all countries have been able to keep unemployment low. For example, as Theda Skocpol points out, at the high point of the interventionist, New Deal, and Keynesian periods in U.S. history, policymakers acted cautiously—in fact, conservatively. American policymakers in Washington were ever mindful of the country's historic traditions of hostility to government (especially central government), *laissez-faire,* both regional and national racism, and "welfare capitalism." [10] As Skocpol observes,

Throughout the postwar period, U.S. macroeconomic managers deemphasized public spending and did not attempt to coordinate manpower and labor-market interventions, or any other sectorially specific interventions, with fiscal and monetary adjustments used to encourage economic growth. The technical and intellectual capacity of the federal government to devise and implement targeted industrial or labor-market interventions were not improved during the era of commercial Keynesian dominance. And little intellectual or political legitimacy was built up for the notion that the federal government could—or should—pursue economic, employment, and social-welfare objectives through the same or deliberately coordinated public policies.[11]

The OECD data reproduced in Chapter 9 (and the discussion about West Germany in Chapter 11) illustrate an important point. It is much more likely that countries that have not been able to follow an effective full-employment policy will have tried to balance labor supply and demand by moving older workers out of the labor force.[12] The economist Juanita Kreps was one of the first to point out the dominant role retirement policies have played in recent years in balancing the demand and supply of labor in the United States and other countries. As she has pointed out, retirement programs have become a major way of dealing with the allocation of labor and unemployment problems arising in market-oriented economies:

Retirement, a relatively new lifestage, has quickly become a . . . device for balancing the numbers of job seekers with the demand for workers at going rates of pay. Insofar as retirement practice is used to drain workers from the labor force, a reversal of the downward pressure on retirement age would seem to be possible only if labor markets tightened. Extensions beyond the usual retirement age are granted when there is a demand for specific talents. Given current levels of unemployment, however, there is no incentive to prolong worklife in general.[13]

And, as Dan Jacobson has expressed it, "more and more governments and unions have . . . come to recognize that adopting employment buffering strategies or developing worker-oriented adjustments and job-replacement strategies are a vital and, indeed, expedient element in human resource policies." [14]

Thus retirement policies in market-oriented, industrialized countries have reflected in a significant way the changing views in these countries with regard to labor-force needs and the changing macroeconomic situations in each country. And the early-retirement phenomenon we see in almost all industrialized countries today should be viewed as part of an uncoordinated market solution to the economic period of stagflation and lower growth that has characterized economic development during most of the years following the OPEC oil crisis.

New Considerations

It is not only historic concerns about the economic insecurity created by market mechanisms used in the search for and promotion of economic growth that are shaping retirement policies today. At least three other relatively new and unique developments are being given increased attention as nations discuss current and future aging policies.

The first development is the significant improvement that has occurred in the economic situation of many older people in industrial countries. As I have discussed in detail elsewhere,[15] not too many years ago it was relatively easy to generalize about the economic situation of the elderly population. Until recently, most older people suffered from economic deprivation; in fact, the elderly were one of the largest poverty groups in all countries.

Today, from a statistical point of view, the elderly in the United States (and most other industrialized countries) are beginning to look a lot like the rest of the population: some very rich, lots with adequate income, lots more with very modest incomes (often near poverty), and a significant minority still destitute. As Smeeding concludes in a recent eight-country[16] study of the elderly's economic status, "the 'elderly' are not badly off in all countries, save Britain. . . . The aged as a group appear to have slightly lower incomes than nonaged households with children but still have 87 percent of the adjusted national mean income."[17] In contrast, as described in Chapter 8, the economic situation of the aged in developing countries such as Poland is still very poor.

The second factor receiving a lot of attention is the phenomenon of demographic aging in various countries. "Population aging" is now recognized as a worldwide phenomenon having an impact on both developed and developing countries.[18] With this increase in older people as a percentage of the total population has come rising concern about the potential economic burden that might arise from such a demographic shift. Chapter 3 provides information on Americans for Generational Equity (AGE) in the United States and the intergenerational-conflict agenda raised by its leadership. But while a lively debate on the political–economic implications of population aging has begun in the United States, Chapter 5 compares that controversy with the lack of controversy in Canada where a relatively generous, income-tested, guaranteed "floor of protection" has been combined with a relatively modest public pension benefit. The result: a set of government income-maintenance programs for the aged that encourage individuals to seek supplemental income from private-sector pensions and other investment vehicles favored by conservatives. In contrast, many conservatives in the United States have reacted with hostility. They think social security has grown too big, that it threatens the private "retirement business" and competes with defense expenditures for the major portion of federal budget dollars.

Finally, there are new economic uncertainties and insecurity arising out of growing international competition and economic interdependence. The world economy is going through a major economic restructuring.[19] In addition to cyclical problems, most industrialized nations have been faced in recent years with large sectoral shifts in productive efforts, a change in the nature of new jobs, and large-scale workforce reorganization. A special report of the secretary of labor in the United States summarizes the American situation:

Despite substantial employment growth in many areas of the economy, the continued loss of jobs in manufacturing industries has displaced many workers from their long-held jobs, often with serious consequences to individuals, their families, and even whole communities. In addition, the increasingly competitive nature of many industries has led to "downsizing"—reductions in the size of a company's work force—and to mergers and acquisitions that often speed up cost cutting, resulting in the loss of jobs.[20]

There has been a need in many countries for first-time and, to a lesser extent, older workers to move away from traditional manufacturing industries into expanding industries associated with the growth in information processing, aeronautics, communication, biomedical technology, and various other service industries. As part of this adjustment process (and for other reasons), unemployment has been at record high levels during the latter part of the post–World War II period, and early retirement has been encouraged in almost all industrialized countries. Increasingly, however, people forecast labor shortages in future years as low birthrates translate into low numbers of new labor-force entrants. Calls for extending retirement ages are now more frequent, and concerns are being voiced about the ability of older workers, if reemployed, to meet the demands of the "new jobs."

A Modest Change in Impact

To what extent are the three factors listed above influencing and shaping future aging policies? To what extent are the reactions in various countries different? My answer: less than one might think, at least based on the research to date.

With regard to the economic status of the aged, all the evidence is clear.

The current economic status of most elderly persons is decidedly modest; no elderly are living "high on the hog" as a result of overly generous social security benefits. Calls for benefit cutbacks in various countries, consequently, have been insignificant.[21]

With incomes above poverty (but still very modest) achieved for most of the elderly, much of the criticism has focused on the fact that some public benefits are given to "those who don't need them." That is, increasingly criticisms have concentrated on the *universal* nature of public benefit programs. There are now frequent calls for *targeting* benefits in the interest of better equity and lower costs. But such proposed policy shifts return us to the familiar and longstanding debate over means testing versus broad-based benefit programs.[22]

Most contemporary critics, however, have little to say about the many problems associated with means testing: saving disincentives, high administrative costs, government intrusiveness, stigma, and lack of participation. Historically, these problems have been the basis for rejection of the means-testing approach, by both policymakers and the public, in most (but not all) countries.

One exception is Australia, which never introduced a social insurance pension, relying since 1909 on a means-tested retirement and other forms of benefit programs. The Australian experience, discussed in Chapter 6, provides us with important insights with regard to the continuing issues that can arise in a country that *seems to* reject universalism. Means testing survived in Australia only as a result of a bipartisan postwar agreement between the major political parties that benefit "tests" should be progressively liberalized. Sheila Shaver has characterized the resulting history as a push toward "incomplete universalism."

Moreover, the more stringent Australian tests introduced in recent years do not reflect growing support in that country for means testing. Instead, according to Shaver, these new deliberalization policies reflect "an accommodation of the welfare state to the diminishing [financial] scope for redistribution."

With regard to the demographic aging of populations, there is a large and still-growing body of literature voicing alarm. In many countries, there is much concern that the demographic shifts now under way will contribute to a loss of competitiveness and general economic stagnation. Moreover, there is a fear of rising financial burdens as a result of "aging populations."[23]

Yet, when one looks closely at this literature, most of the writing is found to be highly speculative and supported by little research. Discussions rest on a very thin reed—the measurement of so-called dependency ratios. Based on these ratios, a kind of "voodoo demographics" has developed that raises the specter of intolerable economic burdens from growing numbers of older people and a resultant rise in intergenerational conflict.[24] The conclusions are based typically on crude demographic statistics and no economic analysis. In contrast, a small but growing body of economic analysis indicates that when we get beyond the rhetoric, the economic "demands" of population aging dictate few changes in the future.[25]

Finally, with regard to the economic transformation currently taking place, again there is a lot of rhetoric but also an obvious need for much more knowledge and a better understanding about what is going on. Certainly the nature of labor-force and job opportunities will change significantly in the future. Many see the future as creating better opportunities for older workers, and more jobs. We must be cautious, however, because such notions, at least as articulated by some professionals and in the media, are overwhelmingly simplistic and probably wrong.[26]

Job opportunities for older workers in the future will depend on many factors. We cannot assume there will be more jobs for older people just because the proportion of younger workers in the labor force is declining. Cyclical and structural unemployment problems undoubtedly will continue in the years to come. The fear must be, then, that policymakers will continue to use pensions and the retirement of older workers as a way of dealing with short-term economic problems. Institutional encouragements to retirement complement a strong desire among many older workers to alter their work situation radically or stop work entirely. Given also the current rigidity of personnel practices, a lack of educational and training opportunities, and assumptions of declining productivity, the future may see these factors combine to create powerful barriers to employment of older workers.

Yet, if we look at the changing composition of industries and occupations, we see that there are not likely to be major "job requirement" barriers to the employment of displaced and older workers. The more important barriers are likely to be the attitudes of both workers and employers, interacting in an institutional environment that discourages work and encourages retirement.[27]

Both Output and More Leisure

Many of the chapters in this book discuss the phenomenon of "early retirement" that has been occurring in most industrialized countries. Again, it is important to see these discussions about specific countries in a broader context.

All the countries discussed in this book (except possibly Poland) have experienced major enlargements in their potential productive capacity throughout the century. Under the familiar title of "the industrial revolution," we can group the breathtaking array of transformations in technology, human capital, and the organization of production that have occurred. The resulting rise in production potential has confronted societies with many new opportunities and, alas, with many new problems. One of the opportunities or problems (we have had trouble over the years deciding which it is) is the potential for spending less time in the paid labor force over one's lifetime. In each country, the expansion of productive potential has brought with it the opportunity either to increase the amount of goods and services available or to produce the current amount of output but with less hours of labor. Historically, of course, industrializing countries have opted for both. Some of the rising productive potential has been used to raise output, incomes, and standards of living (as measured by output levels). Simultaneously, the rising economic potential has resulted in a reduction in the number of hours a particular worker spends in the paid labor force over his or her lifetime. In the United States, for example, the workweek has declined from approximately sixty hours in 1879 to about thirty-nine hours in 1970.

The historic expansion of output and leisure simultaneously is familiar to us all and is by itself not very interesting (at least to those who now take for granted the higher living standards achieved in a tiny minority of the world's countries). What is much more interesting is the fact that *patterns* of increased leisure have changed radically over time. In the United States the workweek has remained relatively stable since 1970; there has been some lengthening of vacation time, but the major change has been longer periods of prework education and, most of all, the expansion of "free time" in the retirement years.[28]

Retire at Age 38!

If industrialized countries had continued to increase leisure by reducing the number of hours worked each week or the number of weeks worked each year, the resulting work patterns today would be very different. In 1966, the economists Kreps and Spengler projected changes in work patterns that could occur as a result of changes in the productive potential over the two decades between 1965 and 1985.[29] Their projections used economic assumptions that, looking back from our vantage point at what actually happened, seem quite reasonable.

The Kreps/Spengler projections indicate what could have been if the United States had used *all* of its increasing productive potential to reduce the hours of paid work. Keeping per capita GNP constant, it would have been possible for the United States to cut the average workweek almost in half, to twenty-two hours per week. Alternatively, the average number of weeks that individuals would have to work could have been reduced to twenty-seven per year.

The United States did neither. Instead, much of the economic growth was taken in the form of increased income (i.e., increased output of goods and services). As pointed out above, both the average workweek and weeks worked per year have declined only slightly over the last twenty years. What has changed is a major reduction in the amount of paid work during the latter years of life—that is, the "institutionalization of retirement" [30] and the growing phenomenon of "early retirement."

But we should again emphasize that much of the growth potential over the years has been taken, not in the form of more leisure, but in increased output–income. In fact, if all the growth potential had been taken in the form of early retirement, Kreps and Spengler estimate that the average retirement age in 1985 could have been reduced to age 38!

The Early-Retirement Phenomenon

Why have we chosen to split our growth potential in only two ways: between increased income and earlier retirement? One would search in vain for any *national* discussion or debate over the work–leisure options that have confronted the American economy in recent decades.[31] That is, there has been almost no general discussion over whether Americans wanted to use their added leisure in the form of more vacation time, a shorter workweek, less hours of work per day, or earlier retirement.

Discussions and decisions did take place. They were highly decentralized, however, and focused mainly on different issues: unemployment, job displacement, promotional opportunities, and productivity changes with age. The early years of retirement have become the "buffer years," and pensions of various kinds (together with lump-sum payments) have been the primary mechanism used to effect the desired results. The result: a steady progression of lower "normal" retirement ages (determined by pension eligibility ages) and "early retirement" encouraged by pension-design provisions and personnel policies.

Strong evidence exists that older-worker labor-force participation is very sensitive to the availability of disability and old-age pensions (both public and private) and the mostly negative work incentives built into these programs.[32] A recent study by Roger Ransom and Richard Sutch found little or no decline between 1870 and 1940 in American male labor-force participation with age.[33] In contrast, statistics for the postwar period show a clear trend downward in participation of older workers once social security and private pensions became widely available.

The strong influence of pension programs on retirement should not be surprising, given that these programs were created by governments, employers, unions, and workers in large part as a reaction to the evolving cyclical and structural employment problems arising in market-oriented economies. Any careful examination of the history of these programs will show that they were intentionally designed to discourage people from working.[34]

A recent study by Packard and Reno focuses on "very early retirees" in the United States—defined as those retiring before age 61½ (that is, six months before social security early-retirement benefits become available).[35] Their analysis shows, again, that pension availability (military, civil service, disability, and private pensions), interacting with health, job loss, and declining work opportunities, strongly affects decision making about early retirement.

The 1980s were not a period of expansive economic growth; quite the opposite. Moreover, nations were confronted with the normal "revolutionary" changes in technologies, products, occupations, and industries that have occurred in market-oriented economies throughout history. At the same time, the new emerging industrial giants of Asia and the international chaos created by the OPEC era added to worldwide instability and economic dislocation.

The resulting years of high job displacement and chronic underemployment caused both public and private decision makers to search for new ways to allocate labor. And it forced millions of supposedly secure workers to confront the necessity of starting a new career. For example, surveys conducted in 1984 and 1986 in the United States found that about 5 million experienced workers lost jobs as a result of plant closings, slack work, shifting jobs, or the abolition of job openings.[36]

Writers disagree over whether the job picture of the past foretells the future. Some think it is realistic to expect labor markets to provide the "good jobs" and rising real wages that characterized the past. Others see the current situation as a transitional period toward a new stage of development.

In either case, what is not likely to change is the use of retirement policies as one (of many) techniques for adjusting the labor supply to current needs. Despite the high price—in terms of lost production potential and growing pension costs—of liberalizing retirement policies, such actions have become very popular with almost all segments of the population. As expressed by one observer, "Everyone is in favor of keeping older people in the labor force except the unions, government, business, and older people."[37]

The Distribution Implications of Early Retirement

Given the major shift that has already occurred in the age of retirement, it is important to remember that *the change has not occurred uniformly across the working population*. Who gets to retire (and how early) varies greatly from one employment setting to another, and sometimes varies among employees of a particular firm. And the terms of retirement—the amount of remuneration, continuing health benefits, reemployment options, and so forth—also vary greatly.

The chapters in this book raise many questions with regard to the distributional impact of various retirement practices and the variety of reforms currently being proposed in different countries. We have few answers. The retirement and pension literature is just beginning to address (but still in a fragmentary and often inconclusive way) the differential impacts as they affect women,[38] "very early retirees,"[39] those without coverage under employer-sponsored plans,[40] part-time workers,[41] and widows.[42] Chapters 9, 11, and 13 in this book provide important new information about some of the major "sorting" mechanisms operating in various countries.

One distributional issue that is sure to receive increased attention in future years relates to the specter of "labor force shortages." Do the demographic shifts occurring in industrialized countries today, coupled with early retirement, imply labor shortages in the years to come? And will the elderly of the future be "forced" to retire later or even go back to work? Much of the popular writing today on this issue conveys a feeling that such happenings are inevitable. But the economist must answer "not necessarily." There are a number of other options to the changing labor-force demography: "capital deepening," retraining, higher female labor-force participation, increased immigration, or the transfer of certain production elements to the younger populations of other countries (if age matters).

The currently voiced "put the elderly back to work" solutions are much too simplistic. They ignore the options. They ignore the fact that most of the elderly do not want to work in regular full-time jobs and will resist such policy changes.[43] They ignore the problem that the productivity of older workers may often be much lower in relation to their earnings than the productivity of younger workers.[44] And they ignore the point we have emphasized in this chapter, that there is a major "buffering role" played by older workers in market economies—economies, given the basic nature of functioning markets, that are virtually certain to fluctuate over time.

The Welfare State: Public and Private

Finally, the discussion throughout this book emphasizes that there are many alternative paths to retirement. More important, there are many alternative paths to *early* retirement, which is often a *transitional* stage en route to the more traditional lifestyles associated with old age.

Most discussions about welfare states, the related retirement process, and economic support for people in old age have focused on social security mechanisms, especially social *insurance*. But one important contribution of this book is to emphasize how important it is to understand the interaction between social security programs and the growing complementary social-protection network associated with *private* firms. This interaction is not new, but only recently has the necessary research been initiated to confirm its importance and growth and to understand its impact. This new dimension to research on the evolving welfare state adds complexity and expands the challenge facing researchers in the future.

Notes

1. Charles E. Lindblom, *Politics and Markets* (New York: Basic Books, 1977).

2. James Fallows, "America's Changing Economic Landscape," *Atlantic Monthly*, March 1985, 47–68.

3. See, for example, Dwight Heald Perkins, "Reforming China's Economic System," *Journal of Economic Literature* 26 (1988): 601–45; and "Selling Off the Communist Shop," *Economist*, February 11, 1989, 17–18.

4. One of the best of recent discussions is in Arthur Okun, *Equality and Efficiency: The Big Tradeoff* (Washington, D.C.: Brookings Institution, 1975).

5. See the overview provided in James H. Schulz and John Myles, "Old Age Pensions: A Comparative Perspective," in *Handbook of Aging and the Social Sciences*, ed. R. Binstock and L. George, 3rd ed. (New York: Academic Press, forthcoming).

6. See, for example, Ezra F. Vogel, *Japan as Number One* (Cambridge: Harvard University Press, 1979); and James H. Schulz, S. Hoshino, and K. Takada, *When "Lifetime Employment" Ends: Older Worker Programs in Japan* (Waltham, Mass.: Policy Center on Aging, Heller School, Brandeis University, 1989).

7. Goran Therborn, *Why Some Peoples Are More Unemployed Than Others* (London: Verso, 1986).

8. Ibid., 14.

9. Ibid., 23, 28–29.

10. "Welfare capitalism" refers to corporate-sponsored and nonunion employee benefit systems, supplemented by the family, local government aid, and/or private charity.

11. Theda Skocpol, "America's Incomplete Welfare State: The Limits of New Deal Reform and the Origins of the Present Crisis," In *Stagnation and Renewal in Social Policy*, ed. Martin Rein, G. Esping-Andersen, and L. Rainwater (Armonk, N.Y.: M. E. Sharpe, 1987), 45.

12. Differences among countries in the availability of and policies encouraging part-time work are also important.

13. Juanita M. Kreps, "Age, Work, and Income," *Southern Economic Journal* 43 (1977): 1423–37.

14. Dan Jacobson, "Optional Early Retirement: Is It a Painless Alternative to Involuntary Layoffs?" in *Early Retirement: Approaches and Variations: An International Perspective*, ed. Shimon Bergman, Gerhard Naegele, and Walter Tokarski (Israel and Germany: Joint publication of the Brookdale Institute of Gerontology and Human Development and Soziale Gerontologie Fachbereich Sozialwesen Gesamthochschule Universität Kassel, 1988), 11–24.

15. James H. Schulz, *The Economics of Aging*, 4th ed. (Dover, Mass.: Auburn House, 1988).

16. The countries are Australia, Canada, West Germany, Norway, Sweden, the Netherlands, the United Kingdom, and the United States.

17. Timothy Smeeding, "Generations and the Distribution of Well-Being and Poverty: Cross National Evidence for Europe, Scandinavia and the Colonies" (Paper presented at the Symposium on Population Change and European Society, Florence, 1988). See also Timothy Smeeding, B. B. Torrey, and M. Rein, "Patterns of Income and Poverty: The Economic Status of Children and the Elderly in Eight Countries," in *The Vulnerable*, ed. John L. Palmer, T. Smeeding, and B. B. Torrey (Washington, D.C.: Urban Institute, 1988), 89–120.

18. B. B. Torrey, K. Kinsella, and C. M. Taeuber, *An Aging World*, U.S. Bureau of the Census, International Population Reports, series P-95, no. 78 (Washington, D.C.: Government Printing Office, 1987); and K. Kinsella, *Aging in the Third World*, U.S. Bureau of the Census, International Population Reports, series P-95, no. 79 (Washington, D.C.: Government Printing Office, 1988).

19. See, for example, M. J. Piore and C. F. Sabels, *The Second Industrial Divide* (New York: Basic Books, 1984).

20. U.S. Department of Labor, *Labor Market Problems of Older Workers*, Report of the Secretary of Labor (Washington, D.C.: U.S. Department of Labor, 1989), 2.

21. R. Klein and M. O'Higgins, "Defusing the Crisis of the Welfare State," in *Social Security: Beyond the Rhetoric of Crisis*, ed. T. R. Marmor and J. L. Mashaw (Princeton: Princeton University Press, 1988).

22. Irwin Garfinkel, ed., *Income-Tested Transfer Programs: The Case for and Against* (New York: Academic Press, 1982).

23. See, for example, Ben J. Wattenberg, *The Birth Dearth* (New York: Pharoo Books, 1987); and Alan Pifer and Lydia Bronte, eds., *Our Aging Society: Paradox and Promise* (New York: Norton, 1986).

24. James H. Schulz, "Voodoo Economics and the Aging Society," *Of Current Interest*, November 6, 1986, 1, 8.

25. William H. Crown and James H. Schulz, *What Will Be the Economic Impact of Demographic Aging?* AARP Public Policy Institute Publication no. 8706 (Washington, D.C.: AARP, 1987); and Henry J. Aaron, Barry P. Bosworth, and Gary Burtless, *Can America Afford to Grow Old?* (Washington, D.C.: Brookings Institution, 1989).

26. For a good overview of the complexity of these issues, see American Association of Retired Persons, *Lifework: Options for Older Workers in the Future* (Washington, D.C.: AARP, forthcoming).

27. Ibid.

28. Fred Best and Barry Stern, "Education, Work, and Leisure: Must They Come in That Order?" *Monthly Labor Review* 100 (July 1977): 3–10.

29. Juanita Kreps and Joseph Spengler, "The Leisure Component of Economic Growth," in National Commission on Technological Automation and Economic Progress, *The Employment Impact of Technological Change* (Washington, D.C.: Government Printing Office, 1966), 2:353–89.

30. Wilma Donahue, Harold L. Orbach, and Otto Pollak, "Retirement: The Emerging Social Pattern," in *Handbook of Social Gerontology*, ed. Clark Tibbitts

(Chicago: University of Chicago Press, 1960), 330–406; Eugene A. Friedman and Harold L. Orbach, "Adjustment to Retirement," in *The Foundations of Psychiatry*, ed. Silvano Arieti, vol 1, *American Handbook of Psychiatry*, 2nd ed. (New York: Basic Books, 1974), 609–45.

31. James H. Schulz, "Issues in Aged Income Maintenance: Population Aging and the Early Retirement 'Time-bomb,' " in U.S. House Select Committee on Aging and the Senate Special Committee on Aging, *Legislative Agenda for the Aging Society: 1988 and Beyond* (Washington, D.C.: Government Printing Office, 1987), 83–97.

32. See the summaries in C. J. Ruhm. "Why Older Americans Stop Working," *Gerontologist* 29 (June 1989): 294–99; and J. F. Quinn, J. F. Burkhauser, and D. A. Myers, *Work and Retirement in America: How the Modern Retirement System Influences Work across Life* (Kalamazoo, Mich.: Upjohn Institute, forthcoming).

33. Roger L. Ransom and Richard Sutch, "The Decline of Retirement in the Years before Social Security: U.S. Retirement Patterns, 1870–1940," in *Issues in Contemporary Retirement*, ed. Rita Ricardo-Campbell and Edward P. Lazear (Stanford, Calif.: Hoover Institution Press, 1988).

34. William Graebner, *A History of Retirement* (New Haven, Conn.: Yale University Press, 1980); and Jill Quadagno, *The Transformation of Old Age Security: Class and Politics in the American Welfare State* (Chicago: University of Chicago Press, 1988).

35. Michael D. Packard and V. P. Reno, "A Look at Very Early Retirees," *Social Security Bulletin* 52 (March 1989): 16–29.

36. Francis W. Horwath, "Pulse of Economic Change: Displaced Workers of 1981–85," *Monthly Labor Review*, June 1987, 3–12.

37. Quoted in Ira Mothner, *Children and Elders: Intergenerational Relations in an Aging Society* (New York: Carnegie Foundation, 1985).

38. Richard V. Burkhauser and Karen C. Holden, *A Challenge to Social Security: The Changing Roles of Women and Men in American Society* (New York: Academic Press, 1982).

39. See Chapter 13; see also Eric R. Kingson, "Retirement Circumstances of Very Early Retirees: A Life Cycle Perspective," *Aging and Work* 4 (Summer 1981): 161–74.

40. James H. Schulz, "Problems of American Pensions: Microsimulation Policy Analysis," *Zeitschrift fur die gesamte Staatswissenschaft*, September 1982, 527–45; John R. Woods, "Retirement-Age Women and Pensions: Findings from the New Beneficiary Survey," *Social Security Bulletin* 51 (December 1988): 5–16.

41. Rosalie F. Schofield, "The Private Pension Coverage of Part-time Workers," Ph.D. dissertation, Brandeis University, 1984.

42. Karen C. Holden, R. V. Burkhauser, and D. A. Myers, "Income Transitions of Older Stages of Life: The Dynamics of Poverty," *Gerontologist* 26 (June 1986): 292–97.

43. See Schulz, *Economics of Aging*, chap. 3.

44. Edward P. Lazear, "The Relationship of Productivity to Age," in Ricardo-Campbell and Lazear, *Issues in Contemporary Retirement*.

About the Contributors

Editors

Jill Quadagno is a professor of sociology at Florida State University, where she occupies the Mildred and Claude Pepper Chair in Social Gerontology. She has done postdoctoral research at Cambridge University and in 1988 was a visiting professor in the Department of Sociology at Harvard University under a National Science Foundation Visiting Professorship for Women. She is the author of *Aging in Early Industrial Society: Work, Family and Social Policy in Nineteenth Century England* (1982), *The Family in Various Cultures* (1985), and *The Transformation of Old Age Security: Class and Politics in the American Welfare State* (1988).

John Myles is a professor of sociology at Carleton University and a visiting scholar at Statistics Canada. In 1980–1981 he was a visiting scholar at the Center for European Studies, Harvard University. He is the author of *Old Age in the Welfare State* (1984) and *Comparative Macrosociology* (in press). He is principal investigator of the Canadian portion of the international class-structure project, a comparative survey now completed or under way in approximately a dozen countries.

Contributors

Gösta Esping-Andersen is a professor at the European University Institute, Florence. He has also held positions as research director of the Swedish Institute for Social Research and as an associate professor at Harvard University. He has published more than thirty-five articles on the welfare state, employment policy, labor markets, and the life cycle, and he is the author or editor of *Social Class, Social Democracy, and State Policy* (1980), *Political Power and Social Theory* (1982), *Politics against Markets* (1985), and *Stagnation and Renewal: The Rise and Fall of Social Policy Regimes* (1986).

Carroll L. Estes is a professor in and chair of the Department of Social and Behavioral Sciences, and director of the Institute for Health and Aging, University of California, San Francisco. She is the author of *The Decision-Makers* (1963), *The Aging Enterprise* (1979), *Fiscal Austerity and Aging* (1983), and *Political Economy, Health, and Aging* (1984). She is past president of the Western Gerontological Society and of the Association for Gerontology in Higher Education. Among her numerous current research projects is a study of the regulation of the quality of home health-care services funded by a grant from the Andrus Foundation.

Anne-Marie Guillemard is a professor of sociology at the Sorbonne, Paris. She has published more than twenty-five articles on aging, retirement, and social policy and is the author or editor of *La retraite: Une mort sociale* (1972), *La vieillesse et l'etat* (1980), *Old Age and the Welfare State* (1983), and *Le déclin du social: Formation et crise des politiques de la vieillesse* (1986). She is currently engaged in research on early-retirement trends in France.

Klaus Jacobs is working as an economist at the Institute for Health and Social Research in Berlin. His special research interest in the field of early retirement originates from his previous work at the Institute for Research on Social Policy at the Free University of Berlin and the Science Center Berlin. He is currently involved in an international project on the past and future role of the social policy of the firm with respect to the early exit of older workers from the labor force.

Toshi Kii is an associate professor at Georgia State University, where he holds joint appointments in the Department of Sociology and the Institute of Industrial Relations. He has published numerous articles on aging, retirement, and the Asian elderly. Former director of the Japanese Studies Program at Georgia State, he is at present on leave to work for DuPont Japan, Ltd., in Tokyo.

Ewa Morawska is an associate professor of sociology at the University of Pennsylvania. She is the author of *For Bread with Butter: Life Worlds of East Central Europeans in Johnstown, Pennsylvania, 1890–1940* (1985), *Poles in Toronto* (1982), *The Maintenance of Ethnicity* (1977), and *Polish American Community Life* (1975). In 1987 she was awarded the Comparative History prize by the American Sociological Association for her paper "Labor Migrations of Poles in the Atlantic World Economy, 1880–1914," and she has recently received a John Simon Guggenheim Fellowship.

Fritz von Nordheim Nielsen has worked for the Danish Ministry of Labour and held research fellowships at the University of Copenhagen, the University of Cambridge, and the European University Institute in Florence. Currently he is working for the Copenhagen Business School and teaching at the University of Copenhagen. His publications include comparative works on labor movements, unemployment insurance systems, public and private pension schemes, and the relations between labor and welfare states in Scandinavia. He is now working on a six-country comparative study of the political economy of occupational pensions.

Martin Rein is a professor of urban studies and planning at the Massachusetts Institute of Technology and a faculty associate at Harvard University. He has previously held positions as a Fellow at the Center for Advanced Behavioral Sciences, Palo Alto, and as a senior Fulbright researcher at the London School of Economics. His most recent books include *Dilemmas of Social Reform: Poverty and Community Action in the United States* (1982), *Women's Claims: A Study in Political Economy* (1983), *Income Packaging in the Welfare State* (1985), *Stagnation and Renewal in Social Policy* (1986), and *Comparative Studies in Social Policy* (1986).

James H. Schulz is a professor of economics in the Florence Heller School at Brandeis University. He is one of the nation's leading authorities on pensions and the economics of aging. He is past president of the Gerontological Society of America and recipient of the 1983 Robert W. Kleemeier Award for outstanding research in aging. His books include *Providing Adequate Retirement Income* (1974), *The Economics of Aging* (1988; now in its 4th edition), and *When Lifetime Employment Ends* (1989).

Sheila Shaver is a senior lecturer in sociology at Macquarie University, Sydney, Australia. She was previously Research Fellow in the Institute of Applied Economic and Social Research, Melbourne University, where she took part in the first large-scale studies of poverty in Australia and investigated social service delivery networks in urban localities. More recently, she has been concerned with class and gender politics in the welfare state. She has also maintained an active connection with welfare politics through board membership of both federal and state Councils of Social Service in Australia. She is coauthor of *Who Cares? Family Problems, Community Links, and Helping Services*. She is currently working on a book provisionally titled "Whose Welfare State: Class, Gender, and Community in Australian Welfare Politics."

Harold L. Sheppard is a professor in the Department of Gerontology at the University of South Florida (USF). From 1983 to 1991 he was director of the International Exchange Center of Gerontology at USF. He served as Counselor on Aging to President Carter, 1980–81, and associate director of the National Council on Aging, 1981–82. He is the author of many articles and books on retirement policy, including *Too Old to Work: Too Young to Retire* (1958) and *The Graying of Working America* (1977).

Harald Sonnberger has taught courses in econometrics and computer science at the Universities of Hanover, Linz, Wien, and Zagreb. He was a guest professor at the University of Groningen in 1985 and 1986. He is the coauthor of a book on the linear regression model with special emphasis on tests for structural breaks and functional form. His current research interests include the development of statistical software and the application of statistics in the social sciences.

Les Teichroew is a graduate student in the Department of Sociology at Carleton University and is currently researching the provision of health services to Third World refugees in Canada.

Alan Walker is a professor of social policy and the chair of the Department of Sociological Studies, University of Sheffield, England. He has been researching and writing on social policy and social gerontology for nearly twenty years. He has authored, coauthored, or edited ten books, including *Social Planning* (1984), *Ageing and Social Policy* (1986), *Caring Relationship* (1989), and numerous journal articles and chapters in edited volumes.

Index